Schooling and Scholars in Nineteenth-Century Ontario

THE ONTARIO HISTORICAL STUDIES SERIES

The Ontario Historical Studies Series is a comprehensive history of Ontario from 1791 to the present, which will include several biographies of former premiers, numerous volumes on the economic, social, political, and cultural development of the province, and a general history incorporating the insights and conclusions of the other works in the series. The purpose of the series is to enable general readers and scholars to understand better the distinctive features of Ontario as one of the principal regions within Canada.

PUBLISHED

J.M.S. Careless, ed. *The Pre-Confederation Premiers: Ontario Government Leaders, 1841–1867* (1980)
Charles W. Humphries, *'Honest Enough to Be Bold': The Life and Times of Sir James Pliny Whitney* (1985)
Charles M. Johnston, *E.C. Drury: Agrarian Idealist* (1986)
A.K. McDougall, *John P. Robarts: His Life and Government* (1986)
Peter Oliver, *G. Howard Ferguson: Ontario Tory* (1977)

Christopher Armstrong, *The Politics of Federalism: Ontario's Relations with the Federal Government, 1867–1942* (1981)
Ian M. Drummond, *Progress without Planning: The Economic History of Ontario from Confederation to the Second World War* (1987)
David Gagan, *Hopeful Travellers: Families, Land and Social Change in Mid-Victorian Peel County, Canada West* (1981)
John Webster Grant, *A Profusion of Spires: Religion in Nineteenth-Century Ontario* (1988)
Susan E. Houston and Alison Prentice, *Schooling and Scholars in Nineteenth-Century Ontario* (1988)
K.J. Rea, *The Prosperous Years: The Economic History of Ontario, 1939–1975* (1985)
Robert M. Stamp, *The Schools of Ontario, 1876–1976* (1982)

Olga B. Bishop, Barbara I. Irwin, Clara G. Miller, eds., *Bibliography of Ontario History, 1867–1976: Cultural, Economic, Political, Social* 2 volumes (1980)
R. Louis Gentilcore and C. Grant Head, *Ontario's History in Maps* (1984)
Joseph Schull, *Ontario since 1867* (McClelland and Stewart 1978)
Joseph Schull, *L'Ontario depuis 1867* (McClelland and Stewart 1987)

SUSAN E. HOUSTON AND ALISON PRENTICE

Schooling and Scholars in Nineteenth-Century Ontario

A project of the
Ontario Historical Studies Series
for the Government of Ontario
Published by University of Toronto Press
Toronto   Buffalo   London

ISBN 0-8020-5801-9 (cloth)
ISBN 0-8020-6717-4 (paper)

Printed on acid-free paper

Canadian Cataloguing in Publication Data
Houston, Susan E., 1937-
    Schooling and scholars in nineteenth-century Ontario

(Ontario historical studies series)
Includes index.
ISBN 0-8020-5801-9 (bound) ISBN 0-8020-6717-4 (pbk.)

1. Education – Ontario – History. 2. Education and state – Ontario –
History. 3. Ontario – Social conditions. I. Prentice, Alison, 1934–
II. Title. III. Series.

LA418.06H68 1988   370'.9713   C88-094550-8

This book has been published with the assistance of funds provided by the
Government of Ontario through the Ministry of Culture and
Communications.

Contents

Picture Credits

Pages of this book on which pictures are reproduced are given within parentheses.

Ontario Archives: Thomas Dick's diary (13) – Personal Diaries Collection, MV 840; John Strachan (73) – Acc. 3077, 52328; Tyendenaga school report (109) and rules, Victoria Central School (261); – RG2 F2, Box 1, Envelope 12, 1842-8; plans for school, St John's Ward, Toronto (207) – Horwood Collection 656, 2; school photo from early 1870s (342) – 9434514861

Metropolitan Toronto Library Board: District School, Cornwall (24) – T30795; Niagara school (48) – MTL 828 R1; Upper Canada College (51) – T30087; sketch (53) – Manuscript Collection: Mills, Alice Maud L.; public examination (80) – BD5 1852 – Examinations; Middlesex County school (171) – T16581; merit cards (265) – Broadside Collection; Egerton Ryerson (311) – JRR 2754; Pinehurst Academy (323) – T13838; Eclectic Female Institute (325) – 376.9713.B67 1863

United Church of Canada Archives, Toronto: Upper Canada Academy (43); Egerton Ryerson (113)

National Archives of Canada, Ottawa: plan of village (52) – Cartographic Archives & A.D., NMC 3667; Grenville County school (59) – Historical Photo Historique C3329 B

Courtesy of Robert Root, private collection: school in Algonquin (59)

Courtesy of *Historical Atlas of Canada*, research funded by Social Science and Humanities Research Council of Canada (artwork by Shelley Laskin): maps (134)

Royal Ontario Museum, Toronto: Normal School (161) – 966 X 298.6; Governor-General in Ingersoll (263) – 88 Can 18 978.359.786

Jackson Library, Ontario Institute for Studies in Education, Toronto: from J. George Hodgins, *The School House: Its Architecture, External and Internal Arrangements* (209, 252, 257)

City of Toronto Archives: Loretto School for Girls (291) – SC 211

Canadian Illustrated News: Central School, Hamilton (229) – 16 May 1863, v. 2; High School, Cayuga (334) – 18 Nov. 1876, v. 14, p. 301

Richard Schofield Historical Collection, Heritage Scarborough: SS 7, Scarborough (341)

The Ontario Historical Studies Series

For many years the principal theme in English-Canadian historical writing has been the emergence and the consolidation of the Canadian nation. This theme has been developed in uneasy awareness of the persistence and importance of regional interests and identities, but because of the central role of Ontario in the growth of Canada, Ontario has not been seen as a region. Almost unconsciously, historians have equated the history of the province with that of the nation and have depicted the interests of other regions as obstacles to the unity and welfare of Canada.

The creation of the province of Ontario in 1867 was the visible embodiment of a formidable reality, the existence at the core of the new nation of a powerful if disjointed society whose traditions and characteristics differed in many respects from those of the other British North American colonies. The intervening century has not witnessed the assimilation of Ontario to the other regions in Canada; on the contrary it has become a more clearly articulated entity. Within the formal geographical and institutional framework defined so assiduously by Ontario's political leaders, an increasingly intricate web of economic and social interests has been woven and shaped by the dynamic interplay between Toronto and its hinterland. The character of this regional community has been formed in the tension between a rapid adaptation to the processes of modernization and industrialization in modern Western society and a reluctance to modify or discard traditional attitudes and values. Not surprisingly, the Ontario outlook is a compound of aggressiveness, conservatism, and the conviction that its values should be the model for the rest of Canada.

From the outset the objective of the Board of Trustees of the series has been to describe and analyse the historical development of Ontario as a distinct region within Canada. The series as planned will include thirty-two volumes covering many aspects of the life and work of the province from its original establishment in 1791 as Upper Canada to our own time. Among these will be biographies of several premiers, numerous works on the growth of the provincial economy, educational institutions, minority groups, and the arts, and a synthesis of the history of Ontario, based upon the contributions of the biographies and thematic studies.

In planning this project, the editors and the board have endeavoured to maintain a reasonable balance between different kinds and areas of historical research, and to appoint authors ready to ask new questions about the past and to answer them in accordance with the canons of contemporary scholarship. *Schooling and Scholars in Nineteenth-Century Ontario* is the seventh theme study to be published. It is a comprehensive account not simply of the early evolution of the public school *system* in Ontario but of '*schooling* itself,' which was from the beginning and continued to be a vital concern to the people of this province. By 1876 Ontario had a system of elementary and secondary education whose 'regulated hours' largely dictated 'the routines of family life.'

Susan Houston and Alison Prentice have written a lively and sensitive analysis of the process by which the 'mania for school promotion' which Ontarians shared with other societies in the North Atlantic world was given institutional form, and the impact of that development on successive generations of students. We hope that scholars will be stimulated by this work to explore other 'aspects of the business of schooling.'

The editors and the Board of Trustees are grateful to Professors Houston and Prentice for undertaking this task.

GOLDWIN FRENCH
PETER OLIVER
JEANNE BECK
MAURICE CARELESS, Chairman of the Board of Trustees

Toronto
26 May 1988

Preface

In 1871 the author of a little Ontario textbook, *First Lessons in Christian Morals for Canadian Families and Schools*, struggled to convey his sense of outrage at what seemed to be an increasing disregard of the commandment 'to honour thy father and mother.' In part, in the author's view, this new careless attitude stemmed from a shallow sense of history: the sacrifices and struggles made in the process of pioneer settlement were all too quickly forgotten as parents painstakingly acquired the means to educate their children, 'perhaps sending their son to college and their daughter to a boarding school.' That such children, when grown up, should disparage their less-educated fathers or mothers was 'inexpressibly contemptible and wicked,' he concluded.[1]

Those fathers and mothers and children and their efforts to get established, to get on, and to get an education in the fledgling British North American colony of Upper Canada provide the central concerns of this book. The author of the little textbook also figures prominently, for the Reverend Egerton Ryerson turned to writing textbooks late in a long and contentious public career. For more than thirty years he was the most powerful personality in Ontario education. In the chapters that follow we have tried to sketch the educational enterprise as it evolved during the period that ends with the Ryerson era: the formative decades of Ontario's first century. This is a tale with many characters – one that touches on the often competing and conflicting ambitions of different individuals, generations, cultural groups, and social classes, and on the uses and abuses of power within families, local communities, and the novel social institution we now know as the provincial public school system.

The importance of public schooling in the history of nineteenth-century Ontario society cannot be overestimated. The advent of publicly funded elementary – and later secondary – schooling has been ranked with the extension of the franchise as a milestone in the evolution of a modern democratic state. Discounting the hyperbole, one must acknowledge nevertheless the audacity of this public policy. In mid-nineteenth-century British North America, Upper Canada (and then Ontario) was a pioneer in the creation of a centrally administered, province-wide school system. Indeed, few jurisdictions in the western world outstripped Ontario's efforts in this regard, although the provision of some sort of schooling, for the working classes particularly, had engaged the attention of most western European powers by the middle decades of the century. The common interest of various national states in the social and political stability that such schooling might help provide was supported energetically by a new breed of public servant. By means of volumes of correspondence and the occasional 'grand tour' of inspection, pioneering civil servants such as Egerton Ryerson ensured that public education policy, within the Anglo-American triangle especially, did not develop in isolation.

The timing of this international agenda for schooling has puzzled historians, economists, and demographers, among others long convinced of its importance. To the power of universal public education has been attributed virtual universal literacy. Both, in turn, at one time or another, have been held to account, in part, for such diverse features of modernism as smaller family size, the rapid expansion of industrial capitalism, and the general acceptance of the consumer ethos and the secular society.

What common experience could account for this shared mania for school promotion, the consequences of which appear to have been so profound? Be it nothing more than coincidence, the striking congruence in time of an unprecedented interest in mass schooling and the social transformation popularly labelled 'the Industrial Revolution' demands explanation. While geographically remote, Britain's North American colonies nonetheless were very much creations of contemporary ideological and economic upheavals, as each struggled to gain a footing. It is too easily forgotten that invasion, rebellion, and cyclical economic development were as much features of Ontario's early history as successful pioneer settlement and the achievement of 'responsible government.' The religious and intellectual turmoil that, from the late eighteenth century, embroiled the educated classes of the Old World in debate was replicated, in miniature, in the colonial society of Upper Canada. Here too 'revolutions' in transportation technology, manufacturing, and commerce conspired in different ways to undermine older conventions of time and rhythms of work. Work and leisure, so intimately linked in the pre-industrial world, soon assumed their modern opposition. The sense of space, too, was subtly redefined. Objectively, space appeared to contract as railroads began to criss-cross the southern Ontario landscape by the 1850s in hectic pursuit of commercial profit. Meanwhile more abstract distinctions between what was *private* and what was *public* space became more sharply differentiated and, by the middle classes, internalized as discrete worlds appropriate to women (the domestic sphere) and men (the public sphere). Earlier in the cities and towns, but throughout Ontario's rural communities by the 1870s, the sensibilities of women and men were becoming attuned to the need for schooling in the new industrializing economy. As parents they would make calculations of the returns from investment in their children's education, and these parental concerns undoubtedly played a significant part in the emergence of public as well as private schooling. Yet their calculations might or might not coincide with those of the men and women who taught in the schools or ran the expanding public school systems. The larger question – what gave to public school systems their distinctive structure and character – remains to be addressed.

In recent years, in analysing the nineteenth-century 'origins' of public education in North America and elsewhere, various historians have generalized about the relationship of public school systems to capitalism, proposing for schools a historically specific social function, particularly in disciplining a future wage-labour force.[2] Such an approach has proved invaluable, sparking as it has the critical analysis of social regulation and an appreciation of the interrelatedness (as well as the pervasiveness) of efforts to structure aspects of the behaviour of different social groups. However, the limitations of too broadly conceived explanations are increasingly obvious. Virtually any social policy, after all, has diverse purposes that are rarely so coherent as to lend themselves to treatment as a single force. In the specific instance of public schooling, themes of social discipline and moral regulation, while of undoubted importance, form strands in a fabric tightly woven of multiple intentions and effects. Thus in 1988 it appears time to begin the historical analysis of public schooling with an investigation of *schooling* itself – a phenomenon of both private and public life long predating the legislative enactments of the mid-Victorian decades that have so preoccupied historians of education in the past.

As will be evident in what follows, we have approached this study of schooling in nineteenth-century Ontario with definable concerns. A tidal wave of words awaits the unsuspecting student who ventures to research the social movements of the Victorian era. In defence we have tried to pay careful attention to words, to their shifting meanings over time and to the ways in which nineteenth-century usage differs deceptively from today's. Words often serve as battlegrounds for competing interests; to borrow a phrase, language is power. In few eras has this been more true than in the Victorian age, and the voluminous record of debate over education has proven to be something of a goldmine. One does recognize, however, that in such circumstances language – the rhetoric in which opinions are expressed – is often chosen for its effect on an audience, added after the opinions are fully formed, more or less as an icing on the cake. Nevertheless some words such as 'character' and 'respectability,' for example, acquired a peculiar resonance over the course of the century as they were volleyed back and forth in public debate. It is in words such as these, rather than in more abstractly defined analytic categories, that we have sought clues to the gradations of social class and the relations between class, power, and education in nineteenth-century Ontario. In a society dominated numerically by farmers and their families, neither the desire for schooling nor the ability to take some advantage of its availability cut neatly along class lines. Nevertheless, the increasingly rigid structures of public schooling do appear to have sharpened the edge of social distinction.

As we have explored how this might have been the case in a province composed of diverse local communities with markedly different economies and cultural traditions, we have broadened a concern to understand class with a concern to understand the role of gender. All too often historians have assumed that schooling has been much the same for boys and girls to the point where 'boys' is a synonym for 'pupils.' Where distinctions were made, girls were treated as the exception to the male norm. What follows does not right the balance by any means, but a beginning has been made.

In our deliberate pursuit of little-known aspects of the business of schooling, we have relied on the fact that parts of the story of Ontario public education are relatively well known. As a consequence we have not detailed, for example, such well-documented political dramas as the separate school controversy. A similar logic has dictated the neglect of various themes – French and foreign-language schooling is an obvious example – that came to the fore after the period with which we are concerned. Nor do we make any pretence of having presented some of our leading characters 'in the round.' John Strachan, Egerton Ryerson, George Brown, Edward Blake – to name only the most obvious – have each been the subject of major scholarly biographies. That the Methodist convictions which so deeply coloured the Reverend Egerton Ryerson's world view receive scant mention does not reflect our sense of their unimportance: rather it is that other aspects of his lengthy public life and character more appropriately fit the telling of *our* tale.

We have tried, in the telling, to convey something of the delight with which we unearthed various archival 'gems' in our exploration of Ontario's nineteenth-century educational history. Vitally important to this history were, in our view, the recorded thoughts and actions of participants other than the almost larger-than-life figures of a Ryerson, a Strachan, a Brown, or a Blake. We hope that the words of these people – women as well as men, girls as well as boys – grace our text with the same life with which, so long ago, they animated the pages now yellowed with age. As they exhorted, confided in, or consoled their friends – or lambasted their enemies – most were innocent of the effect their writings might have on future interpreters of the educational scene. The dominant figures, undoubtedly, wrote more self-consciously with an eye to posterity. Yet whatever their apparent sense of themselves as writers, the characters, both large and small, of Ontario's nineteenth-century educational past found in us fascinated and willing readers. For we must confess to at least one bias. It is not only the written word that intrigues, but schooling; and not just schooling, but people pursuing their multiple goals through schooling. Education for our era too remains an always interesting if occasionally frustrating and sometimes even maddening enterprise. Hence the urge to understand something of its origins in the nineteenth-century past.

We are indebted to many people who share our absorption in the history of schooling. It was an embarrassing number of years ago that Beth Light began an exhaustive study of the educational holdings of the Archives of Ontario and provided us with a systematic analysis of their key records. Her work has been much appreciated, as has that of Rosalie Fox, Margaret Hobbs, Nancy Kiefer, Lise Kreps, Susan Laskin, Liz Good Menard, Elizabeth Smyth, and Judith Zelmanovits, all of whom contributed research at various times, particularly for the chapter on teachers. Isabel Gibb, Marian Press, Jan Schmidt, Shirley Wigmore, Mary Williamson, and Joan Winearls are among the many librarians who offered special help to our project; we are equally indebted to the several archivists and curators whose collections we were keen to raid both for information and for pictures. Mary Allodi, John Crosthwaite, Ian Forsythe, Jeanne L'Esperance, Donald Nethery, Pat Rogal, Victor Russell, and Richard Schofield aided our quest with patience and skill.

Many people supported, kindled and rekindled our interest in the construction of this book. For their conversations, their probing questions, and a generous sharing of their own work, we thank Bruce Curtis, Ian Davey, Nadia Fahmy-Eid, Bob Gidney, Ruby Heap, Michael Katz, Keith McLeod, Wyn Millar, Dick Selleck, and Marjorie Theobald, along with the students who have participated in our seminars at OISE and York. Equally generous with their time and expertise were John Abbott, Ramsay Cook, Chad Gaffield, and Donald Wilson, who read the manuscript in whole or in part and gave us valuable criticisms. We thank them, as we do Jeanne Beck, Goldwin French, and Peter Oliver, of the Ontario Historical Studies Series, whose extraordinary patience and enthusiasm for this study did much to sustain our own. In addition to the Ontario Historical Studies Series, which defrayed our major research and writing expenses, we wish to thank the Ontario Institute for Studies in Education and York University for timely financial assistance to the project. We also thank Susan Hall and Margaret Brennan, who provided not only skilled typing but the knowledge and good humour required to outwit a recalcitrant computer when it seemed determined to outwit the authors. Our work was made much lighter by their efforts, as it was by the skilled editing the manuscript received. Our warm thanks to our editor, Margaret Allen, and to Gerry Hallowell of the University of Toronto Press for the expert attention they gave this book. Lastly, we thank our families and our friends – many of whom are already listed above. They are the people who looked after us while we looked for the missing note or ran after the elusive fact. It is to our families that we dedicate this book.

SUSAN E. HOUSTON
ALISON PRENTICE

Part One:
Interpreting Pioneer Schooling

WHEN SCHOOLMASTER JOSEPH SPRAGG penned the first annual report of the Upper Canada Central School in York in 1822, he noted that most of its pupils had received little previous education. 'During the first year,' he reported, '158 Children, 95 Boys and 63 Girls have been instructed in the School.' Ninety-one of these, he pointed out, 'had never before received any Education'; the others had received 'but very little.'[1]

What did Spragg mean by education? Did he actually wish to imply that ninety-one of his pupils had never received training or instruction of any kind? Or merely that they had never been formally taught their letters and numbers? Or did he simply mean that they had never before attended school? To question the meaning of words like 'education' or even 'schooling' is a vital exercise for anyone who would wish to gain some insight into Ontario's educational past. Certainly it cannot be assumed that our own twentieth-century definitions of these words were necessarily current in the early decades of Upper Canada's history. What is far more likely is that a people whose cultural and material environment and life experience were so different from ours also would have a view of the world, and opinions about the meanings of words like 'education,' very different from our own.

A picture of that early environment and life experience and what it meant for education is not easy to construct. Written records, especially records reflecting the views of ordinary parents, children, or teachers, are relatively scarce. Equally problematic is the fact that the written records that have survived are not necessarily mutually consistent, any more than are the assessments of more recent historians writing on the subject. There has been little agreement about the educational attainment of the thousands of Loyalists and post-Loyalist settlers who made their way, during and after the American Revolution, to the northern shores of Lake Erie, Lake Ontario, and the St Lawrence River. Were these migrants predominantly poor and illiterate as their twentieth-century historian, J.J. Talman, would have us believe? Or were most of them more like the approximately one hundred prosperous and well-equipped German families that settled on Yonge Street during the summer of 1794, who immediately prepared to build not only mills and a church, but 'a school house'? And, later on, when memories of the Revolutionary War were fading, how did the migrants spawned by the War of 1812 and the aftermath of Europe's Napoleonic Wars affect the educational scene? When vast numbers of British immigrants had arrived to join the early settlers, were Upper Canadian households still typically lacking reading material, as the traveller Edward Allan Talbot implied in 1824? Talbot claimed that during five years' residence in Upper Canada he had seen no more than two people with books in their hands, which does suggest that literature was a genuinely scarce commodity. But then there is the opinion of another traveller, Adam Fergusson, who commented on the 'good display' of books to be seen in the Farmer's Inn near Toronto in 1831. There is also the contention of Colonel John Clarke of Port Dalhousie that in those early days every family owned a Bible, which they read, and from which they taught their children.[2] The conflicting evidence about books inevitably draws us to another question, namely how much importance should be attached to the possession or use of books in a culture in which newspapers and the oral transmission of ideas may have ranked higher than 'literature' on the scale of values. By 1836, thirty-eight periodicals were being published in Upper Canada, and one student of the subject estimated that some 425,000 copies of these newspapers circulated among a population of 370,000.[3]

Clearly Upper Canada has had its pessimistic and its optimistic interpreters.[4] For all the travellers, and the later historians echoing them, who have deplored the ignorance and apathy of its inhabitants, there have been equal numbers who saw chiefly intelligence and energy among them. Much commentary, furthermore, was politically motivated. The height of ambiguity was perhaps achieved by the one individual who has figured most prominently in Ontario educational histories, the powerful educational reformer and, ultimately, chief superintendent of the province's schools, Egerton Ryerson. In 1839 Ryerson was convinced, or at least hoped to convince others, of the intelligence of Upper Canadians; but only two years later he would deplore their ignorance. The Methodist missionary and publicist was responding to the stresses of a period of serious political unrest in the Canadas. Political strife, culminating in the rebellions of 1837–8, had not ceased once the rebels were defeated. Ryerson, who was trying to encourage educational development and wanted to put forward a picture of a province greatly in need of but also richly deserving British investment in this cause, was torn between two images: an optimistic picture of educable subjects who were potentially loyal on the one hand; and, on the other, a darker vision of a populace teetering on the brink of dangerous ignorance.[5]

Contradictory evidence of this sort is less daunting than we might initially suppose. It is, more than anything, perhaps, an important clue to the absorbing interest that some early Upper Canadians and travellers to the province had in educational questions. It is true that most of Ontario's first settlers may have been poor; no doubt they possessed few books; certainly the circumstances of those fleeing revolution and war and attempting to carve farms out of the wilderness would suggest that survival rather than literary culture was their chief concern. Yet, both among the Loyalists and among subsequent immigrants to the province were not a few members of the class known as 'gentry,' some of whom earnestly strove to replicate in the backwoods whatever versions of literary culture or learning they had left behind them. As well, there were clearly many individuals with a more humble concern for the fundamental skills of reading, writing, and arithmetic or who, even more basically, felt it was quite sufficient, when it came to education, to impart morality, religion, and the practices of agriculture and housekeeping to the young of Upper Canada. People like the Reverend John Strachan, the Cornwall and York grammar school master who later became the first Anglican bishop of Toronto, might well complain, as he did in 1828, that because of its obscurity and frightful climate (worse, some said, than Siberia's) gentlemen 'of education and zeal' had refused to come to Upper Canada. Others, such as his rival, the young Methodist Egerton Ryerson, had their answers ready. Even if all were not members of Strachan's Church of England, Ryerson argued, persons who valued education were indeed present in the colony. What was more, they were quite as 'respectable' as John Strachan and his Anglican friends.[6]

Certainly, the circumstances of migration and pioneer life mitigated against the possession of large family libraries or the immediate development of elaborate educational institutions. And, for whatever reasons, mobility and hard work continued to be a fact of life for many people after their original arrival in the colony. Joseph Spragg noticed that his school in York was constantly renewing itself; change among the inhabitants of York was 'continually occurring.' Perhaps the urban environment was more unstable than the rural, but even in the backwoods many did not remain on the farms they originally settled.[7] In addition, as Basil Hall reported in 1830, among less wealthy settlers 'all those members of each family who can be spared from field work, [went] off to neighbouring towns, villages, or even to the better class of farm houses, and engaged themselves as servants.' In cash-hungry Upper Canada, whenever families needed money to buy cattle, farm implements, or seed, 'most of the young women' and 'frequently also the boys' were thus employed. There were other reasons for engaging in service. A young boy whom the British traveller Anna Jameson encountered as he drove her from one place to another during her 'summer rambles' in Upper Canada in the mid-1830s said that he and his sisters were in service because they didn't get along with their stepmother. But the shortage of money was probably the chief reason. In the Bathurst District, another commentator of the period found all the women, girls, and boys in a community searching for a lost needle, an object that was highly valued because the nearest replacement was literally sixty miles distant. Few men were present in the search, he noted, because most of the area's males were away working in other regions for badly needed cash. He might have added that the children, who in a wealthier place might well have been in school, were instead very much present and active in the community search for the vital needle. It was hardly an anomaly, therefore, when Indian families withdrew their children from mission schools during the spring hunt or, more drastically, refused to send them to school altogether. Native people were by no means the only Upper Canadians whose attitudes, mobility, or economic needs made them resistant to sustained bouts in institutions called schools.[8]

Even wealthier and less migratory families did not necessarily value formal schooling in the young province. An early correspondent to the *Kingston Gazette* tried hard to persuade the well-to-do in his community of the importance of a more serious approach to education. Riches were so uncertain and so frequently 'changed owners,' this writer argued, that even wealthy families should have the prudence to educate their children 'in habits of industry and economy.' It should be noted, however, that there is no indication even in this discussion that the training advocated should necessarily take place in a school.[9]

Indeed, any history of education in a pre-industrial society such as early Upper Canada that focuses only on formal instruction in schools risks running very wide of the mark. It was not in schools and colleges that the vast majority of Upper Canadian girls and boys learned the skills that they would need to function as adults. Aside from reading and writing, which were frequently taught by mothers and fathers to their own off-spring, or by mistresses and masters to their apprentices and servants, the historian must take into account all the vital social and household skills, the agricultural, hunting, craft, and even professional skills, that were passed on from adults to young people in the family or household setting.

The difficulty is to document this kind of learning. It was traditional and took place in the setting of the household, an institution everyone took for granted. There was little need, therefore, for anyone to describe or analyse it. In 1829, the Anglican schoolmaster and cleric John Strachan would feel called upon to write a treatise on how to run a grammar school, for the edification of other schoolmasters who might benefit from his experience.[10] But no one, or no one in Upper Canada at least, wrote at such length about child rearing, or how to train an apprentice. Literature of this sort, especially on child rearing, does exist for the period, but it was produced elsewhere. And, like so much writing on the subject, it tended to be prescriptive, rather than descriptive of what was considered the norm. It is from snippets of information found in a variety of sources, therefore, that we must piece together the early history of the family and education in Upper Canada.

On the surface, the role of the state in education is somewhat easier to document. As a result the intervention of government in early-nineteenth-century Upper Canadian schooling has been described from a variety of points of view, in political as well as educational histories. Until recently, however, historians focused chiefly on the context and terms of the political debate – pitting Reformer against Tory and dissenters against established churchmen – leaving aside discussion of its significance to the internal history of schooling. We are only just beginning to understand the evolving role of the state in the socialization of young people in the past and to link this role with the important educational activities of other institutions like charitable societies and churches.

From family and state we turn to the schools and their teachers, both of which present problems of another sort. Anecdotal histories of schooling in Upper Canada abound, but we have as yet no clear notion of the way schools really functioned. In our attempt to piece together a coherent picture from fragmentary evidence and anecdote, we face the additional problem of interpretation, as we grapple with the meaning of words like 'private' and 'public' as they relate to schooling, or the meaning of the word 'school' itself.

In the following exploration of family, state, and school in early Upper Canada, then, there is much that remains elusive. Yet one conclusion at least may already be suggested. For a great many Upper Canadians, there was much more to education than the 'three Rs' of reading, (w)riting, and (a)rithmetic. Equally, for most of them, there was much more to schooling than school-books or schools.

1 Family and State in Upper Canadian Education

Looking inside households and families to see how Upper Canadians reared their children is an intriguing challenge. From a rich literature of letters, diaries, and travellers' accounts, not to mention more mundane documents such as apprenticeship indentures, we can learn much. Some of our letter and diary writers, after all, were parents or youngsters themselves. And even those merely travelling through were fascinated with Upper Canadian attitudes towards children who, to the pioneer household in need of labour, were often seen as an exceedingly valuable commodity. Upper Canadian families may not have been as large as we imagine traditional families to have been. But most households seem to have welcomed children – other peoples' if they did not have enough of their own – for there was always work to be done.[1] Through sketches of the schooling of Edward Arthur and Sophia MacNab, we catch glimpses of how the wealthiest Upper Canadians orchestrated the training of their children. In contrast, the stories of Letitia Creighton and Thomas Dick, and of Thomas Dick's friend Ellen Jane Cross, represent the strategies of ordinary families. Although all these young Upper Canadians grew up after 1820, their histories are nevertheless appropriate to our present concern, for they illustrate not only the variety of forms that families could select for educating their children in a pre-industrial pioneer society, but the way in which traditional, informal patterns of education persisted side by side with more modern, structured kinds of schooling, as the latter gradually began to become more widespread in the course of the nineteenth century.

From the particular we move to the general and, perhaps, somewhat away from reality as we examine what a variety of Upper Canadians had to say about child rearing, as opposed to their actual experience. What expectations did the authors of apprenticeship indentures have of the arrangements made for children? What did early schoolmasters and clergymen believe about how children should be treated and schooled? Then, back to the reality. What did observers of the Upper Canadian scene make of these subjects and what conclusions can be drawn about how typical Upper Canadians dealt with the young? Since many early Upper Canadian families looked to the state to help with the schooling of their children, it seems important to introduce the question of state involvement in education at the outset. Here one of the classic problems of educational history emerges, for 'the state' clearly had its own agenda. At its simplest the question is which came first, popular agitation for assistance from the state or the initiative of government? In what ways, we want to know, did state-sponsored or -assisted schooling benefit the British authorities who financed it? In what ways did it affect those that they governed?

As in all educational history, the answers are not clear cut. It is not always easy to fathom the motives of those involved in running the schools or in the creation of government policy. Yet there is no doubt about what happened. Even during this early period of Upper Canada's history, the scaffolding for state intervention in what had once been primarily a family matter was beginning to be put in place.

I

Edward Arthur was the eldest son of Sir George Arthur, lieutenant-governor of the province after the Rebellion of 1837, and his education was fairly typical of that bestowed on the most privileged young men of his time.[2] It began with a tutor at home, an arrangement that was not necessarily ideal, for later Sir George came to the conclusion that the tutor had done his children much harm. Domestic study was followed by a stint at Upper Canada College, an élite boys' school established in the colony in 1831 by the then governor, Sir John Colborne. This period was marred, in the elder Arthur's opinion, by the fact that the college paid undue attention to the older boys who studied there and, as a result, neglected the younger. Perhaps Sir George's reflections on his son's early education were occasioned by the problems he began to have with Edward; for after Upper Canada College the boy was sent, along with his older brother, Charles, to study with William Walton in England, and here his deportment and application came in for considerable criticism. Sir George at this point began to complain of Edward's behaviour and warned him that, unless he applied himself, he would gain neither the admission to military college that he coveted nor a much-hoped-for commission in the army. When Edward did get into Sandhurst, possibly because of an uncle's intervention, his father must have been much relieved.

Sir George Arthur clearly worried a great deal about the progress of his son. Once Edward was in England, however, there was little Sir George could do about specific difficulties as they arose. He wrote fatherly letters to Edward's teacher and to the boy himself, and trusted to God and his English relatives to set Edward on the road to advancement. Only if he applied himself, the elder Arthur finally admonished his son, would he be able to return home and relieve his sister, Kate, who back in Toronto was proving herself a brilliant and speedy clerical assistant to her father the lieutenant-governor.

For information about a typical upper-class girl, we turn to Sophia MacNab, the daughter of the prominent Upper Canadian businessman and politician Sir Allan MacNab. In Sophia's case, we know only what she tells us about her education in her thirteenth year when she kept a diary at the request of her dying mother.[3] From this journal, begun at home at 'Dundurn Castle' on the outskirts of Hamilton, we learn that Sophia and her sisters at one time attended a convent school in Lower Canada. But now her education was conducted entirely at home by her parents, an aunt, an elderly male tutor, and a music master. Under the heading of 'Rules for Sophie and Minnie,' Sophia described a typical day at Dundurn. The girls rose at seven. They were to be dressed and have their night clothes folded and their prayers said by eight. At nine, school began. They studied with their tutor, Mr Thompson, until noon, after which they exercised outside. The girls practised their music and did their school lessons from two in the afternoon until four. The next rule required them to go to bed at eight and have the lights out by nine. On the weekend the schedule changed, for Mr Ambrose, the music master, came on Saturday mornings instead of the tutor. But in spite of this bright spot in the week, Sophia clearly found her schooling dull. She was much relieved when, after her mother's death, the family was able to take a long holiday in Lower Canada, where her father attended the legislature of the united province. Among numerous other amusements in Montreal and Quebec City, the MacNab girls renewed their acquaintance with the nuns at the Montreal convent they had evidently attended a few years before.

How different from Sophia's education was the schooling of Letitia Creighton, the daughter of an American mother and an Irish father who raised their family on a farm near Cobourg. In an autobiography written in her old age,[4] Letitia recalled her first walk through the fields and forest to the local 'common' school. It was 1831 and she was four years old. Terrified by a gander, which seemed about to attack her, but saved and set on her road again by an old woman she had never seen before, Letitia survived the walk and settled down to what seems to have been relatively continuous attendance at the school, until she could learn no more there. No doubt there were many interruptions caused by bad weather or household and farm work, but the only one that is mentioned was occasioned by the presence of a large bear in the neighbourhood, first sighted eating the contents of the school garden. Local parents thought it prudent to hunt down and kill the bear before permitting their children to attend school again.

An interlude at home appears to have followed Letitia's years at common school. But having developed a passion for learning, the young farm girl set her sights on attending the Cobourg Ladies' Seminary, a goal that at the time was quite beyond the means of her family. She won out in the end, however, financing her further education in the first year by teaching common school during the summer months; in the second by living cheaply in a rented room instead of in the expensive academy boarding hall and eating fare brought weekly from the farm by her father; and in the third by promising to teach for a time in the seminary after she herself had completed the course of study. After a stint of teaching in her school, which by this time had changed its location and become the well-known Burlington Ladies' Academy, Letitia moved to a new position at another ladies' seminary in Picton. Her career there was short-lived, however, for a local merchant and widower, the father of eight children, persuaded her to change her marital status (and her name – to Letitia Youmans). As a married woman, Letitia taught first her own stepchildren and then, very briefly, at the local common school. Family duties took priority over the common school, and she gave up the latter, but soon became deeply involved in the Sunday school movement. After another brief return to teaching when she apparently took up an assistantship in a Northumberland County grammar school,[5] Letitia Youmans settled down to her life-long work in temperance reform.

Letitia's case was hardly typical. It nevertheless provides an example of what might be achieved by an ambitious girl who lived near an educational centre like Cobourg and had supportive parents. Her quest for schooling was a particularly avid one. We only know her history because, as Letitia Creighton Youmans, she went on to become a founder of the highly influential Canadian Women's Christian Temperance Union, and was persuaded to record the story of her life. It is also worth pointing out that, prior to 1830, the Letitia Creightons and Edward Arthurs would have had trouble finding colleges and academies to attend in Upper Canada. Like Sophia MacNab they might have been sent to schools in Lower Canada or to the United States for the 'superior' education that they or their parents craved. Institutions called ladies' and gentleman's academies existed, but no colleges, and all such schools were small, family-like institutions and far less prestigious then either Upper Canada College or the Burlington Ladies' Academy was eventually to become.

Our last portrait is of a young man whose life bore little resemblance to the three described so far. Thomas Dick is known to us because, on 2 January, 1867, he decided to keep a diary.[6] From this record of a young Irishman who migrated to Canada with his widowed mother and three sisters in 1856, we catch glimpses of Irish rural traditions preserved in the Ottawa Valley well into the nineteenth century and, also, of rather more casual attitudes to schooling.

Thomas Dick's diary began with the death, as a result of an accident while harnessing a colt, of a nineteen-year-old friend, the day after the two boys had stayed out half the night on a New Year's Eve 'spree.' An important participant at the three-day wake that followed, Thomas recorded that on 4 January he was the only strong 'mail' person in the household of the bereaved family. The dead youth's sister, Ellen Jane Cross, was deeply affected by the tragedy. The only mention of a day school in Thomas Dick's diary occurred on 29 January, when Ellen Jane started in at the local school. Thomas recorded his hope that attendance at school would help 'keep up her mind some.'

After this dramatic beginning to the new year, the young man returned to his normal round of 'drawing wood' or being 'in the woods all day,' punctuated by the odd visit to the mill or 'the office.' More evenings than not during the winter he seemed to visit friends or relatives on neighbouring farms. He attended church, sometimes commenting on the sermon, and went to drill and singing school. On 26 March Thomas was tapping the maple trees, and by 25 April spring ploughing had begun. Singing school, 'stoping' with friends, and walking the girls home provided Thomas with opportunities for courtship as well as sociability. When his friend Bob Walker came home from the shanty, Thomas and he went that very night to the singing 'at McNally's.' 'Bob came home with Ellen Jane and I came home with Mary Walker.' The next night, Thomas visited Ellen Jane. Her family went to bed and he stayed with her until midnight. 'Her and me had a good chat it is the first time I ever sat up with her in that house.' As well as evenings with the girls that spring, Thomas spent evenings with Bob Walker, chatting about 'the girls' or about 'things in general.'

As spring moved into summer Thomas appears to have tired of keeping the diary regularly and from early June 1867 on he recorded, with one exception, only the main events of the year and those very briefly. He went 'to shantie' and returned; he stood up at the weddings of friends; he started or finished the ploughing. The first noise of the frogs in the

January 26ᵗʰ Old Mr. Golden was buried to day he had a Small funeral it was was very Stormy & he did with with the fever I was at the funeral came home & Stopt at home this night.

January 27ᵗʰ Did not go to church is Stormed to day I went to the office in the evening & to john cross's Ellen is not at home She is at R. Mc. cann's Stoped there till eight oclock & then come up to Brocks Jennie is just got home from L'Orignal from the tiamets Stopt awhile thou & then come home

January 28ᵗʰ Broke a colt & went to dull in the after noon come up to Ramleys had Supper Stopled awhile & then come home the roads is very bad.

January 29ᵗʰ R Rennick & me went down to Senning School at the Any had a good time with clark the Senning School master come home at five oclo in the morning Ellen jane cross Started to go to School to day it will keep up her Son mind

January 30ᵗʰ In the woods to day went up to john cross's

Thomas Dick's diary

spring was frequently recorded, as were the first arrival and last departure of the steamboats on the Ottawa River. Local deaths were among the other major events listed and, when members of the family were involved, Thomas noted down the number of buggies at the funeral.

Only the occasion of a first visit to Toronto to see his married sisters in 1873 was thought momentous enough to record in any detail. The journey ended with a comment on the feeling of 'lonesomeness' the still-unmarried Thomas felt on returning home. Rural Irishmen typically married late and, in Thomas Dick's case, the responsibility of a widowed mother and three sisters, as well as the need to establish himself in a new country may have delayed this step even longer than usual. He does not say how old he was when he finally married Maggie Lough of Cumberland in 1881, and there is no other clue to his age. But if he arrived in Canada as a boy in 1856 and was in his late teens when he began the diary in 1867, he would have been in his middle thirties by the time of his marriage, an event that took place some time after the death of his mother at the age of seventy-two and long after the marriages of his sisters.

Growing up, then, could be for some Upper Canadian youths a long-drawn-out affair. Being Irish and an immigrant, Thomas Dick probably represents the extreme end of the curve. Also, Dick, as the only male member of his family, doubtless considered himself quite grown up long before his marriage in 1881. Nevertheless, the North American born, other sources suggest, were probably able to acquire the necessary material means for setting up independent households more easily and quickly than most immigrants and were therefore generally able to marry younger.[7]

But Thomas Dick's story was typical in other ways. His farm work was seasonal, as were his comings and goings to the lumber shanties. If his own schooling was chiefly over by the time he began to write the diary, his reference to Ellen Jane's suggests a use of schools very similar to that described by Joseph Kett for early-nineteenth-century Americans,[8] a use that was governed by the needs of the home, of work, and of the individual rather than the timetable or other exigencies of the school. If Ellen Jane needed a period at school in the winter of 1867, there was nothing to stop her from starting on 29 January. For Thomas himself, the demands of the bush and the farm meant that he had little time for formal education. Yet singing school, drill in the evenings, and sermons on Sundays were available to him and were clearly an important part of his life.

Did Edward Arthur, Sophia MacNab, Letitia Creighton, or Thomas Dick and Ellen Jane Cross have anything in common? In some ways, very little. Edward Arthur and Sophia MacNab were clearly members of the gentry, of an urban élite; their young lives included travel and amusements far beyond the means of most Upper Canadian young people. Their education was privileged and, as schooling went in those days, the formal parts of it were probably very expensive. Letitia Creighton, on the other hand, may actually have had more years *in school*, despite the humbleness of her early education, than either of our two young aristocrats. This early schooling was no doubt relatively cheap, but it would not have been altogether free. Her later attendance at a ladies' academy certainly places her in a more privileged category than the average rural female child, but this further education was apparently achieved without the backing of great wealth. Thomas Dick possibly had little or no continuous formal schooling. Yet he and Ellen Jane Cross were probably as typical of Upper Canadian rural youth as any young people one might find. Their schooling was casual but, at least in Dick's case, we know that a measure of literacy had been won.

What these young people did have in common was the fact that they and their families used educational institutions as they saw fit. Some parents hired tutors; but when it was time for a family journey, the tutoring was stopped; a session at boarding school might be interrupted by a return home to be with a dying parent. If it looked as if a child would not be admitted to a particular school, an uncle's influence could be brought to bear. Other parents might send a daughter to school for a while to help her overcome her grief at the loss of a beloved brother and, if boarding at an academy was too expensive, an ambitious student could find a room elsewhere in town and get her family to bring food from the farm. When a young man had to work during the day, he might look to evening schools for education and entertainment. For all these young Upper Canadians, there was much more to 'education' than attendance, all day, five days a week, at a 'school.'

II

Schooling in early Upper Canada, as in any place or time, depended on society's attitudes to children, and there is no doubt that the prevailing view for most of Ontario's early history was that the young person's principal responsibility was to labour. In 1806, John Strachan complained that, even among the leading families of the province, boys were given only a few years to attend school, because their parents were so 'anxious to get them introduced to business.' The view was echoed by Richard Cartwright of Kingston and by later travellers to the province. In 1824, E.A. Talbot attributed the extensive use of child labour on Upper Canadian farms to the scarcity of adult labour and maintained that boys were typically put to work when they were seven or eight, becoming almost 'as serviceable' to their fathers by the age of ten as they would be at eighteen. Other writers agreed that large families spelled prosperity in a pioneer society, because the children could contribute so much to the family economy.[9] We see an example of the absolute necessity of child labour in the situation of Frances Stewart, whose letters to England about her 'forest home' on the Otonabee River in the 1830s and 1840s itemized on several occasions the work that occupied her girls and boys. On 5 June 1843, she wrote that the children generally rose at five in the morning and worked until eight every evening. Two of the boys were at school, but the three others were shingling the porch roof, with the assistance of a five-year-old sister who fetched and carried the shingles. By this stage in her pioneer existence, Frances Stewart was suffering from 'asthma and weakness,' and her eldest daughters had taken over all the housework except for a small amount of sewing that their mother could still manage; the three older girls had always had charge of the younger boys, each taking responsibility for one of them.[10]

There were critics who, observing scenes such as this one, roundly condemned the practice of putting the young to work. John Strachan, writing in 1812 to the *Kingston Gazette* under the *nom du plume* of 'Reckoner,' complained that parents drove their children 'to work like slaves,' forcing them to labour at a time when neither their bodies nor their minds were able to withstand the resulting fatigue. Another *Gazette* correspondent told the story of a family with five daughters and one son. The daughters were taught to read, write, and 'cast accounts,' according to this critic, but the boy was not. By the time he was six, the child was able to drive a team, and soon afterward he learned 'to plant and harvest, to fodder the cattle, clean the stables and harness.' When, at the age of seventeen, he 'expressed a wish to learn to read,' he was promised a year at school, but in fact was not allowed to go until he was twenty and then the teacher turned out to be a drunkard. This tale, according to its teller, finally ended with a complete rift between father and son.[11]

It would be a mistake to assume that all pioneer parents expected their children to work all the time, any more than they expected to work all the time themselves. Labour many Upper Canadian children did, but it was at least partly because they themselves evidently felt compelled to participate in the productive lives of their families and communities. Nor were their parents necessarily uncaring of their children's feelings or well-being. In his classic study of traditional European childhood, Philippe Ariès suggested that high infant mortality in the past produced attitudes of comparative indifference towards the very young, attitudes that persisted among most classes of society into the nineteenth century.[12]

But his perception may well have been exaggerated even for the society he studied.[13] And we certainly have evidence of Upper Canadians who expressed love for their offspring. John Strachan talked about how he and his wife 'delighted' in their children when they were young, and the Upper Canada College schoolmaster William Boulton noted how the increase in the number of children in a family increased the flow of 'tenderness and affection.' Boulton also alluded to the increased anxieties that a growing family could produce and the fact that children rendered 'frugal and industrious habits more necessary.'[14]

Attitudes to children were in a state of flux in nineteenth-century Upper Canada and were class based. Many children in this pioneer society took on important work roles very young. But educators were beginning to feel that this was sometimes a mistake and could lead to unfortunate results for the children in question. Parents who had aspirations for their children's advancement were warned to consider the effects of too youthful employment or immersion in the world. When it came to male children, especially, educators distinguished between stages of development and expressed concern about the acute susceptibility of the young to good or bad influences at all stages of their growth. Schoolmasters and clergymen who spoke in this way about the innocence of youth and the dangers of too much work too early were reflecting a growing interest in the nature of childhood that was to be found on both sides of the Atlantic. Children, they argued, needed to be protected. 'Do not parents suffer their children to be too much in the streets?' asked Niagara schoolmaster Richard Cockrell in 1795. Cockrell was the author of the first tract on the theory and practice of education to be published in English in British North America, a pamphlet he entitled 'Thoughts on the Education of Youth.' In it he complained that families allowed their children far too much latitude; their exposure to 'loose, illiterate companions' did more damage than was commonly supposed. Parents, Cockrell concluded, should pay more attention to the moral and social development of their offspring.[15]

How did Upper Canadian parents react to advice of this kind? Certainly, only a minority of children actually worked 'in the streets' as Anna Jameson's cart driver did. Most families saw little harm in putting their children to work, but most of this work took place on the farm. If boys learned how to drive a team and to plough, girls were taught to spin, to cook, and to care for the poultry yard and the dairy. Most often it was mothers and fathers who taught them. From parents or guardians who could read or who listened to sermons, however, more was expected. And in a society that was decidedly patriarchal, more was expected in the early days of fathers or male heads of households than of mothers and female housekeepers. It was to the former, at least, that the early teachers and men of the cloth first appealed in their sermons and tracts on the educational needs of the young.

Thus it was to the father who habitually wore his hat in the house or who swore or drank that Richard Cockrell looked for improvement. Such a father should think of the example he set to his children. Israel Lewis, the writer of an Upper Canadian textbook on the law 'for families and schools' published in 1844, felt that the household head (who was clearly assumed to be a man) should act as a magistrate within his family. It was his duty to see that his children, apprentices, and servants understood the laws of the land. And it was Egerton Ryerson, not his wife, who wrote to his brother, George, about the conduct of a young nephew of whom he was temporarily in charge. 'Joseph is broken of his bad propensity,' Ryerson wrote to his brother, 'and is becoming a good boy.' When William Hutton, a schoolmaster and farmer from Hastings County, found that he had little work to do, he decided to undertake the instruction of his own children. Even when this circumstance no longer obtained, Hutton still continued to take a major interest in the education of his son and daughters. His letters to family members in Ireland frequently commented on the academic progress of the children and on what they were doing.[16]

But if fathers and masters were expected to take responsibility for the education of their children and apprentices, women were also beginning to hear growing echoes of a campaign to magnify their role in the educational process. It is in the sermon literature that we find some of the earliest British North American references to an idealized motherhood. 'Mothers! How much depends on you!' the Church of England bishop of Quebec, Jacob Mountain, exclaimed in an 1822 sermon on the family, religion, and education. An Upper Canadian clergyman, the Reverend J.H. Harris, dwelt on the importance of the mother's role in 1833. The early nurture of children and the opening of their minds was generally, according to Harris, the mother's task. 'Christian mothers, think of the consequences which depend on your discharge of this duty!' By the 1840s, the *Canada Temperance Advocate* was printing its advice on 'The Management of Boys by Mothers.' A bad son, the author contended, was about 'the heaviest calamity that can be endured on earth. Let the parent, then, find time to "train up the child in the way he should go." ' If the 'child' in this case was evidently a boy, the 'parent' was no less certainly his mother. In the United States, the periodical press was even quicker to take up the theme of female parental responsibility, and two magazines, *Mother's Magazine* and *Mother's Monthly Journal*, appeared in the 1830s to promote the cause. One cannot know the extent to which their message penetrated the consciousness of Upper Canadians, but it can be assumed that members of the province's reading élite would have been affected. Certainly, the message was a strong one. Mothers were responsible for no less than the moral characters of their children, boys as well as girls. A well-regulated 'conscience,' the internalization of proper Christian morality through the mother's love, and discipline were the goals.[17]

Beyond such exhortations, which were clearly on the increase if not altogether new in the nineteenth century, there is no doubt that, in the ordinary realm of instruction in the household arts, mothers were always assumed to be in charge. It may have been William Hutton who wrote most of the letters home about his girls, but we may be sure that it was his wife, Fanny Hutton, who especially welcomed the return of her oldest daughter, Anna, when the latter came home to spin and help care for her younger brother and her sisters, after a period living with another family as a governess. It is equally certain that it was Fanny who taught her daughter how to spin and do other household chores in the first place.[18] The moving of young people in and out of the household is illustrated by the comings and goings of Anna Hutton. Perhaps the relatively well-to-do, especially, were accustomed and had room to take in each other's children. Sir George Arthur, for example, happily offered to board Sir John Colborne's eight-year-old son so that the latter could attend Upper Canada College as a day pupil in 1838. Poorer children, particularly among first-generation immigrant families, also boarded out, but chiefly as servants.

Especially in the earlier years of the century, formal apprenticeship was also still the lot of many young people. In 1847, the *British Colonist* reported a coroner's inquest into the death of one Richard Walker, a father who had evidently bound out his children before he died. Among his papers were found memoranda indicating where and at what dates these children had been apprenticed 'to various parties.' Then we have Edward Davis, a four-year-old 'poor Boy' who had been abandoned by his parents in Wilmot Township, Waterloo County, and was apprenticed by the municipal authorities in 1839 to Christian Swartzentruber of the same county to be trained as a farmer.[19] No reason is given for the indenture of Mary Ann Thompson of Grimsby, in 1825, at the age of seven. As with Walker's children, presumably, her parents were signatory to the deed of indenture. Mary Ann was to be freed earlier than Edward Davis, at eighteen rather than twenty-one; this age difference was traditional. But in both cases, similar requirements were spelled out for the contracting parties. The children were to obey and work faithfully for their new families. Mary Ann was expressly bound to avoid gambling, drink, and fornication. Above all, she was not to marry. The families, on their side, had to provide food, clothing, and shelter for the children. A suitable education was also part of the bargain. For Mary Ann, this involved instruction in reading and writing, while for Edward it meant three years' 'schooling,' two of them before he turned twelve and one afterwards. When their apprenticeships ended, neither child was to be turned penniless out into the world. Both were to be given appropriate payment, according to their sex, for their labour. At the end of her term as an apprentice, Mary Ann was to receive two suits of clothes, a milch cow, and a bed. Edward, for his part, was to be sent on his way with 'one yoke of Oxon one Chain one ax and one good freedom suit of Clothes.'[20]

If servants and apprentices could expect to get most of their education in the domestic rather than the public sphere, the indenture of Edward Davis suggests that formal attendance at a school could also be an expectation. Nor were children who were bound out in this way necessarily treated all that differently in the matter of schooling from children raised by their own parents. 'Domestic,' 'home,' or 'private' education extended far beyond the likes of the Arthur family or the MacNabs. R.D. Gidney has called our attention to the fact that in Britain, during the first third of the nineteenth century, domestic instruction of the young was still the preference of many families. Advertisements for tutors, governesses, and domestic schools in colonial periodicals suggest that this was often the preferred mode in the new world, too. In 1827, for example, James Durand, Sr, Esq., of Dundas, advertised for 'a person thoroughly qualified to teach a young gentleman in various useful branches of education.' The salary was high and the branches to be taught included French, practical surveying, geography 'with the use of globes,' natural philosophy, and chemistry. A governess seeking a position in 1837 advertised in the *Bytown Gazette* that she wanted to teach young children in a respectable family the 'plainer branches of EDUCATION and needlework.' Sir John Colborne considered Arthur's invitation to board his son so that he could attend Upper Canada College, but finally decided in favour of 'private' education, namely a tutor in Montreal, until he could send the boy to England. At a somewhat humbler level, Mary O'Brien was among the many Upper Canadian women of this period who thought it not unusual to provide the literary as well as the practical training of her own children. She soon extended her domestic teaching to include one older girl, who would help with the household chores and the care of the youngest children in return for her instruction in Mary's 'school.'[21]

Then there were families who decided, for one reason or another, to board their children out with other families on a paying basis. No reason is given in the following advertisement, but clearly the advertiser could not afford the fees of a regular boarding school. It appeared in the *Cobourg Star*, in April 1839.

Any respectable female residing in the country, (the vicinity of Cobourg would be preferred) desirous of taking charge of three girls, between the ages of 4 and 10, to board and educate, may apply to the Postmaster, Cobourg. None need apply whose terms would not be moderate. Boarding school charges would not suit. [22]

The early Upper Canadian family, in sum, was heavily involved in education. There was the requirement that apprentices be taught the skills of their trade. There was the fact that many parents undertook to provide the literary schooling of their own and, sometimes, neighbouring children. There was, in addition, the formal training provided in households by tutors and governesses. Finally, there was the more informal education that naturally resulted when so much of the productive work of society took place within the household, on the family farm, or in the family business. Kate Arthur could hardly have transcribed her father's letters if this work had not been done at home.

Families were also nearly always responsible for what their children read. Well into the middle of the nineteenth century it was parents and guardians who provided the books that children took to school. If many Loyalists possessed no more than a Bible and a copy of Mavor's spelling book, these books were, because of their rarity, all the more likely to be valued household treasures. John Strachan found the scarcity of books such a problem early in the century that he set about writing an arithmetic text for his Cornwall grammar school and had it printed in Montreal. With this exception, all the books his pupils used before the War of 1812 had to be purchased in the United States or abroad, for only gradually did British North America get into the book-printing business in any substantial way. And buying books from afar was not without its difficulties. On one occasion when Strachan sent in an order, the bookseller sent only half of a two-volume work; on another occasion, the vendor was dead by the time the order arrived. The scarcity of books to purchase in Upper Canada was still noticeable in the 1830s. The author of a guide for immigrants published in 1834 counselled prospective Upper Canadians, especially those going to remote areas, to bring their family libraries with them. [23]

Of circulating libraries there were few; only one in all of Lower and Upper Canada combined in 1795, according to a traveller of the time. But very soon some districts of Upper Canada remedied this situation. As early as 1800 there was a subscription library catering to families in the Niagara region, and a surviving catalogue gives some ideas of its growth and contents. Totalling 937 items by 1820, the library contained a variety of serious and lighter works. There was a great emphasis on religion, philosophy, and history. But there were also travel books and a few novels, including Richardson's *Pamela*. It was still too early to find many volumes specifically designed for children, but there was one. Twelve items were to be found in the relatively new and growing genre of women's literature: seven copies of the *Ladies Magazine* as well as five more substantial volumes, such as the rather bluntly titled *Female Complaints*. The Niagara Library did not have a peaceful history, for many of the books were lost or destroyed during the War of 1812. But such setbacks were only temporary. Increasingly, families who had time to read somehow managed to obtain the books they wanted. As Adam Fergusson noted, the family who ran the Farmers' Inn near Toronto in 1831 had a tolerably good 'display' of them. The *Cobourg Star, Picton Traveller*, and *Bytown Gazette* were among the many Upper Canadian newspapers advertising the existence of a book society, circulating library, or news-room in the 1830s. Such informal organizations catered to the individual and family quest for learning long before people were able to acquire many books of their own and well before the growth of public or public school libraries in Upper Canada.[24]

III

For all the emphasis on informal educational institutions and on learning in the domestic environment, there was also, from the beginning, an interest in the development of schools. Most of the children we have discussed so far clearly supplemented their domestic learning with periodic or even regular attendance at schools. And, from the beginning as well, there was agitation for government assistance in the matter of such formal education. It has been argued that a tendency to look to the state for help was particularly characteristic of Loyalists who, having sacrificed much for the British government, felt that the Crown in turn owed its defenders social as well as material support. Certainly the argument fits well with early Upper Canadian requests for assistance in the founding of educational institutions. On the other hand, a tradition of government involvement in the provision of college and grammar schooling – and, in some New England constituencies, even common schooling – was also the heritage of both British and American immigrants to the colony.[25]

It evidently seemed inconceivable to many leading early Upper Canadians that a colony made up, if only in part, of refugees from the American Revolution and the Napoleonic Wars could create entirely without assistance the educational institutions that would be needed to prepare young men for their future professions and life's work. The words 'young men' are used deliberately, for the early quest for government aid focused on advanced schooling for males. Immigrants who belonged to the professional or merchant classes were especially concerned. Where would they educate their sons? It was possible, and numerous families must have followed this course, to apprentice youngsters to clergymen, lawyers, or doctors who had migrated to Upper Canada bringing their professional knowledge and practices with them. Indeed in the colonies and states that the Loyalists had so recently abandoned, for the training of physicians and lawyers at least, this was practically everywhere the common procedure. The Law Society of Upper Canada continued to require a period of apprenticeship of students aspiring to be called to the bar; and until medical schools were founded, a traditional practice could be stretched and accommodated to the training of doctors as well.[26]

But there were at first few trained lawyers, doctors, or clergymen to whom boys could be apprenticed. And there was no doubt that, in the long run, educational institutions replicating in British North America the universities of Great Britain or the colleges of the United States seemed indispensable. There was also no doubt in the minds of leading Upper Canadian promotors of professional education that the government would have to be involved in the development of such institutions. Indeed, Lieutenant-Governor John Graves Simcoe was the first to assert Upper Canada's need for a university. He noted in passing that for the 'people in the lower degrees of life,' education could be cheaply provided. But when it came to the schooling of the 'higher classes,' Upper Canadians would have to depend on the generosity of the imperial government. Accordingly, Simcoe requested a grant of £1,000 a year to cover the costs of two schoolmasters, one each for Kingston and Niagara, and of a university, which would be situated in the colony's capital.[27]

Simcoe's plans were too ambitious for the British government of the day and his scheme failed. Schoolmasters did begin to drift into Upper Canada, but not because of any generosity of the Crown. Richard Cockrell, who opened a school at Newark in 1796, was one of the most popular and best known in the early days. Within a few years Cockrell had moved his school to Ancaster and subsequently taught in Wellington Square (Burlington), Cobourg, and York, before moving back to open another school in Niagara. Shortly after John Strachan's arrival in 1799, the latter took charge, as he put it, of 'a select number of the Sons of the Principal inhabitants of both Provinces,' and as the fame of his school spread, Strachan even more than Cockrell began to be thought of as the leading intellectual light of the small colony.[28]

The District School House, Cornwall, J. Strachan, early headmaster

It was Strachan, by now also a Church of England clergyman, who along with other 'principal inhabitants' finally succeeded in persuading the Upper Canadian authorities to allocate government funds for educational purposes. In 1797, the provincial government had already taken a major step in setting aside vast tracts of Crown land as reserves for the future support of grammar schools and a university. But when Strachan made his appearance in the colony, the actual creation of government-supported educational institutions of any kind was still only a dream. More immediate and practical were the needs of the schools that were already springing up to serve the sons of the colony's élite, in places like Cornwall, Kingston, and Niagara. The Scottish schoolmaster's first foray into provincial politics was in fact a successful bid for funds to pay for 'philosophical apparatus' to be used by schools of this sort and, most particularly one gathers, by his own school at Cornwall. Strachan began his campaign for the money in 1804, and a bill appropriating £400 for the apparatus was finally passed in 1806. But things moved slowly in Upper Canada. 'There has been a new election since the money was voted,' Strachan complained to a correspondent in 1808, 'and my friends are all out.' Indeed, he went on, 'the spirit of levelling' had pervaded the province, and the colony's new legislature would be composed of 'ignorant clowns.' Strachan looked forward to the day when his pupils would be moving into positions of power and he would have more influence on the affairs of the colony.[29]

The schoolmaster did not have to wait that long for his scientific apparatus however. The promised money was finally forthcoming and he was able to order it. John Whitelaw, a grammar school master who taught in Kingston at the time, wrote to a friend in Lower Canada in 1810 on the subject of Strachan's purchases. Rumour had it, he gossiped, that Strachan had added money from his own coffers to supplement the £400. Whitelaw had failed to obtain a complete list of what had been purchased, but he had heard that the apparatus included a telescope, an air pump, a 'camera obscura,' and a 'magic lantern.'[30]

In the meantime, the provincial government had waxed even more magnanimous. The year 1807 marked the passage of the District Schools Act and the beginning of sustained state involvement in formal schooling in Upper Canada. Often known as the 'Grammar School Act,' this law provided an annual sum of £800 for the maintenance of a 'public school' in each of the colony's eight districts. The nomination of the teachers who were to be the sole recipients of the money voted and the regulation of the schools were put, by the act, into the hands of five trustees for each district who, in turn, were to be appointed by the lieutenant-governor. The latter also retained the power to veto the district trustees' nominations for teachers. The act said nothing about the qualifications of the district schoolmasters, except the very important proviso that they had to be subjects of the British Crown.[31]

This first major intervention of the state into Upper Canadian schooling met with a mixed reception. Critics quickly emerged who saw the act as chiefly benefiting those who were already privileged in the colony. Certainly the 1797 legislation envisaging free grammar schools had been ignored, and the act included no provision for controlling the fees charged by the masters who were receiving the government money. It was Kingston's district schoolmaster, John Whitelaw, who, despite his belief that relatively stiff fees were important to the status of a school, nevertheless pointed out privately that Strachan's charge of £10 per pupil for a year's tuition at Cornwall was too high. With fees set as this rate, Whitelaw argued, the 'poor' could not benefit, and the district schools would become unpopular. But even before Whitelaw's charge, the 1807 law had been attacked as unjust. It was chiefly in the appointed Legislative Council of the province that consistent support for the act was to be found, and in fact many in the elected Legislative Assembly opposed it. The Honourable Justice Robert Thorpe of the Court of King's Bench was among those who originally voted against the bill, and later the leading critic of the administration, Joseph Willcocks, led a move to repeal it, succeeding in the Assembly but failing in the upper house. Subsequent efforts during the next few years to repeal the act were also unsuccessful.[32]

A major source of concern to opponents of the District Schools Act of 1807 was the question of control over the teaching appointments. Legislative Assembly member John Mills Jackson bluntly charged in 1809 that the appointments had become sinecures for half-pay officers, and later Robert Gourlay, a persistent critic of Upper Canadian élitism in government, echoed Jackson's point. The nomination of schoolmasters, Gourlay complained, had become a matter of government patronage, a reward for 'convenient persons' who were often quite unfit for their jobs.[33]

Written petitions against the act from the London, Newcastle, and Midland districts have survived. In two of these, a cause of complaint was the location of the district grammar schools: only the inhabitants of the towns where the schools were placed, it was claimed, could really benefit from them. Another issue was the channelling of the fund to one teacher per district, in places where several good schools existed. Finally, some of the law's critics focused on the selection of classical grammar schools to receive the boon. Why these and not the common schools that dotted the province and whose need was so much greater? The District Schools Act, argued the petitioners from the Midland District in 1812, 'instead of aiding the middling and poorer class of His Majesty's Subjects, casts money into the lap of the rich ... A few wealthy inhabitants, and those of the two of Kingston, reap exclusively the benefit from it in this District.' The money should be taken away from the grammar schools, another critic argued, and spent on roads. This would have the double advantage of opening up the province and providing work for the needy.[34]

It must have been as a result of the expression of these and similar concerns that the lieutenant-governor's office was persuaded to conduct, in 1816, an inquiry among the district school trustees regarding the workings of the law. The replies to the government circular were far from encouraging. A trustee writing from the London District pointed out that he hardly ever saw his fellow trustees; none of them were able to visit the school with any regularity, furthermore, as they all lived too far away, in his case a distance of fourteen miles. In a collective reply from the trustees of the Eastern District School, the problem outlined was the difficulty of finding a good teacher. The former master had attracted twenty to twenty-five scholars, but during the tenure of the more recent one the school had diminished from about ten pupils to one or two. Newcastle District did no better. Indeed, reported Trustee Elias Jones, 'in consequence of the great difficulty for these last three years in obtaining a Teacher adequate to the overseeing the Public School, and, in consequence of the delinquency of the one last recommended to His Excellency, there has been no Public School kept.'[35]

If critics were harsh, and even supposed supporters of the district schools less than wildly enthusiastic, true defenders of the law did not hesitate to speak out. An 'American Loyalist' denied that the teaching posts were used as political rewards and claimed that only two of the eight schoolmasters were unable to teach Latin. Also on the side of the school law, of course, were the district schoolmasters themselves and the parents of their pupils. A petition from Cornwall (where Strachan's school was located) sang the praises of the district schools, which, it argued, equipped young men with the 'purest moral and religious principles' and prepared them 'to give the most salutary direction to the general manners of the province, and revive that ardent patriotism, for which their fathers have been so honourably distinguished.'[36] Patriotism was clearly an issue in a colony that had been founded chiefly by people loyal to the British Crown during and after the American Revolution – an issue that would be raised over and over again in defence of government policy in education. Opposition to state-supported grammar schools was alleged to smack of republicanism, supporters arguing that without them parents would be forced to send their boys to the United States for advanced schooling.[37]

Associated with the quest for an identity or loyalty separate from the already potent image of a new world society being fashioned in the American republic was a continuing concern about the training and qualification of the public men of Upper Canada. The ideal of an 'intelligent magistracy' was contrasted with the American tendency to elevate the 'ignorant' in government. In a respectable society, as John Strachan and his friends reiterated on numerous occasions, public situations ought to be filled with 'men of information.' On people like Strachan, the War of 1812 between Britain and the United States had an enormous effect. For three long years, American ideas were more than a minor presence on the periphery of Upper Canadian society. The legacy of the war was a powerfully renewed anti-Americanism among Upper Canada's rulers and an even deeper determination to defend and expand British institutions in the colony. In the light of the war's impact, it is noteworthy that peace should have been followed so quickly by the Common School Act of 1816 and that the ubiquitous John Strachan should have been among those who promoted its passage. In a report that he prepared for the government in 1815, Strachan, who by this time had moved to York and become the master of the Home District Grammar School, still listed a provincial university as first among his priorities, with the continuation of the district schools second. But the most interesting section of his report was that recommending state assistance to the province's 'common' schools.[38]

Strachan's proposal in this connection was not an exceptionally liberal or realistic one. He wanted government funding, in the form of £30 per school, to go only to those communities that had themselves contributed

£50 a year towards the salary of a schoolmaster and had provided him with both a schoolhouse and a 'comfortable residence.' As with the grammar schools, he recommended that an annual report to the government on the state of the school should be required in return for the grant and that any teacher accepting government funds ought to be a 'natural born' subject of the king. To administer the proposed school grants, Strachan suggested the creation of a provincial board of education, which would receive the annual reports from assisted schools and assume the duties held by the district boards of trustees created in 1807, namely the general regulation of the schools and, in particular, of the books to be used in them. The proposed board, the enthusiastic Strachan concluded, might be made up of the judges of the Court of King's Bench, the members of the Executive Council, the Home District school trustees, and, last but not least, the Home District Anglican clergy.

Strachan did not win all his points. With the school act of 1816, state assistance was extended to institutions defined as common schools. But the creation of a provincial board of education was delayed until 1823, and the superintendence of government-aided schools therefore remained for the time being in the hands of the district boards. Moreover, control over the certification and appointment of the common school teacher was given to locally elected boards of three trustees, who were subject to the regulation of their district board only in such matters as the choice of books and school rules. The duties of the common school trustees were very basic: they were required to build or otherwise provide a schoolhouse, and they had to produce at least twenty scholars for the school. They were also to provide some part of the teacher's salary, although not the £50 stipulated by Strachan or, indeed, any specific amount.[39]

Upper Canadians who worried about the susceptibility of their fellow colonials to American influence achieved the restrictions they wanted on the nationality of teachers. But Strachan's apparent hope that only the British born would be eligible to receive the grant was blasted. Instead the act provided that those who were subjects of the king by virtue of naturalization or of having been an inhabitant of the old province of Quebec at the time of cession to the British Crown in 1783 were also eligible, as were those who became subjects by taking an oath of allegiance. The total common schools grant was set at £6,000, to be divided among the eight districts on a scale that presumably reflected their estimated populations. It was left to the district treasurers to pay the individual teacher whatever was deemed an appropriate share of the grant, on the production of a trustees' statement verifying the satisfactory conduct of the school in question for a period of six months.[40]

As in 1807, reaction to the new law was mixed. Its promoters echoed the words of Lieutenant-Governor Francis Gore, who held that 'the dissemination of letters' was vital to all classes. The spread of schooling, this argument went, would promote morality and religion and ultimately ameliorate the condition of the population. 'To inform the common people' was desirable; it made them better subjects of 'both God and man.' A few critics, however, worried that the 1816 legislation had gone too far. The British traveller James Strachan argued in 1819 that the Common School Act had been 'injudicious' in permitting schools with as few as twenty scholars to share in the government bounty. The result, he claimed, had been a proliferation of small schools of the 'lowest description.'[41]

The government attempted to meet some of the criticisms of its school laws by amending the acts of 1807 and 1816. The grammar school amendment act of 1819 introduced obligatory annual reports and public examinations and also made provision for ten free scholars in each district school. The common school amendment act of 1820, however, was evidently a response to the need for financial stringency. Possibly also because of reported corruption and consequent wastage of school funds on the local level, it drastically reduced the annual common school grant to £2,500. A further common school act passed in 1824 made significant alterations in the relations of power affecting the schools. In order to receive the government grant, teachers now had to be approved or certified competent by at least one member of their district board of education. Thus the 1824 measure began to erode the authority of local trustees, previously absolute with respect to British subjects at least, to choose their own teachers. Two further significant features of this act were its provision of some government assistance to both Indian and Sunday schools.[42]

With these revisions, the laws of 1807 and 1816 set the pattern for provincial intervention in local education until 1841. The laws tended to favour, as their critics never failed to point out, the training of boys destined for the professions over the more basic education of the general population by providing much larger individual grants to a limited number of district school teachers than were available to the teachers of common schools. A second feature of the school laws was their formal introduction into Upper Canada of duly constituted boards of school trustees. The district boards were appointed, but for local common school purposes, the standard North American procedure of electing three trustees was established. Whatever their powers at various times in their history, common school trustees clearly stood for local control in education. Thirdly, the school acts of 1807 and 1816 extended the traditional principle of state control over who could teach by stipulating that government teachers must be British subjects.[43] Lastly, the new laws provided for a system of administration. Rudimentary at first and tending to favour local authority as far as the common schools were concerned, Upper Canada's school laws nevertheless began the process of provincial administrative involvement in what had previously been chiefly a local and parental concern. If in 1816 local trustees could certify their own teachers, by 1824 the authority of a district board trustee was required. Money from the government came, in other words, with a price tag attached. The price was the exercise of an authority beyond the family, the teacher, or the local community, an initiative towards the establishment of some measure of central government control.

For the time being, however, both the administrative interference and the financial assistance from the provincial government were to be minimal. In 1822, the Executive Council had approved the establishment of a provincial administrative board, to be known as the General Board of Education, and finally, in 1823, six members, all Anglicans, were appointed to the board. Its existence was confirmed by legislation in 1824. But despite the fact that John Strachan chaired this new body, the minutes of its proceedings suggest that it met infrequently and devoted little time to the regulation of the schools over the ten-year period of its life.[44] The main interest of the board was the administration of the province's reserved school lands. Still, references to education did surface occasionally. In 1823, the year of the General Board's founding, the minutes contain a copy of a dispatch from Lieutenant-Governor Peregrine Maitland to the imperial government, in which Maitland proposed an additional £100 *per annum* for the district schoolmasters, with a view of engaging men 'of a more respectable description' for these positions. Maitland also spoke of the desirability of creating a 'general system of Education' under the direction of the board, consisting of district schools for professional education and 'national' or Anglican-controlled monitorial schools for the general population. Maitland, in fact, succeeded in turning the major common school at York into a monitorial school of the type proposed. But beyond this single experiment, the monitorial scheme appears to have made little official headway in Upper Canada. In any case, it does not seem to have been taken up in any detail by the General Board. Beyond the administration of the school lands, its members had most at heart the promotion of a provincial university and the dispensation of small sums of money for the purchase of religious books and tracts for the children of the poor. Certainly at the point at which the revenues of the school lands, instead of being distributed, were being invested in the Bank of Canada, it was clear that the money was being saved for something other than the common or even the district grammar schools of the province.[45]

In 1829, following visits he had made to the district schools the previous summer, John Strachan made a report to the general board on the state of education in Upper Canada. He had evidently been struck by the lack of uniformity among the schools and the inexperience of the younger masters. His response was to submit an 'outline of study,' which, if adopted in all the schools, would elevate the 'standard' of education in the province. In his report, Strachan argued forcefully that the teaching of Christian virtue ought to come first and that of useful knowledge second; that good public schools were essential to the peace, good order, and prosperity of society; and that neither 'the sick nor the destitute' had greater claims on the public purse than 'the ignorant.' Education, he argued, was like any other charity, and perhaps it was time to go beyond the present means. Upper Canada's leading Anglican educator, in fact, called for a look at the approach followed by the governments of several neighbouring American states, where the law required that sums be raised by local taxation for the support of schools, in return for the government bounty.[46]

Nineteenth-century educational reformers were fond of an agricultural metaphor when it came to the provision of more or better schooling. Even good land, they noted, had to be cultivated; otherwise, 'noxious weeds' sprang up.[47] Government intervention in Upper Canadian education and Strachan's plans to make it more effective derived from such a view. Both suggested that something as important as the education of the young could not be left entirely to chance, or to parents, or even to the teachers that parents hired.

But in 1829 this was still a minority view. In the short term, nothing came of Strachan's report. Parents went on educating their children in a variety of ways, as they had done since Upper Canada had come into being in 1791 and as they had done before it existed. In the 1830s and 1840s, Edward Arthur, Sophia MacNab, and Letitia Youmans took advantage of what was available or went in search of schooling away from home; they also learned a great deal in the domestic environment. On the other hand, each of their stories suggests growing parental concern. Fathers (and mothers) worried; children themselves had ambitions to move beyond what was locally or easily available. This might be especially true if one were in the upper echelons of Upper Canadian society. It could also be true if one had aspirations to rise.

The school that Ellen Jane Cross dropped into when it suited her needs was in some measure the creation of mid-century reform. But her casual use of it, as well as much about the school itself, had roots in the early nineteenth century. Government-sponsored teachers were already available to many of Upper Canada's young before the 1840s, along with teachers whose livelihoods were entirely independent of the state. But parents remained in charge of their children's schooling and, on the whole, chose whether their boys and girls would attend school and when. It was the interplay between their decisions and those of the teachers, the churches, and the state that created the complex mosaic of domestic and public schooling that had emerged in the colony by the time the next school law was passed in 1841.

2 *Creating Schools and Scholars*

From the earliest decades in Upper Canada a variety of interests were brought into play in the development of schools. Spiritual concerns no doubt predominated in the minds of many early settlers and pioneer founders of schools. Certainly that would seem to be the case with Fran- çois-Xavier Dufaux, the Roman Catholic missionary who started one of the very first schools in 1786 when he brought Mlle Ademard and Mlle Papineau to the parish of Assumption near Fort Detroit to instruct the French-speaking girls who lived there. Dufaux established the teachers in a house so that they could take in boarders, paid their wages and household expenses out of his own funds, and did everything he could to encourage the attendance and catechizing of the girls of his parish, while he attended to the boys.[1] Upper Canadian Anglicans, Presbyterians, and Methodists – to name only the most obvious groups – worried that children were growing up without Christian instruction, and increasingly pressed their denominational claims one against the other. But, as Father Dufaux's venture suggests, clerical school founders worried as well about the moral and social improvement of Upper Canadian children: spiritual, social, and moral concerns were for late-eighteenth- and early-nineteenth- century clerics all of a piece.

No doubt practical considerations were uppermost in the minds of most parents, but their motives, too, were multiple – or at least appeared so on the surface. Not long after the Constitutional Act of 1791 created the province of Upper Canada, newly arrived merchants and government officials began to bring in tutors and governesses or to send their children to be educated in schools such as Mr Richard Cockrell's in Niagara. Very soon they had more than one school to choose from; and girls' schools, like that of Mrs Cranahan in Adolphustown, complemented the offerings that were purely for boys.[2] Families who patronized schools of the latter sort expected that their children would receive social as well as academic training. Miss Hussey's day school in Toronto offered not only 'a thorough knowledge of the four rules, but some acquaintance with social deportment.' And teachers too had multiple goals. Mary O'Brien may have taught her own children because it was traditional to do so, or because it was more convenient, or because no other teacher was available. She clearly added older girls from outside the family to her school with another purpose. It was a question of barter: they helped with the household work and child care in return for their education. But many young men and women taught to help pay for their own further education – as did Letitia Creighton – or to save money for a farm. One Oxford County gentleman, John Tidey, took to teaching temporarily when crop failure, illness, and general bad luck threatened to bankrupt his family, while an American immigrant to the same county taught school until she could get her cheese business established on a firm footing. In Martintown, thirteen miles from Cornwall, a Mrs Black combined school teaching with dressmaking.[3]

The founding of schools, the sending of children to school, or the decision to teach school cannot be considered in isolation. On the contrary, all were interwoven with other considerations and, in the case of teachers, with other occupations. Teachers and pupils alike worked, between sessions in the schoolroom, on family farms or in family businesses or trades; schools doubled as kitchens or, if separate from domestic buildings, as churches. There is little sense of a gulf between families and teachers or between 'school' and 'community' in early Upper Canada.

Perhaps the most interesting fact about the schooling that the combined forces of parents and teachers on the one hand, and the church and the state on the other, managed to produce was its apparent variety. There were private venture schools of all sorts, both day and evening; there were schools catering to particular groups, such as girls or native or black children; there were schools intended for the poor. Sunday schools became an important feature of the educational landscape and had goals far beyond the purely religious instruction of their clients. By the 1820s and 1830s, more elevated institutions, calling themselves academies or colleges, had also begun to spring up. Finally, as we have seen, there existed in growing numbers the common schools and, in much smaller number, the district grammar schools, both generally subsidized in part by the state. The difficulty with any attempt to penetrate beyond the surface characteristics of these schools arises with the discovery of their many overlapping features, despite the apparent variety of the overall picture. Early-nineteenth-century educators were anxious to label both schools and scholars. But the boundaries often seem blurred, and the meaning of their labels is not always clear. Still, an examination of the many kinds of schooling available in Upper Canada before the reforms of mid-century reveals, if not the shadowy beginnings of a school 'system' at least some of the educational concerns that would fuel the creation of one.

I

An important distinction that Upper Canadians made when talking about education is the distinction between schooling that was public and that which was private. But their understanding of these words was quite different from ours. To John Strachan a private school was one conducted in someone's household by a governess or tutor or, possibly, a school in the teacher's own house. A public school, on the other hand, was a larger institution with a building of its own. The pupil at a large school was by definition more exposed to the public world.[4] Private education, in the early nineteenth century, then, was private because it occurred in a relatively protected domestic setting. The distinction between the kind of private schooling that was chiefly or entirely supported by private funds and public schooling, defined as entirely government and tax supported, was only gradually to be made in the course of the nineteenth century.[5]

Most early Upper Canadian private schools were proprietary and thus also private in a slightly different sense of the word. Fees were the sole income of these schools, their teacher-owners answered to no one but the parents of their pupils, and the profits belonged entirely to themselves. The phrase most often used to describe such schools is 'private venture.'

Some nineteen Upper Canadian schools have been tracked down for the period before 1800: two each in Kingston, Adolphustown, and Newark, and one apiece in Grand River, Matilda, Port Rowan, Napanee, Fredericksburgh, Ernesttown, Mohawk, Moraviantown, Niagara, Ancaster, York, St Catharines, and Fort Malden. Most of these were probably in the private venture or proprietary category.[6] Mrs Cranahan's was one of the first schools in Adolphustown; William Cooper's was possibly the earliest in York, and Richard Cockrell's the first in Niagara.[7] After 1800, such schools proliferated. By the end of the second decade of the nineteenth century, for example, Kingston had been the seat, for shorter or longer periods, of the following schools, most of them private in both senses of the word: the establishments of the reverends John Stuart, M. Donovan, and John Strachan; Baker's Classical School, Mr Wolfe's day school for girls, and Mrs Hill's school for young ladies; and the schools of Mr Tolkien, Mr Harris, Mr Hodgson, Mr Lapsley, and Mr and Mrs Pringle.[8]

The private venture schools were as various as the names of their teacher owners. Mrs Butler of Niagara advertised that her establishment, founded in 1823, was to be a 'select school' for young ladies, offering instruction in reading, spelling, geography, history, grammar, writing, and needlework, as well as the advantages of Mrs B's 'many years' experience in the tuition of youth whilst residing in England.' Mrs and Miss Ryley's young ladies' school, which opened in the Parsonage House in Port Hope in July 1843, was similarly conducted on 'English principles' and devoted to the 'health, comfort and intellectual improvement' of its pupils.[9]

Some schools had very clearly defined special purposes. In 1847, W. Millar intended in his Cornwall 'Day and Evening School' to prepare some of his scholars for 'the profession of School Teaching.' An early Cornwall day and night school, conducted in the home of Mr Chesley by Chet Raizenne, advertised itself in 1835 as a French school. 'Two gentlemen of the name of GRAY and DODGE,' according to the *Niagara Reporter* in 1841, had advertised the opening of a school for teaching 'an improved system' of penmanship, while Robert McCarrol and son, late of Ireland, devoted their Cobourg school in 1832 to the instruction of ladies and gentlemen in music.[10] Among the special schools that it would be interesting to know more about were the early 'infant' schools. One existed in York as early as 1831 for children between the ages of two and seven, and by the mid-1830s the idea was spreading. The York school had evidently been modelled on similar schools in the United States; a school that opened in Cobourg in 1834 for children two and a half to seven years of age was in turn modelled by its proprietor, Miss Scott, on the schools she had taught at in Toronto and 'other places.'[11]

It was common for the proprietor of a private venture day school, particularly if a schoolmaster rather than a schoolmistress, to teach special subjects in a separate night school. Mr Oakley of Niagara focused on geography, English grammar, and arithmetic in the evenings in 1832; Mr William Tefler of Niagara in 1831 and Mr Morris of Cornwall in 1835 offered to devote their evenings to the teaching of mathematics. On the other hand, James Moloney taught just about everything in his Bytown night school, which was open from five until nine. The subjects offered were reading, writing, arithmetic, bookkeeping, English grammar, geography, geometry, algebra, mensuration, and navigation, 'all according to the precepts of the most modern and approved writers.'[12] Whatever their curriculum, the private evening schools evidently catered chiefly to young people who were otherwise employed during the day.

Most of the charitable schools and schools sponsored by churches also had special clienteles in mind. The school of Mlle Papineau and Mlle Ademard was intended specifically for the French Catholic population near Fort Detroit, the schools inside the fort evidently catering almost exclusively to English-speaking Protestant children. The Toronto school of the Irishman Denis Heffernan started out in the late 1830s as a private venture school attended by both Catholic and Protestant pupils, but eventually turned into a more formal, public institution, with a board of trustees and a special building, and catering mainly to Roman Catholic children. A founder of the Yonge Street Quaker settlement returned from the Philadelphia Yearly Meeting of Friends in 1806 with a parcel of books intended for a local Quaker school to be taught by his son, Timothy Rogers. Timothy was soon replaced by a candidate who suited the community better, but the school continued both to be Quaker and to be conducted in private households until 1816, when a schoolhouse was built. The more formal Quaker school survived for over a decade, only to be 'discontinued' at the time of the Hicksite separation in 1828. The remaining 'orthodox' Quaker population turned at that point to the local common schools.[13]

The Quaker school and Denis Heffernan's were private in the old-fashioned domestic sense only when conducted in private households; Denis Heffernan's alone was private venture as well. But his school lost its private characteristics, in both senses, when a special school building and a school board came into the picture. Now it was controlled by a public beyond the teacher, and it was also public in the sense that it was no longer conducted in the teacher's home. It may also have been supported in part by the donations of subscribers, in addition to parents' fees. The Quaker school, even when it moved into a schoolhouse and in that sense went 'public,' was still oriented to particular Quaker children, their teacher, and their community sponsors, rather than to the new schoolhouse. When the schismatic Hicksites moved away, the 'school' moved with them and the schoolhouse itself was abandoned.

Many of the religious schools dating from the first half of the nineteenth century were public in the sense of having their own quarters, however temporary the attachment to a given building might have been. St Andrew's Presbyterian Church school in Niagara had its own schoolhouse in 1817. In the upstairs room a black teacher conducted a school especially for the black children of the area. Separate missionary schools also existed for native children. These were not always exclusive, however, for occasionally white children attended, as they did in 1849 at the school founded by the Wesleyan Methodist Missionary Society at Alderville in Northumberland County. In this school were registered fourteen white children 'from the Township' in addition to the twenty-six native pupils.[14]

Special schools for particular excluded groups often stressed 'industrial' subjects in addition to the three Rs, although practices clearly varied. In an early Brantford native school, the traveller Patrick Campbell reported that the 'old Yanky' teacher taught only arithmetic and English to his sixty-one pupils in the early 1790s. By 1831, however, the British Society for the Propagation of the Gospel sponsored a 'Mechanics' School' for the native children near Brantford, in which instruction was given in 'handicraft trades'; a school supervised by the Methodist missionary William Case in the same period taught shoemaking and spinning. The Methodist school at Alderville also featured what was known as the 'industrial plan,' and mid-century visitors to the school discovered the children to be 'as proficient in the knowledge of making bread, chopping wood, and in the general management of a farm, as in arithmetic, geography, and the English language.'[15]

Industrial schools were contemplated not only for native children but also for poor children of European descent. A small 'Industrial Boarding School and Polytechnic Institute' near Thornhill advertised the willingness of its superintendent to take in 'destitute' orphans for half the usual fee of £10 *per annum* in 1847. In addition to a long list of regular academic subjects, plus agriculture and gardening, the pupils were to 'have the choice of two or three trades.' All pupils were to spend a portion of each day, except Sundays, 'in the Field, the Garden or the Workshop; a portion in the school room and gymnasium.' The diet was 'principally vegetable'; there were 'no extras, no vacation, no Corporal punishment.' Boarding children in this way seems, even at only £15 or £10 a year, to have been a fairly expensive undertaking, and one wonders to what extent such a school catered to the needs of the genuinely destitute. William Lyon Mackenzie reported the existence of a similar school in the village of Hope, East Gwillimbury, in the 1830s. In addition to an academic school where children were taught the 'ordinary branches,' the institution included a large school for 'the instruction of young females in knitting, sewing, spinning, making chip and straw hats and bonnets, spinning wool; and other useful accomplishments of a like description.'[16]

Charitable societies in the early nineteenth century were often involved in promoting monitorial day schools. Modelled on the British schools designed by Joseph Lancaster, who favoured a non-denominational approach, and Andrew Bell, whose schools were clearly Anglican, these institutions were intended to allow a single teacher to govern large numbers of children by dividing the pupils into classes and employing student monitors to control the rather rigidly prescribed activities of each class. The *Niagara Gleaner* reported the existence of a Lancastrian school in Cherry Valley in 1819[17] and, in Kingston, the Midland District School Society had begun in 1814 to raise funds for a school for four hundred children to be run on the Lancastrian plan. With financial assistance from an English philanthropic society, the Committee for Promoting the Education of the Poor in Upper and Lower Canada, enough money was forthcoming for a building, which was duly erected; after a halting beginning the school operated for about ten months in 1817–18. The schoolmaster, Robert Johnston, had already fallen victim to the demise of a monitorial venture in Quebec city; after a year he was fired or quit the Kingston school, as gradually the supporters of non-denominational charity schooling lost ground to the proponents of the competing 'national' system of Anglican denominational schools.[18]

Information about the Kingston school is to be gleaned in a letter from the Reverend George Okill Stuart to Lieutenant-Governor Peregrine Maitland, arising from the latter's interest in monitorial charity schools. Maitland did not share the Midland District School Society's belief that there should be no interference in the pupil's religion, however, and was anxious to promote national or Anglican schools, following the Bell system.[19] The result of Maitland's own efforts in this area was the founding of the Upper Canada Central School at York. The stated purpose of this charity school was to 'train ... the rising generation in general, to proper and regular habits of application and industry, combined with sound moral and religious notions,' the religious notions in this case being those of the Church of England. From the first years, the numbers at the Central school were large, with well over one hundred pupils registered, although fortunately the likelihood that all of them would attend on a single day was remote, as in any nineteenth-century school. The relative success of the Central School has been eclipsed, in the historical record, by the manner in which Maitland, assisted by John Strachan as superintendent of the recently created General Board of Education, engineered the transformation of the York school into a national school. Thomas Appleton, the Yorkshire Methodist schoolmaster who lost his job in the transition, petitioned for redress of loss of salary to the House of Assembly in 1828 and again in 1835, having failed in his appeal to the Colonial Office in 1832. The issue that sustained this suit was not, alas, justice for Mr Appleton, but rather the political question of whether public monies should be granted (without the approval of the colonial legislature) in support of specifically denominational schooling. The question of church-state relations emerged as a central concern of the colony's 'reform' sympathizers in the years immediately preceding the Rebellion, encouraged in part by a sharpening of denominational tensions and rivalries. In consequence, the vision of non-sectarian schooling for the poorer classes promoted by the Lancastrian model of monitorial schools faltered.[20]

In part, then, ideological and political conflict explains the failure of the monitorial idea to take hold in Upper Canada. In addition, of course, the large-scale barracks-style schools typical of such experiments in popular education were quite unnecessary to the task at hand, given the modest size of even the fastest-growing colonial towns. Nevertheless, in the 1830s, the Kingston school reappeared. One authority dates its revival to 1833 and claims that the Lancastrian method was no longer insisted upon and that a small fee attracted 'members of the better class' in addition to the children of the poor. By the late 1830s, however, Kingston evidently had two genuine charity schools sponsored by the society, schools that were not only free but that provided books and clothing to needy children. In the winter of 1842, some 234 children of sixty-seven families were given clothes so that they would be able to attend one or the other of these schools.[21]

Another approach, and one that was better adapted to the lives of most Upper Canadians, was the Sunday school. Poor children, and even many who were not so poor, had to work. Since such children were unable to attend school on weekdays, a movement developed to provide for their instruction on Sundays. Starting in eighteenth-century England, it had spread to New England and Nova Scotia by 1800; by 1820 it began to be felt in Upper Canada, and the next two decades were the years of its most vigorous expansion. According to a study of the movement by Allan Greer, some ten thousand children in Upper Canada were attending 350 to 400 Sunday schools by 1832.[22] As Greer points out, the instruction of children in moral and religious matters on the Sabbath was traditional. What was new about the Sunday school movement of the eighteenth and nineteenth centuries was its emphasis on basic literacy skills as well as on Christian morality. Children in Sunday schools, in sessions that might be three hours, or in some cases, all day long, were taught to read and write. Some Sunday schools, such as the school opened by the Methodist Church at King and Jordan Streets in York in 1818, actually claimed to be non-denominational, if not altogether secular. When the legislature voted £150 in 1823/4 as a yearly grant for the purchase of books and tracts for Sunday schools, however, the interested parties were probably Anglican and the matter handled by the General Board of Education. According to the *Cobourg Star* in 1832, Sunday Schools in the mother country were 'generally, if not universally, associated with the National Schools' and therefore with the established church. In its efforts to promote such schools, the Cobourg newspaper emphasized not only their religious and spiritual goals, but their 'immediate and temporal advantages ... their never failing attendants in this life.'[23]

As significant in their impact as Sunday schools and, as far as their clientele was concerned, equally practical, were the larger academies, seminaries, and colleges that began to emerge in the 1820s and 1830s.

Some of these have been studied individually, but until recently they have not attracted attention as a group.[24]

Part of the problem is one of definition. How do we distinguish the small 'academy' or 'seminary' of the private venture teacher from the larger, more important establishment, also private venture or possibly supported in part by subscriptions, but employing several teachers, boarding large numbers of students, and occupying something more than a private house? What are the differences, if any, between proprietary institutions, such as the Cobourg Ladies' Seminary (later the Burlington Ladies' Academy) and the Upper Canada Academy, with its corporate Methodist backing? Or what differences were there between the institutions of the period calling themselves 'academies' and 'colleges,' or between both of these and 'seminaries'? Later-nineteenth-century distinctions between public and private educational establishments, that is between those supported by the state and those supported otherwise, or between institutions of higher learning and elementary or secondary schools, simply do not apply. Some of these institutions were proprietary; others were supported by a combination of fees, private subscriptions, and church funding, or state and church funding. Many considered themselves seminaries of advanced instruction, but at the same time took in pupils as young as seven or eight years of age. This latter fact, indeed, may be the major reason for the obscurity of the academy movement. Canadian historians of higher education have tended to focus on the histories of those institutions that gradually evolved into colleges or universities according to twentieth-century definitions of those terms, while other historians of education, concentrating on the history of elementary schooling or what evolved into *public* elementary schooling, have also considered the academies to be outside their purview. We know that the Bishop of Quebec thought it better that John Strachan's seminary should be called a 'school' rather than an 'academy' in 1809, but can only guess that this may have been due to the American or the Methodist connotations of the latter. In American and Canadian usage, according to Egerton Ryerson in 1836, an academy was synonymous with a 'minor college.' But certainly very few schools calling themselves academies had as many as the 170 students that the Upper Canada Academy attracted in its early years. It is no wonder that our knowledge of the academy as a Canadian educational institution has remained shadowy.[25]

Whatever the reasons for its obscurity until now, the academy movement deserves attention because these schools performed an important role in early- and mid-nineteenth-century élite and adolescent education. The attendance of younger children can be explained in two ways. The first is the sense that relatively well-to-do parents had of the superior training, both intellectual and moral, that these special boarding schools could provide even at the elementary level. Robert Sullivan of Hamilton sent his young son to the Upper Canada Academy in 1844 because he worried that the boy was too 'idle' at home; he apparently felt that day schools in the neighbourhood could not solve the problem. The second explanation is the teacher-training function to which academies often aspired. In 1844 this was one of the stated purposes of the Newburgh Academy and, as late as 1865, this 'large and elegant' school, devoted chiefly to the teaching of the 'higher branches of an English and Classical education,' still housed a 'Common School' in its midst. The younger children were clearly there to provide pupils for the teachers in training.[26]

But it is not clear that teacher training was the chief attraction of all the early academies, seminaries, and colleges. Rather, their major distinguishing features were, first, their concern to provide something more than the 'common' or elementary branches of education for their students; secondly, the likelihood that they would be large enough to support more than one or two teachers; and thirdly the possibility of financial aid from a church, the state, or an educational corporation. The *Brockville Recorder* of 26 July 1833, for example, announced the opening by the Misses Kyle of a 'seminary for young ladies' providing instruction in 'English Grammar, Geography, Chronology, History (Ancient and Modern), Writing, Arithmetic and Plain Wk.' For additional fees, students could also study music, French, drawing, the use of globes, bead and ornament work, gymnastic exercises, and dancing. Mr Kyle also intended to open a classical French and English academy, the advertisement noted. Both schools combined, if they actually materialized, would have had three teachers altogether and, with their wide-ranging curricula, have met the first two criteria we have laid out for an academy, if not the third. Yet by 1841 there were at least five institutions in Upper Canada qualifying under all three criteria. The Grantham Academy of St Catharines, dating from 1829, was coeducational, while Upper Canada College of Toronto, founded in 1831, was for boys only. The Upper Canada Academy of Cobourg, founded in 1836, was coeducational until its metamorphosis in 1842 into Victoria College, when women were excluded. Dating from 1841 were the coeducational Quaker West Lake Seminary near Picton (later Pickering College) and Queen's Presbyterian College at Kingston for young men.

Some of the proprietary academies, although they lacked corporate financial support, enjoyed reputations equal to any of these. Perhaps the most famous was the Cobourg Ladies' Seminary. In 1847, by which time it had moved to Hamilton and changed its name to Burlington Ladies'

Upper Canada Academy – after 1842, Victoria College – Cobourg

Academy, this school boasted a 'Board of Visitors' and may actually have enjoyed, as a result, some corporate aid. Whatever the financial status of schools like the Burlington Ladies' Academy, however, it is clear that corporate financing was not necessary for success. When the Upper Canada Academy closed down its female department on becoming Victoria College, it was evidently possible to refer parents and friends to twelve comparable seminaries or academies that took in young women; three in Cobourg, five in Toronto, and one each in Niagara, Kingston, Hamilton, and Cornwall.[27]

This suggests that by the 1830s and 1840s such schools were possibly as numerous as or even more numerous than government-supported grammar schools. The latter, in some ways, were very similar to the institutions described above. Their masters frequently took in boarders, as there was no other way that country youth could attend; girls were by no means totally excluded; and students younger than teenagers were clearly welcomed. The chief distinguishing feature of the grammar schools, perhaps, apart from the standard government subsidy provided by the District

Schools Act of 1807, was that their teachers tended, at least until the 1840s, to be Church of England. The Anglican monopoly of the grammar schools may, in fact, have accounted for the predominantly Nonconformist affiliation of most Upper Canadian academies. Secondly, despite the attendance of some girls, these schools catered chiefly to boys, and their teachers were nearly always men who were supposed to be university graduates. Indeed the male orientation of the district grammar schools[28] clearly accounted for the large number of Upper Canadian academies and seminaries catering only to girls. Curricular differences, with the academies stressing English and commercial subjects and the grammar schools the classics, were more apparent than real in a province where grammar school pupils studied the three Rs, surveying, and the weather – and where at least some academies, certainly those attended by boys, provided instruction in Latin and Greek. It was the intention of their supporters that the grammar schools should be preparatory institutions for university study, but as John Strachan pointed out in 1827, it was also true that the system of instruction was designed to 'qualify young men for the different professions who might not find it Convenient, or not be disposed to pursue their Studies at a higher Seminary.'[29] At least one grammar school master freely used the monitorial system, which raises even more questions about the differences between the various types of schools.[30]

Perhaps the open-ended character of the grammar schools (like the academies) is best symbolized by the failure of Upper Canadians to settle on any one name for them. They were variously called public schools, district schools, and, only rarely in fact, Latin grammar schools. The favourite term for them was 'District School,' which, in the end, placed the emphasis where it belonged. These were simply the schools whose teachers were selected to receive the government bounty for grammar schools in each of Upper Canada's several districts.

More clearly defined than any other type of school were the common schools of the province. These schools were called 'common' for a number of reasons, reasons that appear to have been self-evident to most Upper Canadians. First of all, they aspired to provide only a common or 'English' education, as opposed to a classical one. Secondly, in theory at least, they welcomed all the children of a neighbourhood or community 'in common.' Upper-crust Upper Canadians, in fact, did not send their children to these schools for precisely this reason, interpreting 'common' in its third meaning, as 'vulgar.'

Certainly the earliest common schools were very casual in their origins and organization. In 1797, the residents of the township of Charlotteville, in what was later to become Norfolk County, simply formed a common school when a teacher called William Pitt Gilbert happened to be stranded in their midst. Nine residents banded together to engage the schoolmaster's services and signed up some thirty pupils for his school. A later resident of the county recalled that this mode of proceeding was typical. A teacher, or someone on his or her behalf, would canvas a neighbourhood to 'obtain signers for the school.' Once sufficient numbers were enrolled, fees agreed upon, and plans made, if necessary, for the boarding of the teacher and the provision of firewood to the schoolhouse, the school could begin with no further ado.[31] After 1816, common schools might continue to have such casual beginnings; however, if they wished to receive the government subsidy that the law provided, the schools' 'signers' or subscribers had, in theory, to see that the requirements of the law were carried out. Common schools, thereafter, would be taught by British subjects only, governed by three fully elected trustees, and have on the books a minimum of twenty registered pupils. The government subsidy, small as it was, was a significant magnet in cash-hungry Upper Canada. Even before the passage of the 1816 Common Schools Act, Michael Smith's survey of Norfolk, Oxford, and Middlesex counties turned up between one and four common schools in every township. In 1826, Strachan estimated a total of 350 common schools for the province as a whole. By 1832, some twelve thousand children were registered in 450 government-funded common schools.[32]

II

If it is next to impossible to make sharp distinctions among the different types of schools in early Upper Canada because each type seemed to share institutional or curricular labels characteristic of one or more of the others, it is equally hard to categorize them when dealing separately with their financing, accommodation, or students. Many schools were subsidized by government to some extent, but few entirely, and fees of some sort were charged for nearly all of them. Accommodation varied from a single room to the elaborately institutional, but not always according to the type or status of the school. One can roughly match students to schools in terms of the wealth or occupations of their families, but there remain puzzles about precisely how this worked. Nor can simple categories be worked out in terms of the teachers. Not all the teachers of native schools were 'Old Yankys' like the master of the Brantford Indian school, nor were all the proprietors of ladies' seminaries gentlewomen from the British Isles.

Information about the financing and fee structures of schools is perhaps the hardest to assess. To begin with, we have only the most general, common-sense notion of what money meant in terms of purchasing power.

The sort of detailed wage and price indices that late-twentieth-century economic pundits (amateur and professional) take for granted simply do not exist for much of the nineteenth century. Selective references to wage rates abound, of course, in emigration tracts and travellers' accounts, but these are not particularly useful in isolation beyond confirming the obvious: that unskilled wage labour fetched less in the market-place than highly skilled work. The problem is not limited to the class of wage labour, however. The financial circumstances of the gentry appear equally hard to fathom. In the mid-1830s, for example, gentlemen such as Captain Larratt Hillary Smith, who bought improved farms up Yonge Street, somehow paid the £2 per quarter (with an additional 5s. for quill pens, ink, candles, and firewood) charged by Upper Canada College for a boy's education. Smith's neighbour, Francis Boyd, bred improved cattle imported from England and had a Holbein painting to hang on his wall, but neither Boyd nor anyone else had running water. Nineteen-year-old Larratt Smith struggled to maintain a social life in Toronto appropriate to a young articling law clerk on a monthly allowance of £8 from his father. When he ran out he could always work extra hours for the government: twenty extra hours realized £3.2.6 – not quite enough to pay for the pair of best black trousers (£2.10) and satin waistcoat (£1.12.6) he ordered from the tailor. Quite clearly, then, beyond what one could literally pay for, there was a more complicated notion of what one felt one could – or must – afford.[33]

Secondly, one might assume that private venture schools of the domestic sort would be relatively cheap because no special school buildings were involved, but what little evidence we possess suggests otherwise. The fees, at least of the schools that were advertised, seem to have been on a par with those of the larger academies or grammar schools, both of which were subsidized in a variety of ways. Equally, one might assume that the cheapest schooling would be in a charity school. But it is probable that many common schools were cheaper still, at least when charitable institutions like the Upper Canada Central School or the Midland District School Society institution in Kingston were in fact charging fees.

Our best information in this period is for the schools that advertised, and for them it is possible to make rough comparisons, especially in the 1830s and 1840s. We discover for the 1840s, for example, that the Quaker seminary at West Lake was relatively inexpensive for such a school, with its annual fee for board and tuition starting in 1841 at £12.10 and remaining well under £20 as the decade wore on. The Upper Canada Academy in 1841 charged £22 per annum for board and up to £8, or possibly more depending on the level of the student, for tuition. 'Extra' courses could actually total £28, although few if any students would have been able to attempt all of them. Egerton Ryerson might claim that this school's clientele came from an entirely different class from that of Upper Canada College, but in fact the latter advertised charges of £33.16.0 a year for both board and tuition in 1845 and listed almost no extras. Upper Canada College, of course, was generously subsidized, with an initial grant of some sixty thousand acres of land and further grants from the university endowment as time went on. It is not surprising, therefore, that, when it became Victoria College in 1842, the Upper Canada Academy looked to supplement its original funding (raised by subscription in England and locally) with government aid.[34]

The Burlington Ladies' Academy fees in 1847 were very similar to those cited above, at £27 a year for basic tuition and board, but at this prestigious institution, the extras could apparently add up to almost £100. Here one can only assume that it was impossible for a student to take anything like the full complement of extra courses offered. Although some ladies' schools were probably far less expensive, most for which advertisements can be found seem to have been no cheaper, and were occasionally even more expensive in their rates. Miss Malvo's and Miss King's, two ladies' seminaries in Cornwall, charged £30.10.0 and £50 respectively for basic board and tuition in 1842 and 1845. Earlier in the 1830s, the Misses Kyle of Brockville had charged £31, while Mrs Holland of Peterborough had set her school's fees at between £40 and £60, depending on the student's level. Far cheaper was Mrs Shorter's seminary, which was moved in the winter of 1846–7 to Chippawa. Believing the charges at most schools were 'generally considered too high', Mrs Shorter was attempting to keep her fees incredibly low at £4.10.0 for twelve months.[35]

The cost for day pupils was of course much less than that for boarders. The Misses Kyle charged £6 in 1833, and almost ten years later Miss Malvo's fees were exactly the same, at £1.10.0 per quarter, not counting the extras. The interesting comparison here is with the government-subsidized district grammar schools, which, if Dundas District School in 1846 was at all typical, charged only a little less at £1.5.0 per quarter or £5 a year to the students of 'languages.' Less-advanced pupils who were studying the 'higher English branches' only and beginners paid £1 and 15s per quarter, respectively.[36] Grammar school boarding fees that have been tracked down also seem very similar to those charged by the academies and private venture schools that advertised. The District School in Peterborough, for example, charged £28 for pupils under thirteen years of age and £32 for all others in 1838.[37]

Information about common school fees is much harder to come by, since these schools rarely if ever advertised and trustee minutes or other records dating from the years prior to 1850 are almost impossible to find. Until more evidence is forthcoming, it is sufficient to note, perhaps, that

TERMS
At Mrs. & the Miss RADCLIFFE'S School,
Niagara.

BOARDING with ordinary Tuition, including English Grammar, Geography with the use of Globes, History; Composition, Plain and Ornamental Needlework, &c. &c. &c.   £6   0   0   Per Quarter

Writing & Ciphering, ...   "   10 0   "
Day Scholars, (including Writing
        and Ciphering,) ... ...   1 10 0   "
Music, ...   1 10 0   "

Drawing, Velvet Painting, Artificial Flower & Card Work, charged separately.

No entrance money required.

No Pupil taken for any term less than six Months.

A quarters notice, or a quarters payment expected, previous to a pupil's leaving School.

No allowance for temporary absence.   Each Lady to bring Bed & Bedding, Towels, Spoons, Knife & Fork, which will be returned.

*⁎*Bills paid Quarterly.

Niagara, December 9th, 1828.

Charges at a Niagara boarding and day school for young ladies in 1828

nearly all common school teachers supplemented the government money with fees and that sometimes, in the early days, fees were paid entirely in kind. Probably all pioneer common schools required pupils' families to supply the school with fuel. In the winter of 1831, at the Ernesttown common school, school closed when the supply of wood ran out and did not reopen until there had been a chopping bee. At the same school, the teacher was receiving at least some of his wages in the form of flour and a sheep and was also supplementing his school earnings with clerical and surveying work.[38]

As with financing and fees, the physical layout is a useful clue to the status if not the type of school. Both private venture and early community common schools were frequently conducted in a single room of a dwelling, although many teachers aspired to the more roomy accommodation of an entire house. Yet when it was a question of an entire house, more often than not the teacher, along with his or her family, was also in residence. Almost certainly this was the case with boarding schools.[39]

When it came to individual rooms, a second-storey schoolroom may often have seemed most suitable. E. Taylor's select school in St Catharines was to be in a room above Mr A. Tilden's grocery in 1828; Miss Frances Bartlett's school was in an upper room in Smiths Falls in 1831; the Heffernan School, Toronto, was located in an upstairs front room in 1839. It was sometimes more convenient to have the school downstairs, however, especially if the teacher was a housewife. Such seems to have been the case with the domestic schools conducted by Anne Langton and Mary O'Brien. A really large school might also require a downstairs room, as was the case with Miss Elliot's school in Ancaster, which she proposed to conduct in 'the large Ball-Room in Mr. Kay's Dwelling-house.'[40]

Like Miss Elliot, teachers with insufficient room in their own homes often took space in the houses of others. Dr Baldwin's school in York was located in Mr Willcock's house on Duke Street. After his marriage, however, he expected to have it in his own house. An advertiser in the *Niagara Gleaner* in 1833 informed his friends and the public that he proposed to reopen his school 'in the House lately occupied by Mr. Proctor.'[41] In a mobile society, schools were also mobile. Still, appropriate space was crucial and could be a problem. In the Boulton papers, two letters from the winter of 1833–4 outline the difficulties encountered by the Street family school. The Streets were badly 'disappointed in their school,' one letter noted, 'solely for want of a house, the man which was to have built a house for them having gone off and left them in the lurch, with a great frame standing for which they had paid a great deal.' The solution, evidently, was for Miss Street to take a position as a governess, leaving Mrs Street to carry on alone, presumably in their current, inadequate dwelling. But the next letter, dated a few months later, recorded continuing problems. 'Mrs. S.' had been 'so inconvenienced for want of a proper house for her school' that she had not been able to do justice to her pupils.[42]

Private venture teachers evidently bought and sold suitable houses. If the buildings in which they taught were fitted out to function exclusively as schoolhouses, it was often convenient to have their own dwelling nearby. Such an arrangement was perhaps what the writer had in mind in this advertisement for a schoolhouse that appeared in an 1838 issue of the *Cobourg Star*.

TO SCHOOLMASTERS

A schoolhouse, 18 feet by 35, and superiorly finished and furnished, is now unoccupied and for sale at Port Hope. The lot on which the House is built will be sold with it. The location is one of the best that could be selected, and a most eligible one for a retired residence. This property and situation are well worth the attention of any well qualified teacher, who is desirous of permanently locating in a neighbourhood, in which by a skilful [sic] discharge of duty, he might command an extensive and respectable patronage.[43]

Accommodation for district grammar schools resembled that of private venture schools, was almost equally varied, and was often left entirely to the discretion of the master. A correspondent of the *Picton Traveller*, commenting in August 1836 on the excellent results of the district grammar school examinations recently held in the local court-house, lamented that the Prince Edward District schoolmaster was unable to obtain in the town of Hallowell, 'a sufficiently commodious schoolroom, conveniently situated,' this despite the glowing account of Hallowell's possibilities by the schoolmaster himself the following February. The town selected for the District School, according to this subsequent account, commanded not only an 'elevated, a delightful and healthy situation,' but possessed 'every accommodation, convenience and comfort.'[44] In Niagara District in 1833 the trustees planned the construction of a 'splendid ... academy,' but rented quarters were the order of the day until construction could begin. The housing of the Johnston District School remained, in 1840, in the hands of the principal, and clearly the prosperity of the school led to his being able to afford an especially good building. As he 'respectfully' informed the public, his numbers had increased and he could now engage 'as an Academy the large and handsome edifice on Court-House Avenue, Brockville, lately known as the Commercial Hotel.' The accommodations, he went on to inform his readers, were 'of a most superior description'; the situation was airy and healthy; and the playground 'unsurpassed by any in the country.'[45]

The larger academies and colleges were also able to afford good space. The Toronto Academy, a plain clapboard building 'with a porch and belfry to give importance to its front,' held two hundred pupils. It was not sufficiently grand or well located to be permanent, however, and when the school moved to Elmsley Villa, the old schoolhouse, moved to the rear of its lot, became an 'outhouse, storeroom and kitchen' for the newly constructed Queen's Hotel. Grantham Academy's building in St Catharines, 'a handsome edifice of brick 30 by 60 feet, and two stories high,' was no doubt more permanent. Schools dating from the 1830s, such as the Upper Canada Academy and Upper Canada College, were grander still. Already in 1829, the plan for Upper Canada College included a two-storey schoolhouse and

Upper Canada College, 1835

four dwellings for the masters and boarders; a picture of the college dating from the 1830s shows that this plan was carried out.[46]

The premises used for common schools varied almost infinitely, and many shared their space with other users. Early York schools were sometimes to be found in taverns, and the capital's Market Lane School was held for a time on the ground floor of the Masonic Hall. Indeed, the multiple uses to which early settlers put their buildings is illustrated over and over again in the history of common schools. Brockville's first stone building was at various times, if not simultaneously, a store, a tavern, and a residence, as well as a schoolhouse, while a log schoolhouse in Richmond Hill doubled as a town hall for many years and was also used as a place of worship. Early town plans invariably showed the location of the schoolhouse or school reserve, sometimes adjacent to the parsonage and, indeed, it was not unusual to combine the functions of school and church. A frame schoolhouse in Gananoque was in fact made available to ministers of several denominations, and Baptists, Methodists, and the occasional Presbyterian evidently took turns using the building to hold services.[47]

The contract for this Gananoque school survives and gives some idea of what builders thought necessary for a common school in 1815. The school was to have 'a porch of convenient size with a door,' a chimney

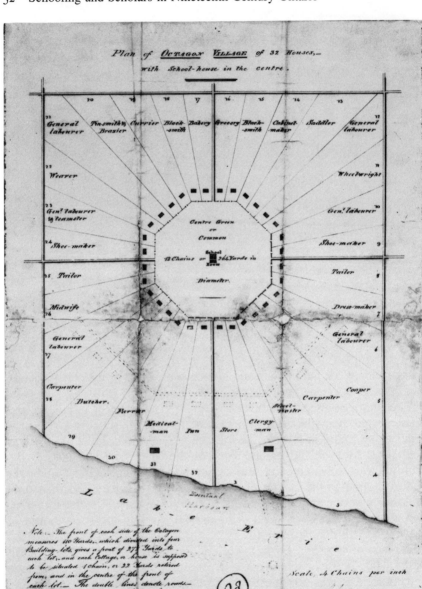

The plan for an ideal village, with the schoolhouse in the centre of town

to be carried up through the centre of the roof, and a 'necessary office' with a 'jointed partition in the middle of the same, with two conveniences and a door to each division.' The dimensions of this office were four by eight feet, and it was seven feet high. The school was to be furnished with a teacher's desk, a table for this desk, and a seat or 'form.' In addition there were to be three scholars' desks along the sides of the room, six forms for the scholars to sit on, and a row of pegs along the wall near the door for their coats. Playground space, if any, depended on the amount of land surrounding the schoolhouse and belonging to it. Oro Township schools of the 1830s were generally on a quarter of an acre of ground, beside a road, but in the case of an 1820 Toronto Township school, the ground was only forty feet square altogether. Even for the Oro schools, however, there were no real schoolyards, and the children played chiefly on the roads. Nor, in the case of the Oro schools, was accommodation provided for 'necessary offices' or 'conveniences.'[48]

Memories of these early schools were not always pleasant. As one octogenarian recalling his early school days reported, prior to the 1840s the schoolhouses were 'generally wretched, ill-ventilated hovels, with rude and uncomfortable furnishings – boards fastened to the walls like shelves for desks – high seats without backs from which the feet of the young children dangled like Mahomet's coffin between heaven and earth.' The difficulty of sitting on such seats was etched in the mind of David Mills, sometime schoolmaster, who while a member of parliament in 1889 wrote a long letter to his daughter describing the schools of the 'olden time.' In the first school Mills attended, some children were lucky enough to sit at the school's single desk, but all the rest sat on 'seats without desks, made out of slabs with the flat side turned up.' These seats 'were often very high, so that small children had hard work to get upon them, and their feet were far away from the floor.' The solution to this problem was to push themselves 'away back' and then to lean forward 'so as to secure tolerable comfort.' Mills illustrated his statement to make the point. The pupils, he said, looked 'something like this:'

The seating was not the only discomfort Mills remembered, because the school was also inadequately heated. Yet it was a cut above an ordinary log schoolhouse. Of frame construction, it boasted seven windows, and 'when lighted up at night ... had the appearance of a pretty large building from our place because one could see the light through four of the windows.' The schools of Oro Township, in contrast, were made of round logs with moss chinking, and oak clapboard roofing, sometimes held down by poles rather than nails. But they may have been warmer, for at least one informant remembered the box stoves 'kept red hot with huge hardwood blocks.'[49]

That there was little concern for the permanence of the ruder of these early school buildings is revealed by the casual approach to the land title. In Oro, the ground on which the schoolhouse stood was usually donated by a family who wanted the school near their own place. The school enjoyed 'squatter's rights' while occupied. But when the building was no longer in use, the land simply reverted to its original owner. Indeed land that was actually school property may have been more trouble than land that was not. In Bayside, District of Victoria, a large acreage granted for school purposes was first squatted on by a blacksmith and then squabbled over by various sets of trustees. For years, no school was built on it at all.[50]

There is also a sense of impermanence about pupils. Joseph Spragg's comments about the constant changing of his pupils in York's Central School suggest that entire families were coming and going with great frequency. But also mobile, it appears, were the children whose families remained stationary. Sometimes they followed a boarding school that 'removed,' as the Cobourg Ladies' Seminary did to Hamilton, or Mrs Shorter's school to Chippawa. Sometimes they stayed in their own communities, but were in and out of school as teachers came and went. Finally, it is very clear that most early-nineteenth-century students entered and left schools at their own choice and convenience or that of their parents or guardians. As a result, advertisements for schools often adopted a plaintive or insistent tone when it came to the dates of their students' comings and goings, since schoolmasters and schoolmistresses preferred their pupils to start at the beginning of a term and stay put for the session, but found this almost impossible to enforce. Even D.C. Van Norman, principal and proprietor of the prestigious Cobourg Ladies' Seminary, although noting that it was 'desirable [sic] that all wishing to avail themselves of the advantages of the school,' should come 'at the commencement' of the new term, had to admit that the school was willing to accept students 'at any time' in 1843.[51]

Who were the pupils who were moving in and out of schools so frequently? The evidence to answer this question is elusive, but not altogether obscure. F.H. Armstrong has tracked down 204 of the boys who studied with John Strachan in the course of his twenty-three years of teaching and attempted an analysis of their backgrounds and subsequent careers. He found that Strachan's Upper Canadian pupils hailed chiefly from York and the two administrative districts of eastern Upper Canada; they kept company at his schools with boys from Montreal and Quebec. Sons of Upper and Lower Canada's office-holding élite, and often attending schools with their brothers and cousins, Strachan's students went on in many cases to become office-holders themselves. His expectation that he and his pupils would go forward together was born out in fact.[52] Overall, there is little doubt that, with few exceptions, only the relatively well-to-do could attend the more prestigious grammar schools, colleges, or ladies' seminaries that charged high fees.

Yet there were exceptions. Strachan himself took at least one orphan, John Beverley Robinson, into his school. And there is evidence to suggest that, while the educational gulf between rich and poor was wide, it may not have been as wide or at least as systematic in early Upper Canada as it would later become. Even boarding schools could cast a fairly wide net. Widows were traditionally poor, and one might expect few widows to be able to afford a boarding school. But those who inherited businesses or properties were more fortunate than others, and perhaps this is why an Irish widow and tavern owner was able to send her youngest daughter to a ladies' boarding school in London in 1835. Ian Davey has shown that the girls who attended the Burlington Ladies' Academy, although not from destitute families, were also not particularly 'upper class' in terms of their fathers' (or, more rarely, their mothers') occupations.[53] Many of the fathers were artisans or shopkeepers. R.D. Gidney has drawn attention to the difference that obtained between urban places, like York, where by the 1830s schools could be distinguished by the class backgrounds of the clientele they served, and most rural places, where cash-poor pioneers of diverse economic as well as denominational backgrounds had little choice but to make do with the local common school. In many townships and villages the classes may well have mingled in the only school within reach.[54] Finally, some day schools were incredibly cheap. It could also be argued that almost any family that could afford to keep young persons unemployed at home could probably also afford to pay the cost of their keep at a boarding school or their tuition alone at a day school. The key, of course, was the ability to support young people who were not engaged in productive or remunerative work, for it is clear that the majority of ordinary families required their children's labour to keep the family economically afloat. The very poorest would have trouble sending their children to school not only because nearly all schools charged some fees, however minimal, but because adequate clothing or shoes might be in short supply. Some might have to send their children to labour or even live in the households of others, in which case even attendance at night school could well be out of the question.

One has a sense that the early private venture schools were very much family affairs. To begin with, most, especially the boarding schools, were probably very small. Mrs Spilsbury's school accommodated from four to six boarders in 1831. The Reverend R. Short announced that he would try to create 'the comforts of a Private Family' for his boarders in 1837, and in 1841 Mrs Brown advertised that her boarders would be treated 'in all respects as members of her own family.'[55] Even at a larger school, like Upper Canada College, boarders appear to have been housed in small family groups, at least in the early days when each master had a number of children in his charge. Some, like the French master J. de la Haye, were able to command fees that were higher than the college average in return for special advantages offered – in his case, presumably, the advantage of tuition in spoken French. In other cases, people evidently not connected with the school at all took in a few boarders on a family boarding basis, as did a Mrs Brooke, who advertised in a September 1849 issue of the *Globe*. For the masters themselves, boarding students was sometimes the hardest part of the work. One gathers that the establishment run by the Reverend William Boulton, a master at Upper Canada college in 1833, was sufficiently large to be labelled a 'boarding hall,' since he had the help of a matron. Despite this assistance, however, things seemed to get out of hand during the absence of his wife in July. Boulton found it unpleasant 'to have a constant bustle with such a set of unmannerly boys.' The furniture got 'knocked about a great deal,' and his time was continually interrupted.[56]

How did parents and pupils regard their schools? Some were duly impressed. Thomas Ridout wrote home in 1807 to the effect that the boys at John Strachan's school in Cornwall stayed up until midnight or 1:00 a.m. every night to complete their work. Equally, Letitia Creighton recalled great dedication to her students at the Cobourg Ladies' Seminary, a school she could barely afford to attend, and that inspired her to rise before dawn to struggle with especially challenging problems in arithmetic. William Hutton wrote to relatives in the old country about his pleasure at his son's progress at Upper Canada College, when the boy 'raised himself 15 on the mathematical form and 6 on the classical in two days.' This, possibly, also reflected Hutton's pride in his own achievement, since he had earlier been his son's instructor. The Hutton case is also interesting because it was young Hutton himself who chose to attend the college. He considered superior schooling to be more valuable than a good piece of improved land. His sisters should get the farm; for himself he asked for nothing but 'an education.' His Upper Canada College schooling and subsequent legal training, in fact, very quickly elevated the younger Hutton to a cash income higher than his father's, at a point when the senior Hutton also commanded a respectable professional salary.[57]

Students at schools like John Strachan's or the Cobourg Ladies' Seminary may have viewed themselves as almost unable to afford such an education, compared to some of their peers. And as we have seen, Ian Davey's evidence suggests that, even in prestigious schools, many students did come from relatively modest 'industrious' backgrounds. But this did not mean that the schools themselves entirely accepted the diversity of their student bodies. Upper Canada College is an interesting example of a school torn between its desire to cater to the variety to be found in Upper Canada and its anxiety to turn out a uniform 'product.' On the side of diversity, we have the principal's policy, stated in 1831, that children of every religious denomination would be accepted and the decision, in 1836, to take in six native boys, to be trained for missionary work among their own people. On the other side, the provincial General Board of Education, whose responsibility the government of the college was until the board was disbanded, was not willing, at least in the early years, to accept any free pupils. Mary Shepperson's request for free tuition for her son was turned down. There was, in addition, a concerted campaign to counteract the necessarily diverse educational backgrounds that many boys brought to the school at the beginning. The college, it was believed, should aim to develop a single, uniform 'plan of discipline and education,' and such reasoning may have inspired the decision to have a preparatory school attached to the college. Parents needed to be disciplined, too, according to the General Board, which felt aggrieved at the assumption that pupils could attend at the 'convenience' or 'wish' of their families. Very early in the college's history, the board proposed a strict enforcement of regular attendance and that parents be required to send notes explaining the absences of day pupils.[58]

With such sentiments we begin to slip away from our earlier contention that there was little or no gulf between teachers and families or between school and society in early Upper Canada. The rules of Oakville's first common school, founded in 1836, suggest the mutual comfort yet potential for disharmony and alienation that even an early common school could combine.[59]

1. School to be open at 9 o'clock a.m. and an intermission for fifteen minutes at 1/2 past Ten, and to be dismissed at 12 o'clock noon – to be called in

at 2 o'clock p.m. an intermission for fifteen minutes at 1/2 past 3 p.m. and dismissed at 5 o'clock p.m.

2. Due regard to cleanliness, and the avoiding of all infectious diseases among the children in School such as the Itch and Whooping Cough, etc.
3. The pupils to be strictly required to observe good order at the intermission and noon hours, to avoid all screaming and useless noises, quarrelling, etc.
4. Good fires to be kept during all wet and damp days –
5. As all good children from their cradle are possessed by enquiring minds, that proper attention be given to all enquiries they may make relative to education in mildness, with an approbation of their conduct in so doing.
6. That swearing, calling of bad names be strictly forbidden.
7. That punctuality in attendance on the regular school hours be particularly required by the teacher, and also that his example in so doing be a sufficient warning to them –
8. That all pupils in the school do not be allowed to whisper and laugh during the school hours, and but one allowed to be out of school at a time, and not then without the consent of the teacher.
9. That the teacher be required to take a paternal as well as pedagogical care over all pupils placed under his tuition.
10. That the teacher require each subscriber to the school to furnish his quota of firewood for the season and have it cut and properly piled for the use of the stove in said school house.

Some other minor laws are actually necessary which should be discretionary with the teacher by and with the advice and consent of the trustees.

In all this the Oakville school trustees were no longer simply the representatives of the parent subscribers but clearly felt called upon to regulate both the teacher and other people's children with formal rules. 'Screaming and useless noises' were ruled out along with unpunctual attendance and even whispering. Yet sympathy was at least expressed for children's 'enquiring minds' and useful questions. Later common school rules do not seem to have been so sympathetic. In Fredericksburgh in 1842 the rules stated bluntly that students too old to 'receive discipline' were simply to be expelled.[60] Still, one suspects that some common schools, especially perhaps the smaller ones, would retain much longer than larger, urban institutions the flavour – if not necessarily the reality – of family interest and involvement. Many of the smaller private venture schools must have been the same.

Certainly, whatever the type of school, families had the choice of whether or not to send their children, on which days, and for how long. Fees (or 'rates') paid by parents may also have helped them to keep the upper hand, especially in those schools whose teachers were entirely

A common school house, dating from the 1830s, in the village of Algonquin

A Grenville County common school house, erected in 1812, abandoned by the time of this photograph taken in the 1920s

dependent on this income. The clientele of Upper Canada's schools could always vote with their feet. When families were displeased, they had the option of simply withdrawing their children from the school. If they were lucky, a better teacher or school might be found in the next street, the next concession – or the next year. Many, of course, felt that they were not lucky. There was always the possibility that an insufficiently supported school would fall by the wayside and, although the point may well have been exaggerated, it is true that many of the schools founded in this period did not have long histories. Then, families looking for 'select' schools or advanced training for their children, particularly families with girls that they wished to educate beyond the three RS – as well as families whose location, ideological predisposition, or means precluded choice – believed that they had reason to complain. Indeed they complained loud and long, and their complaints increased with time. In the final analysis, the number of schools Upper Canadians created suggests that formal instruction was already a much-sought-after commodity in the colony well before mid-century. Even in the early decades of the nineteenth century, and certainly by the 1830s, the competitive quest for educational 'improvement' had begun to affect many Upper Canadian parents and children, and their schools.

3 *Schoolmistresses and Schoolmasters*

One way or another teachers were at the centre of the Upper Canadian quest for schooling. Theirs was an entrepreneurial spirit. Young or old, married or single, female or male, they were often the creative forces behind their schools, and thus were justly styled the mistresses or masters of their worlds. On the other hand, the status incongruity noted by Jeanne Peterson for nineteenth-century governesses, caught between the authority they had over their charges and their inferior status within the households of their employers, was also true for many Upper Canadian teachers. Mistresses and masters of their schools far more than is the case today, they were nevertheless the servants of those who employed them. Even private venture teachers were often forced into a deferential position with respect to the parents and friends of their pupils, for these same parents and friends had the power to send or to withdraw the children on whom their fortunes depended.

Yet whether mistresses, masters, or servants, one fact does emerge from an examination of early Upper Canadian teachers: their closeness to the communities in which they taught. Not by any means necessarily native to those communities, often itinerants in fact, they may frequently have been complete strangers to the pupils and their friends at the beginning of their employment in a given school. But, if they lasted, it is certain that by the end of the year they were known quantities.

I

Who were the teachers of early Upper Canada? What manner and class of women and men taught school? The answer must be all kinds. Certainly teachers were distinguished by very few formal qualifications. Although, roughly speaking, it was a general rule that masters of large academies and grammar schools ought to have had classical educations and university degrees, the latter was by no means absolutely required and even the former was not a certainty. Even after mid-century, the founder and headmaster of a popular academy could be almost entirely self-educated. An example is William Wetherall, who attended a Quaker academy in his early youth in England but taught in common schools in Canada. Wetherall felt qualified to open his own seminary after what he described as a long period of 'solitary' study. Of course there were the legal requirements for the teachers of common and district grammar schools laid down by the acts of 1807 and 1816. But these were minimal and referred chiefly to the loyalty of those undertaking to instruct the youth of the colony.[1] And no such rules applied to the hundreds of private venture teachers who, even by mid-century, may still have been the majority of men and women teaching in Upper Canada.

Once again we turn to advertisements for information. They tell us of course what the teachers themselves wanted their potential clients to know, but are revealing nevertheless. Mr C. Gregor, the master of Ottawa District School, announced in an 1838 issue of the *Bytown Gazette* that he had not only 'passed through a complete course of University Education at Glasgow,' but had studied education with the 'celebrated SHERIDAN KNOWLES.' On quitting his 'very numerous' school in Fontrose, Scotland, to come to North America, Mr G., as he styled himself, had been spontaneously presented by the inhabitants of the town with 'a most ample certificate of character and abilities.'[2]

Some teachers expected their names alone, or the names of institutions with which they had been associated, to convince the public of their merits. Thus Miss Radcliffe simply announced that she had 'taken a share in the direction' of the Cobourg Ladies' Academy in 1831. Details such as teachers' qualifications or even the school's fees were not mentioned in connection with her new academy, where young ladies were to be taught 'all the branches of education necessary to fit them for a useful and elegant life.'[3] Perhaps women teachers in particular felt it unladylike to be specific. In addition, in a period when advanced formal learning for women was rare, few had much of a specific nature that could be mentioned. Could they say that they had had a complete course at a university? Hardly. Or that they had studied with a particularly renowned teacher? Only rarely. Instead, they were forced to fall back on their knowledge of 'education' in the old country, the length of their experience as teachers, their knowledge of particular subjects, or their unsullied character or elevated position in society.

Many men, of course, did the same. One individual, announcing a new private school, pointed out that it replaced Mr Thompson's just discontinued and noted his ten years of experience in conducting a common school. A district grammar school principal mentioned 'as proof of the success' that had attended his teaching, that a very young pupil of his had been a successful candidate at the examinations for Upper Canada College. A private venture teacher who had recently been a 'Student of the University of Cambridge' referred parents to two ministers for credentials 'as to his classical attainments and abilities as an instructor,' also pointing out that he was engaged to teach French at the ladies' seminary conducted by Mrs Fenwich and Mrs Breckenridge.[4]

The prize for the most appealing advertisement of the period goes to Bindon Burton Alton, 'Late Chief Usher in the Feinaglion Institution of Limerick and Contributor to the Albums and Magazines.' B.B.A., as he styled himself, stressed not only the subjects he could teach but the style of his teaching. In his school the ordinary branches would be 'laid down to every capacity in a plain, simple, instructive manner, not heretofore exemplified.' Other more elevated subjects would also be taught, such as the use of the globe, 'that beautiful and entertaining science of which all polite life needs to be acquainted.'

And as the writer has spent several of his juvenile days on the green waters, he will instruct young or old in the Rudiments of Navigation, and lead them by plain and spherical trigonometry to comprehend the most complicated calculations, even in 'Lunar Observations' – not forgetting Algebra, Euclid and the higher branches of Mathematics.

B.B.A. intended to devote himself 'arduously' to winning the patronage of the public. As to his talents and abilities, he referred readers of his advertisement to the 'celebrated institution aforementioned' in Limerick, of which he had been a 'fit Conductor.'[5]

Teachers looking for work in schools already established were usually less flamboyant. They chiefly listed their experience and the subjects they could teach. One ad, shortly after the War of 1812, assured prospective employers of the advertiser's loyalty; in another case, a teacher described himself as 'middle aged'; in a third, the would-be schoolmaster referred to his ability to speak French with a Parisian accent. The latter teacher, who was looking for a post in the wake of the 1837–8 rebellions, felt it useful also to announce the fact that his 'views' were 'moderate.'[6]

School trustees, families, and school proprietors who were looking for teachers emphasized morality, manners, and ability, possibly because most such advertisements were for teachers of common schools, where frills such as French or the use of globes were out of the question. The village of Grafton wanted a person 'capable of taking charge' of their school. Other common school trustees advertised for persons who were

'of sober habits and qualified' or who were 'qualified and respectable.'
Occasionally, however, the ads asked for more. The village of Colborne,
for example, atypically stated a preference for a teacher 'acquainted with
the classics,' clearly with something more than an ordinary common
school in mind.[7]

Colborne was unusual in making this a requirement. A good teacher
of the typical common school was chiefly seen as someone who could
take charge, knew enough to teach the three Rs and, above all, was
reputable. Certainly trustees usually wished to avoid teachers who drank
too much or were for some other reason likely to cause trouble in their
school or community – and certainly such characters existed if we are to
believe the testimony of the period. But common schools were not the
only ones to suffer from teachers with tarnished reputations. Typically
the local press kept a watchful eye, sometimes for political reasons. For
example, a Kingston paper revealed alleged criminal acts in the American
past of Barnabas Bidwell, founder and principal of Ernesttown (Bath)
Academy, who was, in some circles, better known as an outspoken critic
of the government. Other times, the 'scandal' might be quite a local
affair, as when the *Picton Traveller* let it be known that the Reverend
Moses Marcus, district school teacher in Prince Edward, had apparently
absconded, leaving his position vacant and probably taking the government stipend with him.[8]

Almost as interesting as what was mentioned in early nineteenth-century advertisements and descriptions of teachers are the numerous characteristics and questions these documents left out. Fees were listed by
some but not all private venture teachers, but no one on either side
specified the sums to be paid to the teacher working for wages. Almost
as elusive as wages was the question of gender. Private venture teachers
described themselves as Mr, Mrs, or Miss, or, if the school were for
girls only, said as much. Very occasionally, common school trustees
made it plain that they were looking specifically for a man.[9] Many others,
however, either assumed that most applicants would be men or left the
question open. Finally, as we have already noted, questions of pedagogy
only rarely warranted attention. Clearly the issues of the teacher's income,
gender, or pedagogy were by no means so volatile in early Upper Canada
as they were later to become.

No doubt wages were a major factor distinguishing one kind of teacher
from another. At the top were the men who commanded headmasterships
at schools like Upper Canada College or the district grammar schools; at
the bottom of the scale were the young men and, even lower, the young
women who took employment in rural common schools. In between there
were many levels of income. What private venture teachers may have

cleared in a year is anybody's guess, but their earnings probably varied as much as the earnings of those whose salaries were a matter of public record. Entirely outside the scale were the teachers, chiefly women, who seem to have taught for nothing or who, at least, were never paid in cash. In Madoc Township, a Miss Olmest kept school 'for several years gratuitously' until a 'common school teacher' could be found in the mid-1840s. It is probable that Anne Langton charged no fees for the few backwoods students that came to her small private school in the late 1830s. Nor did Mary O'Brien and the many other women who undertook to teach one or two others beyond their own children. In Mary O'Brien's case, the girls' labour was their teacher's payment. Clearly, payment in kind was acceptable not only to housewives but in more formal settings as well. We have noted the common school teacher who recorded payments of flour and sheep; in the *Canadian Argus and Niagara Spectator* of 2 March 1820 an ad for Mrs Roberts's 'Young Ladies' Boarding School' specifically stated that 'produce' would be accepted in lieu of fees.[10]

An idea of how early school promoters felt salaries ought to be distributed can be gained from two documents in which 'ideal' salary scales were set out. The first is a statement covering several types of schools by John Strachan in 1815; the second a discussion of Upper Canada College by Sir John Colborne in 1829. In both cases, the guiding principle was hierarchy. Strachan's plan called for a university principal who would be paid £750 a year, a senior professor at £500, and three more professors at £400 each. The professors of law and surgery could be paid £200 because their income would be supplemented by private practice. A librarian and a gardener were tagged at £100 each. Headmasters of district grammar schools, Strachan felt, should be paid £300, a sum that could be supplemented by fees – but modest fees, as the proposed salary was so high. The salaries of second and 'under' masters would be £200 and £100 respectively. As far as common school teachers were concerned, as Strachan revealed in another document, the government ought to provide £30 towards their income, while another £50 should be raised by the 'people,' for a total of £80. Colborne's scheme for the salaries of Upper Canada College masters was similarly hierarchical. Both plans called for the lowest to make one-sixth or less than the highest on the payroll. Both accepted that other sources of income, such as taking in boarders, would supplement the basic salaries of some teachers.[11]

It is interesting to compare these to Strachan's account of his own actual earnings as the district schoolmaster at York in 1820. His average annual income over the previous two years had been £184.8.1/2, which, with the government salary of £100, meant that he had earned a total of

£284.8.1/2. His expenses, however, came to £242.10.0: £100 each for two assistants, £12.10.0 for the school servant, £1 for firewood and £20 for miscellaneous expenses such as repairs and preparations for the public examinations. After expenses, then, his actual profit from the school totalled little more than £40. Another known salary of the period is Joseph Spragg's for running the Upper Canada Central School, a salary that seems to have been higher, eventually, than even the £100 the government paid to district schoolmasters. In 1821 Spragg was paid £50 twice a year, but by 1822 this had risen to £75, and he was also given considerable sums each year to cover his expenses.[12] The wages of common school teachers were of course much lower than this and also lower than the total of £80 proposed for them by Strachan. The £30 suggested as the government portion was in fact never approached in this period, for the fixed sum the government set aside for the purpose had to be divided among hundreds of teachers who qualified for it and was never enough. It was the rare community, moreover, that could raise £50 a year in fees. Indeed, many communities raised almost nothing.

Still, in an economy in which cash was hard to come by, teaching jobs were an important source of income and were sought after at all levels. More often than not teaching was just one of several occupations engaged in over the course of a year – or a lifetime. For men, the occupation was frequently combined with a career in the church. Of the eight district schoolmasters whose names are listed for 1822, it is surprising in fact to find only three listed as 'Reverend.'[13] Certainly many clergymen found their livings inadequate and were keen to supplement their clerical earnings with 'the labour of teaching a few scholars,' even if they did not engage more formally as teachers of public schools.[14] And Anglicans were not the only divines to combine their clerical callings with teaching. The Reverend Mr Bell pointed out in 1824 that most Presbyterian ministers had to do the same 'to obtain the means of support,' and advertisements by clergymen proposing to take in a few pupil-boarders or to open more substantial private schools appeared in the press regularly.[15]

If district schoolmasters and male private venture teachers often doubled as ministers of the cloth, male common school teachers were more likely to combine school teaching with humbler occupations. According to his 1841 advertisement in the *Cornwall Observer*, Mr Carnegie of Dundas County was both a schoolteacher and a watchmaker. But the most frequent combination was teaching and farming. A farmer's diary of 1796 records a helpful deed to a neighbour who was both a teacher and a farmer: wood was cut for the latter's sugar hut, 'so that he might not be hindered by [outdoor] work from keeping school.' John Tidey was both a farmer and a surveyor, as well as a schoolmaster, in Oxford County in the 1830s, but seems eventually to have concentrated on the latter role.[16]

Perhaps, however, the reverse trend, that is the pattern of teaching for a while before moving on to farming or some other occupation full time, was more common. Letitia Creighton's father taught a common school to save money for a farm; others, including Letitia herself, taught to finance their further education. William Cooper taught for several years in early York and then became an auctioneer. It may have been such youthful, temporary teachers that kept the majority of common schools open and the wages of teachers low. Certainly it was relatively rare for an early-nineteenth-century schoolmaster to be employed exclusively in the occupation or to have a teaching 'career' that lasted an entire adult lifetime.[17]

Any consideration of the part-time or temporary teacher necessarily raises the question of women in teaching because, if career teachers were unusual among men, women who spent a lifetime in teaching in this period were reputedly rarer still. Yet there were women who devoted themselves over many years to the occupation. Marjorie Theobald's detailed study of 'young ladies' schools' in mid-nineteenth-century Australia demonstrates how important, both to their communities and their own families, the careers of such women could be. Women teachers came to the Australian colony of Victoria from continental Europe, Theobald discovered, as well as from the British Isles, although the latter group naturally predominated. Some were married and supported husbands who, for one reason or another, were without means; some formed partnerships with teaching husbands. Others were widows or single women who taught alone or with female friends or relatives. In many cases their schools were far from ephemeral; indeed the instruction they offered was much relied upon by colonial families wishing to educate their daughters.[18]

R.D. Gidney and W.P.J. Millar, in contrast, have emphasized the ephemeral nature of Upper Canadian voluntary and private venture schools, noting that of the 196 such schools that they located for the period between 1830 and 1870, only one-half are known to have survived for more than two years and one-third for more than four.[19] One would like to know how many among the latter group were taught by women of the type uncovered by Marjorie Theobald. Certainly the experience of several Upper Canadian schoolmistresses suggests that her arguments may well have validity for Upper Canada, especially in the province's urban centres. Miss Eliza Hussey of Toronto was able to retire in the mid-1850s on an annuity of £108 a year, which she derived from the sale of her school property after more than twenty years in teaching. Mrs Van Norman, the wife of Victoria College's D.C. Van Norman, appears to have shared with her husband the management of their renowned Burlington Ladies' Academy, to which she brought pupils from the seminary she had run in Cobourg. The Burlington school only closed because the Van Normans moved on to an even more prestigious school in the United States. Or consider Mrs Street and her two daughters, whose struggles to develop a school were finally rewarded with the establishment of their seminary in Ancaster. It is true that there were many women who engaged as schoolmistresses only for a brief period before marriage and then abandoned the occupation. But others managed to carry on teaching when they became wives.

Whatever their marital status, all proprietors of private schools for young ladies were also housekeepers, for every household school needed domestic management. Servants had to be engaged, directed on their tasks, and paid; in the case of boarding schools, pupils needed to be fed; laundry had to be arranged for, fees collected, and accounts kept. Finally, like schoolmasters, some schoolmistresses were also explicitly engaged in more than one occupation. Mrs Black, who advertised her young ladies' seminary in Martintown in the *Cornwall Constitutional* in 1850, we will recall, was also a dressmaker by trade.[20] Unsung by educational historians, but obviously vital to many of the private venture and almost all the boarding schools ostensibly run by men, was another category of women educators, the wives of schoolmasters. These women, too, engaged in the domestic side of school management, looking after the feeding and care of boarders and even – in the case of William Boulton's wife, evidently – helping their husbands keep order.

We have no statistics from which to assess the proportion of teachers who might have been women in the common schools of early Upper Canada. But we know that it was by no means unusual to find a woman teaching such a school. The assumption was plainly that where girls or younger pupils were to be found in any number it was suitable for women to teach them. The strategy of hiring a woman also produced savings for cash-poor school trustees who were anxious not to overspend in these early years, as they would continue to be throughout the century. The same motives may have induced trustees to hire elderly immigrant men ('old soldiers' seem to have played an important role in the early common school teaching work-force) or to persuade married women who were teaching their own children at home to take on the local common school. This certainly happened to Letitia Creighton Youmans, and a similar story was told about Lillian Macpherson Rose, who rode into London on the back of the local superintendent's horse to acquire her certificate, and thus became one of the first common school teachers of Zorra Township, in Oxford County.[21] Finally when school terms were extended over the entire year and male teachers happened to be farmers or were otherwise seasonally occupied, women were often engaged to take the school in the summer-time, turning it over again to a schoolmaster in the winter.

Many of the young women teachers who took on common schools, whether in summer or winter, were often well under twenty years of age, and sometimes problems arose on account of their youth or the combination of their youth and their gender. Susan Cassidy, who began teaching at Bradford in 1837 at the age of fourteen, was unable to manage the 'unruly' boys. But she persevered and, after two years, moved to Tecumseh and a new school. When she married another teacher, Thomas O'Flynn, they 'both taught,' probably taking boys and girls separately at the same school.[22] Susan Cassidy's case was not atypical. The narrator of her story remarks that the man who replaced her at Bradford did little better as far as discipline was concerned, since he tended to fall asleep at his desk, producing 'high carnival' in the school. Nor was it unusual that Susan Cassidy continued teaching after her marriage. Indeed there were many who felt that a husband-and-wife team was the ideal arrangement for a 'mixed' school. An 1838 government report recommending a model school for each township, where teachers might observe in order to learn by example, also recommended that such schools be kept by married couples.[23]

Teaching, in fact, like many artisanal occupations, was plainly a family affair in early Upper Canada, and husbands and wives were not the only possible combinations. Countless mother-and-daughter teams, like the Streets, or fathers and daughters, like the Kyles, or, more rarely, fathers and sons, kept school together. Nor was the assistance rendered by the younger family members merely token. It was the Misses Whitelaw who were prepared to receive young ladies as pupils in 1851, under the 'superintendence' of Mrs Whitelaw; one gathers that the daughters did the actual teaching. Many other examples could be cited.[24]

Indeed assistant teachers played crucial roles not only in family private venture enterprises, but in all the larger schools. The Reverend Thomas Creen, master of the Niagara District School, took as his assistant a local common school teacher in 1828. An editorial in the *Cobourg Star* in 1836 pointed out that expanding numbers had forced the master in Cobourg to employ assistants 'out of his private resources' in order to 'do justice' to his pupils. Petitions were sent to the legislature requesting an allowance to support a permanent assistant in this case, with unknown results.[25] But the need was not new. John Strachan had employed two assistants in his York school in 1820, and John Whitelaw had relied heavily on them in his Kingston school in 1810. By mid-century, in towns and cities, even the common schools were beginning to expand and require assistant teachers.

By and large, however, most schools before 1850 were small enough to get along with one or at the most two teachers – and for this if for no other reason relations between teacher and students were necessarily closer than they would become when schools grew large. The teacher was expected to play a parental role towards his or her pupils. 'It has ever been my conviction,' wrote Strachan, 'that our scholars should be considered for the time being our own children.' Career teachers had important and life-long relationships with some of their old pupils, as Strachan did with John Beverley Robinson, or as John Whitelaw did with Daniel Wilkie.[26] If parental discipline called for corporal punishment, and it seems that it generally did in this period, then it was normal for teachers to administer similar rough justice in the schools. When a teacher of Niagara knocked a child insensible and was himself beaten up by the older pupils, this suggests not distance but close relationships of a hostile nature. In some cases the teacher was clearly under the thumb of parents or trustees. In 1810 Alexander Lilliam Carson's contract to teach at a school in York stipulated that trustees controlled how many and which pupils were admitted to the school and the precise hours and days it would be open. The contract also specified that Carson and no other would teach the school.[27]

Not all employers were satisfied with the teacher, and there is no doubt that collectively and individually the early Upper Canadian teacher was often under attack. A correspondent of the *Kingston Gazette* in 1810 felt the Upper Canadian country schoolmaster to be 'an insignificant contemptible being'; most teachers, this writer believed, were 'unfit for business and too lazy to live by the "sweat of their face," ' hence their choice of occupation. A satirical piece in the *Niagara Gleaner* in 1832 suggested that there were innumerable ways to make sure that children hated their teachers, implying that many teachers had no trouble achieving this state of affairs. A gloomy, negative, uninvolved stance on the part of either teacher or parents was certain to create friction and unhappiness in the schoolroom. One presumes that this writer spoke from experience. Looking back on the early schools in his old age, another somewhat negative witness recalled that it was as well for the male teacher to vote as the community did in old Ontario, or his job was likely to be forfeit in the days before the secret ballot.[28]

Teachers who did not get along with their communities, or at least with all parts of them, occasionally surface in the records. William Case confessed in 1830 that one of his young missionary teachers had seduced some of his Indian pupils. In 1835, a conflict that had grown up between an Upper Canadian schoolmaster and the people with whom he boarded resulted in a petition to the lieutenant-governor. Some teachers' contracts, such as William Carson's of York, provided explicitly for formal, independent arbitration in the case of controversy between teachers and their employers.[29] There is no doubt that the close relations between school and community that still characterized the small world of early-nineteenth-century Upper Canada could occasionally get too close.

II

Two schools of thought plainly existed in early Upper Canada about the appropriate treatment of the young, with the usual range of opinion shading from one extreme to the other. Simply put, there were the hard-liners who believed in adult authority, most appropriately wielded by a mature male and enforced with the rod. Learning, in this view, took place best in an atmosphere, if not of fear, at least of mild apprehension. Then there were those who were beginning to have a more optimistic view of children's behaviour and potential. Instead of forcing learning on the child, exponents of the second school explored less-authoritarian ways of motivating children to learn. Associated with the harsher pedagogy were dreary recitations, memorizing from books, and the unquestioning use of corporal punishment. Connected with the newer approach were questions and answers, learning not just from books but from nature and life, and a preference for shaming children into a contrite state. The latter was held to be the more 'modern' method.

But when we turn from these generalizations to the reality of early Upper Canadian schools, it is hard to know exactly where they applied. A few Upper Canadians did indicate something of their views on teaching methods or school discipline. A correspondent to the *Kingston Gazette* in 1810, for example, made it clear that for him the purpose of a 'well-disciplined' school was the fostering of habits of subordination, which were in turn essential to the 'administration of civil government.' But he gave no details on how such habits were to be cultivated. Fifteen years later, a short piece on the management of children published in the *Niagara Gleaner* argued the value of whipping them. On the other side were the views expressed in Richard Cockrell's 1797 tract on education. Children, Cockrell held, were '"reasonable beings' who could be 'wrought upon best by argument.' Complexities such as arithmetic rules should be explained to them and 'stripes' avoided, except in cases of 'strictest necessity.' Cockrell also eschewed mass recitations, which he said could only be compared to 'the aggregate hum of a beehive.' Following in

Cockrell's footsteps, perhaps, a school in Niagara that opened in 1839 announced its intention of employing the system of Johann H. Pestalozzi, the European educator renowned for a more child-centred approach to schooling.[30]

Aside from tidbits such as these, which serve to indicate merely that both harsh and milder, more thoughtful approaches to children coexisted in the province, we have little to go on, for few teachers or school circulars were explicit about their stances on pedagogical matters. Mrs Crombie of the Prince Edward Ladies' Academy simply pointed out in 1836 that her system for teaching 'the solid and useful branches' was 'the same system ... pursued in the District School,' while a Miss Brampton, advertising the following year, referred enigmatically to her own 'peculiar mode of tuition.' Mr Hagan, along with many others, announced his intention to teach writing 'upon the most approved and modern system.' When it came to arithmetic, however, he did give a genuine clue. By pointing out that 'the shortest method of casting up Merchant's Accounts' would be taught, he declared his belief in teaching practical applications, not just abstract formulae.[31] The practical approach to arithmetic was in fact not as modern an approach as Hagan thought. Certainly, John Strachan insisted that his pupils be made aware of the everyday applications of knowledge. The introductory arithmetic text he published in 1809 included sections on land surveying and the buying and selling of stocks and ended with an appendix on business forms. This practical approach to the teaching of arithmetic was traditional and typical of the time.[32]

The best description of the actual running of an Upper Canadian school was also provided by Strachan in his 1829 pamphlet on the management of grammar schools, a pamphlet that clearly emphasized the practical. In this thirty-page discussion, an experienced grammar schoolmaster not only described how he had organized his own school, but provided considerable detail about daily and weekly procedures.[33] Strachan's school had been a fairly large one. He had therefore divided his pupils into five classes, in this case according to their ages, which ranged from seven to sixteen. The subjects studied in each form or year were not specified, but variety was emphasized, Strachan arguing that additions to the classical grammar school curriculum were essential. The aim was to introduce subjects that were 'not only suitable to the present age' but made it almost certain that every pupil would find at least one subject 'adapted to his taste and capacity, and in which he [might] excel.' The practical came out in the way subjects were taught. Mathematics classes surveyed and measured bays, church steeples, and trees, while bookkeeping classes played store. Boys possibly destined for the provincial assembly or the bar learned how to debate and declaim. Strachan's 'system' was con-

John Strachan, from a portrait painted about 1820

sciously aimed at bridging a perceived gulf between 'the business of the School' and what went on 'out of doors' or 'the business of common life.'

The recommendations for school management were also modern. There were daily and weekly timetables; older boys or 'censors' kept the registers, mended pens, prepared writing books, reported absentees or delinquents and acted as 'monitors.' A formal system of justice prevailed, which was aimed at replacing corporal punishment as far as possible with rewards and punishments and in which the boys participated as jurors. A severe punishment was the placing of a boy 'in Coventry,' although never for more than a week; rewards consisted of prizes, merit for which was computed on a daily, weekly, and monthly basis.

In his involvement with his pupils' practical needs and avoidance of corporal punishment, Strachan might be thought the most up to date of teachers. We have no way of knowing how much memorizing and reciting went on in his school, but it was clearly replaced, at least to some extent, by debating, the conduct of surveys, the taking of architectural measurements, and the like. The division of pupils into classes, and the use of monitors, however, could lead to a rather rigid type of individual ranking that in turn suggests at least some rote learning and the measurement of pupils according to the number of verses learned or Latin words correctly spelled. William Hutton's account of his son's progress through the 'forms' at Upper Canada College suggests that this leading school ranked its students in every subject every day, and Strachan's daily, weekly, and monthly record keeping and 'Book of Merit' imply a similar practice. The promotion of competition for place or 'emulation' was, in fact, accepted as good pedagogical practice and as almost essential to the motivation of children in a large school.

To what extent were Strachan's methods either successful or typical? We know from the testimony of pupils that his schools were admired by many. But that all district schools or other Upper Canadian schools were organized in the same way seems unlikely. Strachan's pamphlet was itself promoted by its author's perception that Upper Canada's district schoolmasters needed advice. Evidence of schools where pupil numbers declined suggests that some teachers at least used different and less popular 'systems' or no systems at all. Teaching methods different from Strachan's were also occasionally described. In the Midland District Grammar School in 1838, for example, the classes were formed not just according to age, but according to 'proficiency, or probable occupation in after life.' Only two 'senior' classes studied the classics, higher mathematics, geography, or history. In fact, the academic, classical students were separated from those aspiring only to an 'ordinary English' education, and two separate schools were effectively run in the same room. Since the numbers at this school were only thirty-two, however, this organization probably reflected either the teacher's or the district's inability to raise a large enough student body uniformly bent on a classical education.[34]

How different were the grammar schools, with their classes and monitors, from other Upper Canadian schools? The school that immediately springs to mind as most similar to Strachan's, oddly enough, is the Upper Canada Central School at York. The similarities were probably the result of size. At the Central, too, monitors were used to 'multiply' the teacher's 'power,' and this 'division of labour' was taken as an important key to success. At this school, also, pupils were placed in classes or grades, the argument being that hope of promotion or fear of 'degradation' were necessary to 'fix the attention, call forth exertion and ... prevent the waste of time.' But the use of monitors and the introduction of classification were also intended to produce the 'progress, good order and silence' so important in a very large school, and the Central School was large, eventually numbering several hundred students.[35]

The schools that seem most different from the larger grammar schools and, above all, the Upper Canada Central School, are the numberless small private schools and the increasingly plentiful common schools of the period. Perhaps very traditional in their emphasis on rote memorizing or on skills like needlepoint and dancing, such schools were unlikely to require the formal organization of a York District or Central School. How formal was the education provided by Mrs Brown, for example, as she instructed a small number of young ladies in English grammar, dancing, or French in her own home? How rigid and authoritarian was the Gore District common school taught by an old man, who lay on a bench and had the children recite to him one by one as they gradually drifted in during the course of a morning? Or what can we say about the common school where the teacher slept and pandemonium reigned or the one where the older boys beat up an unpopular schoolmaster?[36]

Strictness there was and lenience, old-fashioned teaching methods and modern, but it remains hard to say exactly where any of these would be found or even how, precisely, to categorize such well-known schools as John Strachan's. Certainly there was a major difference, as Strachan claimed, between the larger public and the smaller private or domestic school. Some criticized the larger schools and the use of monitors; as the founder of a small private academy put it in the 1860s, the practice was 'in its *essence* a spy system.' Other later critics deplored the 'inefficient' individual instruction that focused on the progress forward (or backward) of the individual pupil through the ranks. Sunday schools might be called 'modern' for using shame rather than corporal punishment, classifying the children, and emphasizing explanations, rewards, and love. But they too placed an enormous emphasis on memorizing – in their case, biblical passages. The most progressive schools of all, in fact, may have been the early infant schools, or the Methodist Indian schools of the Reverend William Case. Case said that his system for instructing the native children was 'the infant system,' which consisted of answering the children's questions.[37]

The Methodist missionary's approach implies a measure of flexibility in curriculum and, compared to what was in store for them later in the century, early Upper Canadian teachers and their clients did enjoy considerable curricular choice, within the limitations imposed by what was available in the way of books or other teaching aids. Bruce Curtis has argued that, after the shortages of the first few decades, the choice of books in fact became quite wide as the steam press and increased availability of paper began to have an affect on numbers of school-books printed. Moreover, items like Mavor's popular *English Spelling Book* and Alexander Davidson's homegrown Upper Canadian speller, among the dozens of other school-books Upper Canadians used, were astonishingly versatile 'general compendia containing stories, poems, songs, prayers, geography, grammar, history and arithmetic lessons, in addition to lists of words and definitions.'[38] There is a sense that, with books such as these in hand (and with individual scholars frequently using different books – whichever ones their parents were able or wished to provide), what was studied in school might be highly idiosyncratic, depending in large measure on the wishes or needs not only of the teachers but of the taught.

Despite the potential for variety provided by the character of schoolbooks in the early nineteenth century, there were nevertheless *expectations* of what would be taught in the different types of school. In theory, district grammar schools focused on the classics and mathematics, and common schools on the 'ordinary branches,' or the 'three Rs.' Academies and seminaries, one senses, were expected to offer a 'practical' education focusing on English studies, although one more advanced than that of the common school. The night schools, especially, appear to have emphasized a practical 'English' education and subjects like surveying or bookkeeping. Ladies' schools, in theory, concentrated on the polite arts of music, French, or needlepoint, in addition to the basics.

In practice, however, the distinctions were never this sharp. Take the Newcastle District Grammar School in 1840. Latin, Greek, algebra, and geometry were certainly taught. But so were the 'English branches' and bookkeeping. Earlier, in 1832, the Peterborough government school advertised its intention to aim for a reputation in 'the classics and the sciences,' but also to pay 'strict attention' to 'those who wish to receive an exclusively English education.' The Cobourg District School's program echoed this approach.[39] An 1839 circular for the Huron District School is more specific about the subjects actually taught; they were twenty in number, starting with English spelling and ending with the elements of astronomy, 'etcetera.' The question is how many pupils were actually studying Greek and Latin or any of the advanced subjects in these supposedly classical schools. The answer is: probably very few. In the Peterborough District School in 1834, all thirty boys studied spelling, twenty-nine also learned writing; twenty-five were in reading, twenty-one in grammar. There were twenty-three pupils in arithmetic, eighteen in geography, fifteen in history, and ten in mathematics. But only six pupils each were actually enrolled in algebra or the classical languages.[40]

The academies for their part wavered between the desire to offer a practical English education and the temptation to teach the more prestigious and traditional classical curriculum. The Ernesttown Academy, in making no pretence of offering Latin or Greek in 1811, was among the few that followed the idea of an alternative approach to education to its logical conclusion. Grantham Academy, on the other hand, offered the traditional as well as the modern subjects in its 'male department,' the curriculum of which included spelling, reading and writing, surveying, navigation, and mensuration, but also rhetoric, logic, natural theology, evidence of Christianity, history, chronology, geography, trigonometry, geometry, algebra, Latin, Greek, and Hebrew. Grantham's 'female department,' however, was more limited. In addition to spelling, reading, grammar, and writing, it offered only arithmetic, geography, and mapping.[41] At the Upper Canada Academy, also, it is clear that girls were intended to have an education that differed considerably from that of some, at least, of the boys; however, as with the grammar schools, the question of numbers arises. One suspects that few boys may actually have enrolled in classical or advanced studies. A student could pursue 'all or any of the various branches,' according to the directions given by his parents or guardians.[42]

The smaller domestic and private venture schools varied in what they taught quite as much as, if not more than, the larger academies. Some were clearly elementary; some emphasized the practical and often the 'ornamental' arts, which in fact may have been very practical indeed for young women wishing to marry well and maintain a proper Victorian household or who would become teachers themselves; a third category clearly paid greater attention to intellectual development and offered advanced studies. Many private venture schools for boys, especially, seem to have offered curricula almost identical to those of the district grammar schools and large academies. The Reverend Thomas Handcock's was typical. In 1826 his advertisement listed 'Greek, Latin, Elocution, History, Geography, Writing, etc. and whatever contributes to a liberal and polite, Education.' A decade later, William Hutton's classical school seemed very similar.[43]

Other private venture schools for young men and women confined themselves to English studies, less advanced arithmetic, and other practical subjects. For boys, there were applied studies, such as surveying and navigation, and for girls, such subjects as music, French, and above all sewing. Mrs Dayley's private day school in 1825 included instruction in plain and fancy sewing, as well as 'Rug, Silk and Worsted Embroidery.' Mrs Fraser's 'extras' were music, drawing, and fancy needlework in 1835, while, seven years later, Mrs Shorter's school added only French and drawing to the standard subjects. However some private young ladies' schools attempted more advanced work. At the seminary established by Miss Anderson and Miss Wilson in Bytown in 1839, girls could study history, mythology, and chronology, in addition to the usual subjects.[44] These schools clearly began to approach the advanced English and scientific studies offered by the larger academies to privileged Upper Canadian girls. In 1837, the course of instruction in the 'Female Department' of the Upper Canada Academy at Cobourg included 'English Grammar, Geography, Arithmetic and Astronomy, and when required, Belles Lettres and natural Philosophy, as also, French, Music and Drawing'; by 1840, the course had broadened to include lectures in Roman and biblical history, natural science, and English literature. Taken together, the offerings of the prestigious private seminaries and the larger academies admitting girls suggest that Upper Canada may have paralleled the colonial province of Victoria, Australia, in its ambitions for women's education. Marjorie Theobald has documented the existence not only of 'career' teachers, but also of demanding curricula in her study of Victoria's 'ladies' schools,' most of which offered 'in the cryptic language of shared tradition,' as she so aptly puts it, 'a sound English education with the usual accomplishments' – modern languages, music, and painting.[45] In Upper Canada, too, at least some girls clearly participated in this tradition, which was serious and demanding, albeit different from the curriculum offered to boys destined for the professions or business.

There was less difference between the studies of boys and girls, or of different children in different locations, in the schools that clearly confined themselves to elementary studies. The Central School at York offered English reading, writing, and grammar, arithmetic, bookkeeping, and elements of geography to boys, and English reading, writing, arithmetic, and drawing to girls. The studies of girls and boys in common schools were even more similar, as far as published curricula are concerned. Perhaps harking back to traditional practices, the odd male teacher might refuse to teach advanced arithmetic to girls, but generally the three Rs were basic for both sexes, in both the winter schools most frequently taught by men and the summer schools often superintended by young women. Occasionally, possibly most often in winter schools, some grammar, geography, or, more rarely, history, might be added to the work of the most advanced scholars. Finally, there were the 'industrial' topics taught in such schools as the Methodist missionary school at Alderville and in an unknown number of common schools, which offered instruction in trades to boys and in plain sewing to girls.[46]

Some features all early- and mid-nineteenth-century schools shared. Perhaps no school of this period could have avoided the ever-popular spelling bee. It was also the rare school, as time went on, that escaped the annual public examination, in which children were tested in their subjects and displayed their abilities in a variety of set pieces. To an early examination at Strachan's Cornwall grammar school were invited 'all the respectable people within thirty miles.' The guests were encouraged to question the scholars, and a 'good dinner' was provided to wind up the festivities. Newspapers of the period are full of announcements for the public examinations of district grammar schools and academies, to which all 'interested' parties, as well as parents and guardians, were invited. Often there were speeches and prize-givings; and, at the Upper Canada Academy in 1838, there was also the young ladies' bazaar, which raised £40 towards the 'maintenance and education' of a young native woman at the school.[47]

The 1839 public examination for the ladies' seminary run by Mrs Kain and Miss Brice in Bytown convinced the editor of the *Bytown Gazette* that these teachers had succeeded in establishing 'an Institute' where 'the highest branches of female education' might be acquired. Teachers made their reputations on such examination reports, and parents and members of the public got a chance at examination time to catch at least a glimpse of what went on behind the doors of the schoolroom. Even the Infant School at York held a public examination of its twenty-four pupils in 1832, an event chaired by none other than John Strachan. At this examination, the account went, all political parties were represented. Indeed, it is clear from all accounts that educational boosters intended public examinations to bring communities together. Those attending a similar event, the installation of a new principal at Upper Canada College in 1839, were encouraged to think of that institution as 'dear to all present.' In 1855, the editor of the *Cobourg Star* commented that the examinations conducted by the master of the local district grammar school could not have failed to impress even the most disaffected critics of the district schools. For once, the editor gleefully went on, Cobourg was treated to 'the anomaly of the united approbation of conservative, whig and radical' alike. Parents and public were brought together, the parents on this occasion having 'united with praiseworthy liberality, in providing the several handsome prizes for the occasion.'[48]

Not everyone approved of the public examinations, and the mixed feelings expressed by John Whitelaw on the subject reveal some fascinating reasons. In December 1810, the Kingston grammar schoolmaster

PROGRAMME

OF THE

YEARLY EXAMINATIONS IN THE LADIES' SEMINARY,

WELLINGTON STREET, TORONTO,

JULY 23, 1852.

ASTRONOMY.
Second Class—The Spheres.

| The Misses E. Driscoll, Benjamin, Ritchey, | The Misses Bosworth, Whitt, Mackenzie, E. Bell, | The Misses Mitchell, Gordon, Kidd. |

FRENCH RECITATION.
Second Class.

The Misses Gordon and Bosworth................Athalie, de la 7e scene, du 11e acte.
Miss Mitchell ....La Statue renversée.
Miss Moffatt ....Essence et Majesté de Dieu.
Miss Ritchey ....La Violette.

GEOGRAPHY.
First Class—Europe.

| The Misses Smith, Driscoll, | The Misses Bell, Taylor, | The Misses Wakefield, Macdonald. |

Second Class—Great Britain and Ireland.

| The Misses E. Driscoll, Benjamin, Ritchey, | The Misses Gordon, Bosworth, Whitt, Moffatt, | The Misses Mackenzie, E. Bell, Kidd. |

ROMAN HISTORY.
Second Class.

The Misses E. Driscoll, Bosworth and Gordon.

GEOLOGY.

The Misses Smith, Driscoll, Beard, Bell, Taylor.

FRENCH RECITATION.
First Class.

The Misses Smith, Driscoll, Beard, Blake,   Zaïre,   Acte cinquieme.

ENGLISH HISTORY.

The Misses Driscoll, Smith, Taylor, Macdonald, Wakefield, Bell, Beard.

HERALDRY.

The Misses Smith, Driscoll, Beard, Taylor, Bell.

ITALIAN.

The Misses Blake, Smith, Blake,   I Fiori.   La Rosa / La Viola / La Violetta.

ASTRONOMY.
First Class.

The Astral and Planetary Systems.
The Moon.

The Misses Smith, Driscoll, Bell, Taylor, Beard.

MUSIC.

FIRST PART.

Exhibition Song—(Chorus)—(Expressly composed for the Pupils of the Seminary) by... (Hecht)	Young Ladies.
Solo—"Tyrolienne,"	(Herz)	Miss E. Driscoll.
Song—"Jenny Lind's Farewell to England,"	(Herz)	Miss Smith.
Duett—"Barcarolle," Weber	(Herz)	Miss Blake. / Mr. Stratit.
Song—Duett—"Happy Days,"	(Glover)	Miss Macdonald. / Mr. Hecht.
Solo—"Blue Bells of Scotland," con. var.	(Wallace)	Miss Smith.
Song—"The Harp,"	(Sir J. Stevenson)	Miss Macdonald.
Song—"Blanche Alpine,"	(Glover)	Miss Thomson.
Duett—"Don Pasquale,"		Miss Smith. / Mr. Stratit.
Song—Duett—"Gently Sighs the Breeze,"	(Glover)	Miss Macdonald. / Miss Smith.

SECOND PART.

Song—"The Indian Maid,"	(A. Lee)	Miss Macdonald.
Solo—"La Violette,"	(Herz)	Miss Driscoll.
Song—Duett—"What are the wild waves saying,"	(Glover)	Miss Thomson. / Miss Smith.
Solo—"Atila,"	(Duvernoy)	Miss Blake.
Song—"Bay of Naples,"	(Donizetti)	Miss Smith.
Duett—(From Norma)	(Bellini)	Miss Macdonald. / Miss Thomson.
Solo—"La Parisienne,"	(Herz)	Miss Thomson.
Song—Duett—"Moonlight Music, Love, and Flowers,"	(Barnett)	Miss Smith. / Mr. Hecht.

GOD SAVE THE QUEEN.
DISTRIBUTION OF PRIZES.

A program for a public examination in 1852

scorned the 'wonderful value' of 'externals' in Upper Canada, suggesting that the public examination was all show, failing to reveal the essence of what went on behind the schoolroom door. What was more, in this case, the teacher and one of the school's most involved trustees, the lawyer Richard Cartwright, were 'not on the best of terms.' Whitelaw was sure that Cartwright, 'an excellent Latin scholar and a notorious proud man' had ulterior motives in calling the examination. Fortunately for the master, he had his supporters as well as his enemies, for Dr Stuart was 'equally determined to support the Domine, as perhaps the Counsellor was to pull him down.' Whitelaw had no idea how it would go, but admitted to 'a good deal of anxiety' although 'no *fear* properly called.'

The schoolmaster's description conjures up a vision of division, of men determined to do battle in the arena of the public school exam. No wonder Whitelaw was nervous, both for himself and, no doubt, for the pupils who would bear the brunt of the trustees' attacks. Interestingly, it all seems to have gone well, possibly because Whitelaw met his critics head on and turned the examination into a three-day marathon. Thus, on 30 January 1811:

Well, we had a pretty smart examination here at Kingston – It was called for by the Trustees – I told them we were at their service whenever they pleased, but added, if they did come to examine the scholars, it was not to be a *triffling* parade. It commenced and continued [for] three days of the most rigid scouring that I have witnessed.

Whitelaw himself was grudgingly won over to the idea of the public examination, it would appear. He had previously preferred private visits from the trustees, but now he acknowledged that the public examination brought the achievements of the scholars to public attention, which in turn prevented 'damage from competing schools.' He put forward the view that they should be held twice a year, and advertised in advance. That the scholars had pleased him was nearly all he cared about, or so he said. But in fact it must also have been pleasing that 'a *haughty ungrateful Republican*' such as himself had won the 'unqualified appro-bation' of at least the '*learned* part of the Trustees.'[49]

What of the hidden curriculum or of 'extracurriculars' in early Upper Canadian schools? Certainly, pupils then as now learned far more than the three Rs, or Latin, or astronomy. In larger schools they learned how to be orderly and quiet in spite of their numbers and, in the more rigid ones, to respond instantly to verbal commands or bells. They learned that men taught older boys 'difficult' subjects like Greek and algebra, while women were often confined to teaching girls or younger children easier subjects and sewing. Students in these schools may have had some sense of control over their learning, as they brought to school their own books, and worked out with their parents when they would attend. In an Oakville common school, graduates remembered hunting for Indian artifacts and buried treasure in the schoolyard, or, more dangerously, digging at the school's foundations. Central School children in York fought the district grammar school boys with sticks and stones and got into battles with their 'mortal enemies' at Ketchum's tannery, with the employees of local breweries, or with the inhabitants of a district known as Irishtown. 'Raising Irishtown' seemed in fact a regular pastime, if we are to believe John Ross Robertson's informants about early days at the school. No less memorable were the single events that etched themselves on the minds of early-nineteenth-century pupils. Such was the occasion when the leader of a tandem team of horses belonging to an English officer broke loose and 'plunged' through the Central School's open doors, 'to the great consternation of teachers and pupils' alike.[50]

How can we assess such learning? Certainly there are many factors that reduced the overall impact of schooling in the province. Among them was the geography, both physical and human, of the place. Distances were great and roads often appalling or non-existent, with the result that many children couldn't get to any school. In most schools, attendance was very irregular, a fact which even modestly ambitious teachers found inimical to 'systematic' instruction. Schools appeared and disappeared as both teachers and pupils came and went or their circumstances changed. Thus continuity in schooling in some areas and among some social classes was a rare commodity. As Edward Talbot exclaimed in 1824, 'numerous are the evils which result from a scanty population, scattered over a wide and cheerless wilderness!'[51] Equally numerous, he might have added, were the problems caused by the fact that much of this population was constantly on the move, or that many Upper Canadian families needed the labour of their children to survive.

For teachers it was no bed of roses. For both the self-employed and those in the pay of others, the income was irregular and uncertain. No bureaucrat existed to sort out conflicts inside or outside the schoolroom. The sought-after district grammar school appointments seemed to depend on patronage, at least in the early years; and distant, frequently unpopular authorities in York controlled government funds for Sunday schools and common and grammar schools, and divided them unfairly.

Parents in early Upper Canada clearly worried. They worked too hard to have time to teach their own children; there was no nearby common school; or the local school was conducted in French or German or English and not in their children's first language. Even if reasonably well-to-do and able to afford an expensive private day or boarding school or one of the large academies or grammar schools, which one were they to choose? Which was better, a domestic or a public education?[52] And, if a boarding school was decided upon who was going to take the child (and his or her bedding) to the school? Were boarding schools healthy, considering the prevalence of infectious diseases in the period?[53]

Whitelaw and other concerned district grammar schoolmasters, as well as critics of these schools, worried about whether poor children had a chance to get the best and most advanced kind of schooling. On the other hand, many teachers may have joined Whitelaw in his view that reasonably high fees kept a school's reputation up and made people value it more. Charges of élitism – and of York and Toronto metropolitanism – were certainly and quite justifiably laid at the door of early Upper Canadian educational arrangements. As Midland District petitioners pointed out in 1812, government educational policies tended to cast money into the laps of the rich.[54]

Even the founding of the Upper Canada Central School at York irritated some, who felt that, along with its building, their school had been simply taken over by a government clique that was determined to foist a particular brand of Anglican education on the public. In 1828, a committee was struck to investigate the situation. A school like the Central siphoned off funds that could have gone to common schools, and many were no doubt pleased when the Central School shut its doors permanently in 1844. The same charges continued to be laid against the district grammar schools, which, although they eventually had some free pupils, nevertheless generally remained schools for the privileged and those who could tolerate Church of England or Church of Scotland teachers. Perhaps the worst criticisms were levelled at Upper Canada College. 'The college was never intended for the people,' complained William Lyon Mackenzie, 'nor did the Executive endow it thus amply that all classes might apply to the fountain of knowledge.' The fact that Upper Canada's largest city had both the Central School and Upper Canada College but only two schools that qualified for the common school grants suggests that, in Upper Canada's capital at least, common schools were not a very high priority.[55] An atmosphere of alienation is suggested by instances of conflict between 'town' and 'gown.' John Whitelaw faced his enemies in Kingston, as Egerton Ryerson did in Cobourg, where it was 'notorious that the worst enemies of the College [had] been "People in Town." ' York's Central School pupils seemed to face everyone, from brewery and tannery employees and the inhabitants of Irishtown, to their more uppity enemies from the grammar school.[56]

If not town *versus* gown, it was simply the pressure of everyday – or not so everyday – life that impinged. During the War of 1812, schools were disrupted as teachers joined the militia and went off to fight, or, as in the case of Kingston, the district grammar school was taken over for a barracks. In London, the disruption was compounded, even when the teacher returned, by the fact that, in any case, parents removed their children from school as soon as they could be 'useful in husbandry,' at about age eleven or twelve. The London District School was certainly not fulfilling its avowed purposes in 1816. A 'few' young men made progress 'with mixed mathematics,' and several had begun the study of English grammar, but only one studied Latin.[57]

Less commented upon at the time, but later the cause of considerable grief, was the lack of public financial support for the advanced education of girls. Girls attended some grammar schools, but many educators disapproved of their presence in these supposedly superior institutions. Admitted largely on sufferance to the study of the classics or advanced sciences, they often drifted away early, and girls who did aspire to higher learning faced the contempt expressed in an American satire, reported by the *Cornwall Observer* in February 1841. The author of this piece admonished young women to replace subjects like chronology or geology with 'cookology' and 'bakeology,' in consideration of their probable destinations in life.[58] A few young women, such as Letitia Creighton, may have paid little attention to such critics, but most were probably aware of them. Much was Letitia's pleasure when, a newly married mother of eight stepchildren, this ladies' seminary graduate was able to prevent sudden disaster in the kitchen by a remembered chemistry lesson.[59]

Families, communities, and teachers were clearly doing what they could to educate the young in early Upper Canada. What they produced was an amazing variety of possibilities in the way of schooling, but a variety that was perhaps more apparent than real. There were less variety and opportunity for girls than for boys and plainly only a very few could manage to acquire formal schooling beyond a basic training in the three RS. But that basic training must have been considerable. Leo Johnson has noted evidence of a decline in literacy during the first few decades of settlement in the townships that eventually became Ontario County. Often the first generation of farmers signed their names to land deeds, while many of their sons were able only to make their marks. The writing and spelling of township minutes also declined. But if there was an initial falling off in literary skills as a result of heavy demands made by pioneer family economies on the time and labour of both parents and children, the decline seems to have been temporary. As Harvey Graff has convincingly shown, the vast majority of Upper Canadians who grew up after 1830 considered themselves literate. They told the census takers this in 1861, and the census takers evidently saw no reason to doubt them.[60]

Since all those over the age of thirty in 1861 must have been educated before the 1850s and many before the 1840s, we can safely conclude that, at least by the third and fourth decades of the nineteenth century, Upper Canada's interesting mixture of schools – some cheap and some expensive, some for girls, others for boys, and still others mixed, small and large, partly public and partly private in their funding – may have had something to do with this fact. But not everything, it is important to remind ourselves. The falling off of literacy in the Ontario County region and its eventual revival may or may not have been exclusively tied to the non-existence or the founding of schools. The rhythms of literacy, and its uses, are complex;[61] the basic literacy of the majority of Upper Canada's early settlers could be expected to have fluctuated according to any number of additional factors, among them religious attitudes, wealth, and the amount of time parents had to teach their children. Schools had other purposes than the advancement of children's skills in reading, writing, and arithmetic, moreover. To the three Rs we must always add memorized catechisms and biblical lore, accomplishments, and good manners and 'morals.'

Most children experienced schooling as a local affair, an activity they could drop in and out of as it suited their parents or guardians – or themselves. If things went well they enjoyed the sociability of the experience and learned to read, spell, write, and perhaps cipher. All sorts of things could go wrong, and of course they often did. Most of the time, a middling state of affairs probably obtained, as they did in a school visited by Mary O'Brien, newly arrived in the province in 1829. Kept by an Irish, grammar school-trained veteran of the Napoleonic Wars who had taught in Upper Canada for eight years – despite a hand that was no longer steady for penmanship – the school charged a dollar and a half per quarter and required the pupils' parents to provide the teacher with board, lodging, and washing.

We found upwards of 25 children, healthy & quick, standing round their master, spelling long words with great volubility; this done the head boy proclaimed 'attention' – a volley of bows and curtseys followed & rearrangement which included several lesser children, all conducted with considerable discipline; then rather a curious jumble of questions in English grammar & Scripture history – including, however, Julius Caesar – brought the dinner hour.[62]

Perhaps much Upper Canadian schooling, to sophisticated observers, would have amounted to a similar 'curious jumble' of amusement and learning.

In Kingston, as late as 1849, there were 738 children in common schools and 826 in schools labelled 'private.' By this time the newer meanings of 'private' and 'public' were taking hold. Twenty years earlier the provincial General Board of Education had estimated that in all Upper Canada one-half of the population attended schools assisted by the public bounty, the other half privately financed schools.[63] Yet it was already apparent to some that public schools – those that were supported by public funds, as well as those that were large – were the wave of the future. The cry for public funding was insistent. The claims of the large school, moreover, had been put forward by John Strachan in 1829 and continued to be advertised by the Upper Canada Academy in 1841. In a large school the younger pupils learned from the older ones; where several teachers were employed there could be specialization and the various subjects could be taught more expertly. In such a school, it was also suggested, different denominations could mingle and children would learn the meaning of tolerance.[64] But parents worried that this was not all they would learn. For some time to come, many Upper Canadian families, by preference or necessity, would place their children in small, domestic or local private schools and ignore the future. To preserve distinctions of class and gender was clearly one motivating force in this endeavour. So were denominational concerns and a preference for the known and familial, however. Schooling in early Upper Canada emerges as a curious jumble in more ways than one, as individual schools appealed to particular segments of society and individual teachers sought to create special worlds where the skills they were able to impart were valued above all others.

Cobourg, the chief town of Northumberland County, was an interesting community in 1841. It was the *Cobourg Observer* that printed the scurrilous comments on 'cookology' and 'bakeology' in 1841, and it was here that Egerton Ryerson and Victoria College were soon to find themselves embroiled in conflict with the 'town.' In 1841, the families of Cobourg enjoyed a wealth of educational opportunity, according to one of the town's biggest boosters, the *Cobourg Star*. There were the Upper Canada Academy (still admitting both girls and boys at this point) and the district grammar school. There were four or five common schools (strange that the *Star* did not know how many) and Mrs Brown's academy for young ladies. In 1842, when Upper Canada Academy became Victoria College and was closed to women, two new young ladies' schools, run by Mrs Van Norman and Mrs Hurlburt, respectively, would appear. The *Star* rightly believed that Cobourg in the 1840s was 'a most eligible place' for the 'education of youth.'[65] The same, with a few caveats, could probably be said about Upper Canada as a whole.

Part Two:
Mid-Nineteenth-Century School Reform

IF COBOURG WAS CONSIDERED a most eligible place for the education of the young in 1841, it was also a thriving community economically. According to Charles Rubridge, a traveller and promoter of immigration to Upper Canada who had come to the town several years earlier, this pioneer port had become, by the third decade of the nineteenth century, a busy and prosperous place.[1] In 1819, Rubridge reminded his readers, there had been no more than 'six or seven wretched houses' in Cobourg. By the time of writing it boasted a court-house and a college 'that would not disgrace any town,' as well as 'other handsome brick, stone and frame buildings,' including two churches, three meeting houses, flour, saw, and carding mills, stores and shops, and, almost last but not least, 'good schools.' Cobourg could also boast thriving newspapers, dating from the 1820s, prominent among them the *Cobourg Star*, which was no less anxious than Charles Rubridge to paint an encouraging picture of the town's progress. And people read more than newspapers, for in 1842 the *Star* felt the need to print a warning to 'heads of families' on the connections between 'popular literature' and 'crime.'[2] Indeed, all the evidence indicates that most people were literate in Cobourg and that children were going to school, in some cases even to college. Blessed with prosperity and educational opportunity, but also home to people who were beginning to worry about the problem of crime, Cobourg illustrates the development that had come to many parts of Upper Canada by the time the upper and lower provinces of Canada were united under one provincial government in 1841.

Yet there had been much economic distress during the 1830s, as the troubles leading to the 1837–8 rebellions made clear. And when the stream of migration from the British Isles swelled to a flood in the 1840s as a result of famine in Ireland, there was to be much more. Two men who lived in Upper Canada during the period left records that illustrate both the stresses and the opportunities of life in nineteenth-century Ontario. Both were married and had children. And both families lived, at least during most of their early years in Canada, on farms.

John Tidey came to Upper Canada from Ireland in the 1820s and married Dorothy Hellums, a woman of local birth and American Mennonite background. We encounter him and, in a very shadowy way, his family, at two moments in time. On the first occasion, in 1838, he is pouring into his diary[3] the despair brought on by a disastrous year on a new farm in Oxford County. Unable to complete the fencing, he had lost some of the stock; the potato crop had failed, and rust had destroyed the wheat. Ill and believing himself and the family to be on the verge of ruin, Tidey vented some of his spleen on his wife. Earlier entries in the diary had praised her contribution to the work of the household and represented his family as a 'beehive of industry'; now he complained that his wife was bad tempered, neglected her weaving, and went about in rags. Worse still, she had hired a 'useless girl' who ate up all the surplus. Dorothy Tidey, for her part, evidently complained that she was forced to neglect her inside work because her time was so taken up with planting and other outdoor jobs. Outraged at their deteriorating relations and desperate at the thought of losing his two sons should he decide to abandon the family permanently, Tidey reluctantly decided to leave home temporarily that winter and take up a school. Evidently the strategy worked to his advantage, for the next time we see Tidey it is as an Oxford County school superintendent, heaping scorn on his mid-century neighbours because of the dreadful conditions in their common schools. By the 1870s Tidey may have retired from both school work and farming. At least some of his time, in any case, was employed with the publication of a farmer's almanac out of Norwich.[4]

If the John Tidey story illustrates the tensions that could arise in times of economic difficulty, when even the feeding of a hired girl could seem an intolerable burden, the life of William Hutton and his family suggests the opportunities that were available to the prosperous.[5] Hutton was also an immigrant farmer from Ireland; he too did his share of teaching and a spell as a school superintendent, in his case in the District of Hastings in the 1840s. The interesting thing about the Hutton family is that in spite of their apparent means (the ability, for example, to send their son to Upper Canada College) William's letters to the old country reported daughters who spent many of their hours and days at home at the spinning wheel. At one point, Anna Hutton left home to be a governess to the family of William's cousin, the prominent politician Francis Hincks; on her return Hutton remarked on the extra strain that her renewed presence put on the family purse. Evidently even a well-off family could feel the pinch of an extra mouth to feed or person to dress, especially if that mouth or person belonged to a teenager or young adult.

The situations of the Tideys in the 1830s and the Huttons in the 1840s may have differed only in levels of luck and initial capital outlay. Nevertheless, John Tidey's story proves that hard times were a possibility even for the educated; both stories indicate the delicate balancing of family economies that nineteenth-century rural life demanded at all levels of society.

In the 1850s, the Huttons gave up farming and moved to Toronto where they installed themselves in a house overlooking the public gardens of the new teacher-training institution, the Normal and Model Schools for which, Hutton remarked, Toronto was 'so famed.' A far cry from the provincial York that had been home to the domestic school of William

Baldwin, Toronto in the 1850s seemed 'all change' to William Hutton. Everywhere, he exclaimed, were 'brick and mortar, brick and mortar.'[6]

The brick and mortar that so impressed Hutton represented more than grand purposes and metropolitan wealth, although they certainly were evidence of the increasing prosperity of Canada West and of those who profited from commercial and urban growth. Like their rural counterparts, however, many urban Upper Canadians also knew stark poverty or suffered the effects of an economy that was characterized more by radical fluctuations than by stability or steady growth. Indeed the Normal School itself had its own 'underside' of perceived deprivation in the persons of its janitors and porters, who felt keenly the inflationary conditions of mid-century and the increasing injustice of their wages.

John Murphy first wrote to request a raise in salary in company with his fellow Normal School employee, James Ryan, in November 1853. Carefully laying out their expenses on a monthly basis, Ryan and Murphy explained their need for help now that winter approached.[7] A year and a half later, on the 5 June 1855, Ryan joined forces with another employee, John Stewart, to plead once again for a raise; the cost of food and rent had continued to go up, and the men found that, even after denying themselves 'many of the comforts of life,' it was still 'almost impossible' to provide for their families and keep out of debt.[8] The most poignant letter, however, was penned by John Murphy a few days later. Murphy allowed that his salary of £100 had been very generous in 1852 when the cost of living had been far lower. But although both his expenses and the work of keeping up the Normal and Model School rooms and grounds had radically increased, his wages had not. In this and a later letter, the school's janitor focused on the ways in which his job had become more demanding as well as on the runaway expenditures directly related to his work. In the former category, he pointed out that new or much increased time and effort were involved in the dusting and sweeping of a large, new building, the running of messages, the cleaning and ordering of the science laboratory, and the patrolling of the school grounds in the evenings. At the same time, he was affected by new or vastly increased expenditure. He had to pay the women who washed the school's 114-dozen towels, as well as those who scrubbed the floors every month; both the work and the women's wages had gone up drastically. Tragically, he also had to pay the doctors who had attended his children in their final illnesses. The children had died that year as a result of intermittent fevers, which, the doctors said, had been brought on by living in the very damp apartment provided for the janitor and his family in the Normal School basement. Murphy's 1855 request for a raise was denied, but the authorities did have the damp basement and the school's leaky roofs investigated by its architects, although the outcome of their investigations is not clear. What is clear is that John Murphy remained dissatisfied with his pay and in 1859 was still complaining of the injustice he suffered because of its inadequacy.[9] Yet many mid-nineteenth-century Torontonians probably earned far less.

The Murphy family's plight could be attributed to the dislocations of the times or to the blindness of the janitor's employers. Evidently Murphy blamed both. Human conflict in the face of rapid change also emerges from Murphy's account of one of his most annoying jobs, the supervision of the Normal School grounds. The enclosure of the grounds, built on a parkland to which the citizens of Toronto had previously enjoyed free access, symbolized the separation of the school from its community and its identification as property. John Murphy and other Normal School employees were the men in the middle, saddled with the enforcement of rules designed to control marauding children and perambulating adults alike. It was no fun patrolling the gardens in the evening or chasing boys who had climbed the walls and damaged the yew trees. Nor was it pleasant to lock the gates, at the insistence of a Normal School master, against equally insistent members of the public who wished to take their friends or children for walks in the grounds. Normal School porters and janitors were accused both privately and in the press of behaving rudely to innocent citizens and visitors, who for their part felt insulted and seemed prepared, as a result, to condemn the nascent education department and all its works. In 1858 the grounds were closed to all children, except those accompanied by their parents, because of the damage done to trees and shrubs in the garden. As always, the janitor was left to enforce the new rules.[10]

The battle between the Normal School and the irate citizenry of Toronto typifies on a small scale what was happening on a much larger scale in schooling generally during the mid-century years. The brick and mortar that William Hutton noticed in Toronto were nowhere more evident than in the multitude of common school buildings that were springing up everywhere, especially in the more settled regions of Upper Canada. Indeed, Upper Canadians seemed to have developed a mania for construction in the middle years of the nineteenth century. And not all their building involved visible structures. Mid-nineteenth-century zeal for construction also found expression in the elaborate legal and administrative edifice that was eventually to become the Ontario public school system, a system that embroiled in conflict many more than the Normal School groundskeepers and the strolling citizens of Toronto.

Early historical accounts of this work told a story chiefly of the 'spread of education.' Out of the political cauldron of the 1830s, following the 1837–8 rebellions and the difficult union of Upper and Lower Canada in

1841, a transformed Canada West, the story went, finally came to grips with the need for schooling for the masses. The non-system of fly-by-night private schools, itinerant schoolmasters, and imported American books was rejected in favour of a stable and truly Canadian system of schools. The system for the people, moreover, was governed by the people. Liberal democracy replaced aristocratic élitism in education. The transformation is symbolized in this early historical literature by the accession of the controversial Methodist Reformer of the 1830s, Egerton Ryerson, to educational leadership in the province. John Strachan, portrayed as representing a distasteful and oligarchic past when Anglicanism and the Family Compact ruled Upper Canada, is shown reluctantly yielding the stage to his one-time critic and enemy, the self-same Ryerson. The latter, as chief superintendent of schools for the province from 1846 to 1876, takes centre stages as the leading missionary and architect of Ontario public schooling.[11]

There is, of course, a measure of truth in this picture. Certainly the 1840s and 1850s did see extensive legislation on the subject of schooling in Upper Canada, and the laws that were passed in fact succeeded in putting into place an administrative structure that set the mould for Ontario public schooling for years to come. Egerton Ryerson wrote a good many of these laws and, under his leadership, an embryonic education department encouraged the growth of a common or elementary public schooling that was, in theory, available to all, that promoted a British and 'Upper Canadian' point of view, and that in some measure reflected the needs and wishes of many communities and families in Canada West.

Recent interpretations of Ontario educational history, however, reveal a much more complex picture of mid-nineteenth-century school reform.[12] They call into question many of the accepted canons of the traditional story, from its too gloomy portrayal of the Upper Canadian educational scene prior to 1841, to the exaggerated emphasis on common school reform, and the part played in it by Egerton Ryerson, in the period following union. As we have tried to demonstrate in part I of this volume, early Upper Canadian schooling was voluntary. A fascinating mixture of the casual and the formal, of domestic and public, it reflected local and parental control of this area of life rather than abject disregard for education. John Strachan emerges as less a reactionary villain than an interesting and practical conservative who was, perhaps, somewhat more progressive in his educational ideas than many of his contemporaries. And Ryerson, in turn, seems less the undimensional saint or hero than a highly complex and powerful representative of his age, a period that favoured an evangelical and crusading style of educational activism. Indeed, both men recede increasingly into their respective milieux the more closely one examines the complexities of motive and ideology, of social and economic conditions that informed educational change in the mid-nineteenth century.

If new understandings have altered our perceptions of the social and ideological background of mid-century reform, they have also affected our view of both its legislative and its administrative history. Yet to untangle ideology from law, law from administration, and all three from their social and economic roots, is no easy task. Nor in the context of this study is it possible to render in detail the politics of educational transformations in the mid-nineteenth-century in all their histrionic splendour. What follows, therefore, is an attempt to capture the flavour and significance, rather than display the legal intricacies, of mid-nineteenth-century developments in Ontario public education. It is a view drawn chiefly from the centre. We begin with an account of the ideology of reform and the legislation of the 1840s that established the provincial school system. This is followed by a discussion of the conflicts and adjustments that resulted in the school laws of the 1850s, along with the burgeoning supervisory work-force that the new and increasingly complex legislative and administrative measures put into place. Finally, we look at teachers. Focusing first on the system's metropolitan show-piece and model of correct teaching – the provincial Normal School in Toronto – we conclude with an examination of the larger work-force of schoolmistresses and schoolmasters who actually laboured in the government schools. Beyond the ideal, as always, lay the reality.

4 Towards a Government School System

Perhaps the most striking initial impression that emerges from an examination of mid-nineteenth-century school reform is the overblown rhetoric of its promoters. School 'promoters' and school 'reformers' were a ubiquitous breed in the middle decades. While they figure prominently in the discussion that follows, it is well-nigh impossible to provide a specific social profile of this pioneering lobby. Known in local communities for a willingness to support – indeed frequently to campaign publicly for – a coherent, province-wide school policy, they appear to have been drawn primarily from an arc in rural and town society stretching from the indeterminately middling to well off. However nebulous their social category, an important characteristic was their collective propensity for arguing in public in print. They wrote with passion and at length, and their messages was often delivered with little regard for what we, from the vantage point of a century and a half later, might understand as the subtleties of the human dilemma or the complexities of history. Indeed they thundered from the press much as the evangelical preachers of their time must have thundered from the pulpit, which is not surprising in the case of at least one of them. Egerton Ryerson, after all, had been an itinerant preacher before assuming the editorship of the Methodist *Christian Guardian* and then the principalship of Victoria College, the two positions he held before taking on the superintendency of Upper Canada's schools. One wonders in Ryerson's case if there was not something of the lawyer in his make-up as well. When he was not preaching – or pontificating – he argued, developing his points in an intricate and interminable prose that seemed designed to exhaust as much as to persuade.

To sift from this massive speechifying the essential kernels of belief and feeling that fuelled the careers of school reformers like Ryerson is an absorbing exercise, not the least because the speechifiers so often contradicted themselves – or each other. They were, after all, a disparate group: not just Methodists, but members of most religious denominations; political partisans, as well as those who disclaimed political affiliation and promoted government schooling as a 'non-partisan' enterprise; obvious centralists, along with individuals who appeared to represent local interests. At the same time, these men generally shared the dualistic vision that was characteristic of Victorian thought. Theirs was a world that tended to be painted in black and white, rarely in the subtler shades of grey. And, for all their battles about the details, the timing, or the means, educational promoters of all stripes converged on one belief: the need for school reform itself. With lesser or greater degrees of passion, they declaimed about the dangers of an 'ignorant' populace; with lesser or greater degrees of hyperbole they sketched the blessings of 'education' or improved schooling.

In analysing their words, we attempt to probe two levels of possible understanding: one must ask what the relationships are between rhetoric and perceived realities, as well as the connections between perception and *fact*. The myriad public reports, letters to the press, and private statements that constitute the decade on schooling in the 1830s, 1840s, and beyond reveal beleaguered men. Certainly they lived in a colony that was under pressure and in a difficult time. The rhetoric of educational reform was their articulated response.

Ultimately we assess people by their deeds, however. When we turn from the rhetoric of reform to the school laws that Upper Canadians passed in the 1840s and examine their character and initial impact, we begin to unravel the meaning of the mid-century school movement. What Upper Canada's leaders were beginning to put into place by the fourth decade of the nineteenth century was a provincial *system* of schools; one that could be controlled, much more firmly than had previously been the case, from the centre. Certainly, the controversy generated by the school legislation of 1841, 1843, 1846, and 1847 was a clue to its ultimate effect. Many felt that the interests of families and churches, of teachers and schools, of old regional élites and new local authorities, and even of the ordinary children that the school laws were designed to affect were not well served by the new laws.

He who pays the piper calls the tune. But it was not always clear who was paying the piper; nor did everyone like the tune.

I

School reformers' assessments of the state of education in Upper Canada in the 1830s and 1840s began with a critique of Upper Canadian families. Mothers were admonished to keep the boys busy and families urged to keep all their children more fully entertained at home. By implication, families that had once kept their children occupied were doing so no longer and, if mothers were increasingly exhorted, it was because fathers were perceived as, unfortunately but perhaps necessarily, increasingly absent.[1] Especially in towns, the idleness of the young was identified as a growing problem.[2] The twin to idleness (and equally the result of parental neglect, according to reformers), was the widespread ignorance of Upper Canadian youth. Both were tied, in turn, to an imagined increase in poverty and crime. Charles Duncombe, whose 1836 *Report on the Subject of Education in Upper Canada* was the first in what was to become a long series of government-sponsored papers on the need for more and better schooling, focused particularly on the condition of the young in Toronto.[3] 'Every person that frequents the streets of this city,' he wrote, 'must be forcibly struck with the ragged and uncleanly appearance, the vile language, and the idle and miserable habits of numbers of children, most of whom are of an age suitable for schools, or for some useful employment.' Significantly, schooling did not have, in Duncombe's statement, any greater value than employment; he associated the problems of Toronto's idle youth only in part with their absence from school. The parents of these children were not only 'in all probability, too poor, or too degenerate to provide them with clothing fit for them to be seen at school'; they also did not know where to place them in order that they might 'find employment, or be better cared for.'

Whatever they ought to be doing ideally, such children were ripe for crime, and it was unlikely, Duncombe seemed to think, that anything in Toronto's social arrangements in the 1830s would prevent their following in their parents' footsteps and becoming degenerate themselves. 'Accustomed, in many instances, to witness at home nothing in the way of example, but what is degrading; early taught to observe intemperance, and to hear obscene and profane language without disgust; obliged to beg, and even encouraged to acts of dishonesty to satisfy the wants induced by the indolence of their parents,' these children were not fully to blame for their condition. In suggesting this, Duncombe reflected a growing nineteenth-century recognition that many social problems had environmental causes.[4] And since most parents were unable to change their children's environment very profoundly, it was necessary for someone else to do so.

Egerton Ryerson took up these themes with particular vehemence when he became superintendent of schools. 'To leave children uneducated,' he predicted in 1847, was 'to train up thieves and incendiaries and murderers.' Later, education department officials would conduct studies of the inmates of Toronto jails, correlating criminality with illiteracy. Finally,

Ryerson would take the correlations to their ultimate conclusion; ignorance not only caused crime; 'voluntary ignorance' – or the refusal to attend school – itself began to be seen as criminal.[5]

But in the 1830s and early 1840s such pronouncements were still to come. And it would be misleading to dwell solely on reformers' perceptions of growing idleness and criminality among the young. Poverty concerned them equally. Perhaps here too they were looking, somewhat less myopically, beyond the volatile and seemingly uncontrollable environment of Toronto or other large centres to conditions in the province as a whole.[6] To some of them poverty in Upper Canada seemed endemic, especially if they compared their own community to what they perceived as the more thriving economies of the American states south of the border. That Canadians seemed forever destined to be economically inferior to their wealthier neighbours was an ongoing cause for alarm. Ryerson wavered between concern to promote Upper Canada as a prosperous colony (and a safe haven for British investment of both people and resources) and an underlying fear that the province might not be as he wished to depict it. Whatever his stance, he repeatedly tied the condition of Upper Canada to the education and energy – or lack of these qualities – among its people. The 'public unsettledness' of the 1830s, he recognized on a visit to the old country, had alarmed educated Englishmen, who wondered if property would be safe in the colony. In 1839, Ryerson publicly defended Upper Canada: the 'general intelligence, morality and loyalty' of its people were beyond reproach; in three districts especially – Niagara, Gore, and Home – literacy and reading were as widespread as they were in England. But a few years later he seemed less certain and wrote to an American clergyman that Upper Canadians were virtually slaves. Under present conditions, the morals and the intelligence of the people were likely to remain 'on a level with their liberties,' implying that the latter were very slight indeed.[7]

Ryerson's concerns – and Duncombe's – were political as well as social and economic. An uneducated public was not only ripe for crime, it was ungovernable. This latter condition, Bruce Curtis argues, provided the central focus of mid-century school reform: the creation of subjects who were capable of being governed – or of governing themselves.[8] Not discounting the importance of the issue of governability, which among historians of eighteenth-century British society especially has provoked lively debate, we argue that in the context of Upper Canada school policy the two strands – socio-economic and political – were part and parcel of contemporary perceptions and are, indeed, inseparable.

The fascination in school reformers' discussions of these matters is the circularity of their arguments. Ryerson saw ignorance, bordering on crime, when Upper Canadian families refused to respond to changes in the school law and the administration of schools that were intended to make it easier for children to attend. Equally, he saw ignorance bordering on disloyalty when he found that local authorities were incapable of following the complex regulations governing the school system as he and others redesigned it. Even the city of London school trustees, he noted in 1846, were quite unable to fill out the forms for the annual reports to the government on their schools. Ryerson continued to blame difficulties in the administration of the school laws on the insufficient 'educational intelligence' of the people. Of course outright opposition to school reform was equally condemned as arising out of ignorance. Increasingly, 'education' was held up as sacrosanct – a subject that intelligent public men ought to place above the corruption and paralysis engendered by party politics.[9]

School reformers seem to have had a particularly negative view of their time. They looked at the body politic and at the society around them and found both wanting. But there was a positive side to their rhetoric. Reformers looked forward to the prosperity, activity, and morality that could result from the increased formal schooling of young Upper Canadians. Their vision extended from the society at large to the individual child. Malleable and terribly vulnerable to influence, any given child faced two possibilities. If exposed to evil or allowed to remain idle, the potential for sin, economic ruin, or political degeneracy was great. But if sufficiently schooled, there was the real possibility of individual improvement and, ultimately, moral, political, and economic salvation. The tendency to see things as pairs of opposites was also expressed in attitudes to teachers, whose power over Upper Canadian children school reformers at once welcomed and feared. Good teachers could change children's lives for the better, but there was no limit to the harm a bad teacher might do. The quest for more schooling, therefore, was equally a quest for better schooling, directed by teachers who were moral, temperate, and competent.

Certainly school reformers put forward a very negative view of Upper Canadian common school teachers as they were. Early in the century there had been complaints of the 'worthless scum' that engaged in school teaching in the colony. In 1831, it was reported to the legislature that the occupation of teaching in Upper Canada had been degraded to a matter of convenience to 'transient persons and idlers.' Egerton Ryerson, who in 1846 became the province's chief superintendent of common schools, echoed these themes. The time had come to rescue the youthful mind of Upper Canada from the 'ignorant and immoral' individuals who taught in the common schools and, more specifically, from teachers who were drunkards, blasphemers, or idlers.[10] A somewhat muted theme was the presence in the province of American teachers who might be disloyal to the British Crown.[11]

Discussion of the need for trained teachers provoked in some Upper Canadians reflections on what was practical in a colony that was still very young. The members of the district council of Gore argued in 1847, for example, that, because of the opportunities available to the young in a country like Upper Canada, the province would have to employ either immigrants or those 'whose Physical Disabilities from age' found teaching the only occupation suited to their 'Decaying Energies.' The advocates of reform recoiled from such a stance. In response to the statement from Gore, the district council of Colborne spoke out in favour of increased state intervention to create a trained teaching force. Existing Upper Canadian common school teachers, the Colborne councillors complained, were often no better than the 'lowest menials' in either manners or intellect. The government should do all it could to alter this state of affairs.[12]

The quest for improvement was also expressed in discussion of the ideal pedagogue. According to Egerton Ryerson, a good schoolmaster was 'affable without being familiar, grave without being morose' and 'a kind friend' rather than an 'overbearing tyrant' in his school. The harsh schoolmaster with his birch rod and rule of iron belonged to the past. On the other hand, reformers clearly believed that the ideal teacher was a man.[13]

And, certainly, both earlier and subsequent discussion of the pros and cons of female teachers suggests that the concerns school promoters had about school children and schoolmasters extended equally to schoolmistresses. In his report Charles Duncombe made clear his belief that the 'most important and peculiar duty' of women was 'the physical, intellectual and moral education of children' both as mothers and as teachers. But he also argued that many women were totally unprepared for their high calling. Duncombe devoted a large part of his report to a discussion of the need for more and better schooling for girls on these grounds.[14] Complaints about Upper Canada's schoolmistresses in the 1840s were often both bitter and blunt. One teacher felt sure that women were driving qualified schoolmasters out of the occupation. Others complained that 'illegal' school trustees had hired a 'female' willing to teach in a shanty that was 'unfit for a sheep pen.' It was a 'pernicious system,' these critics alleged, that encouraged the employment of incompetent women teachers for a few months at a time, just to save a little money.[15]

Ill-concealed anxieties about gender and wages thus permeated much of the discussion of teachers. Reformers also worried about teachers' social class. The argument was essentially that teachers ought to be a higher class than the pupils they were attempting to influence and instruct; otherwise improvement could hardly take place.[16] For both teachers and pupils better schooling was clearly perceived as a way to move up in society. Ryerson's speeches of the late 1840s dwelt on the dangers of downward mobility in a world where sons found it harder and harder to follow in the footsteps of their fathers. Tradesmen could not expect their children to make their way in the world with as little education as they had had themselves. The same message was delivered to farmers. Deprived of schooling, their children would have no chance. They would descend to the lowest orders, to swell the ranks of the degraded and the poor.[17]

School reformers self-consciously proclaimed a new vision of society. The world they put forward was one that was increasingly divided into two classes: those who were educated and those who were not. The essence of their message was that the unschooled were destined to be the menials of the world, the hewers of wood and drawers of water to their better-educated neighbours, whether one was talking of individuals, communities, or nations. To seek education, therefore, was to seek social advancement; to neglect it was to court, however inadvertently, social and economic disaster.[18]

In the light of the vigour with which private interests and local communities in Canada West were busy developing schools of various kinds in the first four decades of the province's history, these threats on the part of the advocates of common school reform seem extraordinary. What are we to make of their rhetoric? First of all, it is highly probable that many voluntary educational efforts were fuelled by similar concerns and fears. Even at the top of the heap, a Sir George Arthur could be anxious for the future of his son, as he waltzed him from his tutor to Upper Canada College and then off to another tutor and further schooling in England. It seems important, therefore, to pinpoint the more concrete causes of the movement for state intervention in schooling at mid-century.

The first point to clarify is that there is no one moment in time that can be singled out as crucial to the decision that the state should intervene. We have seen that the principle of government involvement in education had been accepted early in the nineteenth century and had grown out of a long tradition of government responsibility in both England and the United States. The growth of state intervention in education was a process; and school reformers advocating increasing intervention were responding to a wide spectrum of concerns. Urban poverty and disorder perhaps headed the list, but rural poverty was not far behind. True, the most devastatingly *visible* poverty did not visit the province until the Irish famine migration of the 1840s, but John Tidey and his family were not the only ones who looked want in the face in the 1820s and 1830s. In York, the first benevolent society devoted to helping indigent strangers had made its appearance in 1817; Susanna Moodie wrote about rural starvation in the 1830s; the ravages of intemperance were already starkly apparent in both urban and rural society in the same decade. Educational reformers were thus reacting to real not imagined social distress. They were also reacting to the world beyond the borders of Upper Canada. Charles Duncombe had toured the United States before drafting his 1836 report on education; Ryerson travelled to both the United States and Europe before writing his first major report a decade later. In the larger context of Europe and North America in the 1830s and 1840s, the social and political dislocations caused by the industrial and urban revolutions that were going on in Great Britain and New England were all too apparent. In Upper Canada children were without shoes or went hungry when bad harvests or bad luck struck their pioneering families; by the 1830s and 1840s, cholera epidemics and immigrant sheds betokened the larger misery that was still chiefly beyond the province's immediate borders but that was bound to affect the thinking of its leaders.[19]

The danger they worried about, of course, was ultimately a political one. It is no accident that a renewed resolve to reform Upper Canadian education followed hard on the heels of the rebellions of 1837–8. Poverty, idleness, and ignorance led not only to crime, but to revolution. The safety of property as well as social peace, reformers argued, demanded a population that could be governed. School reforms of the 1840s accompanied legislation designed to increase government at all levels. The point is that Upper Canadians left to voluntarist benevolent and temperance societies the problem of the poor. They could not accept government intervention aimed at either preventing or dealing with poverty and social dislocation at their roots, which were economic and political, for there was no model save revolution (which in the 1840s throughout western Europe was immediate and frightening). Their approach, rather, was to focus on the reform of schools.

Schooling would take care of the idle, urban boys who could not find proper apprenticeships because of the diminishing or wildly fluctuating profits of small tradesmen and the changing nature of production. Equally, it would take care of the idle girls who, especially in urban environments, but even to some extent in the countryside as well, were no longer kept busy from dawn to dusk with tasks like spinning and weaving. Schooling, in addition, would provide both sexes with skills with which to seek new kinds of employment in an expanding commercial economy: for boys, professional, clerical, and factory work; for girls, whose opportunities were far more limited, work as seamstresses or domestics, perhaps, or even as teachers in the expanding common schools. Finally, schools would work on character: energies would be stimulated and channelled; an enterprising *and* law-abiding populace, reformers hoped, would be the result.

What kind of schooling could have these results? To the promoters of educational reform, the casual and fluctuating private and domestic schools, and even the existing common schools, which had once provided and continued to provide so many with the skills they needed, no longer seemed up to the task. Nor did it seem possible, especially in the atmosphere of tension generated by the political reform movements of the 1830s and the rebellions of 1837–8, to contemplate a continuing dependence on 'American' teachers and textbooks, which some claimed were prominent features of Upper Canadian schooling even in the third decade of the century. The American scare may have been less an educational reality than a political debating point for, as Bruce Curtis has shown, most textbooks used in Upper Canada were British; and anti-British American geographies may have been seen by few.[20] But the few mattered to those most concerned to promote more government involvement in schooling. And the American textbook threat may well have been persuasive in moving legislators to act on the recommendations of the school reformers. Whatever the case, it was to a system of state-controlled common schools, supposedly purged of American influences, that Upper Canadian school reformers looked for a cure to the very real ills of their times.

This was hardly a democratic or even, necessarily, a liberal impulse. Indeed the very language in which school reform was advocated reeks of paternalism. 'The relations of the poor to the rich – of the educated to the uneducated,' according to Egerton Ryerson, required 'the cooperation of the latter in the education of the former.' Like most Upper Canadian educators, Ryerson had little trouble looking to the United States for an instructive example to bolster his arguments, despite the somewhat anti-American tenor of both the school-reform movement and the times. The inhabitants of Canada West should take note, Ryerson pointed out, of the 'paternal solicitude' exercised by the founding fathers of New England, where concern for education had resulted in school laws as early as the seventeenth century. The wealth and leadership of Canada would surely do no less. Acting through the government school system, it was up to those who were educated and well-to-do to elevate the poor and the ignorant.[21]

Axiomatic to the campaign for common schools was the belief that it was not only the duty but clearly in the interest of the wealthy classes to see that the working classes were rendered more intelligent. Echoing sentiments expressed by Horace Mann, the American educator who noted that industrial employers found educated workmen more satisfactory than those who had not attended school, Ryerson pointed out that an educated populace also enhanced the value of real estate. A community that was encumbered with 'an ignorant, and therefore unenterprising, grovelling, if not disorderly population' would surely see the value of property fall, in sharp contrast to a place where everyone was 'enterprising, intelligent and industrious.'[22]

From the beginning, there were two distinct strands to the demand for school improvement: a critique of existing legislation and provision for government-supported schooling on various grounds; and a condemnation of the state of education itself, the parents, the teachers, and their schools. By and large, although not exclusively, it was those who were out of power politically who tended to criticize the school laws and the government responsible for them as either inadequate on the one hand or overbearing on the other; those who were in a position to try to effect change tended to be the most critical of the actual state of existing schooling. It was in the interest of the latter to paint as black a picture as possible of things as they were, both in families and in schools, since this was the justification for their intervention. It was more in the interest of the former to lash out against the government and the character of its educational intervention.

Aside from these understandable contrasts in motivation, surprisingly little differentiated school promoters of one political persuasion from those of another. In the 1830s Tories and Reformers alike sought to increase the role of government in common schooling and, most often, for the same reasons. A Reform sympathizer such as Charles Duncombe was no less concerned than a John Strachan or the equally Tory Mahlon Burwell about youthful idleness and the potential for juvenile delinquency in Upper Canada. In the 1840s Reform leaders Francis Hincks and Robert Baldwin were instrumental in getting education laws passed, but no more so than the Conservative William Draper. The issue, when it came to politics, boiled down to the means. What kind of role would government play and at what cost? How were the burdens and the powers in school matters to be distributed among the various levels of government? Could property taxes for education be tolerated or should revenues from Crown lands be made to bear the major burden of financing the schools? How was power to be distributed among families, teachers, and public authorities in education?

In 1833, the government voted to increase the common school fund, but aside from this gesture in support of schooling, the many reports and bills put before the Upper Canadian legislature in the 1830s produced no concrete change. What they did do was prepare public opinion for the major changes that were to come. Common themes and areas of disagreement were certainly thoroughly aired. A Tory committee, chaired by Mahlon Burwell, proposed property taxes, renewal of a government-appointed provincial board of education, and the granting of increased power to existing district boards. But most of this program was anathema to the Reformers. Reformers, for their part, initiated a tour of American educational and reform institutions after the defeat, in the Legislative Council, of their 1835 school bill. The result was Duncombe's *Report upon the Subject of Education*, hardly a radical tract, with its promotion of education as insurance for the 'safety of government' and the prevention of 'insubordination, anarchy and crime.' The accompanying bill proposed a compromise on school finance, with funds from school lands to be used to stimulate local taxation. But it also proposed a more democratic approach to administration, focusing on the powers of local school trustees, echoing in this respect an 1831 bill that had also been introduced by the Reformers. The new bill passed the Assembly, only to be rejected by a committee of the Tory-dominated Legislative Council, which claimed to support it in principle but refused to introduce it because it was late in the session. The Rebellion of 1837 and its uneasy aftermath intervened. A similar bill, proposed two years later, this time by the Tory Mahlon Burwell, was also defeated by the Legislative Council, in all probability because of reluctance to introduce school taxes in a time of economic depression and so soon in the wake of the rebellion. A subsequent report by a commission of inquiry into education instituted by Sir George Arthur in 1839, known as the McCaul Commission, contained more in the way of administrative controls emanating from the centre than had most of the earlier proposals, but by this time Lord Durham's much more ambitious and prestigious report on the state of both Canadas had also been released. The latter condemned educational arrangements in Lower as well as Upper Canada and proposed, as a solution to this and other problems, the union of the two colonies.[23] Educational legislation for the upper province would have to await union.

II

The wait was not a long one, for despite the conflicts of the 1830s, a consensus of sorts had already been reached among the majority of Upper Canada's legislators on the need for a new school law. The Rebellion was over. Many Reformers closed ranks with their former Tory enemies in their unease when faced with the potential for violence that the years 1837 and 1838 revealed. The possibility of American intervention following the uprising and the apparent sympathy of some Upper Canadians for the revolutionaries and their American mentors and protectors suddenly brought into sharp relief most legislator's British loyalties and attachment to the British Crown. School reform could thus proceed, at least in part, as a measure to minimize what many claimed (even if they did not deeply believe) were the pernicious effects of American influence on Upper Canadian schooling. The Common School Act of 1841 was passed in the Legislature of the United Canadas with little fanfare, in considerable haste, and very late in the session. This law, most historians would now agree, nevertheless ushered in a new era in the legal history of Ontario schooling.[24]

Of outstanding importance among the provisions of the 1841 act was the creation of the administrative office known as the superintendency of common schools. The new superintendent was to be in charge of elementary public education in both provinces, and the provision was not really effective until separate superintendencies and administrative support systems were created later on for Canada East and Canada West. Still, the 1841 act established the principle, if not the fact, of provincial administrative leadership for the schools. The provincial superintendent was granted several crucial powers: to apportion monies arising from the government common school fund and to prepare 'suitable forms for making reports and conducting the necessary proceedings' under the act, as well as to promote uniformity in its implementation.

Secondly, the act provided for local administration at the district and township levels, doing away with the trustees of individual schools. District boards were to be responsible not only for allocating the provincial school moneys to local school districts, in amounts proportional to the numbers of children between five and sixteen years of age in each, but also for assessing property in these districts for funds to pay for schoolhouses. They were to report their proceedings annually to the provincial superintendent of schools. Lowest in the hierarchy of administration were the new commissioners, five in number, which each township was now to elect. These individuals were in charge of building schools and deciding what the assessment for local schools should be; they were to control courses of study and books, as well as the examination, hiring, and firing of teachers. It was these township boards of commissioners that established which indigent families would be exempt from paying the one shilling and threepence established by the law as the proper fee or rate for attendance at a common school. The boards were to report annually to their local district board.

Last but not least, the 1841 act laid the basis for religious dissent in common school education. Any group 'professing a Religious Faith different from that of the majority of the inhabitants' in a township, and

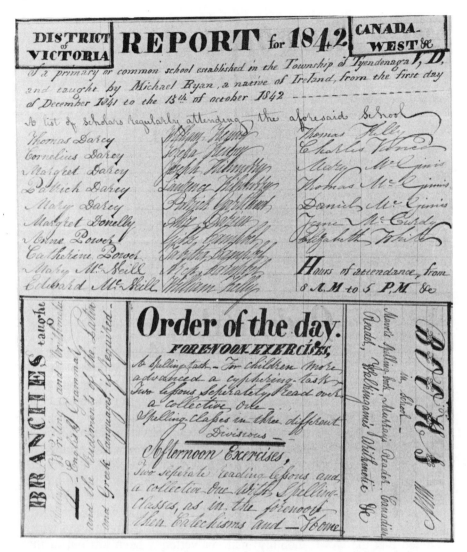

A Prince Edward District schoolmaster reports on his common school: Tyendenaga Township, 1842

dissenting from the 'regulations, arrangements or proceedings' of the commissioners, was empowered to set up a separate school, which could also participate in the provincial fund for common schools.

In three distinct areas the 1841 legislation would prove crucially important to the future of Ontario education: it established, first, a central administrative authority, supported by a hierarchy of administrative bodies at various levels of local government, second, local property assessment to match the provincial government's contribution to the cost of schooling, and third, the principle of religious immunity. The act also established what might best be labelled the paperwork principle: written reports on forms provided by the provincial authorities were now to be required as essential to the working of the system. Continued or reinforced were a number of principles that dated back to earlier legislation: the provincial government's right to specify who constituted appropriate teachers and who should certify them as such, to set the minimum number of pupils that had to be in regular attendance at each school, and to determine the number of months schools should be open.

As R.D. Gidney and Douglas Lawr have pointed out, both the act itself and the conditions of its implementation caused chaos rather than orderly change in the administration of Upper Canadian schools. No one informed local authorities of their responsibilities under the act. When the government finally decided to appoint two provincial assistant superintendents, for Canada East and West respectively, little effort was made to inform the public of this fundamental change. The assistant superintendent, the Church of Scotland clergymen and school reformer Robert Murray, in the case of Canada West, was in his turn given neither financial nor political support. No member of the Executive Council was empowered to superintend the superintendent, receive his reports, or take an interest in any problems he might encounter. No funds were earmarked for provincial education office expenses, such as clerks' salaries, or even for printing the forms that the superintendency was required to provide by law.

At the local level, the situation was no better. Omissions or peculiarities in the act gave rise to considerable confusion, as the new law seemed to imply that children under five or over sixteen were prohibited from attending common schools and that women teachers were ineligible to receive the common school grant. It was also unclear how often the specified shilling and threepence tuition for each child was to be paid. The *Cobourg Star* implied that the amount was to be paid monthly, when it noted that the word 'monthly' had inadvertently been left out of the act when it was printed, but many communities probably remained in the dark on this point.[25] Finally the act made illegal the long-standing practice of establishing union school sections in two adjoining townships where population distribution or geography made this more convenient. This caused much hardship to schools that suddenly found themselves deprived of their accustomed share of the school fund.

Worst of all, perhaps, was the fact that in an effort to provide more 'intelligent' and centralized leadership at the township level, the 1841 act had done away with local trustees for each school. The new township commissioners were given huge powers but little or no guidance or assistance, and the result appears to have been, in some places at least, considerable local tyranny. The responsibilities of the new commissioners, moreover, often proved too large a burden. Receiving no pay for their work and required by law to take responsibility for local teacher hiring and school building, among many other lesser duties, busy farmers, professionals, and commercial men alike complained that the task of managing all the schools in a township was an impossible one.

Certainly there were objections to the powers of the commissioners as there also were to the idea of school taxes. In Emily Township the inhabitants simply closed down their schools rather than pay the tax; in Belleville, supporters of the common school would not allow the teacher to turn in a report on its affairs. In Torbotten, the complaint was that the Dalhousie district council had failed to assess the residents as required, thus depriving them of their share of the school fund, which was tied to the assessment. Waterloo simply reported 'much ill-will' against the new system. In the municipal District of London, according to a traveller, more than 50 of the 177 school districts, or nearly one-third, had their schools closed as a result of 'imperfections' in the 1841 law.[26]

A good many of the problems created by the Common School Act of 1841 were cleared up in the second major Upper Canadian school law of the 1840s, generally known as the Hincks Act of 1843.[27] This legislation verified the existence of the assistant superintendents and appointed the secretary of the province to the post of chief superintendent, thus providing the embryonic education department with an effective link to the provincial ministry. The act abolished the township school commissioners in Canada West, calling once again for the election of three trustees to manage the affairs of each school and providing local communities with at least a semblance of their former autonomy, if not the whole measure they had previously enjoyed. Over the local schools and their trustees and connecting them to the provincial administration were now a core of locally appointed paid superintendents who were empowered to oversee the administration of the school law in their respective regions.

The powers of the provincial superintendent of schools remained similar to those of the single superintendent for both provinces called for in 1841. The 1843 act merely spelled them out more clearly and specified, in addition, that one of his important duties was to furnish local superintendents with copies, not only of the new school act and of the necessary forms for reports, but also of the 'Regulations and Instructions' required for its implementation. This time, in theory at least, local confusion would not be allowed to stand in the way of the law's enforcement.

County and township superintendents were empowered to distribute school funds in their areas and, in the case of the township superintendents, to see to school boundaries. They were also empowered to examine, certify, and annul the certificates of teachers at their respective levels: the county certificate to be permanent, unless annulled, and good throughout the county, and the township certificate valid only locally and for one year. The superintendents were also to take over the task of reporting, the township superintendents to the county, and the latter to the provincial superintendent of schools. What was to be reported was also set out clearly in the act. Finally, superintendents at both levels were to visit the schools and, in the case of the county superintendents, to examine into their 'state and condition' with respect to scholarship and good order, as well as to give 'advice and direction' to both teachers and trustees about the government of their schools and the studies pursued. To the trustees were returned the power to appoint and dismiss teachers, custody over the schoolhouses, the right to exempt indigent families from school fees and to ascertain what those fees should be, and the right generally to regulate the schools and their courses of study. Trustees, however, were no longer as powerful as they had been prior to 1841. They were now required by law to report annually on their schools; their decisions, furthermore, whether on the appointment of teachers or about school regulations, books, and programs of study, were now subject to their local superintendent's approval.

On the other hand, local powers with respect to religious dissent were made more concrete. No child, the 1843 act stated, was to be required in any common school to 'read or study in, or from, any Religious Book, or to join in any exercise of Devotion or Religion, which shall be objected to by his Parents, or Guardians.' Equally, any ten Roman Catholic or Protestant freeholders or householders had the right to establish a separate school, if the common school teacher were of the opposite persuasion. These provisions were more detailed and concrete than what had gone before, but their interpretation and implementation were to prove neither straightforward nor simple, as subsequent decades of religious controversy over the schools would prove.

Somewhat less controversial, but equally crucial, was the introduction by the 1843 act of the idea of hierarchy, in terms not just of educational personnel, but of schools. A superior group of schools, to be designated county model schools, was made possible by the law. Almost entirely severed from control by their local trustees, schools identified as county model schools could receive extra local funds and were to be more directly under the supervision of the county councils and superintendents. The act also looked forward to the eventual founding of a provincial normal

Egerton Ryerson as a young man

school that would supply teachers for the model schools. In fact, while by no means effecting this, the 1843 act clearly envisaged a provincial system of teacher training for Upper Canada.

Except for the idea of township instead of school-section local management, all the principles embodied in the 1841 act continued to inform that of 1843. What the latter added were clarity, detail, and a hierarchy of appointed administrative officers. The possibility of religious dissent remained, as did the requirement that local jurisdictions had to raise from taxes a sum equal to the amount provided by the provincial government in order to receive their share of the provincial school fund. If school trustees were returned to their offices, it was with a diminished power to control their local schools. An embryonic system of administrative authority, with a provincial officer in charge, had been set slightly more firmly into place. Introduced for the first time was the idea of teachers who might be superior to their local employers, either by virtue of their certification by superintendents, or their training in a special school, or both.

If the legislation of 1843 had fewer flaws than that of 1841, it too faced one serious difficulty from the start. This time copies of the act were swiftly printed and circulated; the secretary of state, Dominic Daly, took charge and proved an able superior to the assistant superintendent for Canada West, Robert Murray, and his 1844 replacement, Egerton Ryerson. The problem was caused by the fact that the bill had been planned to go into effect at the same time as Robert Baldwin's proposed municipal reform bill. The failure of the latter left the 1843 school law without the township and county councils upon which it depended for effective implementation, with the result that the responsibilities that the law had proposed for those councils devolved instead upon the province's district councils. As two historians of this period of educational administrative development have noted, even the 1843 act was 'left with a multitude of loose ends, obscurities and conflicting clauses' that were bound to cause problems at the local level.[28] Once again, a new school act seemed necessary almost as soon as the old one had been passed.

Still, three years elapsed between the passage of the Hincks Act of 1843 and Draper's Common School Act of 1846. The intervening period saw the accession of Egerton Ryerson to the assistant superintendency and considerable political turmoil in the Canadas. To many disillusioned early supporters of Ryerson, the one-time Methodist missionary and editor of the *Christian Guardian* showed his true colours as a turncoat and seeker of favours, if not office, from government, when he publicly defended the unpopular Sir Charles Metcalfe in the bitter election campaign of 1844.[29] Whatever the true source of his actions, the end of 1844 saw Ryerson ensconced as superintendent of schools for Canada West, a post he was not to desert for thirty-two years. By 1845 he had succeeded in installing his protégé, John George Hodgins, as clerical assistant in the newly created education department. He also sent the young Hodgins to normal school in Dublin to study the Irish government school system. As well, Ryerson had embarked on a fact-finding mission of his own, one that was to take him to the United States and also to several countries in Western Europe and the British Isles. The school systems of Ireland, Prussia, France, and Massachusetts figure prominently in the pages of Ryerson's massive *Report on a System of Public Elementary Instruction for Upper Canada*,[30] which he published on his return from this tour. This report was quickly followed by the 1846 school law.

Egerton Ryerson's views on Christian, moral, and political education, on social class, and on administration have been analysed from the point of view of both their contemporary contexts and their long-term significance.[31] The resulting portraits have not always been flattering. Single-minded in his concern for Christian improvement and peaceful social advancement, yet arrogant in his contention that Ontario's school system could somehow be immune from either religious controversy or local political interests, Ryerson clearly represented mid-Victorian crusading paternalism at its best and its worst. At its worst, it led him into an embattled and dictatorial approach to school reform. At its best, it led to an ambitious program of legislation and development that even his critics cannot fail to consider staggeringly successful within the context, at least, of its own purposes.

The problem to which the historian always returns with Ryerson is the nature and elaboration of these purposes, and here opinions clearly differ. For some, the Methodist's Christian mission remains paramount, for others his concern for political stability. Other accounts have stressed the goals of administrative or social order. No one has yet undertaken a genuinely probing psychological history of the man, a fascinating challenge considering the volume of his writings and the extent to which his private identity appears to have been linked to his public role.[32] Perhaps the most sensible approach, in the end, is a multifaceted one, recognizing the complexity of forces that were brought to bear not only on Egerton Ryerson, the individual, but that made him so representative of his times. The product of a period of religious, political, and social turmoil, this superintendent of schools for Canada West fastened onto state controlled mass schooling as the motor force that might bring religious harmony, as well as political and social order, out of what appeared to him and to many of his contemporaries to be a state of confusion bordering on chaos. The religious, the political, the social motives were all present, as these forces were present in society.

What is very clear, in the final analysis, is that Ryerson was ultimately most devoted to devising the machinery of educational 'advancement': he saw himself less as a legislator or philosopher of education than as an administrator or facilitator. It was chiefly through their orderly administration that he sought to improve Upper Canada's government schools. Working within a Victorian framework of profound trust in the possibility of Christian progress, and goaded by deep-seated fears of the forces that were at work to undermine and retard that progress, Ryerson looked to 'government' to infuse itself, through the administration of the school system, into what he called the 'public mind' of the province. 'If Government exists for the prosperity of the public family,' he argued, 'then everything relating to educational instruction demands its practical care, as well as legislative interference ... To be a State System of Public Instruction, there must be a State control [sic] as well as a State law.' Ryerson concluded that it was 'now generally admitted' that the education of the people was 'more dependent upon the administration, than upon the provision of the Laws relating to Public Instruction.'[33] The good to be promoted, then, was *government-authorized* and *government-administered* schooling. The resulting education was designed to transform the character of Canada West, to make the place Christian, productive, and safe. The ultimate goal, then, was stable government itself – and the governable subjects that stable government required.

Ryerson came home from his foreign tour, as he later claimed, determined to be eclectic in his approach to educational reform. The school 'machinery' and law would be taken mainly from the state of New York, he said, while the tax system and free schools would follow the Massachusetts model. The government-sponsored textbooks would be Irish in origin, but the Upper Canadian approach to training teachers would draw chiefly on German institutional practice.[34] All this may have been a vast oversimplification of the truth. The 1846 school law,[35] after all, probably drew less on foreign example than on its own Upper Canadian predecessors, the laws of 1841 and 1843. Nevertheless, the new law also made significant departures from these acts. Forty-four clauses in all, it bore the imprint of Ryerson's concern to centralize authority in the education office in Toronto, a concern that the Conservative ministry, led by William Draper, enthusiastically shared. District superintendents, appointed by the district councils, now officially replaced the local superintendents of 1843. These men were to be paid for their efforts and were empowered not only to examine and certify all teachers in their districts and to give advice to local authorities, but also to begin the work of actually regulating what went on in the schools. The power to decide on the content of the regulations was vested in a new body created by the act, an appointed provincial Board of Education, of which the full-time provincial superintendent was to be a member. Gone was the pretence that a political superintendent would oversee his work; Ryerson continued to report to the provincial secretary, but by the 1846 law was himself to be styled the 'Chief Superintendent of Schools.'

The chief superintendent was empowered to 'prepare suitable Forms and Regulations for making all reports and conducting all necessary proceedings' under the act, and 'to cause the same, with such instructions as he shall deem necessary and proper for the better Organization and Government of Common Schools' to be transmitted to the appropriate school officers. The Board of Education, in its turn, was to establish and regulate a provincial normal school, which would be under the direct governance of the chief superintendent, and to disapprove or recommend any books to be used in the schools. Acting on the board's advice, the chief administrator was given authority to do all in his power to discourage the use of improper books in the schools; to promote better schoolhouses and school furnishings, as well as the development of school libraries; and to 'employ all lawful means in his power to collect and diffuse information on the subject of education generally, among the people of Upper Canada.'

As Ryerson often reiterated, under the barrage of attacks to which he was subjected after the passage of this law, many of his powers were advisory, rather than regulatory: the power to diffuse information, for example, or the power to recommend the adoption of better schoolhouse plans. But in the vital matters of school-books and teacher training, the crucial regulatory powers were also there. And from these, indeed from all the powers outlined in the act, a great deal more would follow. Moreover, the law itself began the work of regulation. Following the 1843 act, it clearly established two types of teaching certificates – a special certificate permitting one year of teaching in a given school; and a general certificate good for the district of origin until revoked – and made the district superintendent solely responsible for issuing both types of certificate. By way of replacing the township authorities whom the 1841 and 1843 acts had failed to put permanently into place, it authorized local clergy, district wardens, and township and town councillors, as well as resident justices of the peace, to visit the schools. It required that the teachers of common schools keep 'daily, weekly and quarterly Registers' and that they maintain 'proper order and discipline' in their schools, according to further forms and regulations to be supplied by the chief superintendent of schools. It also required teachers to hold quarterly public examinations of their pupils. The school visitors were authorized to question the children at these examinations and generally to look to the good management of the schools, but their interest was entirely voluntary. The big stick remained the school fund, as administered by the district superintendency. As before, it was forfeit if the school failed to make its annual report, or if it had not been taught for the appropriate number of months (now six) by a British subject duly certified by the district superintendent. It was now also forfeit if any book in use had been 'disapproved' publicly by the new provincial Board of Education.

Ryerson argued that the 1846 law actually allowed more local self-government than had its predecessor of 1843, claiming that outside authorities could interfere less in 'purely local affairs' than had previously been the case.[36] But it is hard to see how this could have been true. Certainly trustees now had onerous duties, largely in connection with the maintenance of schoolhouses and the like; indeed the act contained rather ominous provisions dealing with persons elected to the office who refused to serve. In a letter to William Millar, school superintendent for the Eastern District, however, Ryerson retreated into vagueness on the question of the distribution of powers. Those 'heretofore exercised by the Township Superintendents' were now 'vested in the Trustees themselves and the District Councils.' But crucial powers, including the granting of teachers' certificates and the payment of school moneys, now in fact belonged to the district superintendents. 'Your powers – though not extending to anything which properly belongs to the People themselves or their representatives, unless they appeal to you – extend to what is essential to the improvement of the Schools: – the object contemplated by the Legislative Grant.'[37] What the chief superintendent was perhaps hinting at in this vague statement was what in fact proved to be the case: that energetic superintendents who were willing to use the tools of teacher certification and the withholding of the provincial fund could exercise considerable leverage. The powers of the office clearly depended on the willingness of the incumbent to use them.[38]

Perhaps the most telling evidence of change was the flurry of administrative activity that followed the school act of 1846. Hard on the heels of the law's passage, the education department issued a set of 'General Regulations and Instructions' for the edification of those whose job it was to administer the new legislation.[39] Rules regarding instruction as well as school holidays were laid out in detail, as were the duties of local school personnel: trustees, teachers, and visitors. In addition, instructions were provided for persons wishing to appeal, in the case of any school-related dispute, to the chief superintendent.

The regulations were significant, for in numerous subtle ways they further eroded the power of local school authorities. Their tone was hectoring. Trustees had the right, the regulations pointed out, to hire instructors for their schools, but the 'mode of teaching' was 'with the Teacher.' Only district superintendents and school visitors retained the power to advise the teacher. Trustees could choose the school-books, but only from a list provided by the education department. Trustees were advised to avoid having books 'as various as the Scholars' names,' and the readers and other books published by the Irish National Board of Education were recommended as the best. Teachers were told that it was, among other things, their duty to 'receive courteously the Visitors appointed by Law.' They were 'by no means, to alter, or erase' remarks made in the school visitors' book by these august persons. Teachers were to study the Irish readers and classify and instruct their pupils 'according to the approved method recommended in the several prefaces.' They were to set good examples in matters such as 'regularity and order ... cleanliness, neatness and decency.' The regulations even expanded the categories of teaching certificates from two to three and described them as first, second, and third class, with both the second and the third designated certificates that were good for only a year, the former at the township level, the latter 'at the special request of the Trustees' and only for a particular school section.

Visitors to schools also received instructions. None were to speak disparagingly of teachers in front of pupils. Advice was to be given privately and reported later to district superintendents. As the Irish National Board of Education directed its superintendents, so the latter in Upper Canada were also asked to 'exhibit a courteous and conciliatory conduct' towards all persons connected with the schools and to conduct themselves so as to 'uphold the just influence and authority' of both trustees and teachers.

If we dwell at length on this document, it is because it was typical of hundreds that were to follow. After 1846, hardly a year passed without a host of circulars and instructions from the education department to various local authorities. Both their tone and their attention to detail are evidence of a new regime in Upper Canadian common school affairs. The new chief superintendent of schools was determined not only that there should be adequate school law in the province; he wished also, as his title suggests, to superintend: to instruct, advise, and regulate, down to the tiniest detail, the schools and schooling of Upper Canadians.

The years immediately following 1846 saw no let-up in the momentum that had been established. If anything the advocates of school reform quickened the pace. The 1840s were the years of the district superintendents, many of whom rose to the challenge and made school supervision into something increasingly resembling a full-time job. Speeches, pamphlets, essays, and reports on education multiplied, many of them originating with Ryerson but a good many coming from the pens of these gentlemen. Another piece of common school legislation, the school act for cities and towns of 1847,[40] was put into place and the provincial Normal School began its history in Toronto. In these years also, the education department began to expand.

A great deal of the expansion is directly traceable to the provisions of the school act of 1846. The 1846 law had provided first of all for the provincial Normal School, the creation and management of which was no small task.[41] But more significant still were the powers of regulation given to the chief superintendent and the fact that section 2 of this act specifically enjoined him to use all means in his power to 'collect and diffuse information on the Subject of Education' among the people. The legislators responsible for the 1846 act could hardly have foreseen how strenuously Ryerson and his assistant, John George Hodgins, would work to carry out this part of their task. Finally, the 1846 law had continued the work of a large number of school officers – and created a number of new ones – for whom the education department was the link either to the provincial government or to other parts of the system. Meetings of the provincial Board of Education had to be organized and managed, local school authorities circularized, assisted, or placated, and local disputes arbitrated. To maintain personal contact with the localities, tours of the province for Ryerson had to be arranged and appropriate speeches prepared. It is small wonder, perhaps, that the department expanded.[42]

The school act of 1847 followed immediately on that of 1846 and was clearly considered by its author to be a simple amendment to it. Its provisions were basically twofold. The major thrust and the burden of its first seven sections was the elimination of individual boards of trustees for schools in cities and towns and their replacement by six-person boards, which were to be appointed by the municipal councils or boards of police and were to take responsibility for all the common schools in their respective municipalities, with the exception of model schools, which remained under the jurisdiction of the district councils, as before. Each new urban board of trustees was to appoint a city or town school superintendent, who would take over for his locality the functions previously performed by the district superintendent. City and town boards were to report directly to the chief superintendent of schools. As a circular to urban authorities shortly after the passage of the act made clear, the new law applied to the cities of Toronto, Kingston, Hamilton, London, and Bytown (Ottawa), and also to the corporations of Dundas, Brantford, Cornwall, Brockville, Picton, Cobourg, Port Hope, Niagara, and St Catharines.[43]

The remaining four sections of the act were expansions on the school act of 1846 and had application beyond cities and towns. The bombshell was in the eighth section, which provided that municipal authorities were now permitted to assess taxpayers *beyond* the amounts required to raise the local half of the school fund or to pay for the construction of schoolhouses. The ceiling was removed from local taxation, and moneys could be raised to increase teachers' salaries, repair or furnish schoolhouses, or indeed for any 'Common School purposes' whatsoever. The cutting edge to all this was in what the act failed to include, for there was no provision for permitting the new urban school boards created by the act to levy rate bills (or fees) on parents. The result was that free schools supported solely by the provincial grant and local property taxes were thus imposed by the provincial government on urban councils and taxpayers.

The school acts of 1841 and 1843 chiefly encountered complaints and confusion arising from the inadequacy of their provisions or of local political machinery to make them work; the laws of 1846 and 1847 by their very provisions provoked hostility bordering on rage. Local authorities felt threatened and people who considered themselves reformers betrayed. Representatives of denominational interests were also concerned, as were those who felt that they spoke for the independent working classes, for families, or for taxpayers. Criticisms focused on four major issues. Memorialists from the District of Gore represented the many who believed that the superintendency was a waste of money and that the sums proposed to pay its costs and those of the new Normal School in Toronto would be better spent directly on the schools. A second category of criticism and concern had to do with family and religious interests. There was serious doubt that the denominational or other rights of families could be provided for and protected when single boards of trustees governed all the schools in a city or town. The school act of 1847 in particular appeared to eliminate in urban centres the right given to any ten heads of families to petition for a separate school. But the most explosive criticisms of all focused on two further points. First of all, free schools took away from the 'working man' the dignity of educating his own children. Secondly, their imposition from above impinged on the right of local property owners and householders to self-government.[44]

The opposition to the acts of 1846 and 1847 that made itself felt in memorials to the government was also expressed in pamphlets and articles and letters in the press. It did not mince words. Egerton Ryerson was portrayed as a 'Prussian Dictator' whose chief aim in life was to impose his own particular brand of bigotry on the schools of the province. His office was described as 'useless and exceedingly burthensome,' and the school laws were damned as cumbersome, sectarian, and unsuited to the spirit of the country. A correspondent to the *Globe* summed up his complaint in 1849. Ryerson's statistics were questionable, his district superintendents unnecessary, and the whole school system a complete waste of money.[45]

The memorials and articles were not without their effect, but resistance was expressed most dramatically perhaps by those who chose actions rather than words. The city of Toronto, like Emily Township before it, chose to close its common schools.

Since the 1847 school act simply omitted any mention of rate bills on parents, Toronto authorities first took refuge in queries to the chief superintendent and, through him, to the solicitor-general, regarding their actual legal situation.[46] The first request for information came from the newly constituted Toronto board of school trustees, over the name of the city superintendent, George Barber. Did the board have the right to impose a rate bill on parents and guardians, or were they required to put the whole of their common school estimates before the city council to be raised by assessment? The solicitor-general replied that the latter was the case. Not satisfied, city authorities sent, again via Barber, a second request, this time that the education department submit the case in 'a more distinct and tangible shape,' so that no possible doubts could arise as to the city council's proper course. This time the answer came from

Attorney-General Robert Baldwin himself. Not only did the board have no right to levy rates on parents, but the city council was bound to raise by assessment whatever sum the board of education estimated would be required.

Considerable interest attaches, in the light of this statement, to the new city school board's estimates for 1848. One item had gone down from the previous year's expenditures, the trustees having decided to rent only fifteen instead of sixteen schoolhouses. The provincial fund was estimated to remain the same as the sum granted in 1847. All other items, however, had either gone up or were entirely new. In the new expenditures were estimates for repairs and fuel, maps and books, and a reserve fund for assistant teachers; in the category of old expenditures were an increase of more than £300 to the total for teachers' salaries and a raise of £75 to the original sum set aside for the salary of George Barber. Altogether, the board had decided to increase its annual budget by almost one-third.

The new trustees were clearly following their mandate to improve the schools by making them more comfortable and providing better salaries for their teachers and the new superintendent. On the other hand, the city council, deprived of approximately £900 in rate bills on parents, was faced with the prospect of quadrupling the assessment on property to pay the estimates for 1848. Objecting to the idea that a board they had appointed themselves could turn around and dictate taxes to the people's representatives, the city council also felt aggrieved at the law that permitted this to happen, all the more so since they had never been consulted about it. Indeed, they felt particularly aggrieved, since the chief superintendent resided in the same city as themselves and had had every opportunity to discuss it with the council. The committee of council that concerned itself with the schools reported itself divided with respect to the action to be taken, only one of its members believing that the city was under no obligation whatever to raise the estimates for the coming year. All three members, however, agreed that even if the council acquiesced for 1848, there was no option in the long run but to refuse to levy the taxes, their commitment extending only to the year of the present board's tenure. Otherwise, the 'privilege of municipal legislation in fiscal affairs would be nullity ... for then the people would virtually be taxed, for local purposes, by an authority different from that of their own constituted local government; – an anomaly at once repugnant to British freedom and common sense.'47 The inevitable choice resulting from this logic was to close the schools.

It was an increasingly disgruntled public that concerned itself with Upper Canadian educational matters in the 1840s. From Emily township in 1841 and 1842 to Toronto at the end of the decade, common schools failed to open as confused or irritated local communities grappled with the new laws. Not all were swept away by the rhetoric of common school expansion, teacher improvement, or free schools. Some clearly saw the potential for autocracy in the new educational structures that were gradually being developed and worried that vast sums of taxpayers' money would be spent to no particular effect. Others felt that there might well be an effect, but that it was likely to be a negative one. For their part, supporters of educational reform reacted to such opposition in tones of shocked disbelief. 'In Toronto, the common schools are ... closed,' the *Journal of Education for Upper Canada* complained in May of 1849, 'while juvenile crime increases and abounds beyond all precedent!' School reformers had diagnosed what Michael Katz has identified as a 'crisis of youth'[48] in their chief city, and they thought they knew the cure. Only vastly increased and properly regulated schooling, they believed, would solve the problem. But not everyone agreed with the means adopted to bring this about.

In most places in Canada West in the late 1840s, common schooling nevertheless continued to expand, despite the battles over how it should be financed, conducted, or controlled. The working out of the details of who had power over what was certainly unfinished. But to all intents and purposes, by the time the provincial Normal School opened its doors in Toronto late in the fall of 1847, the essential framework of what in time would be known as the 'public school system' of Canada West was in place. There would be much more said against it, however, before this fact was generally recognized.

5 The Battle for Control over Public Schools

If the opposition to provincial educational policy that emerged in the very shadow of the education department during the 1840s was potent, it was no less so in some of the outlying regions of Canada West. In the Bathurst District, feelings of alienation reached such a height that they finally coalesced to produce what Egerton Ryerson and his supporters identified as a major attack on the entire provincial common school system, the legislative initiative that John George Hodgins later labelled the 'abortive' Cameron school act of 1849. The law (named after the radical Reformer and Commissioner of Public Works Malcolm Cameron, who was evidently its chief promoter) seems in retrospect less an attempt to dismantle Ryerson's school system than an effort to alter its thrust. What its supporters – and anti-Ryerson forces generally – wanted, it would appear, was greater local autonomy in educational affairs.

The ultimate response of the provincial government to the critics of the 1840s school legislation was embodied in the school law of 1850 and those that followed in the same decade. These laws suggest that all concerned perceived the need for accommodation and compromise by the end of the turbulent 1840s. The politics of opposition was complex, cross-cut by local, denominational, and ideological interests. Thus 'political' opponents were not the only ones who needed to be placated. By the 1850s, in fact, the most sustained and effective critiques of Canada West's school system came increasingly from clerics concerned about the loss of control over education by churches and families. Major concessions were sought from the provincial government by the Roman Catholic church in particular, in the form of refinements to the law permitting separate schools for religious minorities in their various communities. And major concessions were in fact won, chiefly because of the political clout of French Catholic Lower Canadians in the legislature of the united province. But it is also true that by the period in question it may have taken one 'incipient bureaucracy' to do battle effectively with another.[1]

The laws of the 1850s did more than effect a compromise between local authorities and central power or between the Protestant majority and the Roman Catholic minority in Canada West. They added the grammar schools to the school system and began the process of developing a hierarchy of government-funded educational institutions, with the common schools at the base of the pyramid and the grammar schools more clearly defined as schools of a higher academic level. They also elaborated the hierarchies among the common schools themselves: 'poor' schools were now to be distinguished from ordinary rural common schools as well as rural from urban, by their different modes of financing. Even schools in the same category would find themselves distinguished from one another by their differing attendance rates, which, in turn, were made to affect their revenues. Teachers too were to be classified, by virtue of certificates that suggested a hierarchy of talent and expertise. This hierarchy was to be defined centrally. For, finally, the laws of the 1850s established more firmly and elaborately than ever the administrative machinery of the provincial government. If the chief superintendent of schools lost some powers in the shuffle, they were few; the upshot was a central office with a great deal of authority to interfere, to advise, and to persuade, if not to coerce.

Indeed, both the reports of the local superintendents and the voluminous manuscript correspondence of the education department are witness to the occasional anguish and the ongoing struggle of thousands of interested parties and local officials, both appointed and elected, to make sense of Upper Canada's mid-century school laws. In the case of the officials, the reports bear witness especially to their efforts to perform their duties correctly and in what they perceived to be the best interests of their communities. The documents are, finally, fascinating evidence of the huge expenditure of effort on the part of the provincial education department to evolve administrative arrangements and divisions of power that would both satisfy local interests and at the same time make the school laws work, more or less as their framers had intended.

I

Eventually rejected by the Baldwin-Lafontaine government that had sponsored it, the 'Cameron Act' has the anomalous status of a school law that was passed by the legislature but never enforced. It was, as John George Hodgins put it, 'abortive.' Still, for all his dismissal of it, the many pages of Hodgins's own *Documentary History of Education* devoted to the battle over this piece of legislation are clear evidence of the powerful feelings it evoked in its day. Certainly no one took it more seriously than Egerton Ryerson, who claimed not only that the bill was intended to dismantle the school system but that its purpose was also to dethrone himself.[2]

If the school laws of 1843 and 1846 were cumbersome, Cameron's law was downright unwieldy. Hodgins described it as 'a sort of composite School Bill' and it drew on several sources. Many clauses were taken *verbatim* from previous acts. According to Hodgins, it also drew heavily on a draft law that Ryerson had submitted to the government in 1848, a bill designed to respond to at least some of the criticisms of the school acts of 1846 and 1847. Without a clause-by-clause comparison of the Cameron Act and Ryerson's draft bill (and the latter is not available), the question of who was really responsible for some of the innovations of mid-century remains unclear. Whatever its origins, Cameron's bill proceeded through the legislature without a hitch and was passed into law.[3]

Its passage was designed to coincide with a new municipal act, which finally succeeded in doing away with the districts and establishing local government at the county and township levels in Canada West. Accordingly, the Cameron Act provided for superintendents at the township, town, and city levels only, although counties could combine forces and hire a single superintendent if they wished, restricted only by the maximum of one hundred schools to be inspected by any one official. The law provided that all schools, without exception, were to be governed individually by boards of three trustees, reporting to these local superintendents. It thus abolished the new city- and town-wide boards. Rates on parents were explicitly permitted everywhere. With respect to free schools and union schools, the act was permissive rather than coercive. With respect to the selection of school-books and the certification of teachers, the Cameron Act did not dispense with controls, but placed them at the county level. Nor did the act dispense with the chief superintendent of schools.

What the chief superindent lost, perhaps, was his dignity. He was now to be 'directed by' the government-appointed provincial Board of Education, which may have been intended under the Cameron Act to loom somewhat more significantly on the educational horizon than it had since its creation in 1846. Certainly no one then or since has doubted that the existing board was purely advisory and took its cues entirely from the chief superintendent.[4] The new act also specified that direction of the new Normal School was part of the provincial board's mandate, omitting any reference to the school's oversight or superintendence by the province's chief school administrator. Finally the Cameron Act brought the grammar schools into the provincial system. This was done by enabling local sections to petition county councils for permission to make local grammar schools into 'senior departments' of their existing common schools.

In sum, the Cameron Act restored considerable power, but by no means all of it, to local authorities, maintaining the momentum of 'improvement' through its appointed county and provincial boards of education. Where Ryerson's approach to such questions as property assessment or the union of urban school sections into single systems had been coercive, that of the Cameron Act was permissive. Where Ryerson had preferred superintendents at the district level, the Cameron Act eschewed even the county level and turned to a township superintendency, albeit with the possibility open that local municipalities could amalgamate their superintendencies if they wished.

According to what one can gather from Hodgins's and Ryerson's own writing on the subject, the Baldwin ministry either assumed that Malcolm Cameron was in fact putting forward Ryerson's own draft law in its entirety, or later pretended that this was the case. Ryerson, for his part, may have been for some time ignorant of the details of the bill. By April 1849, however, as a result of a visit to the seat of the government in Montreal, Ryerson learned that Cameron's proposed legislation had been framed in what he took to be 'a spirit of hostility' to his office and to himself.[5]

The Chief Superintendent lost no time in launching a counterattack. In a lengthy document addressed to the government, he detailed his objections to the bill. The objections were many and sometimes contradictory; they were also revealing. What Ryerson appeared to fear most was fragmentation and drift. What he clearly wanted was uniformity, through as much centralized control as he could get away with.

The Chief Superintendent also seemed to find it objectionable that many sections of the bill were copied from his own draft bill on the one hand, but that it was excessively 'theoretical, cumbrous, intricate, expensive and inefficient' on the other. Although he had evidently been prepared to do so himself, Ryerson argued that it seemed a poor time to introduce a new law 'at the very moment' when the people were learning 'to work new Municipal Institutions.' It was even more unwise to allow such a 'loosely concocted' bill to throw all the labours of the past three years to the winds. Ryerson ended by stating his 'strong conviction of duty' and 'the great importance and variety' of the topics dealt with as an apology for the length of his communication.

Whether the communication was in fact too detailed for busy ministers to absorb or there were other reasons for ignoring it, it had no immediate effect. Cameron's bill was passed, and Ryerson was forced to play his final card. Arranging a meeting with Robert Baldwin, he evidently raised the question of whether he could in fact serve under the new act. Baldwin provided reassurance of the government's support for Ryerson and it was at this meeting that he seems to have given the impression that the government believed all along that Ryerson not only concurred with but had 'assisted' in the preparation of the new law. Baldwin also asked the Chief Superintendent to convey his feelings to the government once again, this time in the form of a letter to himself. In this document on the Cameron Act, Ryerson argued that the abolition of town and city boards of trustees would prevent the grading of schools into the primary, intermediate, and high schools, that were 'founded in every City and considerable Town in the neighbouring States.' He further stated that the provision to make the chief superintendent the 'servant' of the provincial Board of Education was impractical and designed to place the present incumbent in a 'comparatively humiliated position ... denuding his office of the standing and influence' it should command. Finally, he hoped that the government would not allow itself to become, in its support for Cameron's law, the 'instrument of petty intrigue.'[7]

Whether his points were all well taken, Ryerson's statements on the Cameron Act are significant. Forced onto the defensive, he focused in both letters on what it was he wanted most to preserve in the Upper Canadian school system. Paramount, clearly, was his own direct regulation of the system and its Normal School. Of almost equal importance were the preservation of provincial control of school-books and the continuation of urban school boards. The former permitted, through the promotion of a graded series of readers, the classification of pupils within individual schools, the latter the gradation of schools in all communities having more than one. Last, but not least, were the mechanisms designed to ensure that teachers were properly qualified and inspected and that all controls, in fact, were hierarchically organized and, ultimately, 'practical.'

It was undoubtedly on this latter point that Ryerson won the day. His detailed, section-by-section critique of the Cameron Act seemed to demonstrate that the school superintendent of five years' experience knew what worked and what did not. Who were Cameron and his friends, or even Baldwin and his, to gainsay him? Evidently reluctant to lose the knowledgeable administrator, the man who seemed to know more about the system than the ministry itself, the Reform government backed off. Ryerson had suggested an inquiry, and an inquiry was eventually put in motion, in the form of a letter from Francis Hincks requesting the views of former district school superintendents on the school law. But in the meantime the Chief Superintendent was assured that his system would not be interfered with. By the autumn of 1849, Ryerson was already confident of his 'ultimate success' with respect to the principle of free schools and that his name would be 'rescued from the prejudice which misapprehension and calumny have attached to it.' A final letter to the government in early December outlined his views once more, and by the fifteenth of the month a reply from the provincial secretary officially authorized him to carry on under the old system. This letter stated explicitly the government's view that Ryerson's practical knowledge of the workings of the school system made him the best person to frame the new law that the altered municipal government required.[8]

The press covered all these events with varying degrees of thoroughness and detachment. The *Globe* reprinted the correspondence between Ryerson and the provincial secretary. The *Examiner* supported the Cameron Act on the grounds that it took the 'absolutist power out of Mr. Ryerson's hand' and distributed it more 'equitably and fairly amongst the people.' So did the *Ottawa Citizen*, which came down clearly on the side of local control. Other papers hurled epithets at the Chief Superintendent. One, the *Bathurst Courier*, called Ryerson an 'artful dodger,' and expressed the faint hope that Baldwin and his colleagues would not be ignorant of his expertise in 'finesse and intrigue.' Another felt that Ryerson's objections to the Cameron Act showed that 'his Imperial Mightiness, Egerton the Great' had been displeased to see his dictatorship and that of the Board of Education over schoolbooks destroyed. It was his 'love of power' that was the mainspring of Ryerson's critique of the Cameron Act; most of his criticism was 'useless verbiage.' The government's repudiation of its own law was certainly a 'very funny affair.' Hincks's inquiry into the views of the district superintendents was unlikely to help, as the latter were all in the pocket of the Chief Superintendent and very much part of his 'machinery.'[9]

There is no doubt that Ryerson had friends among the district superintendents, as he did among the hundreds of other individuals associated with the province's schools. He had cultivated them assiduously, writing to them at enormous length and visiting them in their districts. His behaviour in the winter of 1850 was circumspect. He informed inquirers that the Cameron Act was 'of course, in force' until it was actually repealed but advised people to carry on as they had under the old laws. They were 'perfectly free and had every right,' however, to make changes if they wished. Evidently some local taxpayers insisted that trustees honour any changes they thought beneficial to themselves.[10]

The incoming correspondence of the education department during the winter months of 1850 brought a number of inquiries, as well as answers to the Hincks circular and a certain amount of free advice. The trustees of a school section in the Johnston District averred that the Cameron Act gave too much power to municipal councils and not enough to trustees and that it would be hard to find enough people qualified to be township superintendents. A minister from Carlton Place wrote spelling out the 'intrigue' in the Bathurst District, where 'thorough going Scotch Radicals' still could not forgive Ryerson his defence of the 'noble, generous but ill used Metcalfe.' It was one Murdoch McDonnell who had helped Cameron draw up 'that abortion of the last Session – the School Bill,' and another enemy of Ryerson's who wrote for the *Bathurst Courier* under the pen name of 'Constant.' A second correspondent on this named another enemy of the Chief Superintendent as the true writer of the attacks in the *Courier*. The man's motive, this friend explained, was to turn Ryerson out of his office in the hope of getting the superintendency for himself. On a more serious and critical note, some correspondents tried to explain to Ryerson what they felt were the good points in the Cameron Act, as well as the bad, or intimated in a general way that the 1846 and 1847 laws did need improvement.[11]

The replies to Hincks's circular, even one from a Bathurst District critic accusing Ryerson of 'the most barefaced lying,' ended up in the incoming correspondence of the education department. This suggests that the government had decided, even before the event, to trust in its incumbent chief superintendent of schools. If the replies contained useful suggestions, presumably these would help Ryerson when he drafted the new bill. Reprinted in Hodgins's *Documentary History*, with 'all irrelevant and extraneous matter' expunged, they confirm that the opposition to Egerton Ryerson and his school laws came not just from fear of Ryerson the man, but from deeper worries about the potential for injustice that the 1840s laws embodied.[12]

II

Ryerson and his assistants in the provincial education department paid at least some attention to the letters. Indeed, the Common School Act of 1850[13] was the result of a decade of learning, not just by local school people, but by the provincial government and its chief superintendent of schools. By the new act the chief superintendency and the provincial Board of Education (renamed the Council of Public Instruction) were preserved more or less intact, as was the relationship of the superintendency to the provincial Normal School. But concessions to local autonomy were made. Although a return to individual boards for each school in cities and towns was evidently not contemplated, by the 1850 act the new urban boards of trustees did have to be elected. These new elected boards retained the power to decide how much municipal councils would have to raise by assessment on property for school purposes; on the other hand, they explicitly regained the right to levy rate bills on parents if they so chose. It was thus in the power of the elected school boards of cities and towns to decide whether the schools in their municipalities should be supported partly by rates on parents and guardians, partly by taxes, and partly by the provincial grant, or whether by eliminating the first of these sources of income, the schools should be made free. In rural schools, the right to make this decision was vested in the annual meeting of the landholders and householders who elected the trustees.

Another area of concession had to do with the nature of the local superintendency. More or less as the Cameron Act had proposed, it was left to county councils to decide if they wished a single superintendent for the county (or if over a hundred schools were involved, more than one) or if they wished to appoint township superintendents. Most chose the latter course, indicating that the preference for known individuals who were close to their communities had not been a chimera. A final area of concession had to do with the certification of teachers. This now rested, as the Cameron Act had suggested it should, with county bodies, rather than individual superintendents. Known as county councils (or boards) of public instruction, the new examining bodies consisted of the grammar school boards of each county, plus the local superintendency. Where more than one grammar school existed, the county could be divided and several examining 'circuits' created. The county boards of public instruction were not totally independent, however. They were to classify teachers according to 'a Programme of Examination and Instructions' provided by the provincial education department.

Where the 1850 act went further than any previous school law of Canada West was in its detailed provisions for auditing the accounts of the various parties handling school moneys and in the minute instructions provided for those involved in the administration of the law. Twelve sections, for example, were devoted to the constitution of rural trustee boards alone, while the section outlining their duties ran to nineteen elaborate clauses. The act also outlined procedures for the arbitration of disputes about school boundaries or between teachers and trustees.

Finally, there was an alteration in the method of allocating the provincial school fund. This was in fact foreshadowed in the Cameron Act and may have been the most significant change the 1850 law introduced. The school fund would continue, according to the new act, to be distributed on the basis of population when it came to the larger political divisions – now the counties. But it was no longer to be divided locally according to the relative number of children between the ages of five and sixteen in the various school sections. The new basis for allocating the fund locally was to be the average number of children actually in attendance in each school. This would reward schools achieving higher average attendance rates with a larger share of the provincial money. The keeping of school registers, which had been introduced in 1846, would now take on a new meaning as the government began to bear down on communities not only to enrol their children in school, but to make them attend, if they wanted a fair share of the provincial funds allocated to common schooling.

How should the school act of 1850 be assessed? Ryerson himself at first claimed that his new school bill was both simpler and more practical than the Cameron Act, a claim that a reading of the two acts does not support.[14] Commenting on the continuing need for explanatory circulars in connection with the law in 1852, John George Hodgins himself did not hesitate to admit that it was in some degree difficult in its practical administration.[15]

Certainly, the act had its critics. Writing before its final passage and from his experience in Hastings, William Hutton had no qualms in pointing out its weaknesses to Ryerson. Hutton failed to see why county treasurers were entrusted with the payment of school moneys to teachers or why the counties were responsible for raising the local share of the school fund. Both jobs, in his view, were better done at the township level. Hutton also felt that the payment of teachers according to average attendance was premature. In back townships where many children had inadequate clothing and the roads were terrible, poor average attendance was inevitable; the schools in these townships would clearly be penalized by a school fund distributed on the basis of comparative attendance rates. The proposal, he thought, was also unworkable because rural teachers (who were supposed to keep the attendance registers) changed so often.[16]

More threatening than such criticisms were demands for the outright repeal of the act. The township of Esquesing in Halton County and the township of Markham 'and other places' in the united counties of York, Ontario, and Peel were still arguing in 1852 that the act's flaws far outweighed its advantages.[17] In Toronto anti-school-law meetings were held and a war of pamphlets was waged against the provincial education department and the Chief Superintendent. Their writers singled out extravagant 'educational palaces' and 'irreligious' common schools for attack. They also condemned the education department's use of taxpayers' money to feed its own version of the truth to the people of Canada West.[18]

The last point was well founded for, like the school acts of 1846 and 1847, the 1850 act was followed by a barrage of regulations, instructions, and advice. Rules were drawn up specifying the new method of classifying teachers, as well as for 'the Regulation, Government and Discipline of Common Schools,' and separate circulars were immediately addressed to local school superintendents, rural and urban school trustees, teachers, and county boards of public instruction, in addition to the mayors, the clerks of municipal councils, the town reeves, and the wardens of counties, outlining their different duties under the new act.[9] These documents explained the workings of the law, exhorted their recipients to exercise their powers fairly and perform their duties promptly, and attempted to awaken in all a sense of their own importance and responsibility in carrying out their duties under the school law. The circulars of the early 1850s were followed over the years by many more such reminders, explanations, and exhortations and were, moreover, only the tip of the iceberg. In 1848 the education department had begun to publish the *Journal of Education for Upper Canada*, a periodical that, like the circulars, was also designed to inspire and inform. 'Controversial' materials were not accepted for the journal and, from the beginning (when it was financed out of Egerton Ryerson's own pocket), it was entirely a mouthpiece of the education department. By 1850 Ryerson had received permission from the government to make the journal an official medium for notices and instructions to local school authorities and thus, in some measure, required reading for everyone involved with the common schools. Since the publication did not sell well enough to support itself, however, a government subsidy was introduced in 1853, permitting the department to distribute it free. By 1855 some 5,000 copies were being mailed every month to a wide readership in Canada West and elsewhere.[20]

Beyond the journal and the official circulars were the mammoth annual and special reports issued by the education department. Running to several hundred pages each, they often reprinted letters, addresses, and circulars by Ryerson or, very occasionally, other educational officials from Upper Canada and abroad. Every year, with a little editing, the reports of the province's many hundred local superintendents as well as the statistics derived from those reports were reproduced within the covers of the annual reports. The statistics illustrated as voluminously as the department could get away with the strengths and weaknesses of the province's schools, as the department perceived them. How many schoolhouses possessed – or did not possess – blackboards, or globes, or maps in a given county or town? The answers stood revealed for all to see, along with such information as the average, highest, and lowest salaries of the municipality's male and female teachers and the number of children enrolled in school. Statistical revelations of this sort were clearly meant to add force to the calls for improvement that filled the pages of the *Journal of Edu-*

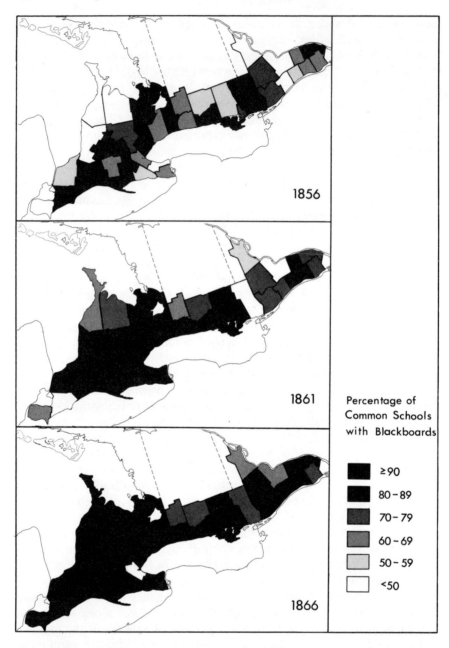

Maps developed from statistics published in the education department's annual reports demonstrate the apparent success of the campaign to promote the use of blackboards between 1856 and 1866.

cation and other departmental publications. Finally, for the benefit of those who wished easier access to Ryerson's speeches or letters to the press, or to be better informed about the contents of his official correspondence, these materials too began to be collected and printed, or reprinted, in their entirety. To the irate Angus Dallas, whose pamphlet attempted to summarize the sins of the province's educational machine in 1857, this was indeed a gigantic apparatus designed, if not exactly (as Dallas would have it) to stifle the expression of free opinion on the school system, then certainly to drown out the voices of opposition by its sheer volume.[21] In the end, perhaps, these amounted to the same thing.

The debate between the *Niagara Chronicle*, which was against free schools, and the *Niagara Mail*, which was for them, was only one of many concerns for these journals. And, if the *Chronicle* felt that tax money spent on improvements calculated to give employment to mechanics and labourers would be infinitely more valuable to the community than free schools or that the whole system was unjust and inefficient, the *Mail* had its arguments for the other side ready made. But supporters like the *Mail* could also rest assured that their side would be repeated tenfold in the pro-system propaganda that poured out of the education office in Toronto.[22]

Perhaps the only organization capable of producing anything like a comparable volume of paper on schools was the growing Roman Catholic Church of Canada West. The arrival in the province of thousands of Roman Catholic Irish, the appearance of immigrant nuns to teach them, and the appointment of an energetic new bishop, Armand de Charbonnel, injected much vigour into the church, and a good deal of this vigour was directed in turn to the question of schooling. Aided and abetted by the amount of controversy over the new school laws, de Charbonnel was prompted to look into the legal situation rather minutely, and soon after his installation in 1850 mounted an intense campaign to consolidate the position of his co-religionists under the separate school provisions of 1841.

The fruits of his efforts were to be found in the Supplementary School Law of 1853.[23] By the new law, separate schools were to share equally with the common schools in the provincial school grants, according to their average attendance rates. Supporters of separate schools were explicitly exempted from the payment of common school rates in their localities so that they would not be taxed twice. Finally, their teachers were specifically excluded from the certification requirements of the 1850 school law, with the provision that candidates could be empowered to teach in any separate school by a majority vote of its trustees.

The position of separate schools was not all that needed clarification by 1853, and the Supplementary School Law went on to deal with multiple question touching on the powers of the various authorities under the 1850 legislation. Many of the provisions suggest a critical and restrictive mood on the part of the government. Clearly not all local authorities were coping with the requirements of the new law. The 1853 act declared, for example, that no superintendent of schools could be, during his term of office, either a school trustee or a teacher. Teachers, for their part, were required to swear an oath before a magistrate every six months verifying the accuracy of their school registers and attendance figures. Stiff fines were instituted to penalize trustees who failed to carry out their duties under the law. Finally, in his capacity of overseer of the entire school system, the chief superintendent of schools gained an interesting new power: the right, in the interest of provincial uniformity, to appeal any legal decision related to the schools and their administration made by the courts of Canada West.

Other provisions, however, suggested a more sympathetic attitude to the problems of local school authorities. A pension or superannuation fund for teachers, the first of its kind in North America, recognized a public obligation to try to assist aging teachers who were worn out in the service of the schools. Superintendents were granted the right to certify teachers on a temporary basis, until the next meeting of the appropriate board of examiners. Local school authorities gained the power to take to law and have fined any persons behaving rudely, noisily, or indecently in the vicinity of a schoolhouse. Common school trustees were permitted to form union schools with local grammar schools.

The latter provision presumed a new legal status for Canada West's grammar schools and, indeed, another 1853 law and further legislation in 1855 were designed to bring those institutions into the general provincial system, as the Cameron Act had earlier attempted. Even before the Cameron Act, Ryerson had foreshadowed his intention to bring the grammar schools under his jurisdiction, arguing the need for more effective government inspection of their activities. Although he admitted that under the then 'non-system' there were a few 'efficient' grammar schools, it was from the beginning his belief that the majority defeated their avowed purpose as superior classical schools by permitting the entry of 'pupils of both sexes, and of all ages and attainments' into their supposedly advanced, male, and professionally oriented programs.[24]

The new laws attempted to remedy this defect. County councils took over from the governor the appointment of grammar school trustees, but here local intervention came to an end. The acts specified that senior grammar schools receiving the annual £100 grant from the provincial government had to be situated in the county towns. While counties might have additional grammar schools (and earlier amendments to the District Schools Act of 1807 had already made this possible), these were to receive subsidies of only £50 a piece, depending on the sums available for distribution and the relative populations of the counties. Pupils were henceforth to be admitted to grammar schools only if they passed an examination in common school subjects and, once admitted, they were to follow a course of study laid down by the provincial Council of Public Instruction. Grammar school teachers had to be university graduates or certified by a provincial examining board, of which the headmaster of the Normal School was to be an automatic member. In order to orient the grammar schools to scientific pursuits, all such schools were required to become involved in a meteorological observation program, the results of which were to be reported annually to the chief superintendent of schools and by him to the governor of Canada. Finally, the law and regulations regarding grammar schools were to be enforced by a provincially appointed inspectorate. The new inspectors were given the authority to investigate minutely the affairs of these schools – from their methods of instruction, their organization and discipline, and the attainments of their pupils, to their 'mechanical arrangements,' including everything from property holding to the drinking water and 'conveniences for private purposes' that the schools provided.[25]

With this law, Egerton Ryerson felt that his major legislative work was over. In his *Annual Report* for 1855, the Chief Superintendent announced that the basic structure of the provincial school system was complete. Although much remained to be done 'in reducing to practice and bringing up to a proper standard, all parts of the system in all of the municipalities' of the province, the 'fundamental principles of the school system, and ... of the school law' could be regarded as settled.[26] Certainly, Ryerson increasingly found it expedient to echo the longing for permanence that had been expressed earlier by many of his critics. If the *Niagara Chronicle* and the *Cobourg Star* had been put off by the somewhat experimental interference in school affairs inaugurated by the school acts of 1843 and 1846,[27] it was now the Chief Superintendent of Schools and his network of school officers who frowned on experiment or pressures for further reform. The province was treated to a lecture on the 'Permanancy and Prospects' of the common school system and told that change in the form of further legislative interference would do much damage to the schools.[28] The legislative drive was spent. After a period when the government itself seemed to alter the basic arrangements for schooling every two or three years, Ryerson and his minions now became advocates of calm in provincial educational affairs.

III

Yet one could hardly expect calm to reign when the subject was education, since schooling affected the lives of so many so intimately. It was, first of all, of at least occasional concern to every family with children in the province and since, in 1851, 44.8 per cent of the population was under sixteen years of age,[29] this must have meant the vast majority of Upper Canadians. There were also those whose positions in the various churches of the province dictated an interest in education. Some of these showed their interest by becoming informal 'visitors' to the schools in the 1840s, and others, as we have seen, by the mounting force of their criticisms of local schooling or of the whole system. Even more intimately involved were the countless local officers whose problems and peccadilloes the Supplementary School Law of 1853 tried to address: the superintendents and school trustees who oversaw the system. All these operated under the watchful and benevolent eye of the chief superintendent of schools.

The office run by the chief superintendent grew mightily and would continue to grow as a result of the new work the school acts created.[30] By 1855 it boasted four separate branches or subdepartments: the Council of Public Instruction and the provincial Normal and Model schools under its immediate jurisdiction; the educational book depository; the map and school apparatus depository; and the education office itself. By 1858 the number of people employed by the four branches came to a total of thirty individuals, counting those who worked in the Normal and Model schools. This may seem a very small number by modern standards, but it was an astonishingly large one compared to numbers typically employed by state or provincial departments of education elsewhere at the time.[31] Even more astounding are the numbers of documents that these employees annually processed. According to Ryerson's *Annual Report for 1858*, the largest part of the department's work consisted in preparing and sending out thousands of copies of its monthly *Journal of Education for Upper Canada*, and equally huge numbers of school registers and forms for trustees' and superintendents' reports and auditors' and treasurers' returns. These were joined, as we have seen, by a multiplicity of circulars to various local officials inspiring and cajoling them or instructing them in how to run local school affairs. To these were added not only the chief superintendent's massive annual reports summarizing the state of the schools but a voluminous official correspondence. When the letters, reports, and forms the department received were added to the documents sent out, the total came to a staggering 38,000 items or so in a single year, more paper than was processed in the same period by the Colonial Office in its management of the affairs of the entire British empire.[32]

Of the recipients of the department's missives, probably few paid more attention than the local superintendents, those stalwarts whose job it was to play on the local level the moral and administrative role undertaken provincially by their chief. Local superintendents responded variously to this task, according to their talents and according to the interpretation put on their role by the local councillors they in part represented. Certainly there was, at first, little agreement on the exact nature of their job, the limits of their power, or the ultimate source of their authority.

Ryerson saw the local superintendents as his watch dogs. It was through them, he wrote in 1848, that the government would 'control the general principles and character' of the school system and, above all, see that the moneys appropriated for schooling were 'faithfully and judiciously expended.'[33] But the supervision of the provincial school fund was not their only job. Ryerson also expected his superintendents to tour the schools and to instruct the children, teachers, and trustees under their jurisdiction. To a particular superintendent whose charge was the town of Cobourg in 1848, Ryerson noted that it was the superintendent's job to bring before his board specific plans for the improvement of the town's schools.[34] In 1856 Ryerson wrote more generally on the 'Duties of Local Superintendents' and published the piece in the *Journal of Education*, now required reading for all school officers. Among the duties he plainly wished to stress were the superintendent's annual school lectures to the various sections, a part of the job that some incumbents apparently found onerous. Here, Ryerson argued, was the superintendent's chance to inspire and invigorate, to awaken 'the *Spirit* and *action* of the *People*.' Through their lectures, the superintendents could participate in channelling the 'moral influence ... energy [and] vitality' that Ryerson believed ought to flow from his own office 'down to the desk of the humblest teacher,' on behalf of education.[35]

If these were the general duties of superintendents, the specific manner in which they were to be carried out – and under whose control – remained somewhat in doubt. Superintendent William Hutton noted that the Hastings District Council required, in 1848, that he visit each of the schools in his constituency twice a year. This was too heavy a demand in his opinion. But who really had the right to prescribe his duties – the local council that had given him his job or his provincial boss, the chief superintendent of schools? Commenting on the nature of the mid-nineteenth-century superintendency, one twentieth-century analyst has argued that the superintendent under Ryerson was a local officer, but one whose duties were 'definitely prescribed by a central authority.' No doubt this assessment of the division of powers accurately reflected Egerton Ryerson's view of the matter. But it did not reflect Hastings District Council's in 1848. The superintendency obviously called for a delicate balancing act between local authority on the one hand and the provincial education office on the other.[36]

Equally problematic was the position of the superintendent when he visited a school. Who was in charge, the teacher or himself? Frequently called upon to pronounce on such questions, Ryerson established in the *Journal of Education* a regular column in which his opinions on various subjects appeared under the title 'Official Replies of the Chief Superintendent.' Ryerson's official reply on the question of school visitation was that the superintendent was 'supreme' in the school while he was visiting it. It was 'absurd' to presume that, when the work of a schoolmaster was being examined, that master should say 'who should do it, and how it should be done'; or that he should feel his 'rights and dignity' invaded when a county or township officer came to perform his legal duties in inspecting the school. The tone of Ryerson's remarks suggests that, indeed, some teachers did feel intruded upon when local superintendents visited.[37]

Conflicting views about the local superintendency had dictated the shift away from township superintendents in 1846 and the shift back again in 1850. Egerton Ryerson himself had had some difficulties with the district superintendency, despite the fact that he had endorsed it in his own 1846 school law. He wanted the district officers to be men of status and authority, but worried at the same time about the potential for abuses of that power. For one thing, it proved dangerous for superintendents to have absolute control over the provincial school moneys. Some superintendents appointed under the 1843 law, as well as under that of 1846, had simply absconded with their schools' share of the fund, leaving their municipalities with no means of paying the teachers the full sums owed to them. Others had been accused of delaying payments to teachers and, in the meantime, using the money to their own advantage. The obvious solution, although it did not find favour everywhere, was to hand over the provincial funds to local municipal treasurers instead of to the superintendents, to be disbursed by the former on the instructions of the latter.[38]

A second issue that concerned the chief superintendent, among others, was the occasional need to dismiss a local superintendent. What was to be done if the person appointed by a local council proved to be utterly incompetent or failed to carry out his duties as specified by the law? The superintendents might collect the salaries provided by their municipal councils and still do next to nothing for the schools. Ryerson argued in 1847 that the governor-general in council should have the power to dismiss local superintendents at least for misconduct, if not for minor incompetence or failure to conform precisely to the rules and regulations.

At the present time, any District Superintendent may, or may not, execute the law, may or may not, apply the School Fund according to the conditions and Regulations required by law, and the Government has no power to prevent him from doing so ... as one half of the Fund is provided by the Provincial Legislature, there ought to be a responsiblility to the Provincial Government on the part of all those, who are entrusted with its management.[39]

In a circular to the wardens of counties dated 31 June 1850, Ryerson clarified the provisions of that year's legislation with respect to the provincial school fund. Treasurers rather than superintendents were to hold the money in question. Trustees henceforth were to write an order to their local superintendent specifying that their teacher was due to be paid. The superintendent in turn provided a cheque, to be presented by the teacher to the treasurer of the appropriate township or county. Though a complicated procedure, this plan nevertheless succeeded in separating the local superintendents from the money whose use they controlled.[40] Whether the government took upon itself or very often used its theoretical right to dismiss a delinquent superintendent is less clear. The same letter to the county wardens implies that Ryerson preferred, in the end, to leave it up to local authorities to get rid of incompetent appointees. He noted that in some municipalities doubts existed about the usefulness of the office because its duties had been 'imperfectly discharged,' but that this was not the case where the office had been filled with 'ability, diligence and skill.' The message was obvious: appoint a good man and the municipality's troubles were over. A good man, Ryerson had pointed out on an earlier occasion, had to be paid a good salary: a cheap superintendent was a poor economy. He had also to be given a free hand and, once appointed, made to feel that he had nothing to fear as long as he performed his duties 'efficiently and *according to law.*'[41]

Certainly there was good reason to want to get rid of some of the superintendents. On the first of April 1850, Ryerson was informed that John Bignall, superintendent for the Huron District, had been found guilty of 'defalcation' to the tune of some £450. Later in the same year, a complaint came from the village of Sandwich. Its author, a French Catholic priest, pointed out that local teachers were poverty stricken and often went into debt on the strength of the money they expected to get from the provincial school fund. When the local superintendent failed to visit the schools and see that the teachers were paid, those who were owed money by the schoolmasters closed in and the teachers had to seek other employment in order to pay their debts.[43] Attacks on the superintendency continued to find their way into Egerton Ryerson's office during the decades that followed. In 1859 two German-speaking school trustees wrote to the effect that their school section had been deprived of its share of the provincial fund because the local superintendent was prejudiced against the teacher, a woman who had been educated in the United States.[44] A similar complaint was lodged by a Roman Catholic rural dean who believed that a local Catholic teacher had been hounded out of his school by the school superintendent who wanted to replace him with a Protestant.[45]

These were very specific complaints. But the superintendency was unpopular for more general reasons. Few Upper Canadian school trustees or teachers welcomed the idea that an individual who was often no better educated than they should be placed in a supervisory role over them. Hamnet Pinhey, when superintendent for the District of Dalhousie, wrote to Ryerson in 1849 that he looked forward to being relieved of an office, the duties of which were completely 'antagonistic ... to the feelings of a large majority of the people.'[46] Fifteen years later, a township incumbent from Leeds County was equally aware of the poor reputation of the local superintendency. Too many superintendents, Henry Lillie believed, had been appointed as 'political favourites,' with little regard for their qualifications.[47]

The superintendents, of course, were not without complaints and irritations of their own. Indeed their reports and the incoming correspondence of the education department constitute a litany of their trials and tribulations during the Ryerson years. The same Hamnet Pinhey who found his office so onerous in 1849 was already very critical of the District of Dalhousie and its people in 1847.

I believe the mass of the people ... of this district less intelligent than in others, and in truth I *hope* this is the fact – I fear there will be both perplexity and perversity to contend with in the 'working' of the [1846 school] act for some time.[48]

Pinhey begged Ryerson, to whom these words were addressed, to keep his confession confidential. But it is unlikely that the subjects of his criticism were altogether blind to his feelings about them. It is little wonder that they were for the most part antagonistic both to the man and to his office. A superintendent writing in 1850 was concerned less with the deficiencies of the people than with those of the job he was called upon to do. The pay for township superintendents, according to this West

Oxford appointee, was totally inadequate. He planned to resign and called Ryerson's attention to the fact that the superintendent for Woodstock had the same intention. Cecil Mortimer may not himself have been a superintendent of schools, but he evidently felt the need to write to Ryerson on their behalf. The focus of his complaint was also the low pay for superintendent's work; but, for this critic, the problem was compounded by the expenses some had to incur on the job. Many local superintendents, if we are to believe Mortimer, solved the problem of having to give annual lectures on education by purchasing a speech ready made. But this cost money. 'Can't you take compassion on the Superintendents,' he wanted to know, 'and furnish them *gratis* with a set of lectures or give them hints for obtaining them at a low rate? The poor fellows only get £5 each ...' Mortimer concluded that, with so little remuneration for their work, the local men could not afford to pay much for the lectures. One wonders how many of the superintendents, in fact, managed to carry out their mandate to lecture the local populace.[49]

Some superintendents wrote to express regret for their own deficiencies. Such was Alexander Dick, from Matilda, who apologized in 1850 because his report was incomplete. He blamed its inadequacy on the reports of his trustees, which were frequently imperfect, incorrect, or 'entirely wanting.' Two years later the superintendent from the Matilda admitted that he had misunderstood the purpose of one of the columns in the form for his report and that this had caused him 'much trouble.' In the same year another local superintendent blamed the 'confused condition' of the schools under his jurisdiction on the carelessness and inattention of the superintendents who had preceded him in the job. But perhaps the most delightful of mid-nineteenth-century excuses came from John Radcliffe who, in 1852, admitted that there was 'a sort of fatality' attending his annual return for that year. A teacher who always assisted him in these matters had put the report in his writing room, where someone had also locked up a dog. The 'brute tore the papers all to atoms' and the unfortunate superintendent was obliged to request that new blank forms be sent to him.[50]

If Radcliffe's troubles were caused by an unusually hungry canine, James Stevenson's seemed largely the work of unusually disorganized local officials. Only his own confession and apology to Ryerson can evoke the sense of confusion on all sides.

I have to trouble you once more with a few lines, because we of the Township of Cambridge is brought into trouble on every hand; on account of the Legislative school grant for the year 1858. We as usewell did not Call on our Treasurer Mr. John S. Casselman for any Cash to pay our Teacher to the end of the year 1858 and when I give orders on him, he said in reply: that he had nothing in his hand to give and that no Grant come his lenth as yet, but that he would write the County Treasurer to find out the Cause; the County Treasurer said that it had: Namely 60 Dollars been granted and withdrew and he thought the reason was that the Sub Treasurer had not filt up his Report and sent it in to him; that he the County Treasurer would transfer it to the Department in dieu time; the Sub Treasurer in hearing this, stated in reply that he had got no Report from any Quarter up to the present for to fill in. On the 21st Inst, – I was at the Council I seen all these Letters with the Sub Treasurer Mr. Casselman.

He filt up the Report neatly, and sent it a way, although long after the time, we are in full hopes that your Reverence will look over our faults and short-comings, – in these beck settlements people is very ignorant for a lenth of time how Common Schools is governed, Also Communications is often long out of time, as you will see by my Report for 1857 did not come to my hand to June the first 1858. Sir I thought it best for to state these things to you, that bad as we are the falt is not ours.[51]

Needless to say, there were more superintendents who complained than apologized, and many of their complaints had to do with the teachers they encountered. What should he do, Robert Galbraith of Orangeville wanted to know, about a teacher who refused to interrupt a reading class when the visiting superintendent was short of time? In the case in question, schoolmaster James Kelly had shown a 'violent display of temper' and said that he would not do as the superintendent asked. A Caledon superintendent expressed his irritation at teachers who objected to the uncertain timing of his school visits. It was true, this individual reported, that he had not notified them about his intended arrival. But this was legitimate because he wanted to see the 'true state' of the schools, not what the teachers and trustees wanted him to see.[52]

If such superintendents had a strong sense of their rights and duties, it is clear that many others did not. To the complaints that these men offered to their chief in Toronto were therefore added scores of inquiries and appeals for help. A.S. Holmes, writing from Raleigh in December 1846, found himself embroiled in local disputes over the correct interpretation of the law. It seemed to him appropriate to apply to 'headquarters' before acting, since duty was 'doubtful.' Joseph Wheeler of Albion, who wrote asking for information in 1850, explained that he was entirely 'ignorant' as to what the duties of his office were.[53]

Most superintendents were probably more confident of their roles or, if they floundered in the beginning, eventually figured out what they were supposed to do. One thing they soon learned was to report at length on the various matters that were of concern to Ryerson and the education department, including the performance and organization of their own jobs. Correspondents complained, for example, about the mode of appointing local superintendents. The superintendent from Charlottenburgh wrote in 1850 that township officers could only be the political tools of the councillors, who appointed them in return for their services at election time. Alexander Winram, of Cayuga North, Haldimand County, elaborated on this argument in his report for 1857. The annual appointment of local school officers by the reeves of townships had been fatal in this person's opinion. Superintendents presently in office dared not give offence.[54] Many who shared this view after 1850 thought that eliminating township superintendents and compelling appointments at the county level might solve such problems. This was the opinion of the Reverend James Godfrey. But Godfrey remained sceptical about the political character of even the county officers, and it is clear that a purely county superintendency was no panacea. William Rath, who served Blanchard, Ellice, Fullerton, Hilbert, and Logan townships in 1868, felt moreover that it was impossible for any county superintendent to cover the field. He would not be able to 'be everywhere at once, at the season when examination soirees, &c.,' were held and would thus lose his best chance of 'meeting the people.'[55]

Of course the geographical extent of their jurisdiction and the nature of their appointments were not the only subjects that local superintendents had opinions about. Their main task was to report on a variety of subjects connected with the schools. They wrote about the quality of the teachers, the pros and cons of female teachers, and whether or not superintendents should have some share in their selection.[56] They wrote about methods of instruction [57] and about whether or not there should be military drill in the schools.[58] There is no doubt, however, that most of the local superintendents simply reported what they thought the Chief Superintendent wanted to know, often giving the most sparse responses to specific questions that they had been asked to answer. John Canning, of Olden, County Frontenac, for example, provided an unembroidered list of local school deficiencies in 1861.

In this township, religious instruction has not been imparted according to the regulations. It has not been practicable to carry out the recent suggested improvements with respect to County Board examinations. I can give no opinion in regard to the influence of prizes, as we have had no examinations, therefore no prizes have been awarded.[59]

John H. Delamere of Emily, County Victoria, had an even gloomier list of responses to departmental inquiries in 1869. The principal cause of pupils' non-attendance was the 'drunkenness, gross ignorance and corresponding carelessness' of their parents. Religious instruction did not generally take place; no school museum had been attempted anywhere in the township; no scientific experiments of any kind were practised; and school libraries were entirely neglected. The *Journal of Education* was received but was evidently not appreciated, for many of the copies were never opened. Altogether the people in the community did not seem to read much.[60]

If such litanies merely spoke to the concerns of the provincial education department, other local superintendents had more original things to say about their regions. Some even dared to express dissident views. Those who were observant noticed that the children of poor and of recent immigrants had difficulty attending school. At least two of the district superintendents joined William Hutton in his criticism of the 1850 school law for apportioning school funds on the basis of attendance, on the grounds that it unfairly favoured the schools in the relatively wealthy, thickly settled regions where school attendance was high and penalized poor backwoods schools and the children who attended them.[61] In a letter to John George Hodgins, J.G. House of Townsend even expressed sympathy for school sections that were constantly changing their teachers, despite the fact that this tendency was much deplored by the central authorities. 'We must not blame them too much,' House argued. The people concerned were only 'human beings, constituted to enjoy changes being always accustomed to them.' The seasons changed, after all. 'Everything changes, we grow old ourselves,' he concluded philosophically.[62]

One would like to know more about the school superintendents who made local educational arrangements their business during the Ryerson years. A great many of them were clergymen. The education department counted how many in 1861 and discovered that, in that year, 142 or about 44 per cent, of the 321 local superintendents in the province were clerics, 63 of them Presbyterian, 37 members of the Church of England, 20 Methodist, and 21 belonging to other denominations. If men of the cloth tended to predominate there were also other professionals or aspiring professionals among the local superintendents, chiefly medical men and a smattering of teachers.[63] In 1869, the Reverend William Lumsden of Hawkesbury, Prescott County, was both a superintendent and a grammar schoolmaster, but reported that he was stepping down as the former since the legality of holding both jobs had been called into question. James Knight of Sheffield, County Addington, was one of ten physicians who were also the school superintendents for their communities that year. Of the remaining superintendents, the majority at any given period must have been farmers. District superintendents in the 1840s and county officers after 1850 may have been, like William Hutton of Hastings, 'gentlemen' with large properties and considerable wealth, but most township superintendents were no doubt more humble individuals who took a brief turn at the superintendency as they did at other government positions that were offered from time to time. In 1869, George Malone, the superintendent for Wolfe Island, was also the local postmaster.[64]

In some ways easier to place in their communities than the superintendents were those other local school officers who multiplied even more rapidly during the Ryerson era, the trustees of the common schools. These men represented Upper Canadian interest in schooling at the grass-roots level and occupied a pivotal position between their communities and the provincial administrative machine. They were the people who hired the teachers and built the schoolhouses. If superintendents found anything wanting in the local schools it was usually the trustees that they blamed.

The most common complaint of superintendents against trustees was that they were 'cheap' and refused to pay decent wages to teachers. Indeed the parsimony of common school trustees was matched only by local superintendents' almost universal condemnation of it. In 1860, the Reverend Edward Sullivan, superintendent for Lobo and London, Middlesex County, noted the 'apathy and indifference' of parents and teachers, as well as of trustees in his region. But with respect to the latter, the problem was compounded by 'a mistaken spirit of economy,' to which the intellectual welfare of the community was largely sacrificed. His counterpart in Winchester, Dundas County, reported in 1866 that the trustees of his locality not only hired the cheapest teachers, but when they did pay high wages it was only to get the money back again in the form of the teacher's house rent. This superintendent also complained about trustees' tendency to hire their own relatives to teach the common schools.[65] The Reverend M.A. Farrar of Asphodel, County Peterborough, described trustees as 'money-grubbing.' According to Farrar, the typical school trustee was 'a perverse animal,' in whom the prospect of spending a dollar usually brought on 'a fit of temporary insanity.'[66] The complaints were endless. Trustees continued to hire unqualified assistant teachers and pay them illegally out of the school grant; others embezzled school funds; one group of trustees allowed a dancing school to use the common school building, despite the fact that some of their constituents believed dancing to be immoral.[67]

Other critics were distressed by the loose way in which some trustees conducted their business. Such was the superintendent from Osnabruck, Stormont County, in 1861. No doubt he would have approved of the *Globe* piece published a few years earlier in which being 'a good and honest man of business' was placed at the top of the list under the heading 'What a School Trustee Should Be.' The *Globe*, of course, wanted more than good business practices in the trustees of common schools. The ideal incumbent, the article went on to argue, should know something not only about school architecture, but about how to 'banish coarseness' and 'develop elegance' in the school environment. He should also be respectable, for children needed to look up to the trustees of a school if they were to think well of the school system. The trustee should be a moral man. Finally, he should be 'educated.' An 'ignorant' trustee was an absurdity.[68]

The issue of the uninstructed or even illiterate trustee was raised more than once during the mid-century decades. Ryerson struggled with the problem in the 1840s but found it hard then and later to come up with a solution that was genuinely satisfactory to everyone. There was no doubt, as he wrote to a concerned correspondent in 1847, that to elect as school trustee a person who could neither read nor write seemed absurd to any thinking person. Nevertheless the law allowed the annual school meeting in rural school sections to elect whomever they pleased and no one had the right to deprive them of that power.[69]

By 1853 there were some nine thousand school trustees incorporated annually in Upper Canada, and to Ryerson these nine thousand represented the power of the 'people' over their own schools.[70] While hindsight allows us to see that the independent authority of trustees had been eroded in important ways by the school laws of the 1840s and 1850s, their powers in some areas remained unscathed and, in the opinion of at least some local protagonists, were still worth fighting over at trustee election time. Some of the fights made their way to Ryerson's desk in the form of complaints and queries about election rules or requests for arbitration. In a York County school section in 1847, for example, a dispute arose because the chairman of the election refused to count heads. When the district superintendent ruled that there should be a new election, the Chief Superintendent was brought into the discussion. According to a letter to the *Examiner* dated 10 March, the latter, in a typically 'Prussian' move, had overruled the district superintendent and reinstated the original trustees.[71] Two years later critics from Haldimand detailed for Ryerson the irregularities they had observed in a trustee election in their community. The source of the trouble was the question of whether or not to build a new schoolhouse. The chairman of the election had allowed 'his party' extra time to go out and collect votes and had permitted two 'under age' young men to vote on the strength of their father's property, not to mention two men living in another township entirely, the latter voting on the strength of an old unoccupied house belonging to the chairman. To compound his sins, the chairman had then voted himself.[72] Two decades later, the queries were still coming in. A questioner called William Pennington wanted advice on the following borderline voters: a widow whose husband had died during the year but had been an assessed freeholder; a young man who was not of age but was on the assessment roll and paid taxes; and a hired man, the brother-in-law and employee of one of the trustees, whose only claim to property was fifty acres of wild land at the back of his relative's farm.[73]

Trustees even more often than superintendents appealed to the education department for advice or information regarding various aspects of their work. Benjamin Hammond, a Yorkville school trustee in 1859, was somewhat vague in his questions about 'irregularities' in tax collection that affected the schools. But trustee correspondents from London were blunt. What were they to do when a very wealthy landowner, none other than the local squire, Colonel Thomas Talbot, refused to pay his assessment for the common schools of the city? Trustees from Windham were equally clear about their problem, which was also a money problem: their local municipal council, in debt over the Woodstock and Lake Erie Railroad, refused to hand over the funds for the schools.[74] What should they do?

IV

The Chief Superintendent did his best to sort out such questions. In January 1846 he gave detailed advice on who could vote in elections for school trustees.[75] By 1849, he was writing to a correspondent in Owen Sound that more 'explicit' regulations would soon be drawn up for the conduct of the school board's annual meeting.[76] But the queries continued. In 1851 Ryerson tackled the question of women voters, arguing that a women who was the head of her household or a freeholder should not be deprived of the vote in school elections just because she was a woman, but that the Court of Queen's Bench would be the final authority on such a question.[77] Robert Hodger, writing from Tillsonburg in 1859, knew about Ryerson's official opinion that women who were householders or freeholders were entitled to vote, but still had a question. Did this include 'married ladies' who were 'freeholders in their own right?' The trouble was that such ladies had voted on both sides, but chiefly on the Protestant side, in a religiously divided community.[78]

If the question of women voters in ordinary common school elections tended to confuse the public, the fact that the rules were altogether different for separate schools surely did no less. Ryerson attempted to clarify the picture for the Roman Catholic bishop of Toronto in 1854. The separate school law, he pointed out, specified that petitioners for such schools ought to be 'resident heads of families' but did not refer to whether they were freeholders or householders. The latter question therefore had no significance when it came to the separate schools and the election of their trustees.[79]

Ryerson and his assistants answered most of the queries they received at great length. Correspondence on local issues sometimes went back and forth for more than a year before the original complainants were satisfied. Other cases could not be resolved by correspondence and, if Ryerson thought them important, he took them to the courts. John George Hodgins studied law during the late 1850s and one can only assume that this was so that the education department would be better equipped to handle the many legal cases in which it became embroiled.[80] Court decisions and Ryerson's pronouncements were considered of such general interest that they often appeared in the pages of the local press. Thus the *Hamilton Gazette* printed Ryerson's advice to a South Dumfries school board regarding its right to maintain school boundaries and have rates collected in the section in spite of township or county boundary changes.[81] Sometimes Ryerson himself wished to reach a larger audience and printed key excerpts from his letters in the pages of the *Journal of Education*. He took this route, for example, when he wished to inform the public that trustees had absolute control over the use of schoolhouses and were not required by law to open them 'for all kinds of public or religious meetings' unless the relevant land deeds had specified such a duty.[82] Pronouncements of this sort multiplied over the years.

Yet much of the correspondence that Ryerson directed to local authorities in Upper Canada appeared to argue for a certain amount of leeway, especially in the running of rural schools. People needed time to adjust to new laws and regulations, as did the superintendents themselves. Thus in February, 1847, he cautioned Superintendent Hamilton Hunter of the Home District against being too heavy-handed in his enforcement of the law, implying that it was possible for a local school officer, in his zeal, to go too far in his 'patriotic' efforts to 'instruct and elevate the popular mind.' Three days later he wrote again to the same superintendent, advising him to settle disputed matters but not to enter into matters that were not in dispute.[83] Another local officer was advised in August of 1849 of the clause in the school law that allowed superintendents discretionary powers in the distribution of unexpended balances, a very useful clause when they were trying to meet 'various special cases' that clearly were exceptions to the general rule.[84]

On the other hand, Ryerson could be both cutting and uncompromising when he felt that important principles were at stake. On these occasions he claimed that the laws and regulations had to be obeyed to the letter and without delay. In 1849, he told Mr. E. Burnham of Colborne that if he did not want his district to appear in a bad light he should do a better job with his annual report; Ryerson had never received a report as 'defective' as the one Burnham had submitted.[85] Ambiguous letters from John Flood of Dalhousie District, at first suggesting that not a cent of the public money would go to areas that had refused to be taxed, and then wondering if Ryerson would not in fact 'wink at' his paying the poor teachers in these sections, elicited first a consultation with the attorney-general and then a very definite response in the negative. Misappropriation of funds would *not* be winked at. In this case, Ryerson went on, it was absolutely vital to maintain the 'great principles' of the law.[86]

There is no reason to think that Ryerson's advice to local authorities was always consistent and considerable reason to believe it was not. If one local superintendent was told in 1849 to go ahead and use his discretionary powers to spend leftover funds, this was not the opinion the Chief Superintendent had offered to the school trustees of ss15, Murray River, in 1847. To these men, Ryerson wrote that district superintendents should not pay out any 'balances remaining from previous years,' not, at least, without first consulting the provincial office. District superintendents were in fact required to keep all such moneys in their hands, 'subject to the order of the [Chief] Superintendent of Schools.' The inconsistency of the two rulings could be attributed to slight differences in the sources of the funds in question. Or it may have been due to their timing. By 1849, Ryerson perhaps realized that he had to give local superintendents more freedom. Alternatively, the contradictory advice may have reflected Ryerson's sense of where his opposition lay or the mood in which his letters would be received. It was tempting to be rigid about what superintendents should or should not do when he was writing to trustees, as in the Murray River letter; it was perhaps less easy to take this stance when writing to the superintendents themselves, especially the superintendents of those districts in which Ryerson knew the school law to be unpopular. The more flexible 1849 letter dealing with the expenditure of extra funds went to the District of Newcastle; in Newcastle the chief superintendent of schools had excellent reason to be careful.[87]

There is no doubt that Ryerson was a beleaguered man. The unpopularity of the local superintendency resulted in hundreds of complaints annually, largely resulting from the efforts of the local men to carry out the law as the education department defined it. Perhaps no run of letters more graphically portrays the tensions that could and did emerge among school sections, regional authorities, and head office than those that passed between Egerton Ryerson and Patrick Thornton, the district superintendent for Gore. Thornton's treatment of local municipal and school officers Ryerson generally found too harsh. An early letter to this superintendent may have helped to produce Thornton's subsequent rigidity; in this interchange, the Chief Superintendent strongly implied that Thornton had actually been too lenient. The problem was a teacher who had been accused of threatening someone's life with a pistol, but whom Thornton had evidently certified to teach.

Assuming that the statements on each side are equal, you have no positive evidence that Mr. Jackson's moral character is such as the law contemplates. The absence of proof that a man's character is bad is no proof that it is good. It is the latter that the law requires ...[88]

This letter was dated July 1846. Two years later, however, the local superintendent was accused of overstepping the bounds of his authority in his refusal to honour an order on the school fund to pay a teacher who, Thornton had evidently judged, was ineligible to receive the public money. In doing this he set aside the opinions of two councillors of the township as well as those of the trustees and thus, according to Ryerson, had acted 'too harshly and disrespectfully of [their] judgments.' The chief superintendent ordered that the teacher be paid. The teacher, a Mrs Merry, may well have been deprived of her share of the school fund by Thornton because she was a woman, for another earlier letter from Ryerson to this troublesome superintendent implied that Thornton had little use for what he considered to be poorly trained 'Female Teachers.' On that occasion the chief superintendent had cautioned his local officer to refrain from interfering in the agreements between schoolmistresses and parents or trustees about what should be taught in the school. Evidence of Thornton's prejudice against Mrs Merry, certainly, was the fact that, even after Ryerson's advice, the affair remained for some time unsettled. Ryerson advised him once again on the subject of this teacher on 19 August 1848. While Thornton's desire to elevate the standards of teaching were laudable, Ryerson wrote, expressing 'contempt' for the 'engagements of Trustees and certificates of District Councillors' and failing to take into account the 'peculiarities of new settlements' definitely were not. Ryerson finally appealed the Merry *vs* Superintendent Thornton case to the governor-general, although it is not clear with what result.[89]

When the difficult Patrick Thornton surfaced again in the fall of 1848, it was for his failure to lay a local dispute before Ryerson. The union school of Saltfleet No. 3 and Grimsby No. 4 had been closed down, the teacher having refused to instruct the black children who wanted to attend. Thornton had disqualified its teacher for a share of the school grant.

Ryerson judged once more that his local officer had been too hasty and recommended the payment of the grant in spite of the teacher's delinquency and prejudice. The same year and again in 1849, Thornton's reporting procedures came under attack. In the first instance he had sent the wrong blank forms to a new school section; in the second, the figures in Thornton's report failed to add up. Finally in 1849, Ryerson became involved in discussions with Thornton and several other superintendents over the expenditure of local funds. In Thornton's case, the Chief Superintendent did not approve of his superintendent's use of unexpended funds and appealed the matter to a higher authority. He failed to persuade the government to interfere, however. Thornton's use of his discretionary powers was upheld and, by implication, Ryerson's tendency to interfere in details rebuked.[90] It may well have been this decision that prompted his relative leniency in dealing with the Newcastle superintendent in August 1849.

There is no doubt that Patrick Thornton had his troubles. One can only sympathize with his refusal to pay the teacher who had rejected black children, and this was by no means his only problem section. In 1848 he wrote to Ryerson about another section where the teacher was a drunk and had seized the goods of local residents for refusing to pay an 'entirely illegal' rate bill. Thornton also had difficulties because of illness. His 1849 report was late, he wrote, because he had been stricken with the flu.[91] But perhaps the most intriguing insight into Thornton's side of the relationship comes from a letter regarding the local superintendent's efforts to develop a series of textbooks for the common schools. Thornton's 'Canadian Progressive System,' containing several reading books and a geography, was 'nearly completed' in 1846, according to one of his letters to Ryerson. But the Irish National Series of school-books, soon to be promoted by the education department, would, he believed, render his own series uncompetitive. One can only wonder if some of the tensions between Ryerson and his lieutenant from Gore were not generated, at least in part, by the local officer's chagrin over the pre-empting of his textbook market by the education department in Toronto, and the latter's reluctance to encourage a district superintendent who had entrepreneurial ambitions in education somewhat beyond the strictly supervisory and inspirational role that the law intended.[92]

Yet there is also no doubt that Patrick Thornton's difficulties were, at least in part, intrinsic to his job. In 1849, trustees complained to Ryerson of a district superintendent who lived fifty miles from their school, failed to warn local authorities of his intended visit, then came when the school was closed, adding insult to injury by listening to the views of local malcontents who were against the trustees. The multiplication of superintendents made possible by the 1850 school act failed to end such criticisms. Local school people complained of superintendents who were prejudiced, who were illiterate, or who based their reports on 'hearsay' rather than on 'actual inspection.'[93]

Local superintendents were clearly resented by many mid-nineteenth-century Upper Canadians, but it remained the chief superintendent who ultimately stood for the imposition of government programs, rules, and supervisory personnel in the local schools. For all that Egerton Ryerson might appear to defend local prerogatives from unduly interfering district, county, or township men, in the final analysis the interference originated with his own office. The effort necessary to enforce the new and increasingly complicated laws governing state-funded schools could hardly avoid appearing meddlesome.

Resistance to this interference took many forms. It was often overtly and actively political, as in the case of the Cameron Act in 1849. Occasionally it took more passive forms. Toronto began the resistance that culminated in the closing of its common schools by failing to send in the reports on its schools in 1847 and again in 1848, forcing Ryerson to cut off the city's apportionment from the provincial fund. The city school board also refused, for nearly a decade, to have much to do with the graduates of the provincial Normal School, which existed in its midst. Toronto preferred to hire teachers from the old country, judging by the origins of the majority who taught for the city in the 1850s. And when the education department saw fit, in 1856, to fire a messenger boy for taking part in a local Orangemen's parade, a mass meeting was held in Toronto's St Lawrence Hall to voice the protests of angry citizens.[94]

Some historians have argued that much of the thrust for the development of educational bureaucracy at the provincial level came from the distress and confusion of local authorities who continually bombarded the education department with requests for help – and even direct intervention – from the 1840s on.[95] However, the evidence suggests, as we have seen, that the local authorities of Toronto, along with elements in the notably dissident districts of Bathurst, Newcastle, Dalhousie, and Gore, would have to be excluded from such a picture. In addition, this interpretation of mid-century bureaucratic development must be questioned on even more substantial grounds. It is true that many requests and complaints suggest a need for help and an equal tendency to bow to the greater wisdom of provincial authorities who claimed to know more than local people did, possibly about education and certainly about the school law. Equally, Ryerson often bent over backwards to placate and encourage school officers at the local level. More often than not, perhaps, he urged local school people to sort out their own affairs. The fact remains, however, that his advice would never have been sought or needed in the first place had not the laws of the 1840s and 1850s created a complex and frequently changing set of rules governing the management of the province's publicly supported schools. The demand for bureaucratic regulation followed, rather than preceded, the school legislation of mid-century. And many people, from Bathurst District to the city of Toronto, had difficulty adjusting to provincial interference in the running of their educational affairs. Nevertheless, in the end, accepting money from the provincial coffers meant accepting the regulation and interference that went with it. Ultimately, the money the province offered was hard to resist, even with the strings that were attached.

Bureaucratic organization was one of the purposes clearly espoused by the architects of mid-nineteenth-century educational change. Education, they believed, flowed down from the top or out from the centre. It may be that in mid-nineteenth-century Upper Canada the problem with this model lay in the failure to create an effective middle management, in the form of a permanent, well-organized superintendency.[96] There is considerable evidence, however, that many Upper Canadians did not want such controls and resented their imposition even in the modified versions created by the school law of 1850. The stronger the controls emanating from the top or the centre, the weaker and more needy, it was implied, were the people at the bottom or the periphery. The inhabitants of those realms – uncertified or alienated teachers, backwoods trustees and superintendents, the poor and the marginal everywhere – did sometimes resent the fact that it was their peculiar habits and slipshod ways that the school system was designed to correct.

But, as Ryerson himself evidently understood, for all the frustrations of bureaucratic organization experienced by the people at the bottom or on the periphery, there was always the advantage that even in incipient bureaucracy one could shift the blame and pass the buck. James Stevenson of Cambridge Township said it best in 1858: 'Bad as we are,' he reminded the chief superintendent, 'the falt is not ours.' What this perceptive man concluded must surely have been the conclusion of everyone who struggled to cope with the incomprehensible laws, multitudinous regulations, and complicated forms of a school system in the process of creation. Someone else, surely, was to blame. And perhaps Ryerson and his fellow designers of the common school system had the last word after all. As the local school officers struggled, they learned. Twenty-one years after the passage of the 1850 school act, thousands of one-time teachers, superintendents, and trustees had been through Ryerson's mill. In what ways the process had been educational it is hard to say. But there is no doubt that it had been. Responsible citizens? Or more governable subjects? They all knew, at least, how to fill out a form. If the thing were done right, the fountains of government opened and the money poured (or trickled) out.

6 Forging a Public School Teaching Force

Educated and effective school officers were the ideal, and school reformers clearly hoped that eventually such officers would sort things out at the local level so that the schools would run more smoothly. But all too often the reality was James Stevenson and the disorganization of Cambridge Township. A second line of attack and one for which educational reformers had more hope in the long run was the campaign to 'upgrade' the people who taught the schools. A more highly trained and respectable teaching force, they no doubt thought, would make the work of the local superintendents and trustees less onerous or, perhaps, even less necessary.

A vital key to the campaign was the Normal School that began to admit students in the fall of 1847. In its structure, organization, and methods the 'Normal' represented what educators argued ought to be the very best, a pattern or model that all Upper Canadian teachers and schools could follow. Indeed, Canada West's chief superintendent of schools saw it as the very 'personification' of public instruction in the province.[1] Normal School promoters hoped that one day all common school teachers would be trained in an institution designed exclusively for their professional preparation, but they did not expect this day to arrive immediately. Rather, they hoped that the Toronto school would have a diffusion effect. Teachers educated there would move out into various parts of the province and would pass on what they had learned to others. These, in their turn, would all 'contribute ... to raise the general standard of intelligence' in Upper Canada.[2]

The campaign to upgrade teachers had further facets. An ideal was put forward, its opposite condemned, and everyone connected with the school system exhorted to see that all teachers lived up to the ideal. A system of certification was put in place and continuously modified or improved upon. The education department and local councils of public instruction also experimented with model schools and teacher-training institutes. These, they hoped, would bring the principles of proper school management, in however brief or truncated a form, to those teachers who could not bring themselves to the training school in Toronto. Finally, the campaign focused on the vexed question of wages and, sometimes but not always more subtly, on the teacher's age and gender.

Continuing complaints about the character of the province's teaching force suggest that reform strategies were only partly successful in effecting their designers' intentions. Assessing their ultimate impact, however, remains a fascinating problem for the historian. Bearing on this conundrum is the question of who actually engaged in the occupation in Canada West in the third quarter of the nineteenth century if, as the old adage went, it was the teacher who made the school. Thus a collective portrait of the province's changing teaching force highlights further the process by which the school system was constructed.

I

Upper Canadian school reformers began to discuss the need for a normal school as early as the 1830s. The idea was mentioned in Charles Duncombe's 1836 report to the provincial legislature, again by Robert McCaul in a similar report in 1839, and in Lord Durham's comprehensive report to the imperial government in the aftermath of the 1837–8 rebellions, in the same year. When the idea was finally on the verge of becoming a reality in the school law of 1846, Ryerson requested a modest annual stipend to get the new school underway.[3] The first students enrolled and began classes late in the autumn of 1847.

Ryerson never failed to take advantage of any occasion that had ceremonial or propagandist possibilities, and the opening of Upper Canada's first public training school for teachers was a prime occasion for both. It was to be followed not long afterwards, moreover, by two equally impressive occasions. The corner-stone laying for the Normal School's permanent new building on 2 July 1851 and the grand opening of the completed edifice in November 1852 provided further excuses for festivity. All three events were duly written up in the local press, and Ryerson made sure that his own reporters also recorded at least two of the occasions in detail for the education department's publications. Indeed, following its usual creed that edifying material could not be used too much, the department continued to reprint the speeches that marked the beginning of the Normal School right into the 1860s and 1870s.[4]

The first ceremony, which took place on 1 November 1847, marked the school's opening in the 'Old Government House,' a building that

dated from pre-union days when Toronto was Upper Canada's capital.
Egerton Ryerson delivered the opening address, outlining the history of
normal schools in general and the new institution in particular. The other
speakers were Thomas Jaffray Robertson and Henry Youle Hind, headmaster and second master, respectively, of the school, and on this occasion introduced to Toronto for the first time.

The day after this event, students were admitted and school began.
But the Government House interlude was short-lived. Within two years,
riots in Montreal sent the union government scurrying back to Toronto
and forced the school to seek new temporary accomodation, this time in
Toronto's Temperance Hall. The disruption and inconvenience must have
provided school authorities with an excellent excuse to press the government for a more permanent structure to house both the Normal School
and the rapidly expanding offices of the education department. Funds
were eventually forthcoming, tenders were put out for a design, and the
winning firm of Cumberland and Ridout set to work to construct another
impressive edifice to add to the new buildings adorning the streets of
Toronto in the early 1850s. The corner-stone laying for this structure
marked the second grand occasion in the school's history and was graced
by the presence of the new Roman Catholic bishop, Armand de Charbonnel, and the governor-general, Lord Elgin, among other Canadian
notables.[5]

The most impressive and memorable ceremony of the three, however,
must have been the final grand opening of the completed building in
1852. The opening was late. Architect Cumberland had the usual troubles,
first with supplies and then with a contractor who had declared bank-
ruptcy. Yet, in spite of the delay (or maybe because of it), Ryerson
apparently forgot to warn some of his guests that they would be required
to make speeches. The president of the University of Toronto, Dr John
McCaul, the inspector-general, Francis Hincks, and Chief Justice John
Beverley Robinson nevertheless all found words for the occasion, as did
of course the ubiquitous Ryerson.

Robinson warned his audience not to expect the results of the Normal
School to be instantaneous, and Hincks pointed out that nothing like
perfection could be achieved until the people of Canada West themselves
gained practical experience in the operation of the school system. McCaul
dwelt particularly on the importance of the Normal School to the development of teaching as a genuine profession. It was Ryerson, however,
who reviewed the history of the school and got down to the nitty-gritty
of its financing. The Toronto school was compared, dollar for dollar, to
similar institutions in the United States – institutions that on an annual
basis cost more and, Ryerson argued, had less to show for it than this

one. He claimed, indeed, that despite the £17,000 cost, it was probable that there was not 'so cheap a building,' on the same scale, anywhere in North America. Ever the politician, Ryerson did not hesitate to end his speech with a friendly request that the city of Toronto hurry up and provide decent access to and sidewalks for the new building.[6]

Money was clearly on the minds of those speakers most responsible for the construction of the school. Hincks pointed out that there had been considerable feeling against the selection of Toronto for the site and that it had been no easy job to acquire the necessary funds from Parliament. And if Ryerson had been able to claim, at the corner-stone laying in 1851, the relative economy of the Normal School compared to University College,[7] he steered clear of such Canadian comparisons in 1852, pointing instead to less well-known American ones. In fact, the delays and final cost of the completed buildings and grounds may have been something of a scandal. In its report of 28 September 1850 on the plans for the new school, the *Globe* had pointed out that the seven-acre block purchased for the project, bounded by Church, Victoria, Gerrard, and Gould streets, had been acquired for £4,500 and that an £8,000 limit had been set on the cost of the building. By the time of the corner-stone laying, however, the grant for the building had already grown to £15,000. Ryerson had to admit in 1852 that expenditure for the school had gone well beyond the original grant, coming in at a final £17,200, and in a later history of the school, the total cost 'including grounds, furniture and apparatus' was reported to have been $100,000, the equivalent of £25,000.[8]

The minutes of the Council of Public Instruction are revealing about its founders' attitudes to the Normal School and the possible causes of escalating costs. Clearly, the institution's promoters were determined to spare no expense in making the building both imposing and permanent. Stone cornices were to be used, and the building was to be covered with slate. Some, if not all, of the stone was especially imported from Cleveland, Ohio. Finally, a landscape gardener was brought in from Hamilton to design the grounds.[9] All this was a far cry from the original Normal School provision, which, Ryerson himself later pointed out, was so minimal that it had been appropriated from the ordinary common school fund and required no 'new, or special grant out of the public revenue.'[10] Taxpayers contemplating this tale might well have received an interesting lesson in how a sum too 'small' to put before the legislature one year before the school's opening in 1847 could become a very large appropriation for the same purpose only four or five years later. Rumblings in the press about Toronto's 'showy' educational edifices certainly referred to the Normal School as well as to the new university buildings or the city's new common schools.[11]

The Normal School

If the expense had been large, all concerned and especially Egerton Ryerson were anxious to point out that Upper Canada had gained a worthy monument. In addition to the main structure, which was to house the Council of Public Instruction chamber and all the various branches of the education department, as well as a theatre and the classrooms of a training school designed for two hundred pupil teachers, there were also the boys' and girls' Model Schools, built for a total student body of six hundred. The grounds included a half-acre fruit and vegetable garden, a botanical garden of one and a half acres, a small arboretum, and two acres designed for agricultural experiments. If slate and stone gave a stately air of permanence to the outside of the building, the inside represented progress, with the latest improvements in evidence, including central wood-fired heating as well as gaslight. Even the furnishings in the school, an improvement on some models purchased by Ryerson in the United States, were intended to be examples for visitors to the school. And indeed, by 1853, the cities of Hamilton, St Catharines, and Toronto had all acquired copies of Normal School desks and seats.[12]

School furnishings were not all that Ryerson had brought back from his travels, and no one claimed that the school was in any way an original invention. They argued, rather, that it copied all the best features of the various normal schools that had already been established in Europe and the United States. During the educational tour that Ryerson made in 1845 the Irish teacher-training school situated in Dublin had made an especially favourable impression on him, and he had dispatched his new clerk, John George Hodgins, to study there for a term before the latter took on his job in the education office. In addition, during the formative stages of Canada West's school, Ryerson and Hodgins sought both counsel and personnel from the Irish school.

In the end, Toronto's school was by no means an exact replica of Dublin's. A crucial difference was the decision, made by the second session of the Normal's existence, to admit women; of less intrinsic importance, but the subject of greater attention in the documents that have come down to us, was the rejection of 'training halls' or residences for out-of-town students.[13] The authorities decided instead that students coming from outside the city should reside in ordinary city boarding houses, a decision that may have stemmed as much from Egerton Ryerson's distaste for institutional boarding as from the obvious need to avoid further expenditure on buildings.[14] It also emerged that the Toronto school's system of training was not necessarily identical to the system practised in Ireland.[15] The Irish influence extended rather to three other areas: the selection of the Irish 'national' series of textbooks as the basic texts for training Upper Canada's teachers; the decision to have a model school attached to the Normal; and the selection of an Irish headmaster.

Thomas Robertson came highly recommended. He had been a classical master in Ireland and had risen to the post of head inspector of the Irish school system before his emigration to Canada West. He clearly also made a good impression when he arrived in Toronto. The *British Colonist* reported that his approach was practical, and the *Globe* was convinced that both he and the mathematics and science master, Henry Youle Hind, were 'accomplished men' at least 'in point of information.' Hind did not last many years at the school, but Robertson's headmastership continued until his death in 1866. It would appear that his performance generally satisfied his Upper Canadian employers.[16]

At least one former student had cause to remember him unfavourably, however, and took the trouble to express to the chief superintendent of schools his view that Robertson's management had seriously hurt the Normal School and its pupil teachers. In a complaint addressed to Ryerson in 1859, Peter Nicol stated not only that the headmaster's morals were 'publically [sic] infamous' but that his principalship had amounted to 'gross mismanagement' of the school. The only concrete addition that Nicol chose to make to these general allegations concerned Roberton's abuse of his powers of recommendation. When trustees sought teachers through the Normal School, Nicol claimed, the headmaster put forward his favourites, preferring them to other claimants who had studied longer at the school or had higher certified standing. 'And what qualities conciliate his good will!' added Nicol enigmatically.[17]

The only sense we can get of Robertson's own perception of his management of the Normal School comes from an essay on the inspection of schools that he published in 1850 and a letter that he addressed to the Council of Public Instruction on 14 January 1851. In the essay, Robertson argued that the essence of all management was careful regulation down to the finest detail. This was true in government, in business, and in the management of a family, so why not in education? The need for control justified inspection, for it was everywhere acknowledged that a 'strict and frequent examination' of the working of all parts of a given machine was essential. Yet if the headmaster believed in control he also believed in kindness, noting in his letter to the council that it was by 'kind and courteous treatment' that he had invariably obtained 'the most complete authority' over his classes.[18]

As the letter from Peter Nicol indicates, however, there was always the possibility of appealing beyond the authority of Robertson to that of Egerton Ryerson and the Council of Public Instruction. On matters of discipline, student boarding arrangements, and Normal School admissions, as well as on other more mundane matters having to do with the management of the building, the headmaster reported frequently to his superior in the education department. And it would appear from council minutes that, in the early days at least, the members of the Board of Education, and of the Council of Public Instruction that succeeded it, concerned themselves minutely with the details of the school's administration. The council paid great attention to the construction of the buildings and made numerous decisions regarding the employment and duties of the school's janitors. In 1854 it responded negatively to a memorial from the students requesting that a month's vacation be granted 'in consequence of the prevalence of disease in the city.' On the other hand, the board delegated to the masters of the Normal School the general oversight of the Model School in 1848 and, in 1853, gave the headmaster the power to readmit students who had been suspended.[19]

By the mid-1850s, in fact, the council seems to have been meeting very infrequently. Several meetings, furthermore, were attended by Ryerson, the chairman, and only one other person. Nevertheless, it is clear that not all powers were turned over to Headmaster Robertson. The council delegated, rather, to the chief superintendent of schools. In 1851, for example, it referred to Ryerson in all matters connected with the preparation or revision of Normal School rules, timetables, and course of study for the coming year.[20] Other indications suggest that Egerton

Ryerson kept a very close watch on the school and considered himself (and was seen to be) in charge. In a letter to Sir Charles Metcalfe outlining the Normal School clauses of the 1846 school bill, Ryerson noted that they provided for the education of young men under the Chief Superintendent's 'oversight.'[21] The internal correspondence between Robertson and Ryerson suggests that the latter interested himself in matters as detailed as the spelling in Normal School applicants' letters as well as in the multitude of discipline questions that arose. And a remarkable number of people appear to have addressed Ryerson rather than Robertson about matters connected with the school. Among the most interesting of the letters in the department's incoming correspondence are those sent by anxious parents and friends to the Chief Superintendent concerning the welfare of young persons about to enrol in the Normal, or, in at least one case, concerning a young master about to be employed there. It is a measure of the continuing personal nature of government in general and education department business in particular during the mid-nineteenth century that Ryerson was asked to take an interest in particular students' lodgings and companions, as well as their religious guidance and morals. As Joseph Bell wrote about a young woman who was both a new student and a stranger to Toronto, he hoped that she would be able to look up to the Chief Superintendent as her '*Protector*' and '*Friend.*' W.H. Poole wrote to Hodgins, rather than to Ryerson, but the essence of the letter was the same. Walter Williams was recommended to Hodgins's particular care with the warning that this student might feel somewhat awkward when he came to the school, 'as most country men do among citizens.'[22]

If Ryerson was sometimes seen as the real head of the school and Robertson as second in command, the internal arrangements of the institution itself also tended towards hierarchy. Ryerson was superior to Robertson, but the latter in his turn reigned over the second master in the Normal School, while both the head and second master had command of the Boys' and the Girls' Model schools, where hierarchy was also the order of the day. Council of Public Instruction minutes for 25 October 1852 list Archibald McCallum as first assistant Model School teacher at an annual salary of £150, John Sangster as second assistant at £125, and Robert Sampson as third assistant with a salary of £100. The first female assistant, Mrs Dorcas Clark, received £75 for her services, while the second, Miss Catherine Johnson, was paid £50. Sensitivity to rank may be seen in Sangster's request that his official title be changed from 'Assistant Teacher' to that of 'Second Master' of the Boys' Model. The council granted the request, although the October minutes continued to list Mr Sangster as an assistant.[23] Archibald McCallum wrote to Ryerson in 1855 to request a change in the substance of his position, rather than in its title. What he wanted was the opportunity to spend more time in the Girls' Model School in order to 'exercise that supervision in the whole school which we all think most desirable.' The present difficulty was that his oversight of the girls' education was more nominal than real. Genuine supervision, he pointed out, would mean the possibility of increasing class sizes from fifty-five children to seventy.[24]

Hierarchical forms and authoritarian modes of government were reflected in both the pedagogical practices and the discipline of the Normal School. The school stressed deference, competition for rewards, and punctuality. Long before it had a permanent building, the Council of Public Instruction authorized Ryerson and the mayor of Toronto to select for the school's use 'a suitable bell of about 112 lbs weight,' presumably to mark the hours of attendance and Robertson worried when the school's various clocks were poorly synchronized, for the school's days were rigidly timetabled. Students received copies of the Irish national schoolbooks as rewards for diligence and good conduct, and certificates upon graduation were by 1859 divided into six possible levels of achievement.[25]

Regulations governing life at the Normal School proliferated. If at the beginning there was room for a certain amount of flexibility, regarding the times of admission, for example,[26] the flexibility seems to have been short-lived. By 1851, late admission was frowned upon, the regulations now stating that students had to present themselves during the first week of term. As Ryerson explained to the father of a prospective pupil who wished to arrive late, the school could not depart from the published regulations without 'endless inconveniences' and 'breaking down the system established.'[27]

The same tendency to increasing rigidity may be seen in the matter of students' ages. The regulations stated that applicants to the school had to be at least sixteen years of age, but it is clear that in the first few years younger people were admitted. By 1850, however, the age of admission for male (although not female) students was raised to eighteen and age rules were more tightly enforced. Other rules governing admission sought to control for character. From the beginning, non-fee-paying students had to declare their intention to teach upon graduation, and all students were required to produce a certificate of good moral character signed by a clergyman. By 1852, further items had been added to the terms of admission, including promises to obey the school's rules and to give back borrowed books. Students also promised to return all lodging subsidies that had been provided should they withdraw from the school for other than medical reasons.[28]

Once admitted, Normal School students had further rules to contend with. The first regulations, passed in 1847, required them to be in their lodgings 'before half-past nine o'clock, p.m., to attend their respective places of worship with strict regularity' and to attend the school constantly and punctually. The Board of Education ruled in 1848 that roll was to be called ten minutes before each lecture and that absentees were accountable to the master in charge. The masters were, in fact, 'invested with authority for enforcing discipline and for ensuring due respect on the part of the students, by public reprimand, and suspension, if thought advisable, 'although permanent expulsion required the sanction of the board. By 1852, a set of revised rules included the regulation that absentees failing to explain themselves satisfactorily were accountable directly to the chief superintendent of education. Further, attendance at Friday afternoon religious instruction was compulsory, as was the residence of students coming from out of town in city boarding houses approved and designated officially by the Council of Public Instruction. Other rules and pronouncements were clearly in response to specific problems that had arisen. Thus an order from the Board of Education in 1848 eliminated the possibility of a Normal School debating society on the grounds that it would interfere with the time needed for study. When the servants of the Normal School were involved in misdemeanours of various kinds they were formally ordered to mend their ways – to be temperate, to avoid gambling, and to keep out of politics.[29] Perhaps the most notorious and hotly debated of the school's rules were those governing the relations between men and women after the latter were admitted in 1848. The admission of female students in the first place has been interpreted as an important gain in the educational advancement of Canadian women.[30] But women were not admitted on equal terms with men and segregation was strict. Male and female students were forbidden to speak to or to meet one another outside class. Separate entrances, separate days for visiting the Normal School museum, and separate model schools for boys and girls were designed to make this separation as complete as was possible in a coeducational institution. By 1853 the rules for boarding required that the female students live in houses that admitted women only.[31]

Evidence of Normal School masters' difficulties in enforcing the rules with respect to male and female students and boarding houses fills the school's registers and the correspondence of the education department, but their problems went far beyond these sensitive issues. There were also numerous incidents arising from students' unwillingness to accept the masters' authority in the classroom. Many older and experienced male pupil teachers found the manner of the mathematics and science master, H.Y. Hind, particularly offensive, and suspensions by this master occupied much of Ryerson's time in the early 1850s.[32] On one occasion a

Normal student was summoned before a Toronto police magistrate, and there were students with drinking problems. Some students got off lightly. For a young man guilty of intoxication and four late nights, Ryerson recommended only a severe reprimand in the presence of his classmates, as expulsion from the school might result in his 'utter ruin.' In the case of another, the Chief Superintendent corresponded with local innkeepers as well as with the clergyman who had recommended the student to the school, in an effort to help him mend his ways. Mr Lanon, who addressed female student teachers in unbecoming terms and was disrespectful to the headmaster, was simply asked to apologize. Equally lenient treatment was accorded in 1849 to Robert Lathy, who was seen in the company of other students at a gathering for the rebel William Lyon Mackenzie, lately pardoned and returned to Upper Canada.[33]

More serious penalties – suspension or expulsion – were meted out to the male student who tickled a female classmate, to those who spoke to women students after class, and to students who were known to have frequented taverns, attended the theatre, or entered a house of ill fame.[34] In general, as Ryerson put it in a letter about a boarding-house fist fight over the ownership of a candlestick, 'lawlessness' could not be tolerated among students at the provincial Normal School. The party deemed guilty in the fist fight was expelled. Long-drawn-out investigations occurred into the case of the student who was accused of entering his landlady's daughter's bedroom and that of the young man charged with making insulting remarks and sending an obscene valentine to the daughter of one neighbour. While female students were less noticeable in the records than such young men, they too were the subjects of inquiry and occasional suspension or expulsion.

If problems of social discipline seemed to dominate the correspondence regarding the school and even the minutes of the Council of Public Instruction, they were of course not the only concern of school authorities. The Normal School had to set a good example morally. But it was equally important that it be – and be seen to be – a model of correct and effective instruction. Indeed, a major purpose of the school was to introduce what seems to have been perceived as a radically new pedagogy into the schools of Canada West as well as an offically trained teaching force. What was offered at the Normal must have seemed a valuable commodity to many Upper Canadians. Students, both male and female, flocked to it.[35]

Yet not everyone wholeheartedly approved of its theories of pedagogy and school government, or of its graduates. Contemporary assessments of the Toronto school were decidedly mixed at its inception and continued to be mixed until the end of the Ryerson regime in 1876. The earliest critics dwelt on the enormous cost of the institution and its contribution to Ryerson's educational empire in Toronto. Ryerson was forced to defend the costs over and over again, for the point remained a sore one.[36] On the other hand, one of the Chief Superintendent's most persistent critics on other issues, the Toronto *Globe*, seems not to have begrudged the money initially spent on opening the school, even suggesting in 1848 that the province could do with four or five such schools instead of one.[37] Of more concern to later critics than initial costs was the extent to which the money spent on teacher training actually came back to the province in the form of employed graduates. 'What has become of the 1,264 students attending the Normal School up to the close of the year 1853?' one critic wanted to know. 'Has the majority of them turned Clerks, or Store-keepers, or gone back to farming?' Angus Dallas, a Toronto merchant, was the sceptic, and his claim was that the graduates had either abandoned teaching or were not considered suitable candidates for the many schools that advertised for teachers.[38] Ryerson was frequently called upon to defend the school's graduates. On at least one occasion he called attention to the number who had won scholarships to the University of Toronto, thus belying to some extent his own contention that Normal graduates did go on to teach in common schools. He generally insisted, however, that the vast majority fulfilled their stated intention to become teachers.[39]

On the usefulness of the school's training for this purpose, opinion was sharply divided. If some trustees scorned Normal School graduates for being too 'showy,' for not being able to spell 'common English words of one syllable,' or simply on the grounds of their general inadequacy, there were others who firmly believed in the school's product. A basic characteristic that impressed those who were favourable to the school was the Normal School teacher's ability to speed up school work. A pleased parent informed the education department of the 'sensation' created in his neighbourhood by the new Normal School teacher, contrasting the efforts of this teacher with the old 'slow coach' system formerly used, while a recent graduate reported that local parents believed their children had learned more in one year under the Normal system than they had previously learned in three.[40]

But if the system was speedy, there were others who thought that it led to uniformity and repetition. The *Huron Signal*, for example, wondered if Normal training resulted in set lessons, taught 'in exactly the same manner as the same lessons would be taught to Parrots.' Perhaps the money spent on the school would be better left in the general education fund. 'We have never loved this Parrot education,' the *Signal* concluded; 'there is something vague in the very looks of it.'[41] Then there were the complaints about the time the Normal School was forced to spend drilling Upper Canada's future teachers in the subjects that they were supposed to teach. One thoughtful commentator suggested that admission be restricted to experienced instructors, who presumably would already know the subject matter when they arrived. Then the school could give up *'cramming'* them and concentrate on instruction in the art of teaching.[42] These criticisms were voiced in 1850, but similar ones continued to be heard throughout the next two decades. The grammar school inspector George Paxton Young was one of those who continued to express concern in the 1860s about the Normal School's focus on cramming content rather than teaching method.[43]

Those in charge defended the school, remaining ever hopeful that things would improve, and trying when they could to 'raise standards.' There were always advantages for the graduates that could be cited in the school's favour. In 1849, Ryerson noted that they were more popular with trustees than others and generally got much higher salaries. They were able to 'perform their duties more satisfactorily, efficiently and usefully' and thus were 'more respected' than other Upper Canadian teachers.[44] What the school did achieve, for many of its graduates at least, was an improvement in confidence, status, and prospects. Most would go forth proclaiming the superiority of the Normal School system. Sophisticated urbanites, like the members of the Toronto Board of Education who, for at least a decade, appear to have hired few if any graduates,[45] may temporarily have scorned the Normal School product. But local trustees in many communities across the province were clearly attracted to Toronto-trained teachers from the beginning.

II

This did not mean that every community would or could hire a Normal School graduate during the middle decades of the nineteenth century. On the contrary, all the evidence suggests that the vast majority of school boards did not. To such boards and the teachers they employed, the education department, its supporters among the local superintendents, and other promoters of school reform directed an unrelenting campaign designed to upgrade the occupation through other means. Their campaign strove to create in people's minds an image of a superior teacher. A major strategy was constant and harping criticism of the unacceptable teachers that trustees actually hired.

Reformers attacked any tendencies that revealed teachers as too low on the social scale. They complained of the lack of gentlemanly manners among teachers and their want of 'due regard to personal appearance, politeness and general deportment.' Also under fire was the habit of transcience. A teacher, it was felt, should be a settled person, a known member of the community. Closely associated with transience and equally deplored was the tendency to regard teaching as temporary work, a stop-gap until something better came along, or as a stepping-stone to another occupation. University students commonly taught in the summer in order to finance their studies in the winter, but they were not the only ones to regard teaching as temporary or seasonal employment. 'Stagnation in commercial affairs' sometimes sent 'clever young men from the city' into the rural areas to become teachers – and these were the first to leave, one local superintendent complained, when better times returned.[46] Other young men, it was reported, engaged in school teaching for a while and then turned to other professions as soon as they had saved a few hundred dollars, while the 'daughters of respectable farmers' gave up school teaching when they got married. Although Ryerson claimed in 1867 that Canada West suffered far less than some American states from young people who taught for a few months and then turned to farm labour or to service as maids or cooks for the remainder of the year, the tendency to regard teaching as a temporary rather than a permanent occupation remained a serious problem in reformers' estimation.[47] A final complaint in the same category was that teaching was used as something to turn to when all else had failed. That it had become the last resort of the 'unfortunate tradesman' or the 'decayed gentleman,' or of 'disbanded old soldiers,' was a common opinion of the 1840s and 1850s, and communications from teachers and others to the education department during the period did in fact occasionally cite physical deformity, weakness of the nerves, ruined health, and subsequent unfitness for other work as reasons for engaging in the occupation.[48]

School reformers were concerned that when teaching became the resort of outcasts, temporary job-seekers, and transients wages were reduced and qualified teachers thrown out of work. Those who were 'offering their services lower than teamsters and herd boys' were supplanting and rooting out the best teachers. Yet the school superintendent for Brock District argued in 1848 that the very low wages paid to teachers were not really out of line, since in fact most female teachers were not superior to 'spinsters or household servants,' and most males not much more qualified to teach than 'labourers or farm servants.' Even genteel immigrants from the old country, who turned to school teaching because of temporary financial need, did nothing for the social status of the profession, according to a correspondent of Egerton Ryerson's from Waterloo County in 1850. The trouble was that such individuals really despised teaching, considering it 'a very subordinate employment, at which they would never have laid their hands *at home*.' The campaign to improve teachers was therefore not only a campaign to raise the status of the

A Middlesex County common school master and his school, sketched by the district superintendent, William Elliot, in 1845

occupation in the eyes of the public, but to raise it in the opinion of the teachers themselves.[49]

Such a quest could, no doubt, be traced back to the first Common School Act in 1816. But it was with the creation of the superintendency in the province of Canada in 1841 that concrete pressures began to be felt. Robert Murray, who held the post of assistant superintendent for two years before the appointment of Ryerson, called upon local superintendents to impress upon teachers the 'great responsiblility of their station in society, and the necessity of the strictest propriety in their walk and conversation, both in and out of school.' The more ardent among the local superintendents responded throughout the years that followed with campaigns of their own. In 1863, the Reverend H. Cameron of Renfrew County was still trying to dissuade teachers from soliciting work around the country like 'mercenaries,' while M.F. Haney of Welland County worked on school teachers' pronunciation of the English language.[50]

But the proper social deportment of the schoolmaster, although indispensable, was only one of several roads to a correct image. Educators and teachers on the rise were also concerned about the actual nature of the employment. Insistently, they demanded that teachers be relieved of manual or unskilled work that could be performed by persons with lower status, and that they be respectably and independently housed.

The question of who was responsible for laying fires and cleaning in schools provoked ongoing debate. In 1848, Ryerson wrote to John Monger, a teacher in Newmarket, that the matter ought to be arranged between the trustees and teacher, 'the law not specifying who shall do it.' The trustees had three options. They could give the teacher a higher salary and make him responsible for cleaning and warming the schoolhouse, grant him a special allowance for the purpose, or agree to its being done by the pupils under the teacher's direction. In 1849, a teacher from Kingston wanted to know what his duties were in this respect and received a similar answer. But the question continued to be raised as a matter of principle[51] and, in March 1861, complaints and queries finally resulted in the printing of the following brief statement in the *Journal of Education*:

Teachers are not required to make Fires. The Teacher is employed to teach the school, but he is not employed to make the fires and clean the school house, much less repair the school house.

This was a distinct change of strategy. Apparently the matter was no longer one of local arrangement but subject to provincial edict. But although the chief superintendent had spoken, the question continued to be raised in rural school sections. In Oxford County, at least, it was occasionally still a bone of contention in the 1860s. The trustees' minute book for School Section 1, North West Oxford, recorded that building fires and ringing the school bell were explicitly contracted to be included in the teacher's duties in 1863. In 1865, however, the superintendent from Oxford reported that the more common solution was to hire a lad to do the 'extra work' or to press it on the pupils.[52]

If it was considered extra work and unseemly for the teacher to be engaged in the maintenance of the schoolhouse, it was considered equally lowering for a schoolmaster or schoolmistress to board 'from house to house like a beggar.' This 'pernicious practice,' according to one school reformer, was wounding the sensitive feelings frequently found in 'persons living so much apart from the world,' as he implied teachers either did or should. Another hoped that soon no teacher would be 'subjected to a strange bed and table from week to week' in a community where the comforts of life were 'so different.' When faced in 1846 with the argument that the provision of room and board should be taken into account when teachers' salaries were being discussed, Egerton Ryerson replied with an attack on the practice itself, which he argued was incompatible with the teacher's need for privacy. The point, according to Ryerson, was that teachers ought to have homes of their own.[53] The promotion of separate domestic accommodation was thus added to the elimination of housekeeping chores and the development of proper speech and manners as part of the grand design for the improvement of teachers. The teacher, wrote one school promoter in 1849, ought to be on a par with the clergyman and gentleman, 'the obsequious servant of none.' To status-conscious nineteenth-century reformers, the distinction between the roles and treatment of boarding teachers and boarding servants must have seemed insufficiently sharp.[54]

All this was part of a larger concern to define the whole relationship between employers and teachers more clearly as various aspects of this relationship came to be seen as degrading to the teacher. Trustees, as well as parents, were urged to act as partners to teachers, to support their plans and interfere less with their work. What went on inside the school was essentially the responsibility of the teacher, who could be *dismissed*, but not *controlled*. Trustees had the power to engage a new schoolmaster or schoolmistress but were urged not to use this power too often and to continue to show an outgoing teacher proper respect while the latter still had charge of the school.[55]

Arguments between trustees and teachers were to be a source of complaint or inquiry throughout the mid-century decades. As early as 1842, Assistant Superintendent Murray had observed that trustees' power to hire and fire could result in a system of 'gross oppression.' Teachers elaborated on the form this sometimes took. In 1846, James Marrs wrote to Ryerson of the difficulties and financial loss to which he would probably be subjected as the result of a fight between two contending sets of trustees. Another schoolmaster, writing to Ryerson in 1846 and again in 1850, complained of the ignorance and illiteracy of trustees and of the drunken abuse inflicted by them on the teachers in their employ.[56] British immigrant teachers sometimes found the relationship particularly irksome. John Ransome, a teacher who had been trained at the Normal School in Dublin, argued in 1850 that as long as they were dependent on trustees there would be an 'unsuperable obstacle' to the formation of a 'proper class' of teachers in Canada West. What independent person would become a teacher, Ransome went on, knowing that he thereby became 'not only the servant but perhaps the slave' of the most 'ignorant and vicious' people in the school section? To an emigrant from England in 1859, the whole situation in the province led to 'sterile' school work. The Upper Canadian schoolmaster, he claimed, was a 'mere hireling,' seen and engaged by school trustees essentially as a labourer.[57]

The wish to free the teacher from the ill-advised interference of trustees (and parents) was expressed on all sides and was clearly an important component of the campaign to upgrade the profession. But as Egerton Ryerson pointed out, there was also the need to protect the public from incompetent teachers. In a letter dealing with the subject in 1847, he noted that the immunity from interference that might be a public benefit in the case of 'humane and properly trained teachers' could hardly be so in the case of teachers who were 'untrained and violent.' Anxiety to increase the independence of teachers thus came into conflict with the fear of what they might do if they really were autonomous. There were movements in the late 1860s to do away with the power of trustees to dismiss teachers, and Ryerson himself occasionally returned to the idea of replacing school-section boards with township boards, whose interest in educational matters, he supposed, would be less personal. But there was no desire to give up controls over teachers altogether.[58]

For in the final analysis, provincial school authorities distrusted schoolmasters and schoolmistresses almost as much as they did parents and trustees. Ryerson made this abundantly clear in a debate that developed in the 1860s over the growing control of textbooks by the provincial education department. The teacher's power in the school was to be a *moral*, not an intellectual (or even a pedagogical) one, Ryerson argued. The selection of schoolbooks, therefore, was entirely outside the teacher's province. To suggest otherwise was to introduce a 'novel feature and a new authority' into the school system and to set the teacher 'above trustees, parents and the Council of Public Instruction itself.'[59]

Clearly it was the usurpation of the latter authority that most worried Ryerson, for the only way to deal with the incompetence of local authorities, whoever they were, was through the creation of outside, superior ones. This had been, and continued to be, the rationale for the gradual building of an administrative superstructure to oversee the schools and their teachers on behalf of the public. The develpment of a system of certification, increasingly controlled by the province, was the result of such thinking. Essential steps were the creation, in 1850, of county boards of public instruction with examining and certifying powers. Three classes of certificates were introduced that county boards could grant, and the government-appointed provincial Council of Public Instruction was given the right to set the minimum requirements for each class. In addition, the provincial council gained the right to grant two classes of certificates to Normal School graduates, certificates that, unlike those of the county boards, were good anywhere in Upper Canada.[60]

Despite the apparent magnitude of these changes, it is not clear that they had any immediate effect on the perceived status of teachers. Composed of the county's senior grammar-school trustees and local superintendents, the new county boards had been charged with the task of ridding the profession of 'unworthy' or 'incompetent' teachers by refusing to certify them. But this they appeared ill-equipped to do. Although from one area it was reported that the county board examinations had raised the standard of education to a respectable status and had done away altogether with the 'worthless dregs of educational society,' many other counties reportedly fared less well. One observer described the applicants for certificates at county boards in 1859 as the 'offscourings of the earth' and, according to another, the boards in the 1860s gave certificates to all comers, no matter what their character or qualifications. 'The axe-man,' this critic charged was as a result 'no longer a chopper in the bush,' nor was 'the mopping girl any longer a drudger in the shanty': both had been raised by 'the working miracle' of a board examination to the 'degree' of common school teacher. There were also complaints against the boards from teachers, who used an argument similar to one that earlier had been used against trustees, namely that to be examined by persons who themselves had little or no knowledge of the schoolroom was degrading. By the mid-sixties a movement had started to restrict membership on county boards to experienced 'educators.'[61]

In the meantime, the education department, acting through the Council of Public Instruction, had begun the process of rendering the boards relatively powerless in any case. This it did by taking over the function of examining and certifying teachers itself. The first step was the introduction of the idea of provincial certificates in 1850, and the implementation of this in 1853 with the granting of the special certificates to Normal School graduates. An important second step was the promotion in the 1860s of written examinations for the county boards. Printed questions and written answers, their promoters argued, were less arbitrary and less subject to favouritism than the old oral questions and answers that had been acceptable for examining teachers in the past. Like all innovations, the idea met with a mixed reception. Frederick H. Rous, a school superintendent from Hastings County, believed that the result of written examinations was 'an entire revolution ... in the character and qualification of our teachers,' and one assumes that he meant an improvement. Others, however, reported that the exams were stolen and seen in advance by the candidates, or that teachers who seemed highly qualified in the written tests had proven totally without talent in the schoolroom. But the use of the written examination continued to spread and, moreover, would eventually make possible the complete centralization of the system of classifying and certifying teachers.[62]

If the government examined and certified the teachers, what role was played by professional teachers' associations? The answer is, very little. Teachers' organizations began to appear in Upper Canada as early as the 1840s. In theory, these were approved by government school authorities and, in his preliminary report on elementary education in 1846, Ryerson underlined the value of professional association to the status of teachers. When teachers assembled together the 'most accomplished minds' among them gave 'tone' to the others; 'roughness and peculiarities of manners' were rubbed off, and each felt 'that he was not solitary and unconnected, but a member of an important body.' The departmental circular to teachers of 1850 again advised that professional associations would lead to increased 'success, enjoyment and social standing' of their members. Teachers were told to value their profession, since, if they did not, others could hardly do so.[63]

But Ryerson also warned the teachers to avoid pretensions or the assumption of 'lofty airs.' Indeed there are indications that the embryo professional associations that already existed by 1850 really were frowned upon by the provincial authorities. In Kingston, the local superintendent wrote to Ryerson in August 1850 that he had 'demurred' when asked to publish the resolutions of a local teachers' meeting, because he considered their proceedings 'improper if not illegal.' The education department had been authorized by the 1850 school law to organize brief training sessions or 'institutes' of its own, and the superintendent evidently succeeded in convincing the teachers of Kingston that it was therefore the prerogative of the Chief Superintendent to appoint 'proper' persons to organize as well as direct all teachers' gatherings. Principal Robertson of the Normal School organized an institute in Hamilton and encountered reluctance on the part of the participants to enter their names 'without some guarantee that the local arrangements would be in the hands of the members.' He explained to them that 'general regulations' at least would 'as a matter of course, emanate from the Chief Superintendent as the Head of the Department.' Clearly provincial authorities were anxious to control whatever associations or meetings the teachers were involved in. In an effort to make this a reality, Professors Robertson and Hind of the Normal School travelled the province during the summers of 1850 and 1851, running local institutes with varying degrees of success. The outlook was not good enough to encourage the department to continue the experiment however; province-run institutes died out, and were not revived again until 1871.[64]

Nor did locally organized teachers' associations manage to thrive in the climate of non-encouragement that emanated from the provincial education department. The Upper Canadian Teachers' Association came into existence in 1860, and from the beginning its meetings produced interesting debate and raised important issues within the framework of the developing school system.[65] But the association achieved very little in the way of power, and in 1865 University of Toronto professor Daniel Wilson spoke to its members of the need for more and stronger teachers' organizations to protect the profession. The teacher alone, he pointed out, was at the mercy of 'mercenary Boards of Trustees' on the one hand, or of 'some overbearing official' on the other.[66] 'Some overbearing official' may have meant the locally appointed superintendents; or it could equally have meant the Chief Superintendent or some of his subordinates. Certainly, there was no love lost between Wilson and the education department. His statement nevertheless identified a new enemy that could be added to the list of the teacher's foes. Trustees, as always, could perform their unfortunate roles. But now, at least in the opinion of some, there were overbearing officials to contend with as well.

In the end the campaign for teacher improvement focused more on teachers' moral and social status and on their permanence or impermanence in service than on any positive orientation towards the ideals of 'professional' expertise or autonomy. Autonomy was promoted only as autonomy from parents and trustees, while expertise (in the eyes of the education department) could be a goal only for the few who could obtain the top certificates. Teachers' professional aspirations would meet even greater obstacles in three more concrete areas of concern: the questions of salaries, of teachers' ages, and, perhaps most importantly, of their sex.

When Egerton Ryerson pointed out in 1850 that teachers could not be 'made respectable' by an act of Parliament but would have to make themselves so, he was no doubt referring to their general deportment. But, like most other reformers, he also believed that genuine respectability would come to the teacher only when good salaries were paid. Trustees were urged in the 1840s to remember that the ideal teacher in the long run was really a *good* teacher, and that a good school was more important than money. If the people wanted able instructors for their children, they would have to pay them as they did able physicians and lawyers. Later, in the early 1860s, the Chief Superintendent hurled abuse at those trustees who, 'deluded by a narrow-minded selfishness,' acted differently when employing teachers than they did when hiring clerks, or even labourers, and sold 'the priceless time and habits of children,' not to mention 'the social interest of the neighbourhood,' just to save a few dollars.[67]

There were some, like the school superintendent from the Brock District in 1848, who, as we have seen, maintained that teachers' wages generally corresponded to the labour received. If teachers were not often above servants and labourers in 'intellect and attainments,' this superintendent ventured, they were doing well when they were paid more than such people. But the vast majority of those commenting publicly on the subject deplored the fact that teachers were paid so poorly. The general burden of their arguments was that if a 'better class' of persons was to be attracted to the occupation, teachers would have to be paid at least as well as people in other 'respectable' employments. The Standing Committee on Education of the Home District, for example, argued in 1845 that able young men would become teachers in common schools only when funds appropriated for their support would allow them to earn as much as 'any ordinary professional man, tradesman, or mechanic.' Better salaries, it was in fact implied by the committee, ought to have higher priority than a normal school. Complaints in more or less the same vein continued to be heard throughout the decades that followed.[68]

Why were salaries so low? A few observers in the 1840s and 1850s answered the question by commenting on the way trustees, especially in rural areas, valued labour. According to John Garnet of Durham County, the 'working farmers' who were the majority in his community judged the value of teaching in 1852 'not by the scarcity of the commodity, or the difficulty of obtaining it, but from the amount of physical labour required in discharging the duty.' They therefore felt that a teacher who earned for six hours of work what a labouring man got for twelve hours of chopping wood was 'munificently paid.' An irate teacher had described a similar situation in 1846. Rural trustees, he had claimed, generally believed that teaching was not real work, but an 'idle, lazy life.' They would always keep the remuneration on a level with that of the agricultural labourer.[69] Another common explanation, however, was that the supply of teachers greatly exceeded the demand for them. In the late 1840s a district superintendent pointed to a large increase in the number of applicants for certificates and attributed it to the easy availability of the government money. Citing instances of female teachers being 'bargained' for, for exceedingly low wages, another critic writing in the 1860s concluded that teachers were generally receiving less for their work than domestic servants. 'As the supply notoriously exceeds the demand,' he reported, 'some trustees consider it not only expedient but right to make an inadequate amount of wages an indispensable condition to engagement.' Finally, and increasingly, the availability of 'cheap' female teachers was seen as a major reason for the low pay.[70]

Solutions to the problem were not easily to hand. One major effort in the campaign for higher wages was the collection of statistics on salaries. No doubt the reasoning here was, in part at least, that public knowledge of what teachers were paid throughout the province might lead to improvement. In 1857, the provincial department began to publish not only the average but also the highest and lowest salaries paid to teachers in the various communities of Upper Canada. Another weapon was the provincial fund, which could be used only for teachers' salaries. In addition, the apportionment of provincial government money according to attendance, the new mode adopted in 1850, was intended to reward the better teacher. If trustees were niggardly, at least the schoolteacher who was popular and attracted lots of pupils would do well out of the provincial fund. It was proposed from time to time that the government should set a minimum wage for teachers, but this suggestion fell on deaf ears. The wages paid to the majority of teachers continued to seem unprofessional throughout the 1850s and 1860s. At the root of the problem were clearly the ages of many teachers and their sex.

According to the official ideal, a good teacher was a mature person and complaints about youthful teachers were endemic. A 'lad in his teens' ought not to set himself up above the parents of his pupils, wrote one critic in 1849, while another in 1858 deplored the entrance into teaching of 'inexperienced persons, many of whom were mere boys and girls.' In Simcoe County efforts were made in the mid-1860s to raise the minimum age for getting a school to seventeen for girls and eighteen for boys.[71] At the same time it was implied that one could be too old for the profession. That older teachers would be discarded as a result of certification procedures and the founding of the Normal School was a not-uncommon accusation.

Is *these men to be cast off*, because they may not be able to answer a few puzzling selected questions by some heady high-minded Examiner – it would be Cruelty – let them labour out their few short years they will soon be gone – or make some small provision for their declining years.[72]

There is evidence that superintendents and examiners were, in fact, attempting to discourage older teachers whose methods seemed out of date as well as men and women who were ailing or disabled. The superannuation fund begun in 1854 was intended to assist such individuals and, at the same time perhaps, permit school boards to let aged or 'worn out' teachers go with a minimum of damage to the collective conscience.[73]

If the employment of adolescent and of old or ailing teachers seemed inappropriate, the employment of women caused even more soul-searching. There were pressures both for and against women in teaching. On the negative side, it was difficult for a profession to have authority if some members of it, by reason of their sex, lacked authority. From its founding in the 1840s, the education department received complaints about female teachers who constituted a threat to qualified males wishing to elevate the position of the schoolmaster in society.[74]

In 1858 a school superintendent from Dundas County stated his belief that female teachers were constitutionally inferior. Few of them, he thought, possessed the 'mental ability and decision of character' that were so

essential to success in the schoolroom; it had been a great error to au-
thorize women to teach at all. His views were echoed by a teacher from
the neighbourhood of Gananoque, who in 1860 complained that, after
eighteen years in teaching, he was being replaced by women who
'could neither read distinctly, spell correctly, cipher accurately, or parse
systematically.'[75]

The complaints against women in teaching focused on two major problems. Critics argued first that, by nature or by training, women teachers
were incompetent, not only intellectually but also in the area of discipline.
They could not manage older pupils, especially the boys. Secondly, their
acceptance of low wages drove the wages down for everyone, sometimes
to the point of driving men out of the profession altogether. On the first
complaint, local superintendents reported variously that the attendance
of the male students dropped when a female teacher was employed, that
females were not competent to 'take charge' when the students were
'grown up young persons,' or that young men were simply ashamed to
be pupils of young women.[76] On the second there is ample evidence both
that women in teaching did accept low wages and that trustees employed
them in the first place at least partly because they did so.

But there were other influences at work as well. An examination of
manuscript census returns for seven Ontario counties in the third quarter
of the nineteenth century shows that, as the proportion of women teaching
common school increased in Upper Canada, the proportion of male teachers who were immigrants declined. Evidently the pool of immigrant men
– the 'old soldiers,' the teacher-farmers like John Tidey and William
Hutton, or the young men like Letitia Creighton Youmans's father who
had taught until he could afford to buy a farm – were either less available
or less in demand in the province's schools after mid-century. Education
department reports and census data also show that counties in the eastern
part of the province moved more swiftly to high proportions of women
teachers than those elsewhere. Most of these counties, the records indicate, were poor; their superintendents confirmed that poverty and a dis-
inclination on the part of the inhabitants to pay school taxes were responsible
for the decline in the number of men willing to teach in these regions.
As one reported in 1855, 'all the teachers in the township are young girls
under 18 years of age, as none other would teach for the salaries that the
trustees are able to pay them.' Young men in these regions were also
close to jobs in the lumber camps, which must have acted as a magnet
to pull them away from work in the schools.[77]

Fascinatingly, as far as the sex of teachers was concerned, the jurisdictions most closely resembling these sparsely settled and relatively poor
counties were the cities of Canada West. There too women quickly took

over the majority of common school teaching posts as school systems centralized and expanded and trustees recognized the savings that could be made by hiring a predominantly female teaching force. Urban school boards invoked the principle of an efficient division of labour: with a male principal in charge and a number of women assistants taking on the junior classes, two birds could be killed with one stone. Schools could be graded and the status of teachers (presumably the headmasters, particularly) could be improved; and at the same time, large numbers of pupils could be cheaply and efficiently accommodated. By the end of the 1850s, the Toronto public school system was neatly organized more or less along these lines. In 1851 there had been twelve male teachers and four female teachers in Toronto's common schools. By 1858, there were eight men on staff and twenty-seven women. There were evidently four girls' schools in the Toronto public system in 1858 and, as a result, there were also four headmistresses. But these women earned only $400 a year, compared to the $700 paid to the six headmasters, and most of the women on staff were earning less than half the amount paid to the men.[78]

The demand for female teachers gradually increased in Canada West. As an anonymous education critic pointed out in 1849, the promotion of education for girls supposed that there should be female teachers to teach them. This critic also suggested that married men should be engaged as teachers so that their wives could take care of the girls and youngest boys. Although few schools may have been able to achieve this kind of sexual segregation because of the costs involved, there is evidence that, during the middle years of the nineteenth century in Canada West, husbands and wives and even parents and children sometimes taught together in the common schools. Teaching thus continued to be regarded, at least by some, as a family occupation, as it had in earlier nineteenth-century schools.[79]

The education department at first gave only guarded encouragement to the training and engagement of female teachers. But women were quickly admitted to the Normal School, and the department in fact made a number of special concessions that may have favoured the general trend. Ryerson, for example, argued that restrictions on the employment of aliens as teachers need not apply to women – fascinating commentary on both the status of the woman teacher and of aliens. Evidently only alien (read American) schoolmasters were considered a political threat; women were essentially outside politics and not a danger. When the age of admission to the school was raised to eighteen for men, it remained at sixteen for women, a move with another ambigious message. Women were perhaps more mature than men at sixteen; equally, maturity in a woman teacher was less necessary if her role in teaching was to assist the men who were running the schools. There is also evidence that the Normal School gradually began to serve two radically different constituencies: schoolmasters who came from afar to upgrade their qualifications and tended to go back to rural counties to teach; and young urban women who, more typically, went on to take assistantships in city schools. With these young women in mind, perhaps, the Council of Public Instruction made a new rule in 1850 that, for first- and second-class certificates, aspiring female teachers were exempt from examination in a number of specified areas.[80]

Gradually the question of women in teaching began to be aired. Samuel Woods, a local superintendent who was interested in the question, set up an experiment in Kingston that he believed demonstrated that a good female teacher could do well not only with the youngest children but even with a class of eleven- to fourteen-year-old boys. Young women, Woods argued, were more able than men to catch 'the salient points in a boy's character.' and could induce him to apply himself 'with more diligence.' Boys tended to be chivalrous with female teachers and did not treat them with levity or contempt. Two years later, an education department correspondent noted that a great many men detested teaching, either because it paid so meanly or because they really saw it as a stepping-stone to something else. Women, on the other hand, did not 'look for anything above their present situations' and were therefore more contented in their work. Why, this writer went on, should women not bring the 'sweetness' of motherhood into the school? Perhaps the most typical approach to the subject, however, was that of George G. Magee in 1860, or of A. MacDonald Lockhart nearly a decade later. Examination and personal observation had proven to both of them that female teachers could teach as well as, or even better than, many males and – more to the point perhaps – 'at a saving of 50 percent.' Clearly, to school boards, a big advantage in hiring women was that by doing so they could get the same amount of 'education' for half the cost.'[81]

Such practical considerations seem a far cry from the lofty sentiments on the profession of teaching expressed by the schoolmen of the Ryerson era. For them the ideal teacher remained a respectable gentleman, a person who was settled rather than transient and, indeed, was probably married and had a household of his own. He was not too young or too old, commanded a decent salary, and saw to it that the housekeeping chores around the school were done by others with lower status than himself. He was not the slave either of interfering trustees or of doting parents. Only in the middle and late 1860s did official opinion and the opinion of correspondents to the education department begin to reflect the powerful imagery, common elsewhere on the continent and earlier put forward by Charles Duncombe, characterizing women as by nature destined for teaching, especially when it came to the youngest pupils.[82] For most of the crucial mid-century years of school reform in Upper Canada, the efforts of school officers focused, rather, on the campaign to elevate the status of men in the occupation.

The concern that was expressed about the growing numbers of women teachers may well have been related to the relative youth of women who taught compared to men. The manuscript census study referred to above shows that, as the teaching force feminized, the average age of teachers dropped. A shift also occurred in household status, for increasingly these teachers were young women living in the households of their parents or guardians, rather than the boarder teachers of the past. Indeed it may well be that the 'boarding around' so deplored by the school reformers of mid-century was chiefly a male phenomenon, which declined as more and more rural teachers tended to be young, unmarried women living in their own communities and therefore able to live at home.[83]

This was less true where urban teachers were concerned. Women who taught in cities, if four Toronto wards that have been studied are typical, were both older on the average and more likely to be heads of their own households or boarders than their rural counterparts. Indeed, within a few decades of the school laws of mid-century, women teachers were beginning to have what might be described as genuine careers in the province's common schools. Perhaps more often in urban centres than in the countryside, but also in rural schools as well, there were now women who worked in the state school system for much of their adult lives. The census studies show a shift towards youth and an unmarried status among both rural schoolmasters and schoolmistresses. Once again, urban schoolmasters tended to be older. In both country and town, schoolmasters were certainly far more likely to be married and heads of their own households than were the mistresses of schools.[84]

The class backgrounds of rural teachers are hard to assess from the census returns because the majority of teachers lived in farm households that are not differentiated on the personal census. But from the urban returns we can see that women teachers probably came from all levels of society, although rarely from either the very poor or the very rich. About one-half of the women recorded as teaching in four Toronto wards in 1861, 1871, and 1881, and who lived with parents or other relatives whose occupations were recorded, had a father or male relatives who were professionals or businessmen. The other half lived with relatives who were artisans or labourers. Many shared houses with widowed mothers. Since most of the male teachers were heads of their own households and were the only or the major breadwinners in their families, their social backgrounds cannot be so easily assessed. But it may be that the new hierarchies that were being forged in school teaching had class as well as age and gender dimensions. Men who became principals of schools, whatever their original backgrounds, may well have assumed that their new positions placed them in a social category above that of their female assistants whose fathers were in trades. When we add this to the fact that, by 1871 and 1881, more than half the men listed as teachers in the four Toronto wards were over thirty and married, their willingness to exercise power over the frequently young, unmarried women who taught in their schools – and the willingness of the latter to accept that authority – can be partly explained.[85] Of course it was the men who married and stayed in teaching, often to become principals, who fulfilled the school reformers' dream of a settled profession peopled by individuals who were not only respectable but mature.

Superannuation files, superintendents' records, and the minute books and reports of school boards show how far this ideal was from being generally realized, however. Two rural school sections in Oxford County, for example, recorded a constant turnover of teachers, with few staying longer than one or two years.[86] A study of five Upper Canadian townships between 1855 and 1870 reveals that each township employed, on the average, twelve to fifteen new teachers every year, a startling figure, since few townships had more than fifteen or twenty school sections and most sections employed only one teacher at a time. The only conclusion one can reach is that most sections were changing their teachers every year or two at the very least.[87] It is important to recognize, though, that the constant changing often reflected teacher movement rather than brief careers. Catherine Plantz taught in ten different schools and two different townships during her twenty-year teaching career in Dundas County. She started when she was fourteen and stopped in 1872 when she married, at the age of thirty-four. After twenty years in teaching, one supposes that she must have felt at least minor irritation that her wages compared so poorly with those of most male teachers. This was certainly the view of one woman teacher who complained to Egerton Ryerson about her low pay as early as 1849. Elizabeth Ann Inglis blamed male teachers and their poor opinion of women for the low status of women in the occupation. Some of the trustees who had employed her in the course of a ten-year career had admitted that she was a much better teacher than most of the men they had engaged. But her pay had never reflected this fact.[88]

Many of the aims of school reform were frustrated as the reality of teachers' lives unfolded in the decades that followed the passage of the mid-century school laws. The very elderly teachers may have been eased out but, especially in rural areas, teachers continued to seem too young.

Transient and unsuitable men were gradually being replaced, but their places were being taken by youthful female teachers. If Chatherine Plantz or Elizabeth Ann Inglis were typical, even women who stayed in teaching for any length of time tended to move from school to school.

The Normal School had a limited impact on this state of affairs. The diffusion effect was inevitably a slow one. As late as 1871 only slightly more than one of every ten Ontario teachers was a Normal School graduate, although the proportion was to increase dramatically during the following decade.[89] Normal School students, moreover, came disproportionately from the counties with large urban centres and especially from the region around Toronto and Toronto itself. Its graduates, especially the women, also tended to teach disproportionately in urban centres. If hierarchically organized school systems headed by Normal School-trained men and staffed by Normal School-trained women were the ultimate goal of school reform, it was in cities and towns that reformers came closest to realizing their ideal.[90]

Various programs were attempted with the aim of reaching teachers in rural schools. The school laws of 1843 and 1850 had proposed county and township model schools, but efforts to found such schools appear to have been largely frustrated. The teacher-institute campaign fizzled out; local teacher associations seemed too dangerous to encourage. Attempts to reduce the number of teachers holding third-class certificates also met with only limited success. The Normal School stopped granting such certificates in 1854, and teachers throughout the province in this category did drop from 34 per cent in 1854 to 6 per cent in 1870. But county boards of public instruction had to balance the desire to raise standards against the need for a supply of men and women willing and certified to teach school, and it is not clear to what extent this shift was meaningful. It is more than a little suspicious that it reversed itself in the next decade.[91]

The major shift regarding teachers in the mid-nineteenth century had less to do with their quality perhaps than with their quantity. Indeed, all the evidence suggests that the expansion of common schooling created a new kind of temporary work for very large numbers of people. An American study has shown that in Massachusetts during the period prior to the Civil War, one woman out of every four taught school at some point in her life[92] and there is every reason to believe that this situation was increasingly duplicated in Canada West. The reform and expansion of common schools also provided new kinds of relatively permanent work for a smaller but nevertheless important number of men and women as well. Indeed the most significant change affecting teachers in the Ryerson era may well have been the division of their occupation into two distinct classes. Victorian dualism was grafted onto the schools of Canada West as a world gradually emerged in which men governed as superintendents, trustees, and headmasters, while women served as assistant teachers. Not all the men were austere and bearded patriarchs; nor, it is clear, were all the women youthful or deferential servants of the system. But given the growing strength of these stereotypes, there must have been considerable discomfort for those who did not fit the mould.

Part Three:
Behind the Schoolroom Door

THE MEASURES PROMOTED by the education department to increase the efficiency of the common school system deserve close scrutiny. One must ask what effect they might have had on the behaviour of young people. After all, the dimensions of the social, economic, and cultural changes that took place over the course of the first eight or so decades of Ontario's history were staggering. By the mid-1870s even the back concessions of most southern townships had lost their pioneer look, while the cities and major towns had become more recognizable to someone who would know them in the mid-twentieth century than to their founding families. Beneath surface appearances, moreover, every aspect of living and believing had been altered. How did such a social transformation, over time, relate to the changing structure and control of schooling? That is a broad but obvious question; surprisingly, perhaps, little in the way of an adequate answer is at hand. There is much room for speculation and theories about how the way in which schooling was organized might affect the uses to which it was put. To ask a very elementary question, for example: was it a coincidence that the numbers of pupils registered at school increased as schoolhouses became healthier places to spend five or six hours a day? Which was the cart ... and which the horse?

One place to begin to answer the larger questions is to inquire about who went to school, for how long, and why. Basic though even these questions may sound, answers to them are not straightforward even for the period in which official statistics abound. By mid-century, Upper Canadians had come to believe in the merits of counting as implicitly as any of their contemporaries and, by contrast to the early colonial period, of counting there was plenty. Census takers now enumerated with increasing thoroughness the general population, the houses, industrial establishments, crop yields per acre, and other sundries; municipal assessors calculated property values; and various anonymous government functionaries recorded all manner of social and economic activities annually. Once average attendance became the basis for apportioning the school fund, the collecting of school attendance statistics became a major enterprise, adding children to the ranks of those special populations – criminals, lunatics, illiterates, and indigents, among others – whose numbers seemed somehow to reflect upon the health of society. The innumerable forms circulated by the education department involved thousands of teachers, school trustees, and local superintendents in the business of enumerating pupils by ages, classes, subjects taken, and days attended. In public debate the claims and counter-claims of champions and critics of the provincial school system were invariably buttressed by appeals to the latest set of statistics in the general belief that they represented some measure of the success or failure of school reform. Belatedly, historians have realized that, whether they are analysing developments in Britain, the eastern-seaboard American states, or the British North American colonies, much of that commentary as well as the numbers on which it was based must be treated with caution. Bias was endemic. Historian Richard Johnson's recent assessment of nineteenth-century British government reports on education – 'that they are full of middle-class people puzzling about the schooling of the children of the working class' – is nevertheless strikingly relevant to the quite different circumstances of the fledgling colonial society of Upper Canada.[1]

It is entirely possible that, given their preoccupation with the view from the centre of educational policy making, historians have exaggerated the impact of the provision of universal, tax-supported common schooling on the intellectual life of ordinary people. Much as it always had, the world beyond the schoolroom provided the experience, information, and mental stimulation from which the majority of the population learned and grew, intellectually. By the early decades of the nineteenth century traditional oral culture was being overshadowed rapidly by the medium of print. The wealth of children's literature, fiction, informed public discussion of politics and current events – to say nothing of a vast realm of 'useful knowledge' – was now no longer confined to the privileged few. Entrance to this new world, however, required the ability to read and write. As we have seen, according to the census takers, at least by the mid-century decades the vast majority of Upper Canadian parents, if not grandparents, were literate. The basic ability to read simple sentences and to write one's name (the commonly used indices of literacy during this period) was the minimum, of course. In the middle ranks of society, successful negotiation of the shifting ground of occupational and social identity demanded more and more skill: an ability to read in the sense of comprehend complex technical or intellectual materials and to communicate, not only in an elegant hand but in persuasive prose, the substance of one's thought. Indeed, with hindsight one appreciates how appropriate it was that his contemporaries among the Methodist clergy remembered Egerton Ryerson as a masterful and memorable writer as much as, if not more than, an inspiring preacher: Ryerson's career itself epitomizes the transition from oral to print culture.[2]

The relationship between literacy and occupational and social stratification in the past is very complex and as yet unclear; however there is little doubt that illiteracy was more and more likely to inhibit upward social mobility. In an oral culture an inability to read or to write is not a handicap, nor does either imply ignorance. Once print culture becomes dominant, however, the implication of ignorance is all too easily drawn. In Upper Canada after mid-century, social reformers were especially quick to associate illiteracy with poverty, dependency, and criminality, and to impute to the lowest stratum of the urban labouring population an 'ignorance' that was both secular and spiritual. Bourgeois caricatures of the poor – particularly migrants escaping the Irish famine – typically condemned their ignorance of self-restraint and self-discipline and their lack of a sense of duty and obedience to parental and civil authority and to God. More slowly, but eventually, the degree of functional deprivation that illiteracy entailed grew too, and the lack of reading and writing skills became one more of the handicaps borne by economically and socially marginalized individuals. While by the 1870s that process was far from complete, the level of literacy required to function effectively in Upper Canadian society had altered dramatically since the 1820s. As late as the 1860s there were still enough illiterate parents that various school officials, now keen to track down truants from free common schools, debated the merits of having tickets printed (in Toronto they read: 'Absent Half a Day') that parents would sign with a cross and give to their children to return to the school. But that was a diminishing problem, and rarely again before the turn of the twentieth century would there be sufficient illiterate parents to attract the serious attention of school administrators.[3] From the 1850s onward, access to schooling was a critical factor in patterning the *distribution* of *literacy skills*. However, the forces propelling the expansion of a literate society lay chiefly outside the school, primarily in the economy and in a flourishing popular culture.

Educators and moralists were concerned about the level of popular taste. Working people may have needed to be encouraged – cajoled even – to learn to read and write, but that in turn posed new problems: the moral consequences of literacy were so great that one could not take for granted the outcome of exposing children and adults to just any kind of printed material. Much official and legislative enthusiasm for establishing public-school libraries in the 1850s stemmed precisely from alarm at the public's perverse preference for 'trashy' novels over more elevating and instructive material. For all the thousands of volumes that would be shipped to local communities over the next decades, however, the market for pulp fiction and pictorial periodicals proved insatiable. Frankly sceptical of the education department's claims to have succeeded in establishing a truly popular public library system where the states of Ohio and New York had failed, a visiting British educator, the Reverend James Fraser, observed wryly at the close of his North American tour in 1863: 'That there should be a general desire for mental culture, or that the attractions of public libraries should be very strong, while elementary education continues to do so little to quicken literary tastes, is a thing not reasonably to be expected.'[4] More disturbing still, most of the periodicals and dime novels so avidly consumed by ordinary Upper Canadian readers were American. A London *Times* correspondent wrote indignantly of a train trip he took from Hamilton in 1861 when 'the people in the carriages were reading paltry pictorial papers which do so much to deprave the taste of the Americans.' Moreover the sides of the train were covered with advertisements from New York and Boston. Outraged, he concluded: 'not a smack of Canada, in book, or print, or journal, or trade, could be detected.[5]

Closing the border to the American press would not have solved the problem, even then. Local newspapers and printers had been catering to Upper Canadians' taste for sensational stories and gaudy details of low life since the 1820s in the form of lurid coverage of public executions and pamphlet publications of prisoners' deathbed confessions. Undoubtedly quite different ends were satisfied by crime reporting: it sold newspapers, it satisfied a quite ordinary attraction to the melodramatic and forbidden, and it may, by inversion, have provided a cautionary tale.[6] Certainly the latter possibility was not accidental. Throughout this colonial mid-Victorian society strenuous efforts were being made by authorities, public and familial, to inculcate by both precept and example very particular moral values. A new kind of Victorian dimension was being added to the long-standing division between the skilled and the rest of the working class. The 'respectable' working class would increasingly distinguish itself from the strata below by adopting a particular lifestyle marked less by skill or income than by a commitment to deferred gratification and self-discipline. The schools especially would attempt to harness the skills of literacy in support of the values of hard work, competitiveness, self-improvement, and sobriety. In this, their ability to reach families in very ordinary and humble circumstances was critical.

How to inculcate discipline – and how to maintain it – became a major preoccupation of Upper Canadian schoolteachers and administrators. In large measure, particulars of school architecture, down to the layout of the schoolyard, were designed to convey the visual effect of order and stability. Interior physical arrangements as well as the timetable of studies were intended to reinforce the message: the placing of benches in rows, the orderly arrangement of hats and coats on hooks, the precise timing of recess – all of it was to be capped by the ringing of the school bell to announce the beginning and end of the school day. In theory, in a well-regulated classroom no detail of the curriculum was too trifling a contribution to the overall celebration of obedience and self-restraint. Keeping discipline, in practice, was altogether a different matter. Sufficient accounts and memoirs of the rule of anarchy in rural one-room schools have survived to belie the reassuring prescriptions offered teachers in the columns of the *Journal of Education*. Education department regulations specifying that a teacher should 'practice such discipline in his school as would be exercised by a judicious parent in his family' were notably vague – in part, perhaps, because for some time prevailing notions of what were acceptable forms of parental discipline had been shifting as they were in respect of the public discipline of soldiers, sailors, convicts, and mental patients.[7] In general the harsher forms of corporal punishment were favoured less than efforts at moral suasion designed to internalize restraint. 'The scholars appear to sincerely love and respect their instructors,' boasted T.A. Ambridge, Esq., the forward-looking local superintendent in Hamilton in 1856; 'we certainly have ground to hope that those whom we can now restrain without the infliction of physical chastisement will grow up into a law-loving and law-abiding people, and that with them punishment will not be necessary to secure respect for wholesome laws and regulations.' All too often, regrettably, the parents of the child presented a major stumbling block to success. Either they failed 'to curb his headstrong passion' or they exercised discipline in 'a very injudicious manner,' with the result that 'the child is rendered all but ungovernable at school.'[8]

The incidence of 'all but ungovernable' school children cannot be calculated, but the evidence of the lecture notes taken by Maria Payne, a student at the Normal School in 1869, is teasing. There young men and women who would soon join the élite corps of teachers were, apparently, warned to avoid flogging, hair pulling, striking a child while angry or on the head ('those who are inclined to consumption may die from a blow on the head'); above all, they must not indulge in such 'cruel punishments' as 'tieing a pupil up by thumbs.'[9] Indeed, the exercise of discipline in mid-Victorian classrooms generated its own arcane vocabulary. Common verbs and nouns acquired fine nuances of meaning at which the late-twentieth-century historian can only guess. The distinctions between whipping / striking / flogging / strapping, one might suppose, connoted either the direction of the blow or its force. Rulers, rods, rawhide, and pointer (often but not always hickory) differed in their fabric and general shape or design.[10] The details of the incidents of severe punishment reported to the education department and in the local press vary markedly, but one particular appears as a constant, as prima-facie evidence of *excessive* punishment: the making of a mark. To make a charge against a teacher stick, one needed a witness. Often, in cases of damaged eyes or large purple welts the evidence did not evaporate quickly. But James Kincaid's father was taking no chances when he paraded his son in the streets of Brockville in April 1860 shortly after he had been strapped by his teacher. All done in 'unseeming haste,' the editor of the

Brockville Recorder commented rather stuffily, but when the charges against the teacher were heard by a full bench of magistrates, the vote to convict the teacher carried seven to six.[11]

The mere fact that incidents of allegedly brutal school discipline were frequently publicized after mid-century confirms the shift in attitudes as well as some 'softening' of the general practice. Much as educational officials had predicted, once the likelihood of a minimally competent teacher and a semblance of home discipline were secured, school discipline became less physical and more indirect. In urban schools especially, suspension for various lengths of time, and the shame and deprivation that that entailed, became popular, and the grounds for it were more finely delineated. An apology made not only to the aggrieved teacher but delivered in public before one's classmates or the whole school became part of the appointed ritual.[12] Should the student refuse to apologize – or, more drastic yet, should the parents support the youngster in his or her refusal – the consequences could be exceedingly grave. Certainly the town of Brantford was badly shaken after Henry Judson's father marched into the school to champion his refusal to apologize for impugning the impartiality of his Central School teacher in August 1859. The Board of School Trustees became embroiled in the matter; the local superintendent was placed in a humiliating position; the local newspaper concluded that 'a serious blow has been made against the best interests of our school': and eventually the Chief Superintendent was drawn into the affair. Ryerson, having taken care to establish that he had no authority to make a legally binding decision in the matter, proceeded to offer an unusually lengthy opinion. The issue was clearly one of *authority*, in his view. 'The teacher has to do, not with parents individually, but with the trustees who employ him,' he advised the principal of the Central School; 'if any parent wishes to see and converse with the teacher, he should do so out of school hours and not before the pupils of the school, where the teacher must be supreme, and be acknowledged as such until superceded.' The alternative was quite unacceptable: 'if every parent is to run to the school, and demand an account from the teacher' there could be neither order in the school nor respect for the teacher. In effect, the school enterprise would be undermined.[13]

Such a spirited defence of the authority of the teacher and of the necessity to contrive and maintain a distant relationship between school, family, and community would appear to Ontario parents and taxpayers living at any time in the twentieth century as quite unnecessary; by the turn of the century such notions were so taken for granted that few thought to challenge them. However, for almost half the nineteenth century, as we have seen, such ideas were virtually unthinkable. Then, once thought of, they remained largely unrealizable goals for far longer than the first generation of school administrators ever let on. Indeed, as one looks beyond the prescriptive literature of school reform one can find enough evidence to warrant revising – if not reversing – the classic complaint about parents' indifference to their children's schooling. As more and more parents, rural and urban, came to view their children's experience in school as time *spent* rather than as time *passed*, it appears that they became all too interested in what went on in school. Once parents took an interest, there was no telling what ideas they would have. In retirement Susan Goodbodey clearly remembered dealing with parents and still puzzled over how she 'got along without any particular training such as Teachers have now-a-days' in her first stint in a common school in the Rideau Lakes area in 1852. Whatever her gift, it stood her in good stead then and again in the late 1860s, when she took a school in Bastard Township where the parents 'were rather peculiar and wished that their children should have a good time in school and be allowed to chew gum during school hours.' In another school, a mile and half west of Mallorytown, she heard much the same line from parents 'rather anxious that their children should do as they pleased.' The fact that many of the parents had lived in the United States seemed to her to account for their 'very strange ideas about school discipline.'[14] There is no evidence of Yankee influence in ss 7, Oro Township, Simcoe County, in the early 1870s, nor was school discipline an issue; nevertheless the new schoolmaster, Neil Campbell, felt he had grasped something important about the limits of a teacher's discretion when he confided to his diary that 'it is impossible for the parents to detect whether you teach Geography right or not like as they can with some other branches, but you ought to from principle to teach Geography right.'[15] However, just teaching grammar *at all* to a twelve-year-old boy got the local Dunnville teacher, N.L. Holmes, into considerable difficulty in the fall of 1856. The issue arose, according to the Dunnville *Independent*, because the father, Mr H. Kellogg, a man of decided opinions, 'would not give the snap of his finger for all any boy will learn about grammar till he is at least 16 years of age because his mind is not sufficiently developed before he arrives at that age to really understand it.' The ensuing drama rivalled the Keystone Cops: father sends boy to school without grammar book; teacher sends boy home until he comes to school with the book; father sends boy back threatening to punish him if he studies grammar, whereupon the teacher hands the boy a grammar book with the injunction: 'I will whip you if you don't study grammar and tell your father that it is not for him to say what you are to study.'[16]

When parents and teachers clashed, the politics of the dispute could be surprisingly complex. A network of relations, neighbours, and any friends and kin of neighbours who might be incumbent local politicians, school trustees, or simply prospective office-holders often were enlisted on both sides. Teachers, especially relative newcomers to a community, were vulnerable but not necessarily helpless in the face of what many of them preferred to characterize as 'made up' or exaggerated stories. Certainly Mrs Rowland, a teacher at York Street school, was not easily cowed when a Mrs Kerr filed in Toronto Police Court a complaint against her for 'having cruelly beaten her little boy' in September 1871; she promptly filed a countercharge of abuse and assault on school premises against the mother.[17] Mr Spotten, headmaster of the city's Victoria Street school, was an able teacher but a stern disciplinarian, whose conduct more than once straddled the line of acceptability. In his case it remained to the indefatigable local superintendent to sort out the troublesome incidents and placate the parents.[18] In fact the diaries in which the Reverend James Porter dutifully recorded his daily professional routine from the first day of his appointment in 1858 to a few months before his untimely death in 1874 provide a remarkable glimpse behind the doors of the common schools in the largest urban centre in the province. On this evidence one can only conclude that a city of more than 40,000 in the 1860s could be a very intimate world indeed. As yet few lines clearly demarcated private from public concerns. Moreover the tentativeness of the notion of public institutional responsibility was mirrored in the absence of well-defined and acknowledged public space in the city. For all the education department might order the enclosure of the Normal School grounds, the fact remained that Toronto's citizens were slow to relinquish to any exclusive authority their proprietary interest in the streets, markets, gardens, or schools of the city.

Consider the events that led to the resignation of one of Toronto's common school teachers in 1865. Although the climax of the tale is extraordinary, the elements upon which the story hinges – the persistent muddle of authorities, official and unofficial; the pervasive lack of privacy; and the non-deferential attitude of parents towards the school – were undoubtedly replicated in communities and school sections across the province. Mrs Elizabeth Mitchell had been trained in England before she secured a second-class teaching certificate from the York County Board of Public Instruction and began working in the Toronto common schools in 1855. When the new local superintendent visited her boys' primary class at Louisa Street school on 12 April 1859, he noted that 'decision and thoroughness, tempered by kindness, are the characteristics of her teaching and discipline.' The first hint of a problem came to the Reverend James Porter's attention in mid-March 1863. Alderman Sproatt and Police Magistrate Boomer arrived to complain that Mrs Mitchell smelled of liquor and was abusing the children (including the alderman's grandson). The incident was resolved quickly and happily when the boy's mother explained that there had been a misunderstanding: she had called at the school only to find that Mrs Mitchell had a toothache for which she had taken laudanum. While her behaviour was unusual, the mother was sympathetic; her father-in-law, the alderman, had simply confused the story.

The next year, in June 1864, another allegation of excessive discipline on the part of Mrs Mitchell made the editorial page of the *Leader* under the inflammatory heading: 'Cruelty at Common School.' This time the local superintendent personally conducted an inquiry. Mr John Johannes of 127 Agnes Street, who had gone to the press with the story, accused Mrs Mitchell of injuring his stepson Ernest's heel. As reported in the press, she 'vented her anger on the unfortunate lad, by placing him across a wood-box and thrashing him on the feet with a cane.' Mrs Mitchell denied it. Mr Howarth, the druggist who had seen the boy's foot, was questioned, as were a handful of seven-year-olds who remembered seeing a barefoot Ernest being thrown from a pig he was trying to ride on Richmond Street. Other classmates, quizzed by the local superintendent in the presence of the headmaster of the school, thought that Ernest had been caned for talking a month previously. To this Mrs Mitchell countered that they were confusing Ernest (who was quiet) with his brother, Joseph, who was 'talkative, restless and often liable to discipline.' Mrs Mitchell was exonerated: the *Leader* published a letter from the local superintendent along with an apology for misrepresenting the case.

It might have been a long-standing problem, then, or just an isolated incident – dealing with one hundred little boys five days a week suddenly proved too stressful, or perhaps the hassles with parents, once one had acquired a certain reputation, were becoming more frequent: whatever the reason the facts were clear. At 3:15 p.m. on Friday, 11 February 1865, Elizabeth Mitchell fell off her chair in the schoolroom thoroughly drunk. Her husband was located in the city and came to take her home. Meanwhile the resources of the school system were mobilized so that hardly a beat was missed. An occasional teacher took over the primary class on Monday; by Friday Miss Hall had been transferred from Victoria Street school. The Reverend James Porter and the Reverend Dr Jennings, chairman of the York County Board of Public Instruction, agreed that rather than fire Mrs Mitchell it would be best if she surrendered her county board certificate. She did, and everything appeared to return to normal.[19]

One does wonder what 'normal' was, and the chapters that follow explore that question. The establishment of a provincial, publicly funded school system in Ontario was not an event, it was a process. Schooling took root in the Ontario landscape and mentality not overnight but over decades. The working out of the blueprint of school reform produced contradictions, compromises, and conflicts the consequences of which remain with us today.

7 *Going to School*

Egerton Ryerson was not far wrong when he foresaw that the establishment of a provincial school system would provide a valuable training ground in civic responsibility. The complexities of changing legislative requirements and administrative directives, the stream of inquiries for information that went back and forth between the education department and local school authorities, the disagreements over local assessments, school boundaries, and school sites that often set neighbour against neighbour – all these brought home to taxpayers and parents the realization that schooling was now public policy as well as a parental responsibility. At the heart of the enterprise, however, were the children, the school-aged population five to sixteen years old. Fears of one sort or another for their futures had encouraged support for taxation reform and the administrative restructuring of the common schools. Accessible and affordable, elementary instruction was now to be the right of every child; equally, it was soon to be the duty of every parent to ensure its acceptance. Replying bluntly to his critics, Ryerson boasted to W.H. Draper as early as 1846 of his goal 'to educate "all the brats" in every neighbourhood.'[1] For the next quarter century the numbers of children enrolled in school became a commonly accepted yardstick by which to measure the success or failure of school policy.

Ryerson was, above all else perhaps, a politician, and in one sense he could hardly lose by setting himself, and the provincial school system, such a standard. The situation in the late 1840s appeared sufficiently bleak that a measure of improvement seemed virtually inevitable. Nor was he mistaken. Trained teachers, permanent school buildings, authorized textbooks, and a longer school year would gradually become part of what it meant to be a 'school.' Over the next decades more and more youngsters of both sexes enrolled in school. Moreover, enrolment in voluntary schools grew infinitesimally; within the provincial school system as a whole, the common school bore the vast brunt of the growth. By the mid-1870s the experience of childhood had altered dramatically for the majority of Ontario's young people. 'Going to school,' at least until the age of thirteen or fourteen, was becoming a habit. Egerton Ryerson, the education department, and their champions would take credit for it all. But how and why this happened is a far from straightforward story and one that reveals much about the lives of children in mid-nineteenth-century Ontario.

I

Between 1850 and 1875 the proportion of children enrolled in the common schools of Ontario increased substantially in all the cities, towns, and country school sections of the province. In raw figures, the numbers of children five to sixteen years of age reported by local superintendents as registered in all common schools rose from 168,159 in 1851 to 451,568 in 1875. Taking the census years, (for which the data are most accurate) over the two decades from 1851 to 1871, the proportion of the school-aged population recorded as enrolled in schools increased from 61 to 86 per cent. To put it another way: over these two decades school enrolment grew by 165 per cent, while the provincial population as a whole increased by only 70 per cent, and the school-aged population by 89 per cent. In the interval, of course, Roman Catholic separate schools paralleling the 'public' common schools became more widely established within the provincial system; however, as late as 1871 separate school enrolment counted for less than 5 per cent of the overall provincial total. Although (on the admission of those submitting them to the education department) the enrolment figures for voluntary or private schools were unreliable, it is fair to conclude that numerically at least these students became an increasingly insignificant element in the overall pattern. The vast majority of children attended common schools, and these schools were in the countryside. For all the publicity accorded the sophisticated organization of schooling in the larger centres of Hamilton or Toronto, the reality for most boys and girls and their teachers was the one-room rural school. In 1871, 80.5 per cent attended rural or county schools; 4.7 per cent schools that were in villages; 8.4 per cent schools in towns. A mere 6.4 per cent were enrolled in schools in cities.[2]

Without belittling the very real growth in school enrolment it is important to note that total yearly registration figures, which the education department started to collect and publish annually from the mid-1840s, probably gave a misleading impression. The incidence of schooling before the 1850s is minimized as the gross registration figures for the period thereafter exaggerate the numerical size of the school population. The distortion need not have been deliberate, for all that it buttressed the arguments in favour of free schooling and provincial administration. Rather, it was a consequence of the statistics themselves. Prior to the 1840s, comparable figures simply did not exist. The basic sources for the calculation of school enrolment – the school superintendents' reports, school registers, and census data on school 'attendance' – came into being with any reliability only after 1850. The eclectic world of private instruction that played such a vital role in the earlier colonial period went happily unenumerated. Once the counting began, of course, it focused on the children enrolled in the government schools, and correspondingly less attention was paid to tracking down enrolments in private venture schools. Once the counting began, moreover, the category of registration included all those who enrolled at any point in the year in any common school. If the parents moved, as was very likely in the middle decades of the nineteenth century, and enrolled their children in a 'new ' school, the children would be counted twice. It was also true that a child who attended only one day, the day of his or her registration, counted on a par with the child who attended two hundred days in a row.

One would very much like to know whether the pace of school enrolment quickened after mid-century or whether it merely continued on an upward trend that might have been established as early as the 1830s. The latter course seems eminently plausible, given what we have seen of the evidence that parents, within the constraints of pioneer life, obviously made efforts and in many cases real sacrifices to ensure a modicum of schooling for their children. And, as we now know, in Massachusetts, where the experience of school reform closely paralleled Ontario's, the expansion of annual enrolments preceded substantial state intervention in schooling.[3]

There were two distinctive patterns of school enrolment, in fact: one primarily urban, the other rural; and these presented very different sets of problems for school reformers. The growth in urban school enrolment appeared truly dramatic. In 1851, when better than 61 per cent of the provincial school-aged population was registered in common schools, a mere 38 per cent of that age group was enrolled in the common schools in the major cities of Toronto, Hamilton, and Kingston. Thirty years later, in 1881, that urban percentage had leapt to 85 per cent, approximating the provincial average of 86.4 per cent. In the interval, enrolment in cities appeared to soar. At least two technical factors accounted for this exaggerated rate of growth. Enrolments in private schools had been higher in urban places at mid-century – understandably, for it was there that one could find the concentration of population essential to the support of private venture education. R.D. Gidney and W.P.J. Millar have estimated that, in the voluntary sector, enrolments of students aged five to twenty-one years averaged approximately 32 per cent of that age group in major centres in the early 1850s.[4] The great increase in common school enrolment was, at least in part, the result of a shift from private to public schooling. Nevertheless, in addition, many more youngsters did go to school. Closer attention to the city of Hamilton, the most exhaustively studied urban community in nineteenth-century Ontario, confirms this pattern.[5] In 1851, barely 40 per cent of the five- to sixteen-year olds in Hamilton were reported to the census taker as 'having attended school during the past year.'[6] Of the seven- to twelve-year-olds – the most likely to enrol in school – a slim majority (50.3 per cent) attended. By 1861 nearly 57 per cent of the school-aged population were recorded as attending, and the figure for the critical years (seven to twelve) had risen to 72 per cent. It was even more obvious by 1871 that a pattern of behaviour had been established: now 68 per cent of the school-aged population went to school some time during the course of the year, and over 85 per cent of the seven- to twelve-year-olds, the group that would be made the target of compulsory legislation that year.

Boys were, however, more likely to go to school than girls. Throughout the 1850s and 1860s boys held the lead in common school enrolments across Ontario, but the gap between the sexes was narrowing. The percentage of pupils registered who were girls grew from 43.6 per cent in 1850 to 47.3 per cent in 1871. The shift was even more evident in urban settings, where by 1871 virtually half the pupils enrolled were female. Although these gross figures seem to suggest that girls had achieved a measure of equality in educational opportunity by the 1870s, the reality was more complex. To enrol required only one visit to the school; to attend – to say nothing about attending regularly – entailed mobilizing family resources in quite deliberate ways. For both boys and girls the differences between enrolment and attendance would remain significant for at least another generation. For both sexes, too, family background and place of residence were crucial factors in simply initiating the experience of going to school.

Close studies of the widely different worlds of rural Peel County and the city of Hamilton in the 1850s and 1860s confirm the significance of both family size and the occupation of the 'head of the household' in the decision to enrol children in school.[7] In Peel, manuscript census returns demonstrate that the larger the number of children in a family the more likely those children were to be registered in a school in 1850, and that pattern continued through the next two decades. The occupation of the household head (as defined by the census) became less significant over time. In 1850 and again in 1860, census returns show the children of 'professionals, educators and highly skilled artisans' as more likely to attend school than the children of farm labourers or unskilled workers, presumably themselves among the less-educated classes of the population. By 1870, the gap produced by family educational background appears to have been reduced. By then, in Peel County, it appears that the children of unskilled and uneducated parents enrolled almost as frequently as did the children of professionals and skilled tradesmen. Yet, if social background was becoming a less important factor in general school enrolment, place of residence remained crucial throughout the 1850s and 1860s in Peel. The school-aged children of rural parents were far less likely to be enrolled than those living in the town of Brampton, where by 1870 nearly 90 per cent of youngsters five to sixteen spent some part of the year in school.[8] Within rural society, moreover, enrolments were less favourable in the newer or economically marginal townships, compared to the established front. In the larger urban communities, by 1870, social background had shifted its point of impact. No longer a dramatic impediment to enrolment *per se*, social class was now affecting the age of school children. In Hamilton, by 1870, seven- to twelve-year-olds from all economic and educational backgrounds were enrolled in school. But among older children social class made a significant difference: the teenaged children of labourers and unskilled workers were far less likely to be reported as attending school than their wealthier counterparts. Statistically, the impact of ethnic background and religion, both significant factors at mid-century, followed the pattern set by gender and class. As recent immigrants, Irish Roman Catholic children in Hamilton were noticeably less likely to attend school in the middle years of the century, but by 1870 they were less likely to stand apart. At least as far as children seven to twelve years of age were concerned, school had become part of growing up.

II

Not surprisingly, it was in the least-developed rural communities that schooling was the hardest to achieve. Geographical barriers to schooling could be almost insurmountable, and their effects were noted in both reports of the times and later memoirs, which invariably highlighted long walks to school, especially in winter. Parents and local trustees were anxious to negotiate a favourable situation for their own children, and evidence of their efforts remains in the endless battles over school locations and boundaries reported in the education department correspondence for the 1850s, 1860s, and 1870s. To the extent that a trustee was powerful or a parent controlled a choice bit of property that could be made available to the school, such individuals worked to see that locations were within easy walking distance of their homes. Many were the complaints of families who lost these battles and found that the school for which they paid taxes was on the opposite side of a swamp or across a river, making the attendance of their children virtually impossible. In the township of Grimsby in the Niagara District, a battle developed between farmers who had lately settled on the escarpment and the inhabitants of the village below, who objected when the farmers wanted to build a second school. William Beamer, explaining the farmers' point of view, expressed more than one concern. Not only were the children forced to walk two and a half miles to reach the village school; they had the additional 'labor of descending and ascending the mountain 350 feet each day,' on a road made dangerous by 'numerous heavily loaded trams that travelled it daily.'[9]

If it was difficult to agree on school locations when there was no school in place, the Grimsby incident suggests that it was even more problematic when it came to altering school boundaries or moving existing schools. Entrenched school trustees and satisfied parents had little desire to lose the school taxes, no matter how complaining or dissatisfied the schools' more distant customers. Even in the case of a school section notably endowed, problems could arise. Lot 19, Concession 1, Sidney Township, in the Loyalist community on the Bay of Quinte was designated a School Reserve in 1789. In time the possession of these 298 acres of land gave the residents of ss 2, Sidney, a considerable advantage over their neighbours, for the endowment ensured significantly lower school taxes. In 1870, for example, the trustees levied no school tax at all. The consequences were, however, unhappy. As early as the 1860s the inhabitants of the adjoining school sections petitioned the township council to dissolve their sections in order that they might share ss 2's good fortune. On at least two occasions the residents to the east and west packed the annual school meetings and imposed an unnecessary rate bill on the children attending the school. Ironically, although its boundaries extended the eleven miles from Belleville to Trenton, the 'privileged' Bayside School had a dismal attendance record: in 1870, fifty of the resident school-age population did not attend school *at all*.[10]

Patterns of settlement could create barriers to school attendance that were both geographical and cultural. In Alfred Township in the Ottawa Valley county of Prescott, British settlers located their farms on high land, carefully avoiding the swampy lowlands they believed were too difficult to cultivate. Later settlers from Quebec, accustomed to working marshy soil, took up the land that their predecessors had scorned. As late as 1871 neither French-speaking nor English-speaking families were heavily involved in schooling. But, as Chad Gaffield has argued, French Canadian children were less likely to be enrolled, in part because the schools were invariably located nearer the anglophone settlements on the hilltops.[11]

Many children and their families well may have avoided schools simply because they were gloomy and unhealthy places. Descriptions abound of low-roofed, unplastered log buildings that were poorly ventilated, dirty, and badly furnished. The 'first' schoolhouse, often of rude construction and dating from the 1830s, typically had fallen into disrepair by the 1850s. Edward Scarlett reported that the schools he visited in Northumberland County in 1856 were so badly furnished that the seats and desks caused 'much unnecessary pain to the pupils who are placed in them.' Indeed he suggested, rather melodramatically, that they might well have been the cause of 'many of those diseases which bring hundreds of youths to premature graves.'[12] In many rural places, sheer poverty explained such mean accommodation. In school districts where the settlers were poor, there were few taxes available: economic improvement led to school improvement. A report from George Murray of Princetown, Oxford County, drew the comparison between the early 1840s and 1857. Schools that had once been built of logs and attended by a modest handful of twenty or so scholars were now all of frame construction and boasted not only triple the number of pupils but authorized readers and Normal School trained teachers.[13] Critics not so sanguine as Murray often argued that it was less a question of economics than of priorities and that many communities put schooling last. John McLaughlin, reporting from Williamsburg, deplored those who placed 'the making and repairing of roads' above 'the making and repairing of minds' in Dundas County in the early 1860s. 'Such is the will of the people,' he concluded; and the people had it 'all their own way.'[14]

Discerning the 'will of the people' was not always easy. As elected officials, school trustees faced difficult judgments: when a compromise was not available only one of several competing constituencies could be pleased. The consequences, under school law, might involve trustees in litigation. That possibility, at least, was on the minds of messrs Weese, Orr, and Graham of Belleville, who inquired apprehensively of Egerton Ryerson in 1858 about judgments of the Court of Queen's Bench in cases relating to taxpayers who resisted compulsory assessment for school buildings. Obviously smarting from the protests of wealthy taxpayers, the trio complained that 'if the Trustees are to be dictated to by the inhabitants as to the specific amount it is impossible for them to build a schoolhouse. They are not representatives of their sections but mere tools to be used only when required.'[15] The political dilemmas faced by trustees did not engage the sympathy of the Chief Superintendent, at least not in public. Governed by 'misguided economy and meanness,' those responsible for school accommodation – both trustees and taxpayers – too often failed in their duty, he charged in 1866. It was not their inability to provide for the comforts of school children and their teachers, but their 'apathy and penuriousness' that stood in the way.[16] On the question of taxpayers' responsibilities, as on many other issues, Ryerson undoubtedly took great delight in pointing the finger at his political adversary, newspaper publisher George Brown. In the late 1850s, Ryerson revealed, Brown had acted the part of the typical absentee landlord, objecting to taxes on his farm properties earmarked for the erection of a brick schoolhouse in the neighbourhood of Bothwell. The tax, Brown had evidently complained to Ryerson, amounted to 'downright robbery.'[17] Beyond parsimony and ignorance stretched innumerable explanations for inadequate school conditions. Newly settled townships and struggling local economies faced more than their share of difficulties, no doubt; but into the 1870s seemingly long-settled areas endured deplorable conditions. Of the one hundred schoolhouses in Lennox and Addington that he visited in 1872, Frederick Burrowes reported seventy-six to be without privies, ninety-three without fenced-in playgrounds or schoolyards, and a scandalous number (twenty-four) of the buildings 'utterly unfit for school purposes.'[18]

Rural communities were not the only delinquents in the matter of school accommodation. Newly elected school trustees condemned the citizens of Port Hope for their negligence in 1850: the premises occupied by the schools were 'fitter to be used as sheds or stables for the lower animals, than as seminaries for the cultivation of the taste, the manners, and the minds of intelligent and rational beings.'[19] Things were not much better in Kingston – where children were reported to be 'packed in their seats as close as one's fingers' – or in London – where the school board had to instruct the janitor of the union school to keep cows, hogs, and geese from pasturing in the schoolyard.[20] Even Toronto schools were dreadful at mid-century. And, despite a much-publicized building campaign, they provided cause for complaint for the next quarter century. In the mid-1860s a number of working-class mothers in St John's Ward simply withdrew their children from Centre Street School, contending that the makeshift rental accommodation was unhealthy as well as inferior.[21] But the new brick schools in other neighbourhoods left much to be desired, too. Beyond the endless and inevitable repairs, inadequacies could prove politically embarrassing, as when the Board of Health was forced to reprimand the school board repeatedly for the poor state of the privies at Phoebe Street School early in 1864. Clearly, winter took its toll and time brought little dramatic improvement in facilities. After more than twenty

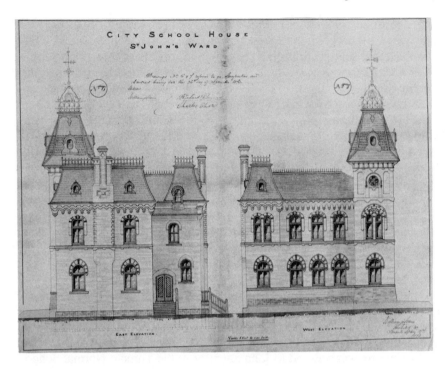

Plans for City School House, St John's Ward, Toronto

years of school 'improvement,' bitterly cold weather – as in the winter of 1873 – could still pose major problems. On 9 and 10 January the junior division boys at Parliament Street School were sent home because the classroom temperature had fallen below freezing, while the outside door of the girls' department at Park School was 'blown from its hinges;' Phoebe Street School had run out of firewood by 21 January; and on 24 February the temperature inside Parliament Street School was recorded at thirty-four degrees Fahrenheit. Most serious was the chronic over-crowding, which not even a massive building campaign in the 1870s could ease. By April 1869, the local superintendent feared that 'both teachers and pupils are exposed to physical injury from insufficient accommodation.'[22]

If such school conditions were often the cause of sickness, poor health itself was clearly a major factor affecting the school attendance of children in the middle decades of the century. A study of absenteeism conducted by the Toronto school board in 1863 revealed that, while 13 per cent of the school-age population not attending were too young or lived too far away from school, 8 percent stayed away because they were sick. [23] With hindsight it seems that one could only have been grateful that they did stay away. Minor epidemics were the scourge of nineteenth-century communities, and school children were effective carriers of infection. Scarlet fever was a particularly vicious killer: four boys and one girl attending Centre Street School had recently died from it, Toronto's local superintendent, James Porter, noted matter-of-factly in his diary for 17 October, 1864; in Hamilton eighty children, many of them 'pre-schoolers,' were killed in the epidemic that raged in 1870–1. Yet tactics for heading off an epidemic were problematical, on both medical and political grounds. In the case of compulsory vaccination against smallpox, the issue would only seem to be resolved, and then the question would be reopened, once again, well into the twentieth century.[24] Less serious than infectious diseases such as smallpox, scarlet fever, diphtheria, or whooping cough were the minor ailments that children brought to schools and that were sometimes the cause of their temporary, and unwilling, suspension. The 'itch' was one such well-known complaint; the common cold must surely have been another.[25]

There is no doubt that the relationship of schooling to health was an increasing preoccupation as notions of germ theory and contagion began to be accepted by medical practitioners and the general public. In 1872 a questionnaire originating with the Board of Health of the State of Massachusetts was referred to John Sangster of the Toronto Normal School because he was 'a Physician as well as an experienced Educationist' and might have a special claim to knowledge on the subject of 'school hygiene.' Sangster's reply was outspoken. While he felt that teenaged girls were most likely to suffer ill effects from school attendance, at least partly because they received less exercise than boys, no child was immune. Eyesight suffered from 'cross-lights in badly constructed rooms' while the 'over-excitement and abnormal positions incident to attendance at school' were the cause of ill health in early childhood. Sangster found fault with tasks assigned to pupils that were too long or too indefinite; even the modes of discipline commonly in use came in for criticism. His conclusion, however, stressed the poor physical condition of schools, which remained 'lamentably defective': systems of ventilation that looked good on paper had proven 'worthless'; heating systems, equally, showed room for 'indefinite improvement.' The list of problem areas yet to be tackled was both wide-ranging and lengthy:

The admission of light, the toning of paper for use in School Books, the arrangements for cleanliness both of School and Out-houses; the moral government and oversight of children in the Play Ground and Offices; the construction and arrangement of School Furniture. No prescribed positions while sitting, or stand-

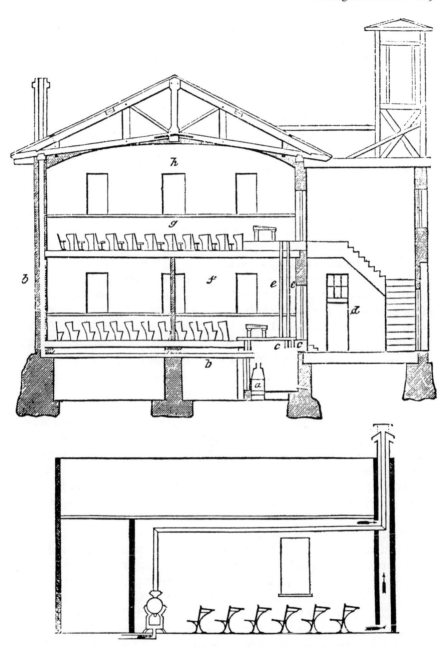

Proper ventilation and heating, according to the education-department-sponsored manual *The School House: Its Architecture, External and Internal Arrangements*

ing; the locality of the School and nature of its surroundings, the whole subject of School amusements, etcetera, are among the more obvious circumstances in regard to our Schools, which demand much more attention than they have heretofore received.[26]

As if the combined ill effects of dreadful school accommodation and endemic poor health were not enough, mid-nineteenth-century communities seeking educational improvement also contended with natural disasters. While at least one school was destroyed by a whirlwind in 1859,[27] by far the most common cause of school destruction was fire. Log or frame schoolhouses, heated by open fires, were incredibly vulnerable. The future provincial archaeologist, David Boyle, took his first school in a rural section just west of Elora, Wellington County, in January 1865. An impatient and idealistic twenty-three-year-old, Boyle was lucky: his poorly ventilated, 'dirty, badly furnished and ill-equipped' school burnt down the first year. The trustees saw fit to replace it with a stone building, now the largest school in the township, outfitted with new seats, desks, and maps to boot. Some communities were not as fortunate. The trustees of SS 1, Bagot Township, Renfrew County were reduced to desperation when fire destroyed the schoolhouse, furniture, apparatus, and 'nearly two thirds of a £20 library' in 1861: the community was exceedingly poor, dependent upon a depressed lumber market, and the fire was the last straw. Compensation from the Poor School Fund for £10 was far from sufficient to pay for a new building, whether in Bagot Township or elsewhere, and school sections that lost their schoolhouses as a result of fire typically went without a school for a period and let their teachers go without pay. The children, one supposes, made do somehow. Arson was sometimes suspected but seldom proved. Arson was endemic in certain parts of Lower Canada and clearly understood there as a form of mid-century protest against local school taxes and government intervention in education. In Upper Canada it was less often publicized or recognized for the resistance it might well have represented.[28]

Two decades after the passage of the 1850 school act, progress in the matter of school accommodation seemed to most professional educators to have been depressingly slow. The education department had done its best, printing plans for improved accommodation in issue after issue of the *Journal of Education* and promoting a copiously illustrated volume entitled *The School House*, written by J. George Hodgins and published in the late 1850s. By 1869, certain concrete improvements had occurred, and these improvements could be counted. The provincial *Annual Report* for that year specified that of the 169 new schoolhouses built in the counties during the past year, 74 were of brick or stone construction and

67 were frame, leaving only 28 constructed of logs. However, of all the schools in the province – now 4,553 – only 1,242 or 27 per cent were made of brick or stone; 1,817 (40 per cent) of the school sections remained satisfied with frame schoolhouses; while 1,469 (32 per cent) still used houses made of logs.[29] In the same year, at the Teachers' Association's ninth annual convention, poor accommodation and its effects on school children came in for an extended attack. A Mr King, one of the keynote speakers, deplored not only the fact that schools were wretched but that so many of their pupils were so very young. He characterized, as typical of urban schools, classes of between 75 and 130 children in which not more than a dozen were older than seven years of age and two-fifths of whom were under six. He pictured them 'huddled together on long benches, in too many cases so high that the children's feet do not touch the floor.' The certain result, he believed, was 'curvature of the bones,' not to mention 'compression of the vital organs.' Confined too long and prevented from breathing pure air, such children were surely affected adversely rather than positively by attending school.[30]

It is hard to know to what extent school promoters were aware of the irony of their position. Not only were children attending school in rapidly growing numbers, as school supporters had urged and, indeed, materially encouraged by tying school-fund apportionments to average attendance figures, but they were evidently moving into schools at rates that far exceeded the capacity of school boards to accommodate them. Through the 1850s and 1860s the school boards built schoolhouses, but especially in villages, towns, and cities the schools continued to be appallingly overcrowded. Whenever the moment came, the arrival of the new schoolhouse often seemed miraculous, for the contrast was so sharp. Australia McBrien, a British army veteran who qualified as a teacher in the mid-1860s, could well remember the old school in ss 1 Cartwright Township, Durham County, as it was when he arrived in 1869. The old log building had a seating capacity of thirty, but by then there were 136 youngsters on the roll and the average daily attendance ranged from 70 to 100 students. Fifteen to 20 of the most junior pupils were routinely sent outside to play – on the road – to make room for the 50 or 60 who were packed together inside. The new frame replacement, erected in 1870, seemed positively palatial. With dimensions forty by twenty-eight by nine feet, the new schoolhouse could accommodate between 70 and 90 pupils 'comfortably' at the new two-seater desks. His excitement scarcely dimmed by a quarter century, in 1896 McBrien detailed the transformation:

There were a Teacher's Desk, a class Platform, a Cupboard for a School Library, which was afterwards well supplied with Books which were lent out to the Pupils once a week. There were Blackboards, Maps of the World, the continents and British Isles; as well as [a] Zoological Map, showing the two grand divisions of the Animal Kingdom with their subdivisions into Classes and Sub-classes.[31]

Not surprisingly, teachers were among the first to complain, publicly, about overcrowding, for they were among those most immediately affected. In 1858 in a letter to the *Globe*, 'A Female Teacher' joined the current public debate over the problem of juvenile vagrancy in the city of Toronto. Too many idle youngsters seemed to be lounging on the street corners. Two solutions had been proposed: enrol greater numbers of the children of the poorest classes in school, and encourage regularity in the attendance of those already on the rolls. More children in the school would spell disaster, this informant warned. In the junior division each teacher already had a minimum of one hundred pupils: under the circumstances she (for the junior division teacher in Toronto was invariably female) could only be delighted when some of her pupils stayed away. Editorial sympathies were less with overworked teachers than with the parents and the taxpayers: the former sought decent schooling for their children and the latter the proper expenditure of their money. It was deplorable, the *Globe* argued, that Toronto teachers should 'take no interest in securing regularity' of attendance, that they felt 'relieved from a burden by non-attendance,' and made no attempt to stop it. Moreover only some schools were overcrowded; other, less popular ones, the *Globe* charged, stood 'half-empty.' Parents knew what they wanted, in other words. They voted with their children's feet and sent them, often in overpowering numbers, to the schools they thought were the best.[32]

As Toronto's anonymous female teacher pointed out, the problem was concentrated in the junior levels. By 1871, when statistics on age first began to be gathered systematically, the province as a whole reported that 47 per cent of school attenders were in the five to ten age group; but in cities the percentage was much higher. Only 40 per cent of the children were over ten years of age in urban schools. Unfortunately education department statistics did not distinguish more minutely the grouping of the five to ten year-olds; however other evidence confirms the 1858 *Globe* correspondent's view. The junior divisions throughout the Ryerson period always were far larger than the senior ones and were likely to remain so. Analysis of the manuscript census for Hamilton reveals, for example, that the proportion of the city's five- and six-year-olds enrolled doubled between 1851 and 1871, increasing from about one-quarter to more than half of all the children in that age group.[33]

City superintendents expressed concern about the effect of schooling on very young children. It was all very well in rural schools, London's

J.B. Boyle commented in 1865; there, the schools might well be emptied in the summer-time if very small children were barred from coming. But in city schools, their attendance was inappropriate. Parents were using the schools to babysit their children. 'In the summer months, children evidently under the legal age are sent to school not to learn, but to be out of the way of the family, and teacher has no recourse but to accept the statement that the child is just "five".' The problem, Boyle felt, was that such children could learn nothing at school and, worse still, confining them in classrooms was simply bad for them. Toronto's superintendent, James Porter, echoed Boyle's sentiments in 1868. Large city schools were not suited for very young children, who needed more space, shorter hours, and a different kind of teaching.[34].

Porter knew whereof he spoke, for Toronto faced a crisis. Serious overcrowding had prompted the addition of a second ten-minute recess, morning and afternoon, for the children in the junior division in 1865. By the summer of 1869 the board had been forced to resort to more drastic measures: a half-day system. Quite simply, junior division classes had become a travesty. Teachers could not attend to all the students at once, and the youngest ones when left on their own either got into trouble or, 'often overcome with weariness,' slept. In defence of this temporary expedient, Porter argued confidently that

when the numbers and the work are dealt with on the half-day system, the pupils are comparatively fresh and active, the interruptions necessary for the preservation of order and discipline are much less frequent, children do not acquire the habit of apparently enforced vacancy of mind, or that of mere mischievous activity: school is, in a word, a reality and not a pretence; a place for profitable employment and not one, to a great extent, of mere confinement.

Soothing explanations could not contain the storm of public protest, however. Too many parents had grown accustomed to sending their children to school all day. Dutifully reporting the litany of parental objections that forced a swift ending to the half-day scheme, Porter noted that 'some have said that they send their children "to keep them out of the way"; and a few have added that "they care not what they learn, if they are only kept off the street".' Even more sobering, perhaps, was the suggestion that some parents were quite prepared to call the school to account for raising expectations, as they charged 'that it is impossible that children can learn as much in half a day as they can in a whole day, and therefore the half-day system must be regarded as depriving the children of one-half of their time and opportunity for improvement.'[35]

The issue came to a head in 1869 at the Teachers' Association's annual meeting in Toronto. Mr King once again went to the heart of the matter, charging that children under six years of age did not belong in schools, which affected them adversely. Estimating that of 400,000 pupils of all ages in Ontario's public schools one-tenth were under the age of six years and calculating a pupil-teacher ratio of eighty to one, King demonstrated that 40,000 small children would require the attention of 500 teachers, plus classrooms and furnishings, at an estimated cost of $400 per teacher. The consequences of pursuing a policy of encouraging five-year-olds were all too clear: $200,000 wasted annually in the schooling of children too young to benefit from it, as well as '40,000 immature minds' annually added to those who had already been subjected to the 'dwarfing, stunting influence' of premature schooling.[36]

III

King's calculations were, in part, a rhetorical flourish and served (as no doubt he had intended) to stimulate an earnest discussion among those present. In effect, the idealists were ranged against the pragmatists. Not surprisingly, Ryerson's lieutenant, John George Hodgins, proposed better schools, more facilities, and an enlightened pedagogy drawn from the English infant school movement, all the while predicting that teachers in cities and larger towns would have 'a very bitter task before them' if youngsters of four to seven years were allowed to roam the streets and acquire their own education. For others, the obvious reality of long hours in a stuffy environment, so patently inappropriate for younger children, carried the argument. Rarely were the very different circumstances of urban and rural schools so sharply etched by an issue. Pressure to accommodate the youngest children and to secure their regular attendance created an extra burden for urban school superintendents as well as urban taxpayers; however, the alternative – raising the school age – would decimate the rural school population. One rural spokesman described the situation succinctly: 'when a Farmer's child comes to nine years of age, he becomes worth money, and is put to work; so that, if they were kept out of school till they were seven, two years would be all the education they would receive.'[37]

Pleas for special recognition of the circumstances of rural farm children were no novelty by 1869. In draft legislation in the late 1840s Ryerson had extended the upper age limit of the right to attend school from sixteen to twenty-one years precisely with the farmers' sons in mind. 'It is justly said,' he recognized,

that if a farmer does not teach his sons to work on the farm before they are sixteen years of age, they will become averse to work, and never make good farmers. But children cannot acquire a proper education before they are sixteen years of age without constant attendance at school. There is also comparatively little for many farmers' sons to do in winter, especially since the introduction of threshing and other labour-saving machines; so that not a few farmers' sons get the greater part of their education by going to school in winter after they are sixteen years of age.[38]

'Not a few farmers' sons' would prove a serious understatement: until the 1870s the practice of balancing work and school (and its consequence, irregular attendance) remained the most striking feature of rural schooling. On this point at least the evidence appears unequivocal. As late as 1872 a solid majority (61 per cent) of youngsters enrolled in the rural schools of the province attended for fewer than one hundred days. While, as we have seen, material obstacles undoubtedly contributed to low enrolment and even lower attendance rates in poorer districts and newer settlements, even in mature counties such as Peel, as late as 1870 a minority of the school-aged children attended for more than half the school year. [39] Significantly, however, irregular attendance was not an aberration of rural society: it persisted throughout the provincial school system, as basic a feature of nineteenth-century schooling as the more common images of one-room schoolhouses, two-seater desks, and brass hand bells. Nor should we be surprised, for the business of 'going to school' and especially of arriving 'on time' – the teacher's time – was only one of a child's many responsibilities, and a recent one at that.

As the discussion of early colonial schooling indicates, childhood in most families was a time cluttered with chores, of helping in innumerable ways to get the family through the day. That reality was not changed by school legislation. In one sense, irregularity of attendance was the price mid-nineteenth-century educators had to pay for their astonishing feat of enrolling most of the province's children in school. For all its improvement, over the next decades the common school continued to have to compete for a child's presence and attention. Enrolling in school was the first step; attending frequently depended on whether or not the child was needed elsewhere. Marginal poverty and economic insecurity dominated the lives of the majority of nineteenth-century families, who struggled, by various means and degrees, to make ends meet at the best of times: periodic trade depressions, crop failures, and other vagaries of the economic cycle simply compounded their intractable vulnerability. Undoubtedly, economic necessities – or as Ian Davey so aptly phrased it, the irregular rhythms of work – dictated in large measure the rhythm of school attendance.

Understandably, the needs of farmers and their sons appeared obvious at a time when agriculture was the mainstay of the provincial economy and occupied more labour than any other sector. As the rhythms of rural life and labour were not random, neither was rural school attendance. In general it was intricately patterned by considerations of age, sex, and season. The feature Ryerson identified – of older boys plodding slowly through their primary lessons, a winter at a time – was especially true of the 1850s and 1860s. As had been the case earlier in rural New England, so in Ontario older boys typically attended in the winter, girls and younger boys in the summer. While obviously the practice lingered longer in some communities than in others, age-specific statistics province-wide after 1871 show that well into the mid 1870s a significantly larger proportion of older students (sixteen years and above) were enrolled in rural or county schools than in city schools.[40]

All farm families relied, as many do today, on their children's labour: the boys helped with the farm chores, the girls with the garden, dairy, and poultry-yard as well as the housekeeping. Once local schools were established, the extent to which that tradition affected school attendance varied; no single explanation can account for the myriad of individual family decisions. However, prosperity undoubtedly encouraged attendance. As previously noted, large families enrolled more of their children in school, as did families of certain ethnic backgrounds. Whether these children attended more regularly is less clear – and precisely what family size has to do with it remains a matter of speculation.[41] On the other hand, one can readily appreciate the impact of a chronic shortage of skilled farm labour and the high price exacted for what was available; a farmer's children were indeed worth money, and in marginal agricultural settlements, opportunities for supplementary wage labour in lumbering or other industries only accentuated the pattern.

Much depended on the local economy. While increased length of settlement worked in favour of school attendance, time alone could not entirely obliterate the handicaps of poor soil or inadequate drainage. As far as regular school attendance was concerned, a second string to one's economic bow could prove a mixed blessing, as the old loyalist settlement of Charlotteville Township, Norfolk County, discovered in the 1860s. The sandy soil, ideal for tobacco in the twentieth century, was then marginal for wheat. In 1860 a disastrous frost wiped out the harvest, but extensive lumbering operations by mid-decade made unusual (and one assumes irresistible) demands upon the time of older male scholars, much to the dismay of the local superintendent.[42] Where lumbering traditionally dominated, the situation was equally unstable. Settlements on the fringe of the agricultural heartland, especially in the Ottawa Valley, were caught up in the volatile lumbering market with few buffers against the vagaries of export demand. In Westmeath Township, Russell County, in 1863, a depression affecting the lumber trade compounded the problems of drought and insects and set in train a local economic crisis that was quickly mirrored in the children's attendance at school. Along the Ottawa River, as in the Bruce Peninsula, Simcoe County, and Muskoka and Haliburton, families on the commercial frontier struggled to combine homesteading with wage labour in the woods and sawmills. In such circumstances, domestic needs were paramount: attending school came a very distant second.[43]

More commonplace than the drama of crop failures or downward trade cycles were the ritual labours of the agricultural season. Each crop and harvest made its own demands. In Essex County, for example, the main crop was Indian corn. A dearth of affordable hired labour meant that most boys twelve years and over worked in the fields from early April to December. Virtually all their schooling was crammed into the months of January to April. As the local superintendent observed wearily, 'their three months' attendance is at an end before they have been brought to habits of order and subordination or of effective study.' In Perth County, on the other hand, farm labour was plentiful in the 1860s, and the families of both labourers and farmers filled the school to overflowing – until the sugar making commenced. Then both young men and girls abandoned the school, their places to be taken by children scarcely five years of age who 'were packed off to school to be out of the way.'[44] Sometimes even the toddlers proved useful. Long-time superintendent J.A. Murdock described a typical scene in the rural settlements of Bathurst Township, Lanark County: 'at certain seasons every child capable of lending even the most trifling assistance to its parents is kept at home. I have often observed very small children stationed at harvest time at a gap in a fence, as sentinels to keep out stray animals from trespassing, while taking in their grain.'[45]

By contrast to the widely accepted need for rural children to contribute to the family economy – to help 'at the times of hay, wheat, oat, apple and potato harvest' and more – in the villages, towns, and cities family demands that competed with school time seemed far less legitimate. Working-class parents of absent children were periodically assailed by charges of criminal neglect and indifference levelled by school trustees, superintendents, and school supporters generally. Not surprisingly, these public remonstrances were to little avail, as the pressures on these children to contribute their time or pittance earnings when the family was in straitened circumstances were as irresistible as they were in rural communities. Unlike the countryside, however, the rhythm of absenteeism in towns and cities was less predictable, for the probable range of family calamities, from death and illness to eviction and loss of job, followed no fixed seasonal timetable. One suspects that what appeared increasingly subversive to urban educators and school reformers appeared quite straightforward to a child. You helped at home when necessary; you went to school when you could. On most days you did both, but sometimes, for shorter or longer periods, you gave up going to school.

Particularly after the age of eleven or twelve, there might be quite a lot of 'toing and froing': for boys, some opportunities for earning wages; for girls, more likely occasions for being of help with younger siblings. But the school was there to come back to, tomorrow or next month, when the crisis had passed, the weather had turned, or the temporary job was over.

To city school officials and the education department, increasingly refined statistics of daily and monthly average attendance revealed widespread chronic irregularity in attendance: to many working-class families there was obviously no need – indeed, perhaps there was a reluctance – to make a clean break between school and work. The exigencies of working-class family life ran counter to nineteenth-century educators' instincts for punctuality, regularity, and permanence. Unprotected in the wage labour market and especially vulnerable when, inevitably, some personal setback occurred, the families of labourers, semi-skilled, and skilled workers were periodically buffeted by something newspaper editors liked to call ''the pressure of the times' – a euphemism for 'things are worse than usual.' Changing jobs and moving one's residence within the same neighbourhood or community were commonplace strategies. Some jobs, particularly massive public-works projects such as canal or railroad building, could mean almost perpetual motion even in the best of times – and little in the way of schooling for one's children. As the railroad children of Goderich discovered in 1857, the school did not want you if your parents were not ratepayers.[46] If, to this definable 'world in motion,' one adds the massive amount of 'moving on' that historians have concluded was endemic to nineteenth-century Canadian society, one begins to share something of the schoolteacher's frustration. Children could be here today and gone tomorrow. For all that mid-century cities were built to the relatively intimate scale of a walking city, neighbourhoods were frequently anonymous places. The Toronto school board's first truant officer discovered just how anonymous when, occasionally, on his daily rounds to the households of school children reported absent without explanation, he had difficulty in finding someone – a neighbour, anyone – who would admit to knowing the family in question. Ten-year-old William Burroughs of Bathurst Street school nearly got away with his minor escapade in 1873 when Truant Officer W.C. Wilkinson found a complete stranger at 192 Bathurst Street, the school's address for Burroughs. After fruitless inquiries among the neighbours, Wilkinson gave up; but a week later he returned to the dogged pursuit of young William and finally located the family at number 210 Bathurst – a short block away. Now it is entirely possible that the neighbours knew of the move but that none would 'fess up' to a truant officer. Perhaps Mr Falaherty [sic] at number 192 was in on the false chase; but on the other hand, after living there for what seemed to him 'some time past,' he might honestly never have heard of the Burroughs family. Various interpretations are plausible, but the incontestable truth of the matter – that the Burroughs family had moved a short block and thereby confounded the school authorities – could well have been repeated literally hundreds of times in the cities, if less often in the towns of Ontario in the 1860s and 1870s.[47]

Working-class mobility (especially in the cities) was more rational than random, for all that it burdened school officials with temporarily mislaid children, inaccurate school registers, and the endless paperwork of official transfers. Toronto provides the example, but the experience was shared widely by all working people who needed to live near their jobs. 'Pressure of the times' could build equally from inflation or depression. By 1854, for example, the provincial economy was badly overheated; breakneck investment in railroads and municipal public works fed high inflation. Rents in the centre of Toronto rose sharply, and increasing numbers of parents 'employed their children at home in assisting in maintaining the family,' quite to the embarrassment of the school trustees, who were in the first phase of opening six costly, new, permanent school buildings. By 1859, the economic situation was reversed: in the midst of a staggeringly deep, continent-wide depression that was to bankrupt more than one municipal corporation, property values in the centre of Toronto fell sharply. The impact on school attendance was immediate, and not unlike 1854: only the direction of the population flow had changed. Working-class families could now afford to vacate the relatively unhealthy and inconvenient eastern extremity along the Don River for a more central location. As well, employment opportunities with the railroad at the opposite end of town drew population south-west.[48]

'Pressure of the times' meant not just family mobility, of course; it also meant that children needed to work: to help their families with a market garden, perhaps, or to get a real, if temporary, job. In 1866, the damage to school attendance caused by the economic dislocations of the American Civil War and the ensuing threat of a Fenian invasion were sufficiently severe that the local superintendent in Toronto canvassed the headmasters of the various city schools for their opinion on the dramatic decline. As many as 120 youngsters had left one school alone. From the answers one can see that the cost of living had taken its toll directly among the oldest pupils: many more than usual were leaving at an earlier age (approximately twelve years) to help support their families; in cases where mothers were compelled to work, girls were staying home to look after younger members of the family. Many families could spare neither their children's time nor the cost of the shoes, clothes, and books necessary for attending school.[49]

While the presence of families chronically unwilling or unable to send their children to school adequately dressed or reasonably groomed surfaced as a major public issue in the 1860s and fuelled the campaign for compulsory school attendance, for many more families the 'pressures' receded and the crisis passed. Families moved on, neighbours and kinfolk helped to tide one over; in time more children grew old enough to leave school permanently. When *exactly* that final school leaving occurred depended substantially on the availability of a job – particularly one with some longevity if not future prospects.[50] At mid-century, job prospects were bleak. Unlike Britain in the early decades of the nineteenth century, Ontario had very few large-scale employers of workers younger than thirteen or fourteen years of age. For boys in towns and commercial cities in the 1850s and 1860s there were too few jobs, and too often those that did exist – messenger boys, delivery boys, newsboys, shopkeepers' helpers, and stock boys – were deceptive 'dead-end' jobs from which one often had to retire at eighteen or twenty years of age. Girls by their mid-teens might be tempted by the insatiable market for domestic help. But the work was not easy, nor was the prospect all that secure. In some families – most notably Irish Catholic families in towns and cities in the decades following the massive Irish famine migrations of the late 1840s – sending teenage daughters into service was a tradition. Increasingly, for girls who could postpone leaving school and leaving home, a little more education could open up opportunites for genteel employment as underpaid shop assistants or equally underpaid school teachers. For the less fortunate, sweatshops began to exploit a growing number of young seamstresses who apparently preferred almost anything to the stifling discipline of domestic service.[51]

Until the 1870s factory jobs for young people in Ontario were very limited and concentrated in tobacco, boot and shoe, and cotton and woollen manufacturing, all highly localized industries. Tobacco manufacturing, for example, expanded dramatically during the American Civil War, with new plants opening in Hamilton, Windsor, and Toronto. When, almost overnight in 1862, the number of firms in Toronto jumped from one to five, the public schools felt the immediate impact as youngsters left school in mid-term to take the jobs.[52] Even without mechanized factories, however, there were often jobs, of a sort. Throughout the 1860s and 1870s the extension of railways and commercial development and the proliferation of small local industries, sawmills, foundries, and the like altered the occupational structures of many towns and villages across south-central and eastern Ontario. By 1871 villages such as Brampton, Orillia, Gananoque, and Hawkesbury were already very different worlds from the rural communities that surrounded them.[53] Invariably school attendance was affected. At Hespeler, the mills caused official confusion by periodically taking children 'of all sizes and age.' According to the local superintendent, boys and girls basically stayed out of school or went to it 'according as their assistance is required or not at the factories.' In the village of Elora in the 1860s, on the other hand, youngsters thirteen years and older from poorer families were the ones tempted to leave school more or less permanently (*more*, it seems, rather than *less*, as few attended the special night school classes offered them).[54]

Depending upon the job one left school to take, of course, thirteen was not an exceptional age at which to leave school permanently. The Provincial Board of Arts and Manufactures estimated in 1866 that 'as a usual practice, boys intending to follow mechanical pursuits, commence the terms of apprenticeship or service at from 12 to 14 years of age.' Exactly what the board envisaged as 'apprenticeship or service' is difficult to assess. The term 'apprenticeship' retained little of its classic connotation by the middle of the nineteenth century. Chronic shortages of skilled labour in British North America had long since made inroads on the formal notion of seven years of service and training. Employers were used to taking boys for two or three years and apparently – so labour spokesmen alleged – some youngsters came and went without learning anything.[55] Generalizations are difficult to draw, since what we see of the social landscape of mid-century Ontario is such a patchwork of competing cultural values and traditions, of local communities of various sizes with varied economies. In the broadest terms the evidence suggests that, materially, the circumstances of youngsters improved: better roads led to better schoolhouses; by hard work and good luck immigrant families 'prospered,' if only in the sense that they 'settled in.' If one lived in a village, town, or city there was more time than on the farm to go to school and fewer alternatives to staying there. However, when 'something better' came along as it did by the late 1860s when the economy moved significantly into the industrial era, the opportunity to leave school for paid employment could seem an opportunity not to be missed. Of course, 'opportunity' came in different guises to boys and to girls and sooner in the lives of working-class youngsters than in those of their more affluent peers. However one point stands out clearly: the timing of leaving school depended on the availability of employment as much as, if not more than, on the necessity to seek it.

The expansion of mechanized production in manufacturing as well as an enlarging commercial sector created employment in the late 1860s and early 1870s for older boys who, a decade or more earlier, might well have been idle and unemployed. The new era of industrial production was most dramatically experienced in Hamilton, where the Great Western Railway shops of the late 1850s proved to be harbingers of extensive industrialization in the late 1860s and 1870s. By 1871 53 per cent of Hamilton's manufacturing work-force laboured in plants with fifty or more employees – a staggeringly different work world than that of the skilled master craftsman and his journeyman assistant. The rapid expansion of the industrial work-force signalled a sharp increase in the proportion of young males between the ages of thirteen and sixteen living at home who were employed. In many working-class families in 1871 teenage boys were significantly less likely to go to school than a decade earlier. While twenty years before more than half of these lads were neither employed nor attending school, and only a small fraction (15 per cent) were employed, by 1871 only a quarter of their number were 'unoccupied' while over 31 per cent had designated jobs. Of all sixteen-year-old males in Hamilton in 1871, two-thirds were employed.

The industrializing economy in Hamilton not only increased employment among young men but also provided new kinds of jobs in the dynamic sectors of the economy at the expense of such older occupations as shoemaking and tailoring, which were being adversely affected by the introduction of machinery. For young women, by contrast, industrialization did little to increase the attractiveness of paid employment; the small minority of young women who worked was merely redeployed among a growing but limited number of alternatives to domestic service. By 1871, its monopoly broken, domestic service employed slightly less than half the female work-force, while industrial work accounted for one-third. However, there were few industrial jobs available to girls under the age of sixteen. School statistics merely confirm this picture. In 1871 a greater proportion of thirteen to sixteen-year-old females were in school than males of the same ages. More and more young women were avoiding domestic service, living at home with their parents, and staying on in school – perhaps as an antidote to boredom or on the chance of obtaining genteel employment at a somewhat older age. Industrialization of the sort experienced in Hamilton, then, brought sharply differing opportunities to girls than to boys, and at different ages.[56]

Within the larger Ontario economy industrialization was a protracted and ragged process. The introduction of machines and steam power, for example, transformed some industrial sectors and firms more decisively than others. Certainly the large-scale factory production experienced by Hamilton heavy industry by the 1870s did not dominate other sectors – nor other communities – in the same way. During the period Toronto was not industrializing to the same extent as its neighbour; nevertheless, by 1871, 10.9 per cent of the industrial work-force was under the age of sixteen (as was 5 per cent of the total labour force). Indeed the *Globe* reported that summer 'the growth in our midst of manufactures, work-shops, etc. where youths and girls from 12 to 15 years of age can find employment.'[57] Inevitably, then, the impact of major shifts in the economy and the occupational structure filtered down through circumstances close to home (such as local labour-market conditions, for example) until they came to be expressed in young people's decisions about school and work. Inevitably, too, social-class attitudes strongly influenced decisions about when to live with parents, attend school, or get a job.

A wage-labour job at sixteen was not the ambition of every young man or woman. Intent upon a future in a profession or a mercantile establishment, the sons of affluent parents had for some time prolonged their schooling in private academies or with tutors. The increased social and economic complexity of Ontario communities after mid-century further encouraged that trend among older boys and, especially, older girls who seemed determined, among other things, to become *at least* intelligently ornamental. These added years of schooling conferred on socially and economically privileged young people one significant advantage: by simply having *more* schooling they preserved, if they did not enhance, their inherited social position. 'The economic benefits of school attendance accrue from the differential advantage it bestows,' Michael Katz concluded from his exhaustive analysis of Hamilton society: 'that is, two levels of educational attainment always co-exist; that reached by most people and that reached by a fortunate minority. It is the distance between the two rather than their intrinsic qualities that counts.'[58] As the patterns of school attendance across the province indicate, extended schooling for adolescents had become, by the 1860s, an increasingly relevant issue for a large number of parents, not merely for the privileged few. Which social classes were willing to patronize the public schools and, correspondingly, how successfully local schools catered to the needs of older school children, depended in large measure on how public schooling was organized within the options provided by the school legislation.

IV

The mounting pressure was felt most sharply by the county grammar schools. Traditional grammar school studies were intended to launch young men on a respectable career, and it was the curriculum – rather than the social background of the students – that notionally distinguished these from other educational institutions. Ryerson had always argued that it was unacceptable policy in Canada to foster the sharp class barriers between elementary and grammar schooling characteristic of England and many western European countries. Much to his dismay, the substantial increase in the number of grammar schools at mid-century represented far more a triumph of middle-class social ambitions than of either an educational philosophy or a conscious social policy.

Pressure to expand the provision of grammar schools beyond the various county seats gained force in the 1840s. Between 1840 and 1851 the number exploded from just over a dozen to fifty-four; by 1855 there were sixty-five; and by 1861 eighty-six schools qualified for the grammar school grant. There appeared to be little rhyme or reason to the location of the new schools. Undoubtedly, as Robert Gidney and W.P.J. Millar suggest, there are tales to be told of political chicanery and official influence as local private venture schools wangled access to a modest government grant. This unseemly race to the trough of public monies was partially self-defeating in that the more schools that were eligible, the smaller the individual grant. Nevertheless, even though the grant might represent only a marginal contribution to a school's total costs (including a schoolhouse, operating costs, etc.) that had to be covered by fees, it did guarantee a basic salary for the master. Even that small measure of stability, as well as the advantage of geographical proximity, obviously proved very tempting. In some cases the influence of one or two families, bent on saving substantial boarders' fees by having a grammar school nearby, was sufficient. But such a handful of scholars and such limited appeal did not necessarily a grammar school make. Reporting on the condition of the schools in 1860, the Reverend William Ormiston deplored this tendency as he detailed some of the confusion that had arisen in the past five years. The school, including the schoolhouse, at Bond Head had been moved to Bradford (presumably the sons of the local élite had outgrown it). The school at Sandwich was still closed and likely to remain so. And neither of the schools proposed at Fingal and Font Hill had ever begun and did not seem to be required, 'neither of them being five miles distance from Grammar Schools already in operation.'[59]

As the grammar school inspectors well knew, the sheer number of new schools with a grant was a poor indicator of the amount and quality of

grammar school instruction across the province. Despite the 1853 legislation and the appointment of qualified, outspoken inspectors, the state
of the grammar schools became more, rather than less, of a thorn in the
side of the education department. Every year some schools did not open
for want of a qualified teacher or a sufficient number of students; others
did open, in schools that were unfit, 'being old and ruinous or (as in one
instance) consisting of a room rented in an improper or unsuitable locality.' The state of the schoolhouses frequently belied the social pretensions of the patrons, for the inspectors' annual surveys suggest that,
overall, accommodation was in almost as precarious a state as that of the
common schools. By 1860 the inspectors could admit to being generally
pleased with recent construction and renovation: now there were a number
of 'elegant and commodious buildings, most of them properly seated,
heated and ventilated, and more, or less, fully supplied with Apparatus,
Charts, Maps and Blackboards.' Yet only twenty-five of the forty-two
schoolhouses in the western section of the province were deemed 'good,
and more, or less, suitably furnished.' Typically the school grounds
remained a wasteland; 'neither Trees, Shrub nor Flower upon the premises, and in cases, not a few, Fences and that neat necessary, out-houses,
are still a desideratum.' The state of the schoolhouse and its surroundings
were critically important in the eyes of the inspectors, who shared a
scathing opinion of local parsimony and neglect 'A trifling expenditure
of time and money might render the School House and Grounds not only
an attraction and an ornament,' they protested, 'but also a pleasant means
of mental and moral culture. A dingy, delapidated or desolate-looking
School House rebukes the negligence which it reveals, and perpetuates
the ignorance and want of taste which permit it.'[60]

That moral lesson was not lost on young W.F. Checkley, appointed
master of the Barrie Grammar School as of January 1857. In a detailed
report to the board of trustees shortly after his arrival, Checkley itemized
the school's deficiencies: no globes, maps, mathematical or scientific
instruments; plaster in need of repair, walls of whitewashing, window-
panes of replacing. In a blitz of activity, a cloakroom had been added to
the entrance porch, a stove, a clock, and a blackboard acquired for the
schoolroom, and a privy 'replaced by one which will permit habits of
decency.' But there was still room for improvement. Most importantly,
the treeless, rugged school grounds could be improved by only a small
expenditure. Like many of his colleagues among the 'improving' educators of the provincial school system, Checkley believed in the sym-
bolism of school arrangements: 'comfortable, commodious and well
furnished schoolrooms were a powerful influence on the formation of
character,' these earnest schoolmen solemnly assured each other.[61]

W.F. Checkley was not entirely representative of the province's grammar schoolmasters, however, for he was especially successful. His stint
in Barrie advanced his career and he became rector of the newly founded
Model Grammar School in Toronto in 1861. The promotion was not
surprising, as under his guidance Barrie Grammar School had come to
rival Upper Canada College for the custom of Toronto's professional
families. Larratt Smith, barrister, for example, was so concerned about
his sons' lack of progress at the Upper Canada College preparatory school,
and about their general misbehaviour and lack of interest in studying,
that he transferred the boys to Mr Checkley's care, hoping that 'they will
learn some manners.' Other ambitious grammar schoolmasters, particularly those providing boarding facilities, recognized the importance of
training in the social graces. The new headmaster of the Cobourg Grammar School in 1859 sketched the new routine: the boys were to master
the classical curriculum during school hours; they could spend their leisure
time in various mechanical employments 'which may in after life prove
useful and agreeable to them'; but after studying they would 'pass a
portion of their evenings in the Drawing-room.'[62]

Some schools were more severely limited. Surprisingly, perhaps, given
the willingness of the élite to patronize Mr Checkley's school in Barrie,
the Toronto Grammar School in the 1850s was no match at all for Upper
Canada College. In terms of attracting students the school was located
off centre, demographically: on a corner property at Adelaide and Jarvis
streets, it naturally drew from the eastern, less wealthy, section of the
city. Moreover the competition was keen. Upper Canada College was a
powerful magnet drawing in upper-middle-class boys; the Toronto Academy competed for the Nonconformist élite; and several private classical
schools, 'down' to the short-lived Model Grammar School, served the
sons and daughters of the middle classes. Nor did the 'delapidated' state
of the schoolhouse, one of the oldest buildings in the city, help. In the
professional opinion of architect Joseph Sheard, by 1860 the school premises were 'entirely unfit, even for occupancy, *with safety*, and in a condition that to attempt to repair would be entirely useless.' With dogged
determination the trustees continued to plead with the city council to
renew its annual grant and struggled to make every possible economy in
the management of the school. They suspected, quite correctly, that many
more than the current eighty pupils would attend if they could but be
accommodated.[63]

One might well wonder why any sensible parent would even contemplate sending a son to the Toronto Grammar under such conditions. In
its favour, however, the school had a sound academic reputation and a
curriculum that catered to a wide range of interests, taught by four full-

time teachers as well as part-time instructors in French and bookkeeping. Elsewhere, some notable schools were able to combine distinguished academic performance with pleasant physical amenities. Under William Tassie, LL D, its founder and principal from 1851 to 1881, the Galt Grammar School became a legend attracting students from various parts of Canada and the USA. With its self-conscious echoes of a British boarding school, Galt Grammar exemplified the best intentions of the provincial regulations initiated in the 1850s. The standard for entrance to a grammar school, established at that time, specified that students were to be able to read intelligently and correctly any passage from any common reading book; spell correctly the words of an ordinary sentence; write a fair hand; work readily questions on the single and compound rules of arithmetic in reductions and simple proportions; know the elements of English grammar and be able to parse any easy sentence in prose; and be acquainted with definitions and outlines of geography.[64]

Not only was this a generally unrealistic entrance standard, but the academic character of much grammar school instruction itself throughout the period only faintly approximated this goal. At the annual meeting of the Teachers' Association in 1865, Ryerson frankly denounced the current trend to social-class, rather than academic, divisions between common and grammar schools. 'Rudimental instructions in English' were corrupting the classical curriculum of the grammar schools, in Ryerson's opinion, and 'wealthy people now used many of them for the education of their children in the English alphabet, while the Common Schools were being left to the children of the poorer classes.' Some schools, he alleged, had no classical pupils at all but were fraudulently reporting twenty-five per year.[65] The villain to which Ryerson alluded was the union school. In some county situations there were striking advantages to be gained by pooling access to the common and grammar school funds and thereby covering the costs of the schoolhouse and the teachers' salaries of a *single* institution. Such official collaboration suited school trustees and county boards of education, but it did not please the inspectors. With hindsight the outcome was predictable: a demoralized common school program and haphazard, mediocre grammar school instruction for a handful of ill-prepared teenagers. As the Reverend Mr Ormiston lamented in 1860, the 'very unsatisfactory state' of many of the union schools in the western half of the province (and they comprised almost half the area's grammar schools) 'not infrequently arises from the fact that there are so few in the School Sections desirous of prosecuting any branch of study beyond those taught in the common schools.'[66]

By contrast, decisions on the part of some urban school boards to unite the common and grammar schools had precisely the opposite effect. The cultural tone and academic standard of the local schools was raised, and the balance between the public and private sectors shifted in favour of the provincial school system. Ryerson had provided a rough blueprint for this development with his 1847 legislation, which considered the special circumstances of school boards in cities and towns. There was a need, if not a demand, for 'schools of a higher order' in cities and larger towns, Ryerson had acknowledged, which ought not be left to 'the hazards of private enterprize.' As a solution he proposed, for the public sector, 'a graduation, and, therefore, a system of Schools: Primary Schools for children from five to eight years of age; a proportionate number of Intermediate schools for children, say from eight to eleven years of age; and one, or more, English High Schools, for teaching the higher branches of a thorough Mercantile Education.'[67] In the 1850s and 1860s Ryerson's idea took form in the guise of the 'central school,' located strategically to draw students from local feeder primary schools, and sufficiently large to offer the higher levels of the basic curriculum as well as elements of traditional grammar school studies.

Invariably, the decision to adopt the central school model was taken in the course of a building campaign. School trustees in the major cities were under considerable pressure to join forces with the provincial education department as the campaign for school improvement gained momentum in the 1850s. Expectations were raised, municipal honour was at stake: rented schoolrooms became unacceptable as the assiduous propaganda of the education department ensured that the average urban taxpayer could distinguish a first-class 'modern' schoolhouse from a leftover hand-me-down. Initial decisions regarding the placement and construction of permanent school buildings set in train a complex series of interrelated decisions that sharply differentiated the quality as well as the quantity of public schooling available to the various social classes in the community. Hamilton and Toronto provide the most striking evidence of the consequences of these initial building decisions. For Egerton Ryerson and the disciples of what was most modern, Hamilton showed the way spectacularly with its decision to build the Central School in the early 1850s; Toronto, the capital, the home of the provincial Normal School and the education department, proved to be a continuing embarrassment.[68]

New brick schoolhouses were fine, but the central school held the key to modernity, for there the latest pedagogical innovations – age-grading, annual promotion, and a sequential curriculum – accompanied the latest in management techniques. Soon the integrated system of age-graded public schools on the 'central' model triumphed in the market-place: in Hamilton (and a little later in London and other communities that followed Hamilton's lead), many private venture schools closed, their clientele

The Central School at Hamilton: a view of the 'north front'

wooed by a public system in which children and teachers were deployed in ever more finely graded categories. Hamilton's particular experience of mid-century school reform appears to have been dictated in large measure by a handful of remarkably well-informed, strong-minded, and well-placed school trustees. What else in this community might have been a factor it is difficult to determine. In any enterprise the interplay of clients' expectations and the provision of a certain level of service is subtle, unstable, and ultimately difficult to unravel. Whatever the dynamics, however, the consequences were unequivocal: considerably better than average for the public sector, Hamilton's Central School very quickly became an 'archetypal urban middle-class school,' showing the exaggerated patterns in the social-class background of the older students in the post-primary classes that would become generally characteristic of urban schooling across the province only in the late 1870s.

By the mid-1850s the system of school organization in Hamilton was already famous and the city a mandatory stop on the itinerary of visiting schoolmen. The system consisted of a number of local primary schools (each housed in a handsome stone or brick building) and a central or high school to which pupils could be promoted once their elementary studies were complete. The Central School, 'with its playgrounds, gymnasia and shrubberies,' occupied two acres in the centre of the city. Architecturally, this 'splendid stone edifice' fulfilled the fondest dreams of the most modern of school administrators. In a rapturous catalogue of its amenities, the local superintendent, T.A. Ambridge, detailed the layout:

on the ground floor, two galleries, four division-rooms, a visitors' room, hat and cloak-rooms, dinner-rooms, & c., and on the second floor, six class-rooms, a teachers' room, and a large examination-hall capable of seating 600 children. The rooms are all heated by hot-air furnaces, placed in the basement, and are fitted up with improved school furniture. The building is surmounted with a tower, in which is placed a bell sufficiently powerful to be heard to the remotest part of the city.

The 'abundance' of the teaching paraphernalia and scientific apparatus and a generous library added but a footnote to all of this.[69]

One of the keys to the administrative success of the Hamilton system was the 1856 decision of the trustees of the senior grammar school in Wentworth County to cease independent operations. Having served for some time as a common school for the wealthier classes, the grammar school, once incorporated into the Central School, became the senior academic department, justifying the boast that a pupil could qualify for matriculation at the university all within the public system. But this privilege was not free! One of the ideologically troubling details of the Central School model was the typical requirement of modest school fees (earmarked for books, slates, and stationery). Hamilton's rates were average: twelve and a half cents per month in the primary schools; twenty-five cents per month at the Central in the higher elementary divisions; one dollar per month in the grammar school divisions. While not exorbitant, such fees could only discourage working-class families from prolonging children's schooling.[70]

In the early 1850s, Toronto school trustees opted for the neighbourhood school model: initially six newly built schoolhouses were located in working-class residential areas, each providing primary, intermediate, and senior classes. Consciously repudiating the era when countless private venture as well as parish schools supplemented the common schools of each ward, the newly created city school board in 1851 set out to obtain the support and patronage of the 'respectable mechanics, the small traders, the honest labourers of the city.' While the snail's pace at which the confidence of the working classes could be attained proved politically embarrassing on occasion, nevertheless this goal dictated the academic and social ambience of the city's common schools.[71] Quite unlike those in Hamilton, by the 1860s Toronto's schools had become awkward and inappropriate places for the children of the professional classes. A.A. Riddell, one-time printer and school trustee and latterly a doctor, believed that parents in his financial and social position faced particular difficulties in trying to educate their children in the city. 'Necessity compelled all my children to attend them [the common schools]; and they might have done well there had I never quitted the printing office,' he recounted to his friend Charles Clarke in 1868; 'when I became a professional, the Schools were made uncomfortable for them and they had to be taken away. My means not allowing me to send them to any private Schools, they were sent to the "Model".' Indeed, as well as the Model School associated with the provincial Normal School – where a fee of a dollar per month virtually ensured 'well-dressed, pleasant-looking, intelligent children' – a raft of private institutions complemented the common schools. Whatever its limitations, by the late 1860s the board's strategy had succeeded to a point; for, according to the *Globe*, the common schools were 'indisputably confined to the children of the industrious mechanic and the tradesman; exclusive on the one hand, of the wealthier merchant and professional man, and, unfortunately, on the other hand, to some degree, of the children of the poor and vagrant classes, who stand most in need of the free education they supply.'[72]

Through the 1850s and 1860s various urban boards of school trustees considered the pros and cons of the central school model: London, Belleville, and Ottawa were attracted by Hamilton's experience; Kingston remained closer to Toronto in organization and ideology, although even in the case of the latter board, the issue was hotly debated. In Toronto's all-age ward schools the number of older pupils in the senior division appeared insignificant, and only a limited amount of specialization was possible given the scattered pockets of senior pupils. Determined to counteract the weight of heavy enrolment in the earliest years and lowest grades, Charles Brooke, chairman of a trustees' select committee on school attendance in 1865, campaigned publicly to reverse a policy that discouraged professionals and businessmen – that is, the middle class – from patronizing the city schools. His committee concurred, with restraint: their final proposal was to centralize the senior levels into the nucleus of a central high school for older pupils doing senior work, and to use the proposed weekly fee of twelve cents per pupil to defray the cost of more teachers in the overcrowded primary levels.[73]

The local superintendent, the Reverend James Porter, was immediately and adamantly opposed, and his views carried the majority of the board. Porter understood the ideological implications of the various organizational arrangements available within the provincial school system. Central schools did indeed encourage the patronage of the professional as well

as the middling classes and significantly, previewed the 1871 legislation
that transformed grammar schools into collegiate institutes and local high
schools. On the other hand, a system of neighbourhood schools entailed
a greater commitment (in terms of public policy if not resources) to the
common schools' classic mission to educate (and socialize) the children
of working-class families. To quash enthusiasm for a central school,
Porter offered a frank assessment of the experience of many of the city's
youngsters caught up in balancing family responsibilities, going to school,
and finding a job. 'Many parents are necessitated and glad to avail themselves of the earnings of their children, as early as they are qualified for
any kind of employment,' he reminded the trustees. Ambitions to give
older students advanced work in the senior divsons were singularly mis-
placed: 'many being compelled to leave for active life before they have
made such advancement ... the supposed higher education to be thus
aimed at would prove a delusion and would end in disappointment.'[74]

V

Discrepancies in the patterns of school enrolment and school attendance
in mid-Victorian schools have alerted historians to some of the contradictions that mark the province's social and institutional development.
There is little evidence to support contemporary allegations that persistent
irregular attendance was the result of widespread parental neglect or
indifference, for example, and much to suggest that irregularity necessarily accompanied the material deprivation with which many families
and local communities had to cope. In new and struggling settlements,
the relative inadequacy of the schoolhouses and teachers frequently matched
that of the roads, bridges, and local gaols; in families and in the lives of
children, schooling was simply one of a number of responsibilities and
one that, at times, could well seem an unaffordable luxury. It is difficult
not to conclude, given the very real gains in school enrolments in the
third quarter of the century, that public schooling enjoyed general support.
Historians have ransacked the record for evidence of explicit resistance
to universal schooling, especially on the part of the working classes –
and have found very little.[75] Typically, it appears, resistance was deflected
and disguised, expressed in a refusal to attend school regularly or for
longer than appeared useful or in a challenge to what went on in some
schools or how they were organized. A *willingness* to take advantage of
local educational facilities is not synonymous with the *ability* to do so,
of course. But the evidence does support the contention that in Ontario,
as indeed throughout the northern United States in the early decades of
the last century, support for elementary schooling was widespread before

the classic innovations of the Ryerson era. Criticism of the details of the provincial system as it developed after 1846, and especially debate over the meaning of 'common,' was not prompted by any rejection of the values of universal elementary instruction. On the contrary, as is frequently the case with family feuds, shared values simply heated the debate. In one way or another the mid-century common school movement satisfied both collective (societal) and individual ambitions. The argument that the money spent on common schools reduced the cost of policing convinced ordinary citizen taxpayers, as well as self-styled classical economists, and for good reason. By and large taxpayers, as parents, shared the vision the common schools promoted: a vision of individual self-development and modest advances in social and economic standing. The ability to participate in that future varied enormously and systematically, however, depending on whether one lived in a rural or an urban community, on one's social class, ethnic (or racial) origin, and, indeed, on one's sex. Most significantly, patterns of school attendance obviously, *but by no means exclusively*, reflected the variable impact of economic change. Then, as now, in comparable circumstances families behaved very differently; some worked strenuously to ensure that their children went to – and stayed in – school; others did not for reasons that are not now, and were not then, easy to fathom.

While it is instructive for historians to calculate the benefits of increased participation and improved educational opportunities in terms of grand themes such as social order and social mobility, one should not forget the children. How might a mid-Victorian youngster have viewed the local common school? The confusion, discomfort, or sheer boredom of it all might well have put some off; conversely, the companionship, or just the chance to get out of the house, as well as the endless occasions for mischief going to and from school might have encouraged attendance.[76] Questions of motivation, on the part of children and their parents, are particularly tantalizing because it was in these critical mid-century decades that 'going to school' became part of childhood and the experience of growing up. Once that pattern had been established, the motive for going to school became insignificant; indeed, that behaviour would then be taken for granted and only the exceptions – of 'not going to school' or of being in a different school – would attract attention.

Ironically, the widespread acceptance, if not enthusiastic support, of the notion of universal publicly supported elementary schooling created political problems for Egerton Ryerson, as chief superintendent, and successive provincial governments. The public school system as it consolidated provincially and locally in the quarter century after 1858 became more than the sum of its buildings, teachers, and student population: it was a powerful cultural institution. As Ryerson and his supporters had intended, that culture was self-consciously exclusive: Protestant, bourgeois, indeterminately mid-Atlantic. Hence the classic political issues of educational policy after mid-century would involve pressures on the provincial school system to ensure comparable services for religious and ethnic minorities and to accommodate those on widely divergent economic and social margins of society: the 'street arabs' and also girls. While the absence, in the historical record, of significant vocal resistance to the idea of public education may appear to diminish conventional over-blown assessments of the achievements of mid-Victorian educators, consideration of the audacity of their self-imposed task to educate, in the sense of socialize, the next generation at least prompts one to pause. The more one appreciates the conditions under which instruction took place (characterized by overcrowding, irregular attendance, and inadequately trained teachers) the more intriguing becomes the question: what might a typical mid-Victorian youngster learn from going to school – occasionally?

8 *What One Might Teach and Another Learn*

As 'going to school' became an expected, if often abbreviated, experience of Victorian childhood, what one might expect to learn from elementary instruction became more predictable. The provincial school system triumphed in the market-place in the mid-century decades, but more was at stake than the displacement of a tradition of private venture and voluntary schooling. A less obvious but more profound revolution in the very nature of schooling accompanied the property taxes and numerous regulations to which communities and families adjusted. In contrast to the familial ambience of earlier colonial instruction, 'public' schooling was deliberately formal in structure as well as content. The new style of public instruction, best exemplified by developments in the common schools, centred on the teacher, a prescribed curriculum, and the rational organization of children. As Ryerson readily admitted, little of 'the new' was home-grown. Beyond a few minor details the classic mid-century innovations in curricula, pedagogy, and school management formed part of an internationally shared technology of elementary instruction. Series of school readers, blackboards, object lessons, and proficiency prizes quickly became the stock-in-trade of progressive school administrators around the world. A revolution of sorts was indeed in the making, but, as the Reverend William A. Caldwell of Dundas shrewdly observed, 'many things look well on paper which, in their practical details, are found not to answer the ends contemplated in their establishment.' In the long run (certainly by the end of the century), the provincial school system and public instruction had become, in the opinion of a new generation of critics, stiflingly formal, mechanistic, and bureaucratic. The journey to that end, however, took an erratic course.[1]

In many if not most Ontario families, decisions about schooling proved inseparable from a raft of other decisions (about work and residence, about moving on or staying put) relating to the particular demands of the family economy. Not surprisingly it seems that, when they could, families and individual pupils approached the common schools with hazy and widely differing expectations. Indeed, one might well ask: what could one legitimately expect? In January 1867, we know, Thomas Dick, the young Irish shantyman in the Ottawa Valley caught up in the tragedy of his friend's death, hoped that going to school would help Ellen Jane Cross 'keep up her mind some.' In Kingston that same year, the sympathetic school inspector found others with expectations so nebulous as virtually to defy expression. Inspector Woods inquired of some of the city's poorest parents about their problems finding the necessary clothes in which to outfit their children for school. Having sounded them 'pretty thoroughly,' Woods asked whether, if they had the clothing, they would see that the children did attend. 'In several instances I have seen the gleam of hope light up the dim smoke-begrimed face,' he reported, 'and an answer came too quick to have time to be a sham. "God knows I would." ' However poignant, inarticulate faith in the unknown was undoubtedly less common by the 1860s than the no-nonsense reaction of William Hutchinson, a carpenter living on Dummer Street in the west end of Toronto. He had two boys, Robert, aged nine, and James, aged seven, in the junior division, male department, of Elizabeth Street school. It seemed to Hutchinson that his boys had not learned anything, and in September 1868 he complained to the local superintendent about the teacher (who had also, in his opinion, unduly punished James). Miss McBride countered by charging that the boys 'were unusually dull.' Nevertheless, she was cautioned. The superintendent managed to placate Mr Hutchinson, but the issues raised by this encounter were disturbing. There were as yet no firm answers to such questions as: What might pupils reasonably expect to learn from spending time in school? or What does it mean to be a 'dull student'?[2]

Typically the behaviour of children and the reaction of their parents prompted such questions, and the responses of teachers and school administrators in individual cases helped frame general answers, often unwittingly. After mid-century, the more informal institutions of learning, such as Sunday schools and craft apprenticeship, did lose ground to the provincial school system, but until well into the 1860s formal education, represented by common schooling, remained quite tenuously organized. To meet the various, and rising, expectations generated largely by their own assiduous propaganda, public educators worked to define a standard measure of a 'thorough English education.' Not only was the notion of a general, publicly verifiable standard novel, but the authority of public educators – and, ultimately, of the state – to dictate and enforce that standard had to be won. In the process, some rights of parents, taxpayers, communities, and, most frequently, children, were curtailed; but not without incident.

I

How best to bring some semblance of order, some system, to common schooling in the province was the challenge Egerton Ryerson faced as he assumed the superintendency in 1844. The anarchy had become proverbial: virtually no two schools were alike; facilities were haphazard at best; the teachers untrained, pupils of all ages (and both sexes) generally were jumbled together and, worse still, each attended according to necessity or whim. From the very outset, school textbooks proved to be a key element in Ryerson's design for school improvement. The immediate target was American textbooks. Undoubtedly, there were a number of American publications in circulation in the province, concentrated where late American settlement predominated (although the oft-repeated charge that American textbooks dominated the common school curriculum in the 1820s and 1830s is not easily substantiated). Nevertheless, allegations of the insidious political threat posed by numerous American imprints in the schools became commonplace after the rebellion activity of the late 1830s. Virulent anti-American feeling was rife in certain circles, especially among Tories; moreover, a more temperate version of pro-British sentiment was instinctively shared by the tens of thousands of recent immigrants from the British Isles who had chosen to set down roots in this British North American colony in the previous decade. For all the objections to various details of Ryerson's administration over the years, few quarrelled with his 'leading idea': 'to render the educational system, in its various ramifications and applications, the indirect, but powerful instrument of British Constitutional Government.' Thus there was a political argument to be made for replacing American schoolbooks, an argument that justified the introduction of a comprehensive textbook policy in the mid-1840s. To help set the stage, as of 1 January 1847, all *foreign* (that is, *American*) books were prohibited – with the exception of the as-yet-indispensable editions of Morse's *New Geography* and the desirable *Kirkham's English Grammar*.[3]

What could be put in their place? In retrospect one best appreciates the genius of Ryerson's policy on textbooks in the context of the overall structural weakness of the fledgling provincial school system. Imagine this small world as a chess-board and ask: what single move could accomplish *all* the following – compensate for inadequately trained teachers; classify pupils according to ability and prior knowledge; meet the challenge of endemic pupil-teacher mobility; minimize sectarian animosity; provide affordable and universally available reading material to families and local communities before the advent of a viable domestic book trade? *Answer:* prescribe the series of school readers published by the Irish Commissioners of National Education. Within a month of his official appointment in 1844, Ryerson tipped his hand and encouraged the Montreal publishing firm Messrs Armour and Ramsay in a scheme to reprint the Irish readers for Canadian use. After his year-long European tour he moved swiftly. He commended the readers in his influential 1846 report and, on his recommendation, the newly appointed Board of Education approved a prescribed list of textbooks for the common schools, composed entirely of twenty-six publications of the Irish commissioners' series, including the famous readers. Adoption of the new texts was voluntary: local school trustees retained the right to choose schoolbooks, but now they risked losing the government grant if they persisted with unauthorized texts. Although the board ordered Ryerson to tread softly and 'to recommend a delicate treatment of the subject' in any correspondence with school trustees, 'rather permitting such [unauthorized] books to fall into disuse than to exclude them altogether,' the impact of the legislation and board regulations was immediate and decisive. Within a year nearly one-half (1,317 of 2,727) of the common schools had adopted the Irish readers; at the height of their popularity in 1866, all but 54 of the province's more than 4,000 common schools had succumbed. Of course, no edict could instantly resolve the textbook muddle. Inevitably individual school trustees, teachers, and parents remained confused and, occasionally, simply adamantly opposed. But in this instance Ryerson's basic administrative strategy of encouraging voluntary local compliance with central policy initiatives was remarkably successful.[4]

The series of Irish readers and the Irish commissioners' other publications had two advantages over their competitors in the schoolbook field. For their time they were remarkably good, and they were very inexpensive. Cheapness, in this case, was clearly related to merit. The Irish commissioners had over the decades created a domestic demand for their books by a shrewd combination of regulation and marketing strategy. The result: attractively low prices – and from there the advantages of economies of scale in production and distribution multiplied. Regarded as superior to the ponderous and heavily religious publications used in schools catering to English working-class children, by the 1840s the Irish national series were the most popular school-books in the British Isles. The Irish commissioners deliberately fostered export sales by selling books at or near cost outside Ireland and by granting reprinting rights to independent foreign agents. It has been estimated that during the 1850s the commissioners exported almost as many books as they kept at home.

The special arrangements that Ryerson negotiated with the commissioners in 1846 were, on the Irish side, simply grist to the export mill; from the Canadian standpoint, however, they were extraordinary. Having devised an elaborate system of incentives to local publishers and booksellers, Ryerson improvised: to ensure that local schools throughout the province were supplied adequately and swiftly with books and other equipment, in 1850 he opened the Educational Depository, in essence a government-owned mail-order bookstore. Local school trustees thus had a choice: should the local book trade raise prices on the authorized Irish school texts, they could buy directly from the depository the edition that the education department imported directly from Dublin at cost.[5]

The decision to adopt the Irish national series for Ontario schools had a profound impact on generations of youngsters. Arguably, none of the much-publicized mid-century innovations – the legislative framework, the Normal School, the Educational Depository – was more important. For much of the century, school-books were *the* central feature of the common school. In rural schools especially, but, until very late, almost everywhere, the school-books available dictated the 'curriculum.' For two or more generations so few of the province's teachers had real professional training that when much else failed, as we know it frequently did, memorizing the textbook could pass the time and placate the school trustees on examination day. School-books were counted upon to convey the 'useful knowledge' necessary to deal with the practicalities of life and to provide an inkling of the standards of belief and behaviour expected by adult society.

The Irish readers were exceptionally effective on both counts. Typically, instructional books in the late eighteenth and early nineteenth centuries were self-contained and unrelated to each other. Lindley Murray's *The English Reader* is a prime example. A staple of the Upper Canadian common school through the 1830s and 1840s, Murray's *Reader* ran through scores of editions in England, Ireland, the United States, and Upper Canada between the 1790s and the 1840s. It was essentially a literary anthology, arranged as 'Narrative Pieces, Didactic Pieces, Argumentative Pieces, Descriptive Pieces, Pathetic Pieces, Dialogues, Public Speeches ... and Promiscuous Pieces.' Murray sampled some of the best, and most morally improving, examples of literary culture but catered very little to the ages of his readers. That the Irish readers did do. Conceived as an integrated sequential series, each reader built on the content of the previous one, increasing in difficulty as well as in volume of information. In effect, pedagogy became inseparable from content once the Irish readers were adopted. Children could pass from learning the alphabet to simple stories of biblical history to the elements of natural history and physical science and the principles of political economy. Ryerson's breathless characterization captures something of the scope:

in the fourth and fifth books, the most important subjects of Physical Geography and Geology, of Jewish History and Political Economy, of General History and Chronology, of Vegetable and Animal Physiology, of Natural History, including elementary Mechanics, Astronomy, Hydrostatics, Pneumatics, Optics, Electricity, and Chemistry, are treated in a manner both attractive and scientific, and adapted to the intercourse and pursuits of life – the whole being interspersed with miscellaneous and poetic selections calculated to please the imagination, to gratify and improve the taste, and to elevate and strengthen the moral feeling.[6]

A true compendium of the latest Victorian intellectual enthusiasms! And that in large measure explains the extraordinary popularity of the Irish texts. For working-class school children, in Britain especially, the content of the Irish readers vastly extended the range of basic information available: it mattered little that very few youngsters would ever reach the fourth or fifth books. By comparison to the typical fare of the Bible, scripture lessons, and religious tracts, the Irish series appeared notably secular and its 'useful knowledge' proved so irresistible that the major school societies – Protestant and Roman Catholic – in England had produced their own versions, close copies of the Irish series, by the early 1860s. But *secular* in the sense of *non-religious* the Irish commissioners' books definitely were not. The Irish readers were intentionally (and conspicuously in their time) 'non-denominational' in that they had the approval of both Roman Catholic and Protestant authorities in Ireland (a critical point for Ryerson, which he would stress repeatedly as the debate over separate schools in Ontario quickened in the 1850s). Non-sectarian, nevertheless, was Christian; the world view presented to children by the Irish readers was carefully constructed around Christian conceptions of God and the duties owed to Him.[7]

The First Book of Lessons opened with a section of seven lessons 'designed merely to make the Child familiar with the *forms* of Letters'; the remaining lessons advanced through two-, three-, and four-letter one-syllable words, laying the groundwork of basic language skills. Dogs, cats, rats, and pigs made an early appearance, but so too, as one of the first sentences that children learned to read, did the adage '*To do ill is a sin.*' The message was swiftly enforced in subsequent lessons by 'If I sin, I am bad, Let me not sin, as bad men do' and 'It is a sin to do ill.' As the prefatory note to teachers recommended that their pupils be 'perfectly acquainted with one Lesson before they proceed with another' and that they 'exercise them as much as possible on the *meaning* of such words and sentences as admit of being defined and explained,' one can probably assume that the concepts of good, sin, and evil were drilled early in each child's school career.[8]

The Second Book of Lessons followed naturally; after a review of words of one syllable, experience in reading and spelling advanced via moral fables and biblical stories to the stage of fairly complicated words, such as *innumerable*, and the first principles of grammar. The illustrative stories exhibited the virtue of having been written for children, exploiting situations and terms they could relate to; but however simplified the vocabulary, the message was never ambiguous: the divine order of the universe was mirrored in civil society. In the tale of 'The Daw with the Borrowed Feathers,' in which a humble jackdaw is vain enough to want to dress like a peacock, the moral is made devastatingly clear: 'It is wisest and safest to pretend to nothing that is above our reach and our circumstances, and to aim at acting well in our own proper sphere rather than have the mere appearance of worth and beauty in the sphere which is designed for others.[9] The corresponding selections of verse had no literary pretensions. The opening and closing lines of 'We Must Not Be Idle' still stir memories:

How doth the little busy bee
  Improve each shining hour

...

For idle hands some mischief still
  Will ever find to do.

By the end of the *Second Book* it was assumed that youngsters had acquired basic reading skills. Nevertheless, the original step between the second and the third book – with its selections from contemporary literary figures such as William Wordsworth, Robert Southey, and Sir Walter Scott – proved sufficiently difficult that *A Sequel to the Second Book of Lessons* was interposed. The sequel, which was used in Ontario schools, caught the attention of William Sherwood Fox, a political science professor at Queen's University in 1932. Intrigued by the extent to which national character and national political culture might be attributed to the socializing effect of differing school curricula, Fox saw the 'balance, sanity, clarity and simplicity' of the Irish books as a glaring contrast to the extravagant jingoism of the comparable American classics, McGuffey's readers. Overall, he concluded, the 1859 Canadian edition of *A Sequel to the Second Book of Lessons* was 'one of the most remarkable common school textbooks I have ever seen.' Inevitably, after another half-century the perspective has shifted, and our judgment is less benign: it does not matter that the information is even more outdated with the passage of time, the moral preaching now seems obvious in ways it did not to Sherwood Fox in the 1930s. For example, one of the notable features of the *Sequel* was its beginning section devoted to a discussion of the principles of a sound education written in language children could understand. The prospective reader (typically nine or ten years of age) is asked to remember not being able to read or write, and then going to school for the first time and learning habits of cleanliness, order, respect, silence, and self-discipline – the things taught first 'because they are necessary to the peace and comfort of others, and therefore to the order of the school.' In a confidential tone the author reminds his reader: 'You know how disagreeable it is to sit by a dirty child.' Indeed! What ripples might such a remark cause in colonial schoolrooms in newly settled rural communities or burgeoning commercial centres? Might the behaviour of Miss Mary Ann Kennedy, a teacher at Victoria Street school in Toronto, be related somehow as she accused Mira and Faithful Murdrew, of 4 Bond Street, of being 'uncleanly in their persons' and told other children not to sit near them? She acted on 'hearsay,' as it turned out, and was duly reprimanded; but could some of her students have taken that particular lesson too much to heart? One cannot help but wonder.[10]

By the 1860s many common school students in Ontario would get into, if not through, the *Third Book*; markedly fewer got to the end of the *Fourth Book*; and the astronomy, hydrostatics, and pneumatics of the natural philosophy section of the *Fifth Book* found only a tiny audience, being remote from even the majority of teachers.[11] That being the case, the overall character of the intermediate-level readers takes on a particular importance, for these were among the last – and the most demanding – instructional materials to which ordinary mid-Victorian Ontarians would be exposed. Following the now-familiar format, the third and fourth books advanced instruction through increasingly sophisticated lessons in spelling, grammar, natural history, geography, and literary appreciation. *Third Book* teachers were advised to have their pupils memorize the best pieces of poetry and that they 'be taught to read and repeat them with due attention to pronunciation, accent and emphasis.' A single reading lesson might well combine instruction in a number of areas. One *Third Book* story about how glass is made introduced students to concepts such as *brittleness* and *transparency*, the geography of the Middle East (Syria and Sidon), the spelling of *manufactured*, and the details of the invention of glass. By the *Fourth Book* a selection about Linnaeus, the famed Swedish naturalist, cloaked a lesson on the Latin and Greek roots of

English words ['What is the Latin root of *naturalist*? What is the first affix added to *natura*?'] in a discussion of the tripartite division of nature as animal, vegetable, and mineral.

In the late twentieth century even the physical size, printing, and illustrations of these little Victorian books seem quaint. Two contrary impressions of their content stand out: the factual material and information is eclectic and surprisingly contemporary, while aesthetic or literary values are largely ignored. In the critical sections of prose and poetry the selections were chosen for their didactic qualities rather than their stylistic merit. Almost none of the excerpts from the classics, ancient and modern, that had graced the early readers remained. To be sure, an obligatory smattering of Shakespeare survived (mostly as obscure stanzas from unnamed plays), along with a little Milton (the highlights of *Paradise Lost* proved irresistible), but in the company typically of the minor works of minor talents. No reasonable interest in near-contemporary authors could produce that end result naturally. Clearly the object was to cultivate the reader's moral, not aesthetic, sensibilities.

Culturally, then, elementary education was quite probably impoverished by reliance on the Irish readers. Certainly they offered predictable gruel when compared to the richness possible in earlier times when one might learn much of what the teacher happened to know, from whatever books could be mustered for the purpose. In other ways, however, as we have noted, the Irish readers brought the curriculum 'up-to-date.' One of the most striking features of the *Third* and *Fourth* books of lessons was the introduction of current liberal economic theory in the form of lectures on political economy. The basic tenets of nineteenth-century *laissez-faire* doctrine, in considerable measure an apology for the class relations and political alignments of the emerging industrial capitalist economy, were promoted by the Irish series. The Reverend Richard Whately, the author of an 1833 tract for schools, *Easy Lessons on Money Matters for the Use of Young People*, somewhat unexpectedly became the Anglican archbishop of Dublin, an Irish education commissioner, and chief proponent of the Irish national series of textbooks. In the form of lectures on such topics as Money, Exchange and the Division of Labour, the *Easy Lessons* were reproduced in the Irish readers: the first four sections in the *Third Book*, the remaining six sections in the *Fourth Book*.[12]

In the 'unsubtle, pre-digested morality' of Whately's lectures (to borrow J.M. Goldstrom's phrase), the virtues of hard work, perseverance, and thrift were applauded; backsliding or lack of will invariably doomed one to poverty or worse. The forces fragmenting the traditional work processes of the self-employed craftsman or small producer were heralded as signs of civilization: 'when everyman does everything for himself everything is badly done,' *Third Book* readers were reminded.[13] Unfettered, the laws balancing supply and demand worked to the benefit of both worker and employer, and the seemingly glaring discrepancies between rich and poor were often deceptive. A long lesson in the *Fourth Book* on the rich and poor (and the 'cheering thought that no one is shut out from the hope of bettering his condition and providing for his children') included a story on the complex economic functions performed by a rich man as he employs others, buys objects, etc., etc. The conclusion was meant to be reassuring: 'the rich man, therefore, though he appears to have so much larger a share allotted to him, does not really consume it but is only the channel through which it flows to others. And it is by this means much better distributed than it would have been otherwise.'[14]

In truth, the Irish readers were saturated with a very specific social and political philosophy. Labelling a discrete section structured in a distinctive lecture format 'Political Economy and the Useful Arts' was a misleading editorial device, in that it implied that these values and this kind of material could be excluded from the curriculum by omitting the specified lessons. That was hardly the case. The importance of social harmony and the corresponding futility – indeed immorality – of radical social protest were common themes in even the earliest readers.[15] By contrast to the past, the present was characterized as a time of restless energy and striving after dreams. The economic (and social) system would prove a hard but just taskmaster to those who dared to grasp the nettle: various sagas of male achievement attested to that. A Birmingham entrepreneur, William Hutton, and the explorer Christopher Columbus, for example (whose stories appear in the *Sequel to the Second Book*), were both very poor but virtuous and persevering youths who gained wealth and respect. However far-fetched such stories might have seemed when read in the Canadian countryside, they evidently appealed to Ontario educators. Toronto's local superintendent, for example, examined the city's common school children in the mid-1860s more often on these two biographical lessons than on any others in the *Sequel*.[16] More generally, the tenets of political economy accorded perfectly with the ideal of the common school as a place where the son of the manufacturer might sit next to the son of a doorman. Indeed, Ryerson, the chief publicist of that myth, wrote his own textbook version of Whately's *Easy Lessons* late in his career as *Elements of Political Economy or How Individuals and a Country Become Rich* (Toronto: Copp Clark 1877).

With time the Irish readers became less exceptional.[17] Eventually, as some material became dated and factual inaccuracies were exposed, pressure mounted for Ryerson and the Council of Public Instruction to arrange for their replacement. On 4 January 1868, a new series of six books was authorized: the *Canadian National Series of Reading Books*, otherwise known as the 'Red Series' or the 'Ryerson Books.' Faithful to tradition, the new series responded to growing nationalist feeling by being in all essentials a made-in-Canada version of the Irish texts.[18]

Readers were the key element in the new common school curriculum for they provided the vehicle for instruction in reading, spelling, and grammar as well as more general knowledge. But they were not the only school-books. The basic elementary fare of the three Rs had, whenever possible, relied on books other than a reader and the Bible. Spelling books, English grammars, and arithmetics abounded in the common schools to the point of nuisance by the mid-1840s. Under pressure from the Board of Education's authorized list the number of these texts was trimmed, but uniformity throughout the province was never as critical a goal for Ryerson in the areas peripheral to reading. For writing (penmanship), geography, and history – even spelling, grammar, and arithmetic – the teacher's command of the subject matter and teaching skill mattered more than any single text. As Ryerson admitted in 1847 with reference to mathematics, he believed that 'the Teacher is the true, and the best, "arithmetic" for the Schools; and, if he cannot teach and illustrate its principles and rules without references to a particular Textbook, very little of the science of numbers will be learned in his school.'[19]

In the mid-1840s one arithmetic text, Francis Walkingame's *The Tutor's Assistant*, dominated the field, being used in over 42 per cent of the common schools. A late-eighteenth-century production, Walkingame's book went through countless editions over more than half a century. The 1818 Montreal edition (based on the fifty-first London edition) was widely used in the 1830s and reportedly until 1845 in Middlesex County, while an even later edition was reprinted in Picton in 1849.[20] Such longevity was feasible because the substance of arithmetic instruction changed very little over time: addition, subtraction, multiplication, division, vulgar fractions, decimals, square and cube roots – these and more were illustrated by examples and learned by memorizing rules and answering practice questions. Often the illustrations were eminently practical. From weights and measures the student advanced to details of basic business practice: the nature of bills of sale or how to calculate single and compound interest. Ryerson's major reservation about the various texts in current use in the 1840s related to the alien and necessarily somewhat abstract quality of the examples used to explain the various rules. Much more desirable to have illustrations 'selected from the statistics and commerce of the Country in which it [the textbook] might be used,' he observed in 1847. As he well knew, authorization of the two Irish arithmetics changed very little, for their examples were British. The situation became critical in the late 1850s when Canada switched to a decimal currency. Among the first Canadian texts authorized to supplement the Irish commissioners' publications were two new editions (1859 and 1860) of the Irish arithmetics now 'adapted to the decimal currency.' For students, substituting texts meant little more than that they were now drilled in converting pounds, shillings, and pence into dollars and cents, in addition to reducing days, hours, and minutes to seconds, miles to inches, and writing the current date in Roman numerals. Roman notation was so popular with Toronto teachers in the mid-1860s that members of the committee on school management protested that the pupils were 'not young Romans of the 2nd and 3rd century, but Anglo-Saxons living in an intensely practical age.'[21]

Allegations of impracticality were not limited to arithmetic classes. Controversy over spellers and the way in which spelling and reading were taught had been brewing for some time before Ryerson's intervention. The traditional spelling books that came under fire had often been little more than disembodied lists of combinations of syllables to be memorized and of words to be spelled, sometimes – but by no means always – followed by short definitions. Typically, little effort was made to introduce young students to words that might relate to the world with which they were familiar.[22] To try to teach spelling effectively while divorcing it from reading and comprehension appeared nonsensical to a new generation of educators. Ryerson, in his 1846 report, came out firmly on the side of the modernists. The Irish national readers were specifically designed to accomplish the task of teaching spelling through reading. A short list of new words to be learned prefaced each lesson text, which then set the words in context. As a deliberate statement on this point, the Irish series did not include a 'speller' as such. According to the Irish method (which Ryerson and the Normal School promoted), when students had advanced to a certain stage they were introduced to a supplementary book, *The Spelling-Book Superseded*, compiled by Robert Sullivan, master of the Dublin Normal School. Designed to help students with some of the anomalies of the English language, this 'little book' offered practical rules for spelling and pronunciation and, as well, explained how some words similar in sound differed in spelling (bough/bow); how words identically spelled could be pronounced differently (bow/bow); and how words spelled and pronounced alike could differ in meaning (bat,n./ bat,v.).[23]

English grammar, too, had its rules, which students diligently memorized and then practised by answering prepared exercises. The more senior students grappled with the Latin and Greek roots of words, prefixes, affixes, and suffixes, and the distinctions among phrases, clauses, and sentences; but for the majority the heart of grammar teaching remained *parsing*: the description of words in a sentence in terms of grammatical rules, as parts of speech, and in their relationship to one another. Accuracy became increasingly important as popular speech became standardized and mistakes in grammar and mispronunciations threatened to betray dubious social or ethnic origins. At the same time, educators continued to regard grammatical drill as a form of mental discipline by which students learned to think in an orderly fashion as well as to communicate effectively. Increasingly, too, after mid-century, emphasis shifted to the ability to write as well as to speak correctly. The grammar in the Irish series directed students to do their work almost entirely in writing, presuming at least some attention had been paid to acquiring the skill of writing or penmanship. Practice in forming arabic numerals and then letters on slate began as the alphabet was learned and, gradually, depending on the availability of school desks on which to write and paper or exercise sheets on which to practice, the student progressed from 'large' to 'small hand' to a 'bold free handwriting' that was as legible as print.[24]

The poverty of many mid-century schoolhouses affected all instruction to some degree, but the study of geography was especially hampered by the lack of blackboards, maps, globes, and pens and ink. As the Educational Depository supplied these items in large volume through the 1850s and early 1860s, geography became more widely studied; but a serious problem remained. British publications – even the Irish national series – typically focused on Britain as the centre of the world, neglecting the entire North American continent and ignoring the Canadas altogether. The most commonly used American texts, on the other hand, often appeared to promote republicanism, and Olney's *A Practical System of Popular Geography*, an attractively illustrated, outrageously chauvinistic political tract, aroused legitimate political concern in Canada. Convinced of the importance of geography, the Board of Education capitulated to popular interest in North America and permitted the continued use of the most neutral American text, Morse's *New Geography*, published in New York by Harper and Row. The weakness of the Irish texts, which had been authorized in 1846, was met temporarily in 1857 by John George Hodgins's *Geography and History of British North America and of the Other Colonies of the Empire*. While this, his first attempt, came under fire for gross inaccuracies, by 1865 Hodgins had produced a trio of Canadian texts that successfully supplanted both the American and the Irish geographies: *Lovell's General Geography*, *Lovell's Easy Lessons in General Geography*, and *History of Canada and of Other British North American Provinces*.[25]

Of all the subjects that Ryerson desired to see in the common school

1865 Hodgins trio (Lovells)

curriculum none approached the importance of religious instruction. 'The Christian religion should be the basis, and all pervading principle of it,' he wrote confidently in 1846; but at the same time, as a pioneer champion of Methodism he was not unware of the depth to which sectarian feeling scarred communities throughout the province. The Irish example had attracted Ryerson from the outset precisely because it seemed to offer a resolution to sectarian differences; for there Roman Catholic and various Protestant church authorities had been able to collaborate in the establishment and regulation of the national schools. In the matter of regulations for religious instruction in the province's common schools, Ryerson followed the Irish precedent and consulted with a number of leading Protestant and Roman Catholic churchmen before drafting the regulations of 1846.[26] The mood was conciliatory, but the question remained: where in this provincial context might common ground be found? One risked denominational wrath by being too prescriptive, too authoritarian; on the other hand, diffidence only invited charges of promoting a 'godless' school system – an allegation that Ryerson personally could not tolerate. The ground he chose, in 1846, was the local school section: legislation was put in place to protect the freedom of conscience of any child whose parents objected to whatever form of religious instruction the local school trustees authorized. Similar assumptions underlay the 1850 legislation and regulations, but already the 'common ground' was shifting: religious instruction proved to be a bone of endless contention. Decisions about the extent and content of the observances depended on thousands of locally elected trustees, their personal convictions, doctrinal beliefs, and political connections with local ratepayers and parents; day to day, the knowledge and religious commitment of the teacher often determined the outcome.

By 1855 the education department was forced to retreat. The new common school regulations were made to conform to those recently devised for the grammar schools: neither assumed nor required anything, but recommended daily opening and closing exercises, which might incorporate non-denominational prayers, a reading from the Scriptures, and, ideally, the Lord's Prayer and the Ten Commandments. By 1857 the position of the local trustees was clarified further in that schoolhouses were to be made available once a week, out of school hours, to local clergy 'of any persuasion, or their authorized representatives' to offer religious instruction to pupils of their faith.[27] The new regulations reduced local tension by offering trustees, parents, and communities an avenue of retreat, with the result that by the 1860s there was enormous variety in the ways religious instruction was carried on. The teacher's responsibility, however, became less clear once religious instruction was replaced by moral lessons. Neil Campbell, who took over ss 7, Oro Township, in 1871, confided to his diary a sense of the difficulties teachers faced in trying to inculcate moral values: 'some teachers give moral lectures once a week &c, but few can do this who do not as it were preach to their pupils by uttering truisms and if you do you will soon lose the respect of your pupils and might as well be silent.'[28]

Egerton Ryerson had set an ambitious agenda for the province's common schools in 1846. 'What the child needs in the world he should doubtless be taught in the school,' he proposed, and the appropriate yardstick of need was to be neither the past nor the present 'but what ought to be, and what must be, if we are not to be distanced by other countries in the race of civilization.' His ideal 'system of common school instruction' included:

Reading, Writing, Drawing, Arithmetic, the English language, Music, Geography, elements of General History, of Natural History, of Physiology and Mental Philosophy, of Chemistry, Natural Philosophy, Agriculture, Civil Government & Political Economy.[29]

A flight of fancy, really, and easily ridiculed when many schools at the time he was writing were not unlike those in Dundas, where in 1850 'the amount of grammar, geography, dictionary and meanings taught ... [were] not worth mentioning; and as for history, composition, geometry, natural philosophy and the like, they were never thought of.'[30] By the 1860s a scaled-down version of Ryerson's blueprint had taken shape, owing in large measure to the Irish readers and the requirements set for the county board second-class teaching certificate held by approximately 48 per cent of common school teachers. To read 'with ease, intelligence and expression'; to write a 'bold free hand'; to know the principles of reading and pronunciation and the rules for teaching writing, 'Fractions, Involution, Evolution, and Commercial and Mental Arithmetic', as well as the common rules of orthography; to be able to parse, write grammatically with correct spelling and punctuation the substance of dictation, and be familiar with a school geography – these were the demands made of prospective teachers and, invariably, they shaped and limited what was taught in the individual schoolroom.[31]

That at least was the conclusion the Reverend James Fraser drew from his visit to the province's schools on behalf of the British Schools Inquiry Commission in the summer of 1865. Having arrived from the American leg of his journey in late July only to discover that many schools (including those in Hamilton) were already closed for the summer vacation, Fraser visited schools in Ottawa, Toronto, Clinton, and one or two other villages. So confident was he of his impression that 'they were characterized by a remarkable similarity of system, and the differences observable between them were differences of degree rather than kind,' that he doubted whether more examples would alter his opinion.

In effect it was all very familiar, much like ordinary English elementary schooling. In the range of subjects taught, for example, the best schools in Toronto equalled most English town schools in providing solid daily doses of an hour each of reading, arithmetic, writing, and grammar, supplemented by classes in geography and history, oddments of singing, drawing, and drill, and, where appropriate, higher mathematics such as algebra and Euclidean geometry. The lessons struck Fraser as long and, particularly in reading, pupils were expected to 'possess themselves of the matter of the lesson.' Quick answers were generally discouraged by giving students time 'for reflection and thought.'[32] The Irish readers provided the framework that carried the students from the most elementary to advanced work as the course of study became more elaborate at the stage of the fourth and fifth readers. By the end of the *First Book of Lessons* youngsters should have known the simple rules for addition and subtraction, perhaps the multiplication tables, how to print on the slate, and, if there were maps or a blackboard, perhaps a little geography. By the *Third Book* one was very likely to be writing with pen and ink and studying the elements of grammar, parsing easy sentences, and beginning world history and natural history. By the *Fourth Book* arithmetic lessons reached vulgar and decimal fractions and square roots, and geography now required an atlas as well as a textbook. Only with the *Fifth Book*, however, came the separate lessons in natural philosophy, algebra, mensuration, geometry, bookkeeping, or linear drawing with which to cap 'a thorough English education.'[33]

Instruction for girls had always differed somewhat from that for boys, but bigger schools and an enlarged curriculum accentuated the gender gap. The public debate in the 1860s over whether some subjects were appropriate for young women or whether girls were even capable of learning certain things related primarily to the issue of girls' attendance at grammar school. Common school practices elicited little discussion, but the incidence of sexual segregation and special treatment ranged in degrees from blatant to subtle. The education department encouraged explicit separation into single-sex classrooms or schools and, in the 1850s and 1860s, that became standard practice in town and city schools whenever space and teaching staff permitted. Typically, intermediate and senior boys' classes were taught by men; the girls' division by women (there was even an authorized Irish reader 'for the use of female schools'). The vast majority of youngsters, especially those in one-room country schools, experienced the differences as a matter of emphasis. One suspects that more frogs were caught by boys than girls for a natural history lesson, and certainly girls typically began needlework (which they brought from home) along with the alphabet. Even in Toronto schools, where boys and girls worked through the readers at the same pace, the local superintendent examined only boys on the *Second Book* lesson on cruelty to insects (section IV, lesson 5) while the tale of 'The Theft of the Golden Eagle' (about a stolen baby and a mother's bravery) was a favourite of the girls reading from the *Sequel*. By the senior division, boys studied bookkeeping, practical mensuration, and, perhaps, the first two or three books of Euclid; the girls, meanwhile, polished their crochet skills and did worsted work and embroidery instead of mathematics. Their accomplishments at plain and ornamental needlework, map and watercolour drawing, and penmanship were often displayed during midsummer and winter holidays.[34]

The introduction of military drill at the height of the American Civil War highlighted these obvious gender divisions. In December 1862 Ryerson urged all male common school teachers to start drill for boys over the age of ten years. Nothing too fancy was possible, he realized, for he could not count on the teachers' having any experience, but 'they might be taught to face right and left, to march, and to form fours deep.' In Toronto in 1863, under the tutelage of a prominent local citizen, Major R.B. Denison, the senior common school boys were drilled an hour a week; 'a few parents have objected,' the local superintendent honestly admitted, 'but generally the Drill has been equally acceptable and beneficial.'[35] Ryerson was convinced, as were many of his British and American contemporaries, that military drill provided an indispensable lesson in citizenship and patriotic duty, and in 1865 he even flirted with making military studies compulsory in the grammar schools. As the threat of military action receded, the moral value of drill came to the fore. Over the years educators and their publicists had lost few opportunities to applaud habits of obedience and discipline among school children. As the *Globe* once described it, the sight of children returning to their places 'as regularly and soberly as soldiers' was 'the very best evidence that could be given of the healthy state of the school.' 'Nothing else is so well adapted to secure those habits,' Ryerson forecast in 1862, and that message was heard in the depth of Huron County where regular drill in ss 1, Howick, reputedly lent 'a tone of regularity to all the exercises of the school.'[36]

Enthusiasm for military drill proved short-lived and by 1870 had become virtually extinct even in the grammar schools.[37] But interest in the 'regularity of the movement and the aim at perfection on the part of every scholar,' that so pleased Cyrus Carroll about the Howick school children did not evaporate; it was transferred to gymnastic exercises for boys and

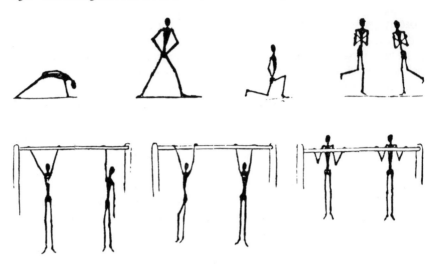

Early gymnastics, illustrated in *The School House*

a genteel form of calisthenics for girls. Vocal music was another special case, in that the teacher's interest and talent, much more than the availability of *Hullah's Music* textbook, determined whether it was taught. In most instances, however, subjects were added to, not dropped from, school curricula in these decades. As schoolhouses improved, maps, blackboards, and perhaps a globe or abacus appeared to make the study of geography, history, or mathematics something more than memorizing the textbook. In country schools there was often a battle to persuade parents to buy new textbooks (some expected a set to last at least a generation). But by the late 1860s, as additional texts were authorized along with the new Canadian readers, even rural teachers offered algebra, geometry, or bookkeeping occasionally.[38]

The Irish readers played such a central role in shaping a uniform curriculum for common schools across the province that one might expect their replacement to have caused at least a mild disruption. It did not. The Canadian series, authorized in 1866, took their place with scarcely a ripple. For all their additional Canadian content, the readers continued essentially unchanged, still primarily repositories of the 'useful knowledge' upon which public educators had placed great store since the 1820s. Even making allowances for the fact that some things cannot be counted and could not otherwise have been measured by the education department in its ceaseless documenting of the 'progress' of education, one retains the disquieting impression that for all its expansion in quantity, common school instruction did not become appreciably more generous, intellectually. Amid the accumulation of facts and memorizing of maxims there was precious little for the imagination.[39]

II

Very few common school teachers had time to nurture a child's imagination; whether they were in one-room country schools or 'modern' age-graded city schoolrooms, they had their hands full elsewhere. Ellen Bowes remembered inheriting about forty-two students with her first school in 1855. 'Some reading aloud, some talking, some had Slates, some stood up by the Teacher and read to him ... The Teacher kept order by the vigorous use of a cane,' she recalled. Her first step was to classify the school with the aid of the Irish readers, then to impose silence ('reading aloud or even whispering could not be tolerated'); finally, she recounted with relish forty years later: 'I was able to bring the School to order, and to teach the several branches of Reading, Writing, Spelling, Arithmetic, Grammar and Geography.' In fact, the job of bringing order to a rural schoolhouse in Middlesex County might actually have been easier than teaching in one of Toronto's schools in the 1850s. Classification according to the Irish readers created three broad divisions in the city's six new schoolhouses, but the teacher (female) of a 'First Division' (or elementary) class invariably had charge of more than one hundred pupils who might be at any stage from learning the letters of the alphabet to finishing the *Second Book of Lessons*. The result was predictable: 'so much time is inevitably occupied by the teacher hearing so very many children reading that not much can be done, though some little is done in the way of elementary arithmetic and geography,' James Porter concluded after visiting Louisa Street school in 1859. Until the mid-1870s Toronto teachers wrestled with as many as nine levels within one classroom: at most, each student was 'actually taught' during only one-third of the school day. The new superintendent, James Hughes, observed sympathetically that 'the work of the teachers in disciplining and teaching their classes was more than double what it should have been.'[40]

It is not surprising that questions of how to manage a classroom and how to teach effectively preoccupied mid-nineteenth-century educators. Views on pedagogy (the art of teaching) were often linked, intellectually, to certain philosophies of education and theories of human psychology, but there was also a very practical side to the matter. Few theorists would have quarrelled with the instinctive first move of Ellen Bowes to classify and order that classroom environment: it was with the moves after that that debate began.

Discussions about curriculum and teaching methods were not new in the 1840s, even in British North America. The Reverend John Strachan's views on matters of discipline, the importance of emulation, and the role of incentives appeared positively avant-garde to many of his Georgian contemporaries. By the 1820s and 1830s the mechanical metaphor so perfectly reproduced by the monitorial system came under fire from British, German, and American critics as outdated, as 'too eighteenth century' to meet the demands of a new era and new societies. Significantly, Ryerson devoted more space in his 1846 report to reviewing current controversies about how to teach a given subject than he did to justifying that subject's inclusion in the basic curriculum. Information was important, indeed critical, in this most practical age, but inherently subordinate to training the child's faculties. As early as 1846 Ryerson clearly articulated a theory of mental discipline that prevailed among Canadian educators for the remainder of the century. 'The harmonious and proper development of all the faculties of the mind is involved in the very method of teaching, as well as in the books used, and even irrespective, to a great extent, of the subjects taught,' he contended. Moreover, 'it cannot be too strongly impressed, that Education consists not in travelling over so much intellectual ground or the committing to memory so many books, but in the development and cultivation of all our mental, moral and physical powers.' Too often traditional schoolmasters proffered a shallow brand of 'mere word knowledge,' and even that inefficiently. 'A knowledge which penetrates little below the surface, either of the mind, or of the nature of things – the acquisition of which involves the exercise of no other faculty than that of the memory' is not really knowledge; and as it 'has no existence in the mind apart from the words in which it is acquired ... it vanishes as they are forgotten.'[41]

The job of introducing a radically new pedagogy to the province's common schools was given to the Normal School. Exactly what changes the Normal was promoting are difficult to specify; little that is explicit on the subject has survived. But two developments appear obvious: the emphasis, first, on new, more 'intellectual' methods of instruction, and, secondly, on improving the content of instruction, on preparing students to teach additional subjects at the senior levels of the common school. In his lecture at the school's opening in 1847, Thomas Robertson criticized the monitorial system of teaching, charging that 'it made teachers indolent, and teaching too much a matter of routine.' He advocated the simultaneous method of instruction in which the teacher dealt 'directly' with all pupils. The crux of allegations of 'mechanical' teaching related to the traditional teacher reliance on verbal memory work. In the old rote memory methods, a single teacher could set students to work memorizing texts. While he or she instructed pupils individually, a monitor (a senior pupil or beginning teaching assistant) would 'hear' other students individually recite the lessons as they learned them. It was this individual instruction that progressive educators deplored on principle. The mere sight of it was a reminder of the bad old days. Even Toronto's local superintendent, no particular champion of the Normal School method, reacted strongly. He was dismayed in 1859 to discover that one of his most experienced primary teachers, trained in England by Samuel Wilderspin, the founder of the renowned infant school system, gave 'more individual instruction to the members of her classes than is usual or, perhaps, generally practicable.' His diary notes reveal his dilemma: appreciating her success with an incredibly unwieldy class (in which forty of the ninety-four little boys present were at the alphabet stage), he felt compelled nevertheless to register his disapproval of her teaching technique.[42]

The new intellectual method required the teacher to engage the entire class in discussion and, through lectures or questions and answers, gradually enlarge the understanding of the pupils. 'Natural' methods of teaching provided the key. When one viewed the child's mind as active, rather than passive, then the metaphor for instruction changed from one of *filling up* a receptacle to *engaging* a lively entity in a mutual – but far from equal – enterprise. The new pedagogy was determinedly teacher-centred, but the image was more that of an orchestra leader than an oven-stoker cum slave-driver. The much-touted 'object lesson' captured the essentials of the new methodology. Instead of asking students to memorize facts about the physical sciences, for example, teachers were encouraged to use a more concrete approach, to bring real things into the classroom to be examined, discussed, and analysed. Instead of learning in an objectless void filled only by the printed word, students in a truly 'modern' classroom were to be exposed to the physical world around them and encouraged to spend at least some of the time studying from nature rather than from books. In part the object-lesson technique – honed to a science by Edward A. Sheldon in Oswego, NY, in the 1860s – built on common-sense tactics familiar to anyone who has ever tried to instruct a beginner: first count apples or daisy petals before dealing in abstract numbers; then half and quarter the apple or divide the petals into piles as a way of introducing the notion of fractions. As formal pedagogical technique, object teaching became highly fashionable in North American educational circles as public school attendance became more universal and more regular. School might just seem less alien, initially, when pupils and teacher shared a common vocabulary. Ideally, the teacher could then build on, rather than deny, the child's own experience as the world of the classroom became formalized and more unlike home, and the concepts to be learned became more abstract.[43]

The new pedagogy, and object teaching in particular, received strenuous support from all the branches of the education department. While the *Journal of Education* reprinted inspirational 'how-to-do-it' hints for teachers, the Educational Depository extended its policy of a 100 per cent matching grant from books to maps, charts, models, and objects of natural history. In announcing the move in 1855, Ryerson explained its rationale; 'persons of all ages, and especially children, learn and understand much more readily and remember much more perfectly, and permanently, what they see than what they acquire in any other way.' Though there is 'no royal road' to knowledge,' he admitted, 'there is a natural road to it; and the more the nature of things is exhibited in the course of teaching, the more rapid and thorough will be the progress of the pupil.' The message could not be repeated too often. 'It is now conceded by everyone,' Hodgins reminded the readers of *The School House*, 'that we can best understand those things which we can see and handle, as well as talk about.'[44]

A map, a coloured picture, or even an arrowhead found in the schoolyard could not guarantee a successful lesson, however. Object teaching could deteriorate as easily as any other technique into mechanical recitation. In the study of geography, for example, an area that notionally benefited from visual aids such as maps and the physical concreteness of a spinning globe, the promised transformation in learning often proved something less than miraculous. Children could answer elementary questions simultaneously, but when called upon individually were often at a loss for words: or they were unable to illustrate on a map what they could say from memory. In large classrooms, such as those in Toronto, where youngsters were taught simultaneously but worked their way through various levels in the room together, only the most senior, who had rehearsed for the 'umpteenth' time, could perform adequately for the local superintendent or answer intelligently on examinations.[45] Even under ideal conditions, with master teachers and carefully selected pupils, object teaching exhibited the strain of attempting to encourage simultaneously both accuracy in factual knowledge and understanding: the thin ice of mechanical recitation was obviously never far away. A description of a natural history class deserves to be recounted in full.

A picture [was] chosen upon which a camel and a cow were represented. Questions were asked relating to the class of animals to which the camel belongs, the character and habits of those animals; in what they are alike, in what unlike; the peculiarities of the cow and its uses; those of the camel, and the countries

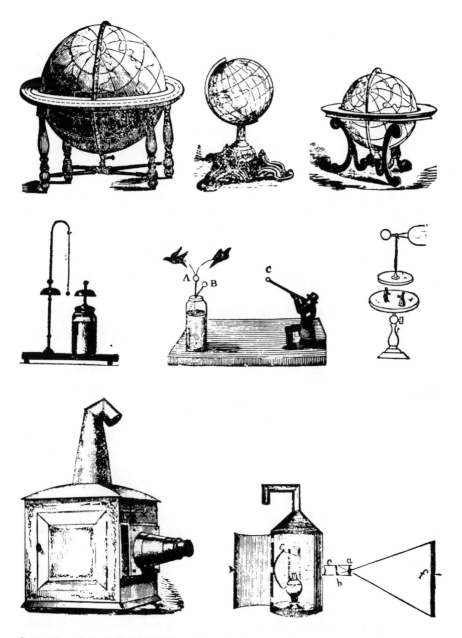

Suggestions from *The School House* for equipping the schoolroom: globes, electrical apparatus, and the magic lantern in which it lives. The little pupils described, with surprising accuracy, the qualities that adapted the camel to the climate and conditions of the countries it inhabits, its use in bearing burdens and in crossing the deserts, the peculiarities of its stomach, in the cells of which the animal carries water sufficient for a supply of several days, the adaption of the cushion-like arrangement of its foot to the sand or dust of the desert. The answers were generally promptly given, and if there was any hesitation in the class it was removed by the encouraging voice and manner of the teacher.[46]

Proponents of object teaching were never easily discouraged, and by the mid-1860s they vigorously promoted its extension throughout the curriculum, as a better way to teach grammar, arithmetic, and natural history. Reservations were brushed aside, inadequacies blamed on inexperienced teachers, not on the theory itself. So committed was J.B. Dixon, MA, after travelling on behalf of the Teachers' Association to Oswego, NY – where he saw 'the system in full and beautiful operation' – that he reported that nowhere in Canada was the system as yet thoroughly carried out. Oswego's success Dixon attributed to the five months' special training given to prospective teachers; no one, apparently, in the amiable atmosphere of the Teachers' Association meetings chose to comment on the obvious discrepancy between that situation and the typical training provided Ontario's teachers.[47] The fortunate few who attended the Toronto Normal School were armed with some very practical suggestions. But the notes kept by Maria Payne, a student at the school in 1869, suggest that in this new era a successful teacher needed to be something of a paragon: a charismatic personality with endless energy and infinite patience. One could not suppose it possible to let students 'grow inattentive and then straighten them in a minute,' Payne had been warned, but there were ways to attract and maintain the interest of the pupils.

They must have an appetite for what you are telling them. The teacher must have a pleasing manner. The subject must be adapted to their comprehension. At the beginning of the lesson ask them 4 or 5 questions on what they have gone over to connect with the last lesson, and to interest them. Give the questions to the least attentive members of the class. Plant 3 or 4 facts and then drill 2 or 3 more and drill over the whole.[48]

Of course it was hard, indeed virtually impossible, to make reality match the ideal. Poor Mary Robinson did not have 'a pleasant manner' when the Reverend James Porter visited her Victoria Street gallery class. She needed to be 'more calm and collected and less noisy and emphatic' when dealing with the children, he explained to her, without acknowledging that having the company of one hundred little boys all day might have something to do with the unpleasantness of the atmosphere.[49] Even for teachers with encouraging voices and manners there were pitfalls. 'In the art of questioning most of the teachers are sadly deficient,' James Fotheringham observed from his vantage point in Hibbert, and for Ryerson's benefit went on to describe the making of a disastrous class: 'a teacher asking of a class promiscuously, say, 100 questions, and answering 80 or 90 of them himself, not in brief and simple propositions, but with many explanations and much lecturing which drown their [sic] pupils apprehension and destroy their interest and attention.'[50] The growing fashion for 'Mental Arithmetic' posed particular hazards of this sort. While written arithmetic retained the textbook formality of rules and abstract number problems, mental arithmetic was geared to calculating solutions to questions drawn from real-life situations – problems relating to time, currency, weights, and measures, for example. A typical question to a twelve-year-old boy went as follows: 'a well was dug three-fifths through the clay, one-fifth through the sand and nine feet through the solid rock, how deep was it?' Much like object teaching, mental arithmetic was thought to excite the students' interest and encourage spontaneity and logical, rational thinking. Invariably, an enthusiast warned the editor of the *Journal of Education*, teachers introducing the subject start with questions that are too difficult and everyone becomes discouraged. It was not the fault of mental arithmetic; 'preachers, teachers, parents, masters are constantly falling into the same error' of rating 'too highly the capacity of their pupils.'[51]

With such high ambitions the proponents of the new 'intellectual' pedagogy required a second line of defence, a position of retreat. Certainly the Normal School recognized that and spent what some critics by the late 1860s considered an inordinate amount of time instructing students in the fundamentals of the common school curriculum. Normal School students were drilled as they in turn would drill their pupils in grammar and the content of the authorized volumes of the Irish national series.[52] Toronto common school trustees were equally clear-headed. 'Education may be either mechanical or intellectual: the best education has a proper amount of both: it should be intellectual from the very beginning, then every step the pupil takes will not only become easier to him, but will be a constant source of delight,' the committee on school management intoned, in terms calculated to please the most progressive-minded of the taxpayers to whom they were responsible. 'But' they continued, 'no important lesson should be unaccompanied with such an amount of mechanical drill as will enable every pupil of each class to master thoroughly every part of the subject, in every way in which it can be viewed.'

Teachers may become weary and parents complain of slow progress, but there was only one way to teach *en masse*, the committee concluded from its school inspection: 'that teacher is always the most successful who possesses the greatest power of patient and unremitting drill.'[53]

Victorian educators saw no contradiction in simultaneously espousing natural teaching methods designed to animate students and praising endless drill and rigid discipline. After all, the purpose of public instruction was generally acknowledged to be the training of the child's several faculties and then, as now, the notion of training implied purposive action, some element of discipline and structure in the experience. Otherwise faculties could be said to unfold like so many water-lilies, which was not an image most Victorian Canadians would recognize. Certainly not J.B. Dixon, for whom the highlight of his Oswego visit was witnessing 'with what diligence and perseverance the Teachers keep their classes at a simple sentence till every Pupil knows every word at sight, and can read the whole in a clear, distinct and natural tone of voice.' We may shudder a little as we imagine the scene from the vantage point of the late twentieth century, but Dixon was supremely confident that here legitimate ends were being met: all the children could 'thoroughly understand, pronounce and spell the words of every sentence they were being taught.'[54]

Evidence from other occasions and in other contexts does suggest that mid-Victorian educators were not always preaching to the converted. Restraint and discipline were widely shared values, but not everyone agreed on how to achieve the necessary control. 'The great mistake, I fear, on this continent, is the idea that education may be had without discipline – forgetting that this discipline itself is the most important part of education,' the Reverend George Blair reminded the common school teachers, school trustees, and parents of Durham County in 1866. Obviously suspecting sentimental indulgence in the ranks of his audience, he was adamant. It was fine for teachers to be constantly cheerful and kind and to try to make school tasks 'as attractive and interesting as possible,' but '*patient silence and respectful attention are perhaps the most valuable lessons which a child can learn in school.*' Blair was certainly cantankerous, but in this he stayed close to the official education department position on the need for strict discipline and orderly school management.[55] Ideally, the teacher in this new era commanded attention by dint of a natural ability to govern and sound training in the latest Normal School methods. In addition – or perhaps just in case – the department determinedly pursued a number of procedural innovations to help regiment the erratic rhythms of school life.

An orderly environment was a basic necessity. If the reminiscences of

RULES AND REGULATIONS OF

Victoria Central School !

SANCTIONED & APPROVED BY THE BOARD OF TRUSTEES.

SCHOOL HOURS.

1st. The hours of Tuition shall be as follows:—Morning, from 9, A.M., to 12—Afternoon, from ½ past 1 to 4, P.M.
2nd. The bell shall be rung every day as follows:—At ½ to 9, A.M.; 5 minutes to 9, A.M.; 5 minutes to 12, A.M.; 25 minutes to 1, P.M., and 5 minutes to 4, P.M.

DUTIES OF PUPILS.

3rd. After having entered their respective Class Rooms, not to leave them without permission. To be seated in their own seats at 9, A.M., and at ½ past 1 P.M., and any coming after those hours will be marked late.
4th. To present themselves at School at all times neat and clean in their persons and dress, and all failing in those particulars will at once be sent home to have the matter attended to.
5th. To take the necessary Books home to enable them to prepare their lessons for the succeeding day.
6th. Always to pay proper attention and respect to the instructions and admonitions of their Teachers.
7th. No pupil will be allowed to remain in the School House during the time allotted for dinner unless he or she live at a distance from the School, and then only during unfavorable weather, such distance to be determined by the judgement of the Teacher, according to the age, constitution and sex of the pupil.

DEMERIT MARKS.

8th. Demerit Marks will be recorded against pupils for the following offences, viz:—Absence from School without leave; whispering or talking during the time of prayers or during School hours; chewing gum or anything else during School hours, opening the folding doors without orders; being in any other Room than the pupil's own; leaving seats without permission; using improper language either in or about the School House, or in any manner treating teachers with disrespect; defacing the walls of the School rooms, marking or injuring any of the furniture; injuring the property or person of any fellow pupil or other individual; neglecting to study; disobedience to Teachers, and in general for any improper conduct—1 Demerit Mark for each offence. It being discretionary with the Teacher to record any number of such Demerit Marks against offenders, as he or she may deem advisable.
9th. The scale of deportment shall range from 0 to 6—6, shall denote perfect; 5, very good; 4, good; 3, indifferent; 2, bad; 1, very bad; 0, disgraceful, and it shall be regulated in the monthly reports by the Demerit Marks as follows:—

0 Demerit Marks	shall denote	Perfect.
1 to 5 (inclusive)	" "	Very Good.
6 to 11	" "	Good.
12 to 17	" "	Indifferent.
18 to 23	" "	Bad.
24 to 29	" "	Very Bad.
30 and above	" "	Disgraceful.

DUTIES OF TEACHERS.

10th. To be in their respective Class Rooms at ½ before 9, A.M., and at 25 Minutes past 1, P.M., for the reception of pupils.
11th. To open and close the School with prayer, not occupying more than 5 minutes on each occasion.
12th. To teach the branches required in their respective Divisions, according to the standard of promotion adopted by the Board of Trustees.
13th. To keep in the books provided for that purpose, a record of the attendance, recitations, and deportment of each pupil, and to furnish each parent or guardian with a correct transcript thereof on the 1st Monday of each month, and at the same time to furnish the Principal with the aggregate attendance for the month of the boys and girls separately.
14th. In no case to grant leave of absence to any pupil except in case of sickness or some pressing emergency, without a note from his or her parent or guardian. This rule, however, not to interfere with the dismissal of the Junior pupils in Class No. 6 at 3, P.M.
15th. To take turns in staying in with those pupils who are permitted to remain in the School House in unfavorable weather during the dinner hours.
16th. And generally to conform to all the duties of Teachers as laid down in the Common School Acts for Upper Canada.
17th. The Principal shall have the oversight of every Department of the School.
18th. In all cases when any doubt may arise as to the most effectual method of carrying out the spirit of those regulations, application shall be made to the Principal in the matter.
19th. Any flagrant misconduct or repeated misbehavior on the part of any of the pupils shall be referred to the Principal, who alone shall have power to suspend if he deem it advisable.

Rules and regulations of the Victoria Central School

retired teachers and elderly public officials can be believed, mayhem once ruled in local schools. James Kelly and James Elliott, both teachers in the 1840s, independently recalled their students throwing their predecessor out the window. Canniff Haight's memory of exactly how many schools and teachers he had encountered was a little hazy after fifty years, but he retained the clear impression that 'the greatest disorder prevailed.' 'One might as well try to study in the noisy caw-caw of a rookery,' he noted in his memoirs in 1885. John George Hodgins, by then in his retirement, agreed with Haight about the noise and disorder, although, he recalled, they were accompanied sometimes by a kind of rustic courtesy of boys doffing their caps to their elders and girls curtseying.[56] By the early 1840s more and more local communities issued regulations governing the manners and morality of common school pupils. The township of Caradoc, for example, was troubled by profane language, swearing, quarrelling, telling lies, and even talking in school in 1842. In the Gore District the issue was chewing and smoking tobacco in the schoolhouses. Regrettably, even if all fragmentary pieces of such evidence could be marshalled, it would be difficult to gauge how anarchic school conditions actually were: obviously some were more so than others.[57] The evidence leaves one in no doubt, however, about the unprecedented reaction of the new Ryerson administration. In 1845 the education department issued the first general guidelines on student behaviour and, following the 1850 school legislation, the Council of Public Instruction devised and widely publicized comprehensive province-wide regulations detailing the duties and responsibilities of teachers and trustees, and of pupils and their parents. Although the wording was revised periodically, a preoccupation with the cleanliness, promptness, and good behaviour of pupils remained constant over the next decades. Urban boards of school trustees typically followed suit, providing their own gloss on the general rules that specified the consequences of non-compliance: for example, lateness by more than fifteen minutes required a note from home, and persistent absence without explanation could lead to suspensions, then dismissal, in Toronto by the 1860s. While even the closest regulation of conduct could not achieve an overnight miracle, teachers and local superintendents obviously felt reassured by the printed text: now at least it was harder for children and parents to plead successfully that they did not know the rules.[58]

The education department radiated regulation in these years. Urban school systems were most affected as the impulse became contagious, and they added their own layers to the growing government pile; but the intrusion reached even county school trustees and remote rural schoolhouses. Much school business – from the days and hours schools were to be opened, to how a student transferred from one school to another, to when in the year pupils might be promoted from one level to the next – could be rationalized and, in time, would be; but not immediately. The confusion over holidays, whether on Saturdays or in the summer-time, was not helped by what appeared to be conflicting departmental regulations. Local custom persisted even in the cities, as the visiting British schools' commissioner discovered to his annoyance in 1865 when Hamilton's famed common schools simply closed for the last two weeks in July in addition to the regulation four weeks in August. Added to the major term breaks, of course, there were always odd days when the school closed – after a blizzard or for an annual examination, the county fair, the circus (maybe), when royalty visited (certainly), or if and when

The Governor-General visits Ingersoll

the trustees locked the teacher out. By 1867 there was sufficient disorder in the system to prompt more rigid regulations specifying that schools must be open a certain number of teaching days a year.[59] Student transfers, most noticeable within urban school systems, continued to frustrate the best efforts of administrators to freeze the mobility of working-class families. As for promotions: despite the built-in structures of the Irish texts and theories of finely graded and classified teaching units, considerations of age clashed with measured achievement, both were compounded by gender, and all were overridden by the reality of overcrowded classes. As James L. Hughes admitted, after taking over as Toronto's local superintendent, even in 1874 'promotions depended more on the capacity of the schoolrooms than the capacity of the scholars.'[60]

These were the real but predictable stumbling-blocks in the way of fashioning more than 4,000 school sections into a smooth, routinely operating system. However, innovations such as incentives for local school trustees to single out and reward meritorious pupils proved more disruptive than Ryerson and his departmental colleagues anticipated. From their point of view, the awarding of prizes simply gave public expression to the values of personal striving and healthy competition upon which Victorian society was based and which the public school system quite appropriately inculcated. In this case, they argued, pedagogical practice was in accord with biblical teachings and current political theory. Ryerson stated his opinion bluntly in 1869: the objection to rewarding meritorious school children 'is an objection against all competition, and is, therefore, contrary to everyday practice in all the relations of life.'[61] By then Ryerson was more than impatient with what he termed 'the hackneyed objection' that prizes and merit cards excited envy and dissatisfaction among the children (and their parents). But by then he had been hearing that objection from teachers and experienced local superintendents for nearly a decade, despite the department's attempts to drown opposition to the official policy.[62] The education department had not initiated prize-giving (some local schools had developed that tradition already), but in the late 1850s the Educational Depository began to promote and subsidize book prizes.[63] The outcome was all too often a shambles; whatever ideological point was to be made it was lost in an orgy of favouritism, if not by teachers, then by school trustees. Books were still such a scarce commodity in local communities and immigrant families that the stakes had been pitched too high. Without publicly admitting as much, the department introduced instead a system of merit cards in 1865. The principle of competition remained, but now there would be more 'winners' and, it was hoped, the process could be abused less easily. Illustrated with biblical scenes and mottoes, merit cards came in different denominations (five, ten, fifty, one hundred ...) in four categories: punctuality, good conduct, diligence, and perfect recitations. Students collected the cards, normally awarded each week, and at the end of term the pupils who had the largest number of merit cards in each category received a book prize.[64] The new scheme did little to mollify the growing rank of critics of schoolroom competition; whether or not the business of prize-giving became more orderly, or more honest, is difficult to judge. Certainly the experience of Ellen Bowes in a rural school in Middlesex County suggests 'not much more,' for in her opinion prize-giving was 'a most unsatisfactory piece of work.' 'When given for marks for good work, the Trustees would interfere,' she recalled; 'when given for tickets, the pupils would beg, borrow and steal from one-another, and parents thought them clever for doing so.'[65]

Over the years the Ontario education department and local school boards devised various schemes to signal the importance of emulation and competition: Ryerson's merit cards were, after all, the precursors of the bronze and silver medals that Toronto school children could earn by good conduct and regular attendance until the early 1970s. In the form-ative decades of the 1850s and 1860s, competition and awards formed part of a school system and school discipline that deliberately mirrored the values of the society it served. To later generations – and particularly our own – Victorian educators have seemed slavishly devoted to order, authority, and efficiency. Certainly, in broad outline the Normal School blueprint for Ontario's common schools appeared to mimic an industrial environment: from the ringing of the teacher's bell in the morning, the

Toronto Public School Board merit cards

school day marked its time by the minute details of an official timetable and discrete lessons in a prescribed textbook; silence, punctuality, and regularity prevailed. It is important to recognize that this ideal of modernity was seldom met; but even granting that, the industrial analogy can be (and has been) overdrawn. In Ontario, as in the north-eastern American states a decade or so earlier, the rational organization of public schooling preceded large-scale mechanized production as a significant employer, especially of youth. The new school discipline, if and when achieved, did tend to inculcate habits congenial to industrial work, but the independent, small-scale producers who dominated the local economies of rural and urban Ontario appreciated those work habits as much as any textile magnate might. Carl Kaestle has argued recently with respect to public schooling in the United States that American common schools did not deliberately replicate factories so much as incidentally resemble them: both institutions faced similar problems of organization and shared a similar 'ethos of efficiency, manipulation and mastery.'[66] Much the same comment could be made with respect to Ontario's schools.

The rituals of prize-giving and annual, or semi-annual, public examinations to determine scholastic merit appear to have had a double purpose: to incite youngsters to achieve excellence and to measure and applaud, when appropriate, the effort of teachers. While the education department and urban school administrators and trustees were convinced of the energizing role played by these public spectacles, the departmental regulation stipulating a public quarterly examination in each school was widely ignored. In the face of a dramatic decrease in the number of examinations held (a drop of 500 or 15 per cent in the previous two years) Ryerson conceded in 1869 that half-yearly exams were more feasible; but he was in an unpleasantly defensive mood. Lashing out at 'incompetent and indolent teachers' who shrank from the publicity that public examinations entailed, he charged that their criticism of competition, whether as public examinations or prize-giving, merely reflected their own incompetence or unwillingness to be judged by their peers.[67] His remarks were unfair and, more importantly, misleading. Certainly, in larger communities with two or half a dozen common schools, public examinations were highly competitive between teachers and individual schools (contemporary descriptions suggest something close to a modern elementary school track-and-field meet). But more often than not an annual examination provided an excuse for a community picnic and some local politicking.[68] They were, by and large, occasions for indulgence, marked by much showing off on the part of the children (and their parents vicariously), the teacher, and trustees. The image of community cohesion that such a scene provided – and that was so easily and so often sentimentalized – was misleading, however. The school was on display but, most often too, the school system was in command. The local superintendent, the school trustees, the teacher – even the pupils – were all players on behalf of the school system, and it was their show: the audience of parents, taxpayers, and well-wishers was composed of 'outsiders.' Seen in this light, the annual public examinations become critically important for the countless ways in which they actually reinforced the mystique of a distance between the special world of the classroom and family and community life.

Public instruction took hold, first as an idea and then as a reality, in these decades in Ontario as the school and community inched apart. It was essential to the success of the whole enterprise that both educators and the public acknowledge that distance. Teachers had to be trained to a sense of it and in ways of asserting it: in that would lie the first stirrings of professionalism. A curriculum built around special books, textbooks that not just anyone in the family would wish to – or even could – read, provided a critical wedge, while the school bell and official school hours could do double duty and keep out those who had no legitimate business in the school between 9:00 a.m. and 4:00 p.m. quite as well as confine and regulate those who did. The most daunting, but essential, move was to create a *standard* as the ground upon which only the school system could stand. Anyone with common sense thought he or she knew about standards, of course; pupils and parents instinctively characterized a new teacher as either having them or not. But as long as schooling remained almost entirely a local affair, with teachers coming and going, to say nothing of children arriving from other schools, there was little chance that a sense of a common or predictable level of attainment and performance would develop naturally, let alone be enforceable. As one superintendent put it: almost annually 'pupils have to unlearn the method of their late, and acquire that of their new, preceptors.'[69]

Much of the discussion of educational theory and policy in the decades after mid-century touched on the notion of *standard*, in the singular. To define a sense in which it could be applied province-wide to the public school system was an extraordinarily difficult task, not least becuse there were as yet few precedents. The fact that in common usage the word had multiple and ambiguous meanings simply added to the confusion. Exactly what promise, if any, was implied in the expression 'an ordinary English education'? Or, to put it another way: what could one legitimately expect from a service that advertised that product? Could it be weighed? Measured? Had the meaning of the terms changed between 1850 and 1870? The historian glimpses public educators talking past each other as they probed for answers: some preferred the inspirational meaning of *standard* as 'a definite level of excellence, attainment, wealth or the like or a definite degree of any quality viewed as a prescribed object of endeavour'; others (call them minimalists) focused on its sense 'as the measure of what is adequate for some purpose.'[70] Intelligent discussion was hampered further by the lack of systematic evidence of actual school performance.

The grammar school inspectors were the only educators in a position
to have a grasp of the level of common school instruction across the
province, as they had been examining grammar school pupils since the
mid-1850s. Annually their reports documented how inadequately prepared most students were, particularly in the English language. By implication the common schools must have been in as bad, if not a worse,
state. Thomas Robertson had not minced words with his 1856 judgment
that 'rapid utterance, careless and slovenly pronunciation, complete neglect of intelligence and expression are so common, as to be all but
universal.'[71] A decade later, the Reverend George Paxton Young was
equally scathing. By then it had become the inspector's duty to examine
all pupils for entrance to a grammar school, and 'ignorance of the rudiments of English grammar' entirely accounted for the very high failure
rate in 1865 – in some schools of more than 50 per cent. In successive
reports through the mid-1860s Young repeated his point, complete with
examples of the sentences students failed to parse and some of the more
outrageously incorrect guesses offered in specific schools. Although he
was not blamed for the fiasco, the young Normal School graduate who
had recently taken over the common school department of St Mary's
union school must have cringed as his friends and colleagues read of his
students' feeble attempts to parse 'I always do my work well':

First boy: 'I' third person singular, nominative to 'always.' 'Always,' a noun.
On second trial: 'always,' an adjective. And so on.
Second Boy: 'I' third person singular, nominative to 'always.' 'Always,' a regular
transitive verb. And so on ...[72]

Faulty grammar was only part of the problem. Too few youngsters
could read properly. At best, by the senior division they might read
correctly, in the sense of accurately, and that was important (too pronounced a dialect or carelessness had increasingly unfortunate social
consequences) and could be drilled. But nothing was more defeating than
the monotone of the primary schoolrooms – 'the hard, metallic tone, the
imperfect enunciation, the utter inflexibility of voice' – that had become
proverbial by 1870.[73] By then, too, complaints about students' reading
without expression, in a sing-song tone and mechanical manner, had also
become commonplace among American educators. It was difficult to tell
whether the pupils understood the meaning of what they were reading or
whether they were simply refusing to pretend to be interested in the
contrived diet of the schoolroom. By the late 1860s, with major new
school legislation pending, the issue of actual performance had become
critical. 'Is this low attainment in the English language to be the highest

measure of Common School work in that department? Is it to be the standard of admission into the High School?' the Reverend J.G.D. MacKenzie, Young's successor, asked bluntly.[74]

After years of quizzing each class in each school in turn, virtually every school-day morning, the Reverend James Porter of Toronto had an answer to MacKenzie's question. Porter was a 'minimalist' in the sense that he recognized that the reality of large classes, erratic attendance, and early school leaving necessarily dictated what was possible. From the outset of his superintendency he had been preoccupied by what one could reasonably expect of students who were unlikely to go beyond the intermediate division: 'they have early to work for their bread, and it is well, if while they are nominally at school, their attendance is not interrupted by occasional employment of a more active kind,' he observed in 1864. Over the years his position did not alter; his constant objective was 'to inspire the pupils with a desire for mental improvement and to put them in the way of making such improvement in after life.' The way to accomplish that end was through the basics: 'children will not become prodigies of learning in our schools,' he admitted in 1868, 'but what they have acquired they will grasp and retain and be able profitably to employ.'[75] Porter was not alone in his views; Goldwin Smith, among other prominent spokesmen, joined the debate with his address to the Teachers' Association in 1873. 'There is no use pitching anything too high,' he cautioned; 'the first duty of a school must be to teach the elementary subjects which it purposes to teach, and by its record of that kind the school must be mainly judged.'[76]

Despite its attractions, however, this line of argument had troubling implications when pushed too far. The notion of a *minimal* standard of achievement could quite easily be translated into the notion of an *optimal* standard: what any twelve-year-old (that would be Ryerson's designation in 1871) needs to know.[77] Once one had attained it, off one could go. In England, the notion of an educational optimum for working-class children gained prominence through the involvement in 1862 of the eminent Victorian public servant Edwin Chadwick in the deliberations of the Newcastle Commission on Popular Education. Chadwick presented a lengthy brief in favour of half-time education and military drill, and in 1865 his views were publicized in Canada by E.A. Meredith, a distinguished colonial public servant, in a paper given to the Literary and Historical Society of Quebec. In Meredith's opinion, Chadwick's intervention, in the form of a lengthy appendix, dwarfed the commissioners' report: 'no part of their able and voluminous Report is so suggestive, none so certain to bring about eventually a radical and permanent revolution in the whole system of education.' In Chadwick's case, however, as historian Harold Silver has pointed out, 'the argument for a "sufficient" education was an interpretation of the class function of education.' In England, the term 'elementary education' meant education for the children of the working classes, not 'elementary' in the sense of primary. This semantic distinction escaped many Victorian Canadians who were anxious to display their hard-won familiarity with current English educational practice.[78]

On the other side of the debate about an appropriate standard there were many who would peg it high. The Reverend Dr Samuel Nelles, president of Victoria University, captured their feeling when he urged educators to 'believe in the possibility of something better.' 'In educational matters the true motto is to be thankful and rest not,' he told an audience of teachers in 1869; 'it will be time enough to talk of resting when we have reached something like a settled science of the mind and an education in harmony with that science; time enough to rest when the leading Educators in Europe and America have come to something like agreement as to what should be taught, how it should be taught, and when it should be taught.' The danger inherent in this position, as Nelles well appreciated, was a reliance on structures and engineering to achieve what had yet to be arrived at intellectually. 'There is some danger of "red-tapeism" even in the School Room,' he cautioned, and went on to compare 'the abstractions of the system builder' to 'the fancies of the Poet': both needed 'to be corrected by constant reference to the actualities of life.'[79]

Nelles, then president of the Teachers' Association, had an astute sense of his audience, which was almost entirely composed of 'progressive' educators (many of whom were Normal School graduates, virtually all of whom were male) committed to the rational organization of schooling. To them, Hamilton's school system most closely approximated the ideal. But at least some of what purportedly went on in Hamilton's schools was sheer bluff – at least so the visiting British schools commissioner, the Reverend James Fraser, hoped. In Canadian terms Fraser was a minimalist; in English terms the views he expressed as an assistant commissioner on the Newcastle royal commission were 'a classic exposition of the government view of elementary education for much of the nineteenth century.'[80] To his credit, Fraser came to North America eager to observe, and he found much to admire and also to criticize during his tour of the north-eastern states and the Canadas. Disappointed in being unable to assess the Hamilton system firsthand (he had heard it was 'the best organized and most fully developed'), Fraser studied the local superintendent's annual reports. Incredulous, he quoted at considerable length from William Ormiston's 1861 description of life at the Central School:

'once a month pupils change seat ranking; twice a year half the class is promoted; ''there are hundreds attending the Central School who never speak to one another; if they know the division to which they belong that comprehends the extent of their knowledge respecting them. Those who are acquainted at home and only those are bosom companions at school.'' '
' ''Paradoxically as it may appear,'' ' the superintendent had written proudly, ' ''fewer associations are formed in the Central School, with its 1,100 pupils, than might be formed in a school of 50 pupils.'' ' Fraser sympathized with the superintendent who, he suspected, felt compelled 'to vindicate the free school system from the reproach of corrupting tendencies' – but he could not believe it. By comparison to the military efficiency of a New York school, Canadian school discipline seemed to him fairly relaxed and all rather English. 'If Dr. Ormiston's picture be drawn to life,' he concluded, 'a more wretched little being than a Hamilton school boy, ''never left alone on the School premises,'' never mixing with his school fellows ''except in the presence of his teachers,'' with ''any associations already existing broken up'' and ''the possibility of forming new ones precluded,'' it is difficult to conceive.'[81]

The quest for a standard that would help define a common school education was intimately linked to the success of the provincial school system and of the common school in becoming, for ordinary people, the only schooling worthy of the name. In the process, an educational tradition was lost. The old alternatives – the ephemeral private schools, the Sunday and evening schools – slowly shrivelled in public estimation, overwhelmed by the vastly greater financial and organizational resources of the public school. By the late 1860s something quite distinctive had been created in the common schools of Ontario. The variation in quality (material and otherwise) was enormous, but James Fraser had understood. 'That the actual results should be unequal, often in the widest possible degree, is true of education under all systems, everywhere,' he noted sympathetically in his report. Fraser, in fact, was as informed and disinterested a judge of the Ontario scene as one could hope to find. He was willing to be impressed, but he was not gullible. He admitted that his first impression, having come from the United States, was 'one of disappointment – one misses the life, the motion, the vivacity, the precision – in a word, the brilliancy.' On reflection, however, he concluded that 'plain, unpretending' teachers successfully communicated 'real, solid knowledge and good sense' to their pupils: 'the whole teaching was homely, but it was sound.' For their part, Canadian students were not very quick, but they knew what they knew quite well.[82]
Unpretentious, cautious, diligent: common schooling was undoubtedly

all of those; but it was also limited and limiting. 'Useful acquirements, and a vigorous discipline, limit the horizon of the most popular idea of education,' the Reverend John Ambery had observed in 1860.[83] Those limitations were not imposed entirely from without. Even as the common school and local community moved apart in these years their relationship retained its intricacies. This was still a very intimate world in which, to a significant degree, the values and attitudes of parents and local taxpayers were recreated and renewed in the school environment, whether that was a common or a grammar school. But public education has never been the sole creation of its immediate clientele. With increasing success the curriculum, teaching methods, classroom organization – indeed, all the rituals of the school day – were being fashioned by public policy. The result: a very particular cultural environment, which for many was congenial and sufficient; but significant elements in the population were excluded in one way or another. Thus efforts by some to fit in, by others to create an environment more appropriate to their convictions, race, or gender provide a counterpoint to the dominant theme of public schooling in these mid-century decades.

9 Exceptions to the Rule

City politicians and prominent and not-so-prominent local ratepayers met with the Toronto Board of Common School Trustees in the St Lawrence Hall on the evening of 9 January 1852. The occasion was one that, in substance, was repeated through the 1850s and 1860s in nearly 4,000 school sections across the province. This particular meeting had been called in response to a petition critical of the trustees' decision to defray entirely by property assessment the expenses of running the city's common schools, over and above the government grant, and to forgo the income received from the monthly charge – or rate bill – imposed on the parents of children attending the schools. In short, the city's common schools were to be free – and (once again) some citizens objected. Egerton Ryerson diplomatically took a back seat on this occasion; it was, after all, a local not a provincial decision. However at an appropriate moment in the course of the meeting he recounted an incident on an official trip he had paid to Boston. He was touring the high school (which was free) with the Mayor of Boston, who pointed out to him 'two lads who occupied the same seat.' One was the son of Abbott Lawrence, the great manu-facturer and now the American minister in England, Ryerson recalled, and the other was the son of the door-keeper of the city hall. 'They were enjoying the same advantages, the son of the millionaire and the son of the door-keeper,' he told his audience pointedly; 'and that was what he wished to see in Canada.'[1] Indeed, at the beginning of his career as chief superintendent, Ryerson had fastened on the idea that the whole operation of the provincial school system could contribute to the ideal of social harmony. Not only would neighbours in countless communities find com-mon cause in local school affairs but, he hoped, a shared recognition of the value of the school system would help bridge the gulfs of nationality, religion, occupation – and class – that divided Upper Canadians. Finally, as his Boston story underlined, Ryerson believed that the school experience itself would contribute by its 'commonness.' Free schooling, he and its many proponents argued, simply helped to realize this common school idea.[2]

In fact, the notion that schooling should be free was much more radical than its supporters ever admitted. In Britain, generations had been taught that to pay for the education of one's children was both an obligation and a right of parenthood. Not only were families accustomed to paying, and to having that measure of control over the enterprise that even a modest financial contribution entailed, but *not to pay* appeared to have the same devastating consequences as taking charity: one risked losing one's *own* sense of independence. Memories of both the practice and its meaning would have accompanied immigrants to British North America and thus, by the 1850s, a tradition of some force was in the process of being overturned. No wonder so many speeches, which sounded so much the same, were repeated year in and year out across the province. The principle of free schooling was radical, too, in that it entailed an element of compulsion. The obvious line of argument led to compulsory attendance: if taxpayers were assessed whether or not they used the common schools, children not attending the school supported for their benefit should be required to do so. What was less widely acknowledged in the public debate that developed in the 1860s over the appropriateness of compelling the poor parents of neglected or delinquent children to send them to school was the fact that the provision of 'free' schools made it progressively more difficult for all but the most privileged of parents to refuse or resist the terms on which common schooling was offered. Parental influence over the content and manner of schooling diminished as the various strands of discipline, pedagogy, and curriculum in the common school system were woven together.

Furthermore, the goal of standardization to which the education department aspired was not simply a bureaucratic phenomenon. Standardization was an integral part of a crusade that asserted one set of values at the expense of others. In a very real sense, in the immigrant society that Upper Canada would remain until well past mid-century, everyone belonged to a minority; some were either instinctively or from experience more conscious of that status than others. Under the circumstances, it appeared to matter less that the cultural values the common schools promoted were truly held in common to begin with than that they represented a common set of values the next generation would share. Kingston's local superintendent, R.S. Henderson, was particularly distressed by the social distance that separated rich and poor in 1852 and, consequently, described the challenge free schooling faced in somewhat florid but not unfashionable terms: 'Education is to be the lever ... that will elevate the social state of the poor – assimilating them in habits, thoughts and feelings to the rich and educated – giving them the same intellectual tastes and pleasures; and endowing them with the same sentiments and feeling.'[3] In increasing numbers Upper Canadians came to share Henderson's preoccupation with social-class relations in one form or another. For many Protestants the common values inculcated in the local common school related directly to a social milieu in which the traditional boundaries of family and ethnic community were gradually being demarcated by social class. Roman Catholics did not dispute this view of society, but many of them, especially recent Irish Catholic immigrants, considered other religious and cultural values to be paramount. As the campaign for free common schooling gained momentum in the 1850s, their determination that the schools their children attended should foster their own value system stiffened. At the same time, the circumstances of other minorities on the extreme margin of this mid-Victorian society – blacks and the destitute urban poor – tested the common schools' claim to be universal. Thus the issue of separate schooling within the provincial common school system claimed the stage along with free schooling after mid-century.

I

The expression 'separate school system' has been associated for so long with Roman Catholic schooling in Ontario that one tends to forget that the initial 1841 legislation provided for dissentient schools in both sections of the newly united province of Canada whenever requested by 'any number of inhabitants of any township, or Parish, professing a religious Faith different from that of the majority.' Such separate common schools were to be subject to the same conditions, rules, and obligations governing other common schools and, in consequence, would qualify for government grants in the same manner as government-funded common schools.[4] Such a wide-open – if not reckless – mandate betrayed what John George Hodgins later characterized as 'the peculiar circumstances' in which the requisite clauses were drafted, 'a result of deadlock in the legislature, and of an effort, in consequence thereof, at compromise and conciliation, under strong pressure from various opposing influences.'[5] Nevertheless the principle of publicly funded denominational schools within the framework of a common school system, once articulated in law, endured. At play in the 'peculiar' circumstances of that 1841 legislative session were many of the political forces that would attempt to contain and reshape the provision of separate schooling over the next quarter century. In the Union parliament, with its delicate political balance of francophone and anglophone, Catholic and Protestant, in an era before political parties and party discipline had acquired their modern meanings, the spectre of deadlock on cultural issues such as church-state relations and public schooling was ever present. In the highly polarized climate of the 1850s the 'various opposing influences' to which Hodgins alluded shifted their ground – and new ones were added – but to much the same end. 'Compromise and conciliation' became obscured by a barrage of stylized belligerence and calculated misunderstanding.

Legislators abandoned quite quickly the attempt to devise a uniform system of elementary schooling for both sections of the province. Within two years Francis Hincks had introduced a school bill pertaining to Canada West alone, for reasons that were entirely pragmatic. Given differing municipal administrations, it was simply administratively impractical to pursue an omnibus sytem. In fact the bases of common schooling in the two sections of the provinces were irreconcilable: much misunderstood, this point would prove to be of critical importance in the ensuing political controversy over the legitimate rights and privileges of Roman Catholics in Canada West. Apparently analogous, in fact the two common school systems were 'reverse images of the same coin.' In Canada East 'public' common schools were denominational (that is, Roman Catholic) and the provision for separate denominational schools acknowledged already existing arrangements whereby the Protestant (anglophone) minority provided separate facilities for non-Catholic children. In Canada West, following the 1841 school bill, the 'public' common school system was explicitly non-denominational and, initially, separate school privileges were intended as a measure to ensure the civil liberties of the minority – as 'a protection against insult' – in those few local communities where intense ethnic and religious antipathy might place them in jeopardy.[6] Notwithstanding the marked differences in the respective social and political positions of the two religious minorities within the united province, however, the implications of a possible parallel proved politically irresistible. Alleging that school arrangements and tax privileges enjoyed by Protestants in Canada East but not accorded to the Catholic minority in Canada West were unjust, by the 1850s Catholic leaders came to regard any rumoured alteration in status as grounds for renewed negotiation to extend Catholic rights.[7]

In the early 1840s, however, the critical issue had not been the separate education of Catholic children in predominantly Protestant Canada West. Divisions within the Protestant community itself forced the hastily conceived compromise in the 1841 school bill. Confronted by the prospect of an entirely secular common school system, Protestant and Catholic appeared united in their appeals to the Legislative Assembly: both agreed that popular education was important and that it must be based on sound

Christian principles. Among themselves, however, the several denominations quarrelled over the appropriate methods for achieving that goal and hence over administrative control of the common schools. For many Protestants the end could be met only by prescribing the Bible (the King James version) as a textbook in all publicly funded schools, although even the staunchest supporters of this measure recognized (some with regret) that it might pose insurmountable difficulties for Roman Catholics. The official Anglican position, championed by the Reverend John Strachan, now bishop of Toronto, followed current English practice in proposing state financial support for denominationally based elementary schooling. For the next two decades the aging Bishop led a protracted but futile campaign to secure tax support for Church of England schools 'in proportion to their respective numbers.' At this early juncture, the Church of England's decision to oppose a provincial common school system administered by secular rather than religious authorities was of singular importance. Ironically, it strengthened the position of the Catholic minority even as it hardened the resolve of the supporters of public schooling to resist the extension of separate school privileges.[8]

The Church of England was viewed with grave suspicion in certain quarters by the 1840s. Powerful still from its long association with the old compact Tory regime, the church was under increasing pressure to relinquish claims to special status with regard to the clergy reserves and the university endowment. In the aftermath of the 1837–8 rebellions and Lord Durham's *Report*, during Lord Sydenham's tenure as first governor of the united province, significant political forces mobilized that were antagonistic to any legislatively sanctioned privileges for the Church of England. Given this climate one can appreciate the clarity and precision of the relevant clauses pertaining to separate schools with which Francis Hincks's 1843 school act replaced the indiscriminate rights so blithely granted in 1841.[9] Henceforth, provided the common school teacher adhered to the other major branch of Christianity, a separate school could be requested by either *Protestant* or *Catholic* freeholders and would be entitled to a proportional share of the government grant calculated on the basis of school attendance. The Protestant-Catholic duality of the 1843 separate school provisions, a duality that persisted through the various school bills of the 1840s, effectively denied the Church of England's claim to equal status with the Roman Catholic Church. The major school legislation in 1850, reaffirming Catholic privileges, relegated to local school trustees any decision to establish denominationally specific (that is, Church of England) Protestant schools within the publicly funded common school system.[10] Supplementary separate school legislation – from the Taché Act in 1855 to the 1863 Scott Act, which became the basis of constitutionally guaranteed denominational school rights after Confederation – referred exclusively to Roman Catholic schooling.

During the 1840s relatively few separate schools existed. Estimates vary, but it is quite likely that the number of schools fluctuated fairly dramatically from year to year and even declined late in the decade. Reporting for 1850 Ryerson noted the existence of forty-six separate schools of which, he estimated, more than half were Protestant – and of those the majority were in all likelihood Church of England.[11] While the leisurely pace of separate school establishment was, as expected, intimately keyed to local community tensions, a more general debate intensified. Arguments in favour of denominationally based schooling advanced by religious leaders carried intellectual force in mid-century Canada. Ryerson's early efforts on behalf of the common school system were being met with widespread criticism and scepticism in communities across the colony. The pamphlet wars of the late 1840s and early 1850s that fanned that scepticism found John Strachan's Anglican followers allied with doctrinaire voluntarists – who preferred independent sectarian schooling to any state involvement – as often as with Roman Catholic publicists.[12] A shared commitment to the primacy of parental responsibility for children and their education and, more abstractly, to a parental model of state, church, and social-class relations muddied denominational, ethnic, and class divisions. Moreover, a truly secular common schooling was virtually unthinkable at the time. On the other hand, while in the abstract one could conceive of a role for both the state and sectarian interests within a public school system, the experiences of the north-eastern American states a generation earlier had already demonstrated just how elusive that ideal could be.[13] Ryerson vigorously promoted the solution of a common school that would serve a religiously mixed population by being innocuously, but definitely, Protestant. Uneasiness persisted, however. Even the ultra-Protestant Orangemen, not renowned for the subtlety of their perception of church-state issues, were troubled. At the Grand Lodge meeting in Toronto in June 1849, a committee that had considered the feasibility of a proposal for separate Orange schools felt compelled to raise what appeared to be the most formidable question: 'What constitutes a Protestant education?' While there could be no doubt about the Orange Order's antipathy to Catholicism, the report concluded that it was not possible to devise a uniform system of instruction acceptable to all Protestant sects, despite the fact that the term 'Protestant education' clearly implied something more than 'a course of merely secular tuition.'[14] Thus, over a decade, the number of tenable positions on the common/denominational school issue shrank, as in a game of musical chairs. By the mid-1850s deepening religious bitterness hardened denominational loyalties across Canada West. Most Protestants (including many, especially low-church, Anglicans) suppressed their alarm at how little commonness there was to a common Christianity, trusting in opening exercises of prayer and optional Bible reading to ensure the Protestant ambience of the common school.[15] Having commandeered the public school system, the Protestant majority ensured the vitality of Roman Catholic school ambitions.

II

Acrimony replaced relative tolerance in Protestant-Catholic relations during 'the fiery fifties.' On the political scene, a newly militant Catholic hierarchy, determined to strengthen and extend Catholic separate schools, was opposed by equally militant Protestants, whose most active spokesman was George Brown, politician and editor-publisher of the Toronto *Globe*. Determined above all else to preserve the educational system, Ryerson was forced onto the middle ground. Visibly uncomfortable, battling first one side then the other in seemingly endless public debate, he nevertheless sought a compromise that would contain the expansionist ambitions of the Catholics and at the same time preserve the principles under which separate schools functioned.[16] For soon there were more such schools. The terms of the Supplementary School Law of 1853, which relieved separate school supporters of the burden of double taxation and clarified other financial details, undoubtedly accelerated the expansion. From a modest 41 schools in 1855, separate schools grew rapidly, numbering 108 by 1858, 115 by 1860, and 161 at Confederation. Enrolment increases were equally apparent. In 1856 the 7,000 or so students in Catholic separate schools represented 2.9 per cent of the total public common school enrolment; by 1861, Catholic enrolment having grown at twice the total public school rate, that figure reached 4.1 per cent, and by 1866 it stabilized at 4.8 per cent. While in absolute numbers enrolments in the common schools and separate schools increased steadily through the 1870s, for both the drama of pioneering was over. In effect, after little more than a decade – between the mid-1850s and the mid-1860s – the outline of Catholic separate schooling was in place, predominantly in cities, towns, and village municipalities.[17]

But Roman Catholics, like Protestants, could be found almost everywhere. What, then, is one to make of the marked rhythm and concentration of separate school expansion? One might ask who wanted separate schooling? Who could afford it? How might 'affording it' relate to 'having it'? To raise and then attempt to answer these sorts of questions entails stepping back from the details of the political controversy and compromise that culminated in section 93 of the British North America Act. That ground has been thoroughly documented and ably interpreted by historians and legal advocates in recent years.[18] In a very real sense the origins of Ontario's Catholic school controversy lie outside British North America: it was the emotion that was homemade. Ireland played a large part in sending to Canada West a population that dominated the immigrant community and a school system that Ryerson adopted more in theory than in practice. Intellectually, the response of British and American Protestants to Catholic militancy and the conservative papacy of Pius IX provided Protestant Canadians with well-polished arguments. Regrettably, the virulent 'No Popery' crusade conducted through the columns of the *Globe* and many Upper Canada newspapers through the mid-century decades becomes no more palatable with time and the realization that most of its substance was imported. After all, the audience was here.[19]

If one considers only parents, not children, as the audience for this school debate, then it was a very Irish affair indeed, even before the massive immigration of Irish during the famine years of 1846–9. In the early 1840s barely half of the Upper Canadian population was native born (correspondingly nearly half – 46 per cent – was under the age of fifteen in 1841). The British – English, Scots, Welsh, and Irish – made up at least half the population: the Irish alone accounted for at least a quarter.[20] Throughout British North America for much of the century the Irish were the largest immigrant group. Any immigrant stream that substantial would command attention; but the Irish case is doubly significant, for 'Irish' immigrants were drawn from two distinct communities. Ireland was then, as it is still, a land riven by deep economic and cultural divisions rooted in religious conflict, the legacy of occupation. The duality of Catholic *vs* Protestant divided the country geographically as well as socially. Protestants tended to concentrate in the north-eastern counties, in the cities, in the worlds of commerce and domestic textile manufacturing. While there was a middle ground in border counties and tenant farming, where the two communities coexisted, the Catholic majority became overwhelming further to the south and west, where subsistence argiculture dominated the local economy. Reference to Ireland is essential, for in a country such as Canada where immigration has played such a critical part, history cannot begin at the seaports or border crossings where some other country's emigrants become our immigrants. And in no case is this generalization more true than with the Irish in the nineteenth century. As we know more of how profoundly divided along religious, political, economic, cultural, and social-class lines Irish society was, we must ask: which of these 'Irish' came to Upper Canada, and when?

In fact, the Irish migrated to Upper Canada in remarkably consistent streams through the mid-century decades, despite the tragic disruption caused by the Great Famine. Overall, Irish Protestants outnumbered Irish Catholics two to one. Those who arrived before the Famine, religion aside, came from strikingly similar backgrounds. There were extremes of course: a sprinkling of well-connected Anglo-Irish families, professionals (notably Church of Ireland [Anglican] clergy), and persons of some substance and modest education, on the one hand; and families and single young adventurers with little but the clothes on their backs, on the other. Paupers there were, of both religions, but the majority in all likelihood had known at least marginal comfort. Preponderantly from the economically advanced north-eastern counties, many may have feared (if they had not already known) reduced circumstances as tenant farmers and rural craftsmen. Once in Upper Canada Protestant and Catholic joined the season's 'immigrant take,' typically passing time in a port town or city before taking up land or locating work for wages in the country. Little of this often-protracted migration process was entirely random. One's destination could be dictated by family, kin, emigration companions, or whatever township was opened for settlement that summer. Whatever the sieve, by mid-century the Upper Canadian landscape was a chequerboard of particular ethnic and religious identities. There was a 'Scotch' block here; an old New England Loyalist settlement there. The timing of arrival mattered. Scottish Catholics, who migrated in the late eighteenth century, shared Glengarry and Stormont with Scots Presbyterians, while Irish Catholics, led by Peter Robinson, settled Emily Township near Peterborough as early as the 1820s. There were some townships – Cavan, Manvers, Adjala, and Williams, to name but a few[21] – where Irish Catholics feared that their Protestant countrymen might burn their barns or harass their children in school, but there were more where Irish Protestants and Catholics, Loyalists, Scots, and English muddled along, clearing the land and building a local economy. The relative wealth or poverty of any particular group explained less about local ethnic relations than the timing of arrival, the peculiar interplay of personality, or traditional cultural competition.

As by and large unexceptional settlers, the Irish joined the brigade of 'invisible immigrants' to the rural townships.[22] In the towns and cities, however, that was less true. By the 1840s immigrant poverty was a known quantity in the larger towns and commercial cities of Upper Canada. Both Protestant and Catholic Irish were included in the ranks of the urban poor, dependent on the irregular rhythms of an unskilled labour market on terms that were barely subsistence level. As early as the 1830s certain blocks in Kingston and Toronto had been identified as Irish Catholic enclaves – 'slums' notorious for their rowdiness, grog shops, and prostitutes.

However, the majority of the poor, Catholic and Protestant, Irish or otherwise, lived less flamboyant lives distinguished primarily by their peripheral connections to the centres of political, economic, and social power. Typically, this remoteness was expressed geographically. By 1845, for example, the Roman Catholic population of Toronto, substantially Irish, represented 20.6 per cent of the city's population, but that figure was five percentage points higher in the poorest ward, St David's, on the eastern perimeter of the city. Invariably, the migrants fleeing the Famine who landed in the port cities in unprecedented numbers in the summer of 1847 bloated an already substantial population of their fellow countrymen in the lower economic strata.

More than 100,000 Irish landed in British North America during the 1847 shipping season, two and a half times the previous year's number. The material and emotional destitution occasioned by the ravages of famine had been compounded by the epidemics of cholera and typhoid that accompanied their transatlantic passage. Of those who remained north of the American border, the majority settled in the rural townships, villages, and county towns of Upper Canada. Initially the port cities bore the brunt of the destitution, straining every resource to support the sick and dying in hospitals and immigrant sheds. In Toronto alone 4,355 were admitted to hospital and 423 were processed by the Widow and Orphan Asylum. Tragically, as a consequence of the strenuous efforts that were made to locate the immigrants outside the major cities, cholera and typhoid moved inland late that summer in the wake of immigrants sent to the country. Indeed, much of the emotion generated by the image of a destitute and diseased Irish depended precisely on a widespread experience of meeting, seeing, or hearing of such a figure.[23] In fact, however materially destitute they were on arrival, these migrants were far from being the 'dregs' of Irish society; they came by and large from the same geographical area and economic strata as the pre-Famine migrants and, like their predecessors, were more apt to have been small tenant farmers than landless labourers (who never could have afforded the passage to British North America). Concluding his exhaustive re-examination of the emigration data, Donald H. Akenson recently maintained that Irish migrants arrived in Ontario in terrible condition, but that their 'bodily emaciation should not be equated with cultural impoverishment or with technological ignorance.' While the religious composition of the Famine migration must be inferred from its congruity with pre-Famine patterns, as Akenson demonstrates, the religious composition of Ontario's population in 1871 so closely approximated that of 1842 that it is difficult indeed to characterize the Famine migration to Upper Canada as a Catholic affair. In this, as in other matters relating to the Irish, Akenson persuades us, Canadians have been beguiled for too long by an Irish American version of the story.[24]

The crisis of 1847 sparked a flight from Ireland that did not stop. Australasia soon outdrew British North America, as the United States absorbed the overwhelming preponderance of the heavy transatlantic immigrant traffic. The relatively modest annual post-Famine migration to Upper Canada may have included, finally, more of the classic poor than previously, but the outline of the Irish immigrant community had been set. The emotional complexity of Irish cultural relations was reproduced in Upper Canada, only the majority-minority positions of Catholic and Protestant were now reversed. Protestants were dominant among Canadian Irish. At the same time, Catholicism in Upper Canada was stamped indelibly as Irish. Traditional centres of Catholic settlement, such as the francophone communities dating from the eighteenth century around Windsor and Sandwich in the west, and the Scots in Glengarry on the upper St Lawrence, continued. Dotted here and there were settlements of recent non-Irish Catholic immigrants. But overall, the consequence was that the assumptions of older established Catholic families to social leadership seemed no longer quite so natural, however temporarily necessary. A significant minority of the Irish in Upper Canada now not only depended upon the strength of Catholic institutions for material comfort and support but looked upon the church as a cultural champion. Orphans, the sick, the elderly, and the destitute, in urban areas particularly, commanded attention as the shock waves of the Famine migration threatened to overwhelm traditional voluntary resources. But no issue appeared more urgent than schooling. To many in the Catholic community in Upper Canada in the 1850s Catholic schools appeared essential for both spiritual salvation and cultural survival.

Coincidentally, the issue of Catholic schooling gained prominence in the most powerful circles of the church. In Europe, by 1848, the intellectual and political forces of nationalism and liberalism reached flashpoint. Shaken by the outbreak of revolution, the Roman Catholic hierarchy moved decisively to counter both developments. The abrupt change in mood of the papacy of Pius IX was echoed swiftly by church leaders throughout the Anglo-American world in the face of increasingly defensive Protestant reaction. Many British Protestants, shocked by the conversion to Roman Catholicism of prominent Church of England theologians at Oxford University in the 1840s, were outraged by the re-institution of the papal hierarchy in Great Britain in 1850. The ensuing 'Papal aggression' controversy spilled overseas and was followed by Upper Canadians with a passion that, if possible, exceeded the British debate.[25] The appointment of a new bishop to the Catholic diocese of Toronto in 1850 to replace the much revered Michael Power, who had died ministering to the Famine immigrants, compounded the tension between Protestant and Catholic. The Most Reverend Armand-François-Marie, Comte de Charbonnel, was a French aristocrat and a strongly ultramontane cleric. Bishop Power's tolerance of religiously mixed schools in the 1840s has been variously interpreted by historians: by contrast the position of Bishop de Charbonnel has never been in doubt.[26] Initially, as far as the education department was concerned, however, nothing appeared to have changed: Bishop de Charbonnel graciously assumed Power's seat on the Council of Public Instruction and future co-operation seemed assured. Alas, to protest (as Ryerson and common school supporters frequently did through the 1850s) that Roman Catholic separate schooling would not have been an issue had Bishop Power lived was to miss the point. The times and circumstances had changed.

The 1850 school act did not help matters. The ambiguous wording of crucial sections (notably clause 19) relating to separate schools guaranteed a certain jockeying for position among common school trustees and Catholic school petitioners. Whether intentional or not, the effort to consolidate the initiatives of the various school bills passed since 1846 resulted in the reduction of certain privileges that Roman Catholics had enjoyed previously. In a climate of suspicion and grudging tolerance, confusion now surrounded both Catholic rights to more than one school in cities and towns where various established school districts had been consolidated under a single board, and the meaning of the term 'school fund' to which Catholic school trustees had legitimate claims. The Toronto common school trustees' rejection late in 1850 of a Catholic application for a third school was merely the opening scene in a drama that quickly became all too familiar. In this as in some other instances the parties resorted to the courts for a legal opinion, but invariably the offending clause or contradiction sparked a campaign for remedial legislation.[27] Surprisingly, in that he recognized the force propelling Catholic demands, at each successive stage Ryerson mistakenly assumed that a concession on the point at issue would settle the question permanently. He had an acute sense of the political minefield awaiting government action. The complex political alliances demanded by the Union, not to mention Strachan's powerful Anglican lobby, left little room to manoeuvre. Counselling the Hon. Francis Hincks and Dr John Rolph in August 1851 in favour of the proposed remedial legislation, Ryerson argued that Catholics would not benefit unduly from it because separate schools would not be able to compete with the increasingly popular free common schools. However, not to meet Catholic concerns at this point was, in his opinion, a mistake. He could foresee that the Catholics, if not satisfied, would simply escalate their demands and broaden the issue 'and then a coalition will be formed between the Roman Catholics and the High Church party, and which you may be sure will have reference to the University, as well as to the Elementary Schools, and, of course, to the Clergy Reserves. But by settling this really small affair now,' he observed, 'you prevent any such coalition, and you strengthen the bond of union between the Roman Catholic Members of Lower Canada and yourselves in Upper Canada.'[28]

What other advice could he give? A collision was inevitable. The Catholic church now officially objected to religiously mixed schooling, the matter having been debated by Irish prelates at the Synod of Thurles in 1850 and at the Council of Roman Catholic bishops in Baltimore that de Charbonnel attended in 1851. Subsequently the Bishop referred publicly to the Baltimore council as his authority for embarking on an aggressive campaign to ensure that Catholic children received Catholic schooling; but by then Ryerson could not have been surprised.[29] More than a year before he had had an inkling of the impact on Upper Canada of 'the late proceedings of the Pope & Bishops in regard to Separate Education in Ireland.'[30] In the new climate under the influential leadership of the archbishop of Armagh (after 1852, of Dublin), Paul Cullen, the vaunted mixed schools of the Irish national system became denominational, effectively *either* Catholic *or* Protestant.[31] More importantly, the example of a powerful champion of Irish Catholic schooling was close at hand in North America. John Hughes, Catholic bishop of New York, had been battling for the public funding of parochial schools in New York city since 1840.

The objections voiced by Upper Canadian Catholic clergy to religiously mixed common schools echoed the American debate for good reason: in both instances they were rooted in cultural as well as religious differences.[32] Textbooks were an obvious irritant. The authorization of the unobjectionable Irish readers did not eliminate alternate texts from local schools and some – notably Pinnock's edition of Oliver Goldsmith's *History of England* – were flagrantly anti-Catholic.[33] Conversely, books by Roman Catholic authors were allegedly censored by Protestant school trustees, who controlled local school library collections.[34] While both Protestants and Catholics believed that education without religious teaching was incomplete, in mixed schools local practice in using the Bible caused dissension. Which Bible would be used? The King James or the Douay version?[35] Daily opening exercises that included prayers were potentially even more inflammatory. The school law clearly gave Roman Catholic children the right to absent themselves during religious exercises, but what if the law were not followed? Maurice Carroll's children in the

Georgetown common school quite evidently had been intimidated by their overly zealous young Methodist teacher in 1852. Perhaps it was, as Ryerson protested, an inexcusable but rare occurrence, although in the township of Williams a community of newly arrived Scots Catholics also felt harassed by a zealous missionary teacher sponsored by the Presbyterian Free Church Society of Toronto.[36] But even well-meaning teachers continued to be confused. A young Miss Ullman ('young' one presumes because her father, Adam, wrote to Ryerson on her behalf in December 1869) gained a new student, a fourteen-year-old Catholic boy whose mother was in service in the neighbourhood. An obvious anomaly, the boy had been excused from coming to school until after the opening exercises were over. All went well until the local superintendent's visit. He insisted that the boy attend the full regular school day but gave him 'the liberty to do just as he pleased, sit, stand or kneel' during the prayers; moreover, so could any of the other pupils, as he personally preferred standing to kneeling! His daughter having been threatened with suspension if she insisted on the children's kneeling, Mr Ullman felt compelled to ask Ryerson's advice on what position of the body was preferred, if the Catholic lad remained during the proceedings.[37]

It is unfair but true that the historical record tends to heighten the pettiness of local misunderstandings such as these. Considered together in an archive, rather than singly as each was experienced, specific grievances, however numerous, appear contrived, the arguments on both sides stylized and unsophisticated. Nevertheless, the issues of Bible reading and school prayer lay at the heart of the conflict between Protestant and Catholic school supporters. The majority of Protestants could comprehend a common, truly non-sectarian religious and moral teaching that would not offend the belief of any specific Christian group. The Bible provided the obvious vehicle for such instruction: it could be read in school without comment or doctrinal interpretation. Roman Catholics, with equal sincerity, believed that that very notion was a distinctly Protestant one: interpretation, which only the Catholic church could impart, was an essential element of moral education.[38] On this point there was no ground for reconciliation, and Bishop de Charbonnel was no more inclined than Bishop Hughes or Archbishop Cullen to be conciliatory. Thus local misunderstandings related to Catholic schooling often were magnified by both sides, and Ryerson was drawn into local conflicts as reluctant arbiter or interpreter of the school law. The mood of his correspondence in these situations ranges from cautiously sympathetic to mischievous to patronizing to sanctimonious.[39] Personally he was far from being a conventional Protestant bigot. He sent his eldest daughter, Lucille, to a convent school in Montreal in the late 1840s and took young Sophie along on his audience with Pope Pius IX in Rome in 1856 – a side trip that would have scandalized his fellow Methodists had they known of it.[40] There is no doubt, though, that his Catholic critics sorely tried his patience. That failing – if it was one – and his passionate commitment to the idea of the provincial common school system, as well as to its existing structure, explain much of his behaviour over this issue.[41]

It is virtually impossible to explain the behaviour of ordinary Catholic families. Their experience of local religious tensions was necessarily immediate and personal: grievances that divided neighbours seldom appeared 'petty' to the parties involved. James Feagan's encounter with the Orangemen of Tyendenaga Township, a fairly well-settled Irish community in Hastings County, suggests that sometimes the 1841 legal phrase 'protection against insult' could carry real force. Apparently the school trustees, the schoolmaster, and some of the students in SS 21 in 1859 were among the Orange Lodge members who staged something of a charivari in front of his house and subsequently frightened his horse into bolting. Indeed, as he informed Ryerson, for the past five years he had been afraid to send his children to school.[42] One must ask where James Feagan's ordeal might 'fit' on the spectrum of Catholic experience in rural Upper Canada? Was he a relative newcomer? Were the Catholic Irish in Tyendenaga a mere handful scattered among the Protestant majority? Did Hastings County harbour a particularly lethal brand of Orangeism? Regrettably we do not have answers to these questions. Yet they are important ones, for not very far away, in rural Leeds and Lansdowne Township, it appears that there were few hazards awaiting the children of the Catholic minority in the local mixed common schools. In one school section, the largest landowner, a Catholic, provided the local stone schoolhouse for the common school system; Protestant and Catholic children attended the school while the teacher was sometimes, but not always, a Catholic.[43] To have a common school that was effectively, if even only temporarily, a Catholic school was a not uncommon compromise in rural townships.

Roman Catholics were a minority among common school teachers (numbering fewer than Anglicans, Presbyterians, or Methodists, but more than Baptists, for example); however, through the late 1860s, after the hectic pace of separate school expansion had eased, the number of Roman Catholic teachers employed in common schools exceeded the total number of teachers in the separate schools. In 1869, 566 Roman Catholic lay teachers altogether were employed throughout the public school system, 338 in common schools and 228 in separate schools (which were served by an additional 73 members of religious orders).[44] In predominantly Catholic settlements the hiring of a suitable Catholic teacher was easily accomplished, although problems did arise over 'nominal Catholics,' whose devotion came into question. Inevitably, however, personality conflicts could create a 'rumpus' in seemingly straightforward situations. The quarrel in Eganville, Algoma Township, in 1861 was quite unexpected. The majority of the community was Roman Catholic and got on well with the five local Protestant families: the common school trustees and the teacher were Catholic. In 1860 the local families asked the trustees to fire the 'obnoxious' teacher who was a drunk and a severe disciplinarian. Foiled by two 'obstinate' trustees with whom the teacher alternately boarded, the Catholic families devised a scheme to leave the common school (plus the immovable Roman Catholic teacher and trustee allies) to the Protestants and to petition to have a Roman Catholic separate school. Understandably, the Protestants objected to being saddled with the whole tax burden of the common school since they, as much as anyone, objected to the teacher. 'Anxiously waiting' a reply, the local superintendent wrote to J.G. Hodgins in the hope that the education department could devise an appropriate remedy for the situation.[45]

Like most Protestants, the majority of Catholic families lived in the rural counties and sent their children to the local common school. Contemporary estimates of the proportion of Catholic children in the common schools varied from three-quarters to two-thirds of all Catholic youngsters by the end of the 1860s; however neither figure is surprising.[46] The sparseness of Catholic settlement in many townships simply precluded any significant provision of rural separate schools. The local superintendents (invariably Protestant) who commented from time to time on the success of their religiously mixed schools were not necessarily prejudiced. There were undoubted benefits to having children of all faiths learning and growing up together.[47]

Certainly, something about John Phililps' [sic] memories of teaching in the early 1850s in Petersville, across Blackfriars Bridge from London, rings true. The school population was divided half and half, Protestant and Catholic, but apparently there was no hint of sectarian bitterness. The basic school curriculum posed few problems and, when it came to moral and religious instruction, Phililps had his own working definition: 'by "religious," I mean, such as all good, God-fearing people were agreed upon.' Too-easy assumptions about God-fearing people can lead to grief, but Phililps (rather unselfconsciously) promoted mutual understanding. 'I asked, while talking about Sabbath observance, "what works may lawfully be done on the Sabbath?" ' he recalled: 'a Protestant boy answered "Those which cannot be done on Saturday nor left off until Monday." A Roman Catholic boy replied "works of necessity and charity.'' Everyone saw at once that both answers were good and essentially the same.'[48]

One can only surmise, in the absence of detailed studies, that many rural Catholic parents were content to live with such arrangements. Overall it appears that neither Irish nor Catholic children were notably less likely to be enrolled in rural schools than children of different ethnic or religious backgrounds.[49] The experience of Peel County suggests an exception that perhaps proves the rule. There David Gagan found that the Catholic population, largely Highland Scots and concentrated in Caledon Township, appeared reluctant to patronize the local common schools. It is not entirely clear, however, whether the critical factor was religion or geography: Caledon was among the most remote and least-developed townships in the county – an area where low enrolment might be expected.[50] Certainly, in time, some rural parish priests and their parishioners disagreed on the necessity of supporting separate schools. One missionary priest complained to the bishop of Hamilton in 1864 about the reluctance of Catholics in the Scots settlement around Arthur, in Wellington County, to support a second separate school. 'The *true* objections with all the opponents,' he reported, 'are a desire not to displease their Protestant neighbours, political and pecuniary interests, and a fear of having to pay one or two Dollars for the erection of New schools, together with certain Tavern Keepers' profits, with whom some of the former Teachers ''eat and drank'' the most of their Salary.'[51] The keenness of the local clergy is understandable, but so, too, is the reluctance of ordinary families to assume the extra burden (which would amount to more than a dollar or two) of providing something that appeared to be scarcely different from the 'improving' local school.[52] Ellen McGeehan taught in the Roman Catholic school in Arthur village in 1865 and remembered it as 'an old Dwelling-house, poorly ventilated, miserably furnished, and much too small for over seventy pupils.' Moving back and forth between separate and common schools in and around Wellington County from 1860 to 1877 (when she went to high school to study for a second-class certificate under the new regulations), Ellen did not alter her routine very much. In the Arthur school she used the separate school readers (which followed the format of the Irish texts, substituting appropriately Catholic homilies and biblical selections) along with the public school textbooks.[53] Certainly, it is to be expected that the doctrinal issues at the heart of the separate school controversy worried religious leaders more than parents and children, to whom anti-Catholic slurs in the schoolyard or in textbooks were especially hateful. Since whatever anti-Catholicism the common school curriculum conveyed likely occurred in history lessons, notably when those dealt with the history and culture of Ireland, non-Irish Roman Catholics may have felt this cultural assault less sharply. The likelihood of such a selective blunting of the experience of cultural bias in the common school system, when added to their personal religious liberalism, does help to explain the strenuous opposition that John Sandfield Macdonald, the prominent Roman Catholic politician (and future premier of Ontario), and his brother, Donald (future lieutenant-governor of Ontario), mounted to the establishment of local separate schools among the Scots Catholics in Glengarry in the mid-1850s.[54]

In the larger towns and cities, by the 1850s, the situation was very different. Catholics were numerous and in many communities overwhelmingly Irish. Parish life was increasingly in the charge of Irish-born clergy. Critically evident, moreover, was the poverty of so many of the recent immigrants. Irish Catholics, collectively, appeared to stand apart from the rest of the urban population. Both the leaders of the Catholic community and its Protestant detractors painted a similar portrait at mid-century of a marginal class of menial labourers who recognized themselves as the proverbial 'hewers of wood and drawers of water.'[55] Catholics and Protestants differed, however, in the inferences they drew from what was so inescapably true. Cultural stereotypes encouraged some to project the contemporary physical debasement of the Irish Catholic population into a future drama of contagious social demoralization that would be averted only by determined Protestant proselytizing, notably through the common school. Roman Catholic sympathizers and defenders preferred to find inspiration in the demeaning circumstances of the recent immigrants. Here was a challenge to the Catholic community and its own institutions to assist the Irish to overcome a traditional image of inferiority. In the meantime, the physical endurance of Irish labourers and the sacrifice made by many men and young women for Canadian development were not to be ignored, for they rebuked the financial exploits of Protestant capitalists and the disdain of anti-Catholic bigots.[56] Roman Catholic labour had built Toronto's finest buildings, 'Patientia' boasted to the editor of the Toronto *Mirror* in 1856: if 'such a class as that which "carries up our cities on their shoulders" did not exist, how otherwise could they be carried up?'[57]

Catholic and Protestant commentators publicized the material poverty of urban Catholics in the early 1850s, but the population in fact was not homogeneous. In many towns and cities (as in the rural townships) there were already Catholic families well established and others 'on their way up.' Preoccupied for a time by the disabilities endured by Irish labourers and servant girls, by the mid 1850s the *Mirror*, for example, returned to address 'the talented lawyer, the successful merchant, the honest farmer,'

Loretto School for Girls, Toronto, 1868

daring to boast of the 'normalcy' of 'this artizan and labouring and professional population.'[58] For education the Catholic élite had relied traditionally on select convent and seminary schools (as, indeed, had many of their Protestant neighbours). The growing middle ranks of aspiring entrepreneurs, tavern keepers, builders, and small businessmen – the 'lace curtain clique,' as Murray Nicolson has described them – patronized voluntary 'select' schools and commercial academies, which the Catholic teaching orders established outside the separate school system. In Toronto in the mid-1870s it was alleged that 'there were certain "select schools" which employed the best teachers and which taught the children of the more substantial Catholics, leaving the great percentage of the Catholic children in poorer schools. Wealthier Catholics then had "no inducement to take an interest in the schools for the children of the mass of their co-religionists." '[59] The ambitions of the Loretto School for Girls, 'patronized by some of the most respectable families in Toronto,' must have been an inspiration to any Catholic crippled by feelings of collective social inferiority. In its new Gothic surroundings in 1862, this school for young ladies offered 'a finished and elegant education, including besides a thorough course of all English branches, a proficiency in the current languages (French, German, Italian, Latin), with all the accomplishment befitting a lady's education (Vocal and Instrumental Music, Piano, Harp, Guitar, etc.), Painting of all kinds, Drawing, and every variety of fancy work, in addition to a high moral training and exercise in the rules of politeness and etiquette.'[60]

Separate common schooling, on the other hand, was defined until late in the century by the twin burdens of poverty and cultural vulnerability imposed by the heavy famine immigration. It took a decade or more for the impact of separate school legislative provisions in the 1840s to be felt, as local urban communities ceased to rely on the private exertions of individual Catholic teachers and established boards of separate school trustees. Private venture Catholic schools had gone beyond the scattered enclaves of established Catholic settlement earlier in the century. In York in the 1830s, for example, various schoolmasters known to be Roman Catholic took pupils. In the early 1840s a two-storey frame schoolhouse on Richmond Street, built by philanthropist John Elmsley, provided Toronto's Catholic community with its first officially designated separate school. Denis Heffernan taught approximately forty boys, aged seven to sixteen years, while his wife took a few female pupils in another room.

Elmsley's generosity soon extended to supporting a commercial school and a Catholic classical academy.[61] Through the 1850s, the support of local Catholic élites and private donations, large and small, remained critically important to the separate schools in all urban communities. Sorting out access to the government grant and a share in local taxes was essential, of course; but if the Catholic community had had to rely solely on those resources school expansion undoubtedly would have been curtailed. More than anything the work of the members of the various teaching orders (the Christian Brothers, the Sisters of Loretto, the Sisters of St Joseph, to name only the most obvious) and their recruits sustained the schools over time.[62] The separate school might assume the premises of an earlier educational venture or occupy unused church property, but invariably it was located near if not in the midst of a Catholic neighbourhood. Often youngsters attended who had not gone to school before, their parents having barely found their footing in a new community. Over the years, each community followed its own strategy. In Kingston, for example, by 1868, 23 per cent of the city's total common school population attended one of the two separate schools, female and male, which had been in operation since 1853. Toronto, with a larger general population to start with, also had proportionately more youngsters (32.7 per cent of the total common school enrolment) in separate schools. The opening of another new school on the city's perimeter drew students immediately from the common schools, although until the 1890s the farthest reaches of the city's limits were also remote from a Catholic school. Indeed, by the mid-1850s, once separate schools had been established in and around the heavily populated core of the city, few Catholic parents sent their children to the city common schools.[63] Bishop de Charbonnel, in a Lenten pastoral message in 1856, had declared that 'parents not making sacrifices necessary to secure [separate] schools or sending their children to mixed schools' were guilty of mortal sin.[64] That message was heard clearly in urban parishes across the province; separate school enrolments skyrocketed, and then by the mid-1860s stabilized. Of course, there was a substantial variation from city to city and town to town, reflecting the religious make-up of the local population as much as its financial resources. At the extremes, Ottawa's separate schools served 52 per cent of the total common school population in 1868, while in London the figure was a mere 12 per cent.

The poverty of financial resources persisted, however, despite the 'success' enrolment figures measured. Its effects were reflected in attendance. The problem started with accommodation. From there one could detail the lack of amenities such as maps, globes, or even 'commodious seats and desks.' The last, while noted, appeared relatively insignificant in the list of things lacking in the Brockville separate school in 1873. Three teachers were attempting to teach, on average, 150 pupils in *one* room in the old Catholic church. A registration of 300 represented one-quarter of the total common school population; understandably, however, average attendance at the separate school was less impressive than in the common school system, with its two ward schools and six-room Central School. Nor was Brockville's problem unique. While the condition of the separate school in certain localities might have been inferior from the outset (as in Paris, for example), so might that of the common school have been. The more serious problem arose over time, as common school accommodation improved and that of the separate schools did not. The contrast between the two – and with that the problem of 'catch-up' – in fact sharpened. Reporting on the state of separate schools in 1865, George Paxton Young, grammar school inspector, was as generous as he could be. Some of the buildings were very poor, he acknowledged, but others – notably in Hamilton, Cobourg, Belleville, and Kingston – were very good indeed. In Toronto, despite an attendance increase envied by common school trustees, accommodation increased only marginally from 1862 to 1877. Matching the city's substantial investment in two-storey brick buildings was out of the question; as late as 1876 five of the nine separate school buildings remained wooden structures. In one schoolhouse of not more than twenty feet square 146 children tried to learn, and then to play in a yard six feet in width. To add to the problem, in Toronto as elsewhere by the early 1870s, the qualifications and abilities of members of the various religious orders to be teachers came under increasing scrutiny.[65]

Nevertheless, poor and not-quite-so-poor Roman Catholic parents did send their children to separate common schools whenever and for as long as they could. At an earlier age, often, and for not as long – but it cannot have been easy.[66] Were they coerced? Intimidated by their priest and bishop, as some anti-Catholic agitators alleged?[67] Were their children so harassed by Protestant youngsters that common schools had become impossibly uncomfortable places for Catholic children?[68] Perhaps; but the absence of systematic evidence suggests that it is unlikely to have been true on a large scale. In Toronto, at least, the isolated reported incidents of Protestant *vs* Catholic schoolboy scuffles sound more like just that – schoolboy scuffles – than significant sectarian strife. At the most one might venture an allusion to what by the 1860s had become ritual encounters between Protestant and Catholic Irish on St Patrick's Day and the 'Glorious Twelfth.' Certainly during and after school hours Protestant and Catholic children could be found loitering together by the waterfront or in a vacant lot.[69] It is more plausible to look to the separate schools themselves for an explanation of the solid support they apparently enjoyed. It is easy to imagine their appeal, especially to Irish Catholic immigrants. They were *familiar* places. There was little distance to speak of between the parish church, the local separate school, and the households they served. They were allies in perpetuating a faith in Irish Catholic identity. Catholic devotion would have pervaded a classroom taught by a member of a religious order. The artwork, songs, and stories reinforced formal lessons in the Catechism. The teacher likely prepared youngsters for the critical rites of first communion and confirmation.[70] The homeliness of the classroom – the rudeness of the building and its furnishings – would appeal to a child. Certainly it would seem less formidable and alien than a two-storey brick building with a confusion of entrances, some for boys, others for girls. The teacher's authority was understandable, being akin to that of the priest. When it came to academic matters, the separate school curriculum differed little from that of the common school. If anything, it was probably slightly more basic, more practical – and thus conceivably more attractive to working-class families for whom a child's time spent at school was money. The Christian Brothers designed their schools in the 1850s 'to fit youth to grapple with the solid realities of life and prevent them from hankering after positions which neither nature nor circumstances entitle them to hope for.' Separate school trustees who could not rely on religious orders for staff were advised by the bishop's office 'to select good teachers, and principally females, who, though not read in the stars, nor understanding Newton's Theorem, are generally more economical and better able to attend even young boys and teach them prayers, Catechism, piety, modesty, good manners, reading, writing and ciphering, etc.'[71] An editorial critique of the common school curriculum in the *Mirror* of 21 March 1856 echoed the philosophy implicit in the Bishop's ordering of the teacher's tasks. 'We are firmly convinced that the whole system is fraught with danger to the future of the people,' the editor lamented. 'Religion, ethics, history, philosophy and every other study which tends to enlarge the superior faculties of our race are totally subordinate to the cold formal one of mathematics.' The priorities were wrong and the consequences bleak: 'the generation which comes forth from the common schools of this Province may have heads but no hearts.'

There could be no rebuttal. Free common schools were designed for a world that valued 'heads' over 'hearts.' A 'cold, formal world' it might be, but it was absorbed with practical affairs and social competition. For their part, common school supporters claimed to fear that 'inferior' separate schools would jeopardize the future of Catholic youngsters in just such a world. Behind sectarian differences there was a critical issue of class segregation. For Dr Joseph Workman, chairman of the Toronto common school board in 1852 and soon superintendent of the provincial Lunatic Asylum, separate schools were objectionable precisely because they were intended to be separate Irish schools. Since Irish Catholics were the poorest class, the schools would serve in effect to segregate the lowest socio-economic class in society. If the Irish had comprised the wealthiest elements, Workman concluded, separate schools would be acceptable. Ryerson repeatedly stressed a similar point in his correspondence with separate school advocates throughout the 1850s.[72] Outraged by the unjustified barriers to personal ambition and accomplishment erected by social prejudice, he was provoked to express his convictions about the relation of schooling to society with uncommon clarity in his 1857 *Annual Report*.

Isolated from the rest of the community during the whole period of their education, they enter into the connexions and competitions of business and compete for elective and other public distinctions, almost as strangers, and aliens, and foreigners, in the very place of their birth. In isolating their children from intellectual competitions and friendships with the other children of the land during their school-boy days, Roman Catholic parents place their children at the greatest disadvantage in commencing the race and pursuing the prizes of life. It is on this account, almost on this account alone, that the existence of Separate Schools is to be regretted.[73]

III

Immigrant Irish Catholics had little choice in the early 1850s but to endure with dignity the bigotry promoted by the cultural stereotype of the drunken, hapless 'Paddy.' By 1858, however, characterizations of the Irish as the 'White Niggers of Canada' were repeated in the Catholic press defiantly, expressing new-found confidence in the ability of the Irish to overcome their typecast inferiority.[74] When one was black, the burden was considerably heavier. As we have seen, sectarian and cultural sensitivities ran perilously close to the surface of local community life in mid-century Upper Canada. The additional element of racism made the mix more volatile. Black settlement was concentrated in the western part of the province where there was access to the American border. The Detroit River area and the Niagara peninsula served as northern terminals for the Underground Railroad network that assisted fugitive slaves. Racial prejudice emerged as an issue in local school districts in various forms, but black education was never a provincial issue, despite the reluctant involvement of Ryerson in the matter. Indeed, for all their passion for statistics, education department officials enumerated neither black schools nor black enrolment on a provincial basis. In its very localism and dependence on such general factors as the timing, character, and volume of immigration and settlement, however, the problem of racial segregation in the schools in these decades highlights central themes in the free common school movement.

Black immigrants first came to the territory that would become Upper Canada as slaves of the Loyalists.[75] Through the 1820s and 1830s free blacks and fugitive slaves arrived, as abolitionist forces in the United States stepped up their campaign and pro-segregation interests countered with increased legal discrimination, particularly in northern states bordering on slavery. In 1829 the first of a series of planned communities began at Wilberforce, near Lucan, from a nucleus of 800 to 1,000 fugitives from Cincinnati who were being harassed by a revival of Ohio's discriminatory legislation known as the Black Code.[76] A steady trickle of more individualistic migration soon created black communities in towns such as London, Hamilton, and Toronto. Fifty or so families from Virginia provided a core for the Toronto settlement; by the late 1830s blacks were fairly prosperous and busily establishing church congregations and small businesses.[77]

Already by the 1840s the central political question of black settlement had emerged. Which was preferable – or possible: integration or segregation? There was something to be said on each side. A vision of the pride and independence possible in all-black communities of yeoman farmers and local craftsmen attracted support from black leaders, white abolitionists, and various religious denominations – most notably the Baptists, Methodists, and the American Missionary Association. As one floundered, another black communitarian experiment began; for all the risk involved, nevertheless it seemed preferable to abandoning fugitive slaves to bounty hunters in the United States.[78] A church and a school were often at the centre of the enterprise. The Dawn settlement grew up around the British American Institute, a manual-labour school for blacks founded near Dresden in 1842, and by the early 1850s as many as five hundred immigrants had settled in the vicinity.[79] In 1849 what turned out to be a most exceptional settlement started at Buxton Mission just south of Chatham. The inspiration of William King, a Scottish slave-owning Presbyterian missionary, the Elgin settlement, as it came to be known, initially faced a vicious pro-slavery vigilante campaign led by an aspiring Chatham politician, Edwin Larwill.[80] However, the very success of the venture as much as the support it received at the highest levels of provincial society soon smothered the local opposition. After 1850 no significant incidents of racial prejudice marred the community's development; at its height late in the decade more than two hundred families (more than one thousand individuals) were farming around Elgin. However successful racially segregated communities might turn out to be, many of their most dedicated advocates nevertheless recognized that they were – and only could be – stepping stones to integration. As fugitives, black immigrants in Upper Canada needed every imaginable kind of assistance; but none was more essential than training for a life of freedom in white society. While a number of factors contributed to the success of the Buxton Mission, the fact that King screened his recruits carefully and that few were recent ex-slaves or immediate fugitives undoubtedly helped.[81] The hurdles faced by these latter groups were especially high.

Until 1850 there were too few blacks in Upper Canada to cause more than an isolated disturbance or two. One event then triggered an unprecedented influx, ironically hard on the heels of the crisis-induced Irish migration. The passage of the Fugitive Slave Act by the United States Congress on 8 September 1850 put British North America in an entirely new position. Henceforth runaway slaves apprehended in northern 'free' states might be claimed and returned to their southern owners. There was always the risk of extradition, but by comparison Upper Canada was relatively safe. Within weeks the trek north began. All the numbers we have are estimates, but the best guess places the size of the black population in Upper Canada at the end of 1851 somewhere between 30,000 and 35,000; as many as 6,000 or roughly one-fifth probably had arrived within the year.[82] Enclaves of blacks, especially in towns, expanded rapidly as refugees clustered together or were forced into islands insulated from and by their white neighbours. In Chatham, blacks comprised 17 per cent of the town's population in 1851 and 28 per cent in 1861; in St Catharines, the proportion was estimated at 25 per cent as early as October 1851, but from that high point it declined.[83] While their impact on the larger centres of London, Hamilton, and Toronto was less dramatic, blacks in the 1850s became a sizeable urban minority. Fortunately, for much of the decade the province enjoyed buoyant economic times. In the Lake Erie – Detroit River corridor, commercial expansion and the building of the Great Western Railway meant employment for unskilled black labour. Advertisements were placed in the black newspaper, the *Voice of the Fugitive*, for example, offering the equivalent of ten dollars a month and board to railway workers. By November 1851 the paper estimated that more than 2,500 blacks worked for the railway in south-western Upper Canada.[84] Everyone was not as easily employed, however, nor was employment always regular and secure. In centres such as Chatham and St Catharines especially, the problem of poor and now often un-educated fugitive slaves assumed menacing proportions.[85] While prom-inent white citizens had notable success in mobilizing support for anti-slavery societies in London and Toronto (one experienced black publicist commented that the anti-slavery movement was more popular in Toronto than in any city 'save Syracuse'),[86] local black leaders struggled to provide essential material support for indigent families. One tactic was to solicit charitable donations for various black mission activities. 'Agents' trav-elled throughout Upper Canada, to northern American cities, and to Eng-land canvassing anti-slavery sympathizers. The 'begging issue' provoked into the open long-simmering differences of opinion among black leaders over the desirability of promoting segregated black institutions.[87]

Black schooling was at the centre of the controversy. 'Separate schools and churches are nuisances that should be abated as soon as possible,' H.F. Douglass, editor of the *Provincial Freeman*, wrote in March 1857; 'they are dark and hateful relics of Yankee Negrophobia.'[88] Five years earlier, Henry Bibb, editor of the *Voice of the Fugitive* (published in Sandwich), had sketched for an American black audience the conditions that awaited fugitives in Upper Canada. Stressing the civil liberties en-joyed by whites and blacks equally, Bibb noted the one exception. Blacks had asked for, and been granted by the provincial government, the right to establish separate schools 'for coloured people.' 'The request, however, was not made by the intelligent portion of the coloured population,' he assured the convention delegates, 'but by a lot of ignoramuses who were made fools of, and who knew not what they were doing.' 'Such men are hardly fit to live or die,' he charged melodramatically, but then went on to conclude: 'we are happy to inform you that there is no compulsion or necessity in Canada for coloured schools or coloured churches and that every man who respects himself will be respected.'[89] Could this have been a fair comment? How had a 'dark and hateful relic' of racism become government policy? Why did the government bow to pressure from 'ignoramuses'?

From the beginning of settlement black children had gone to schools much as white children had, when and where they could. There were local pressures, more or less intense, to segregate black youngsters either on separate benches in the schoolroom or in separate schoolhouses, but the issue was not raised as a question of official policy until the late 1830s. John Strachan strongly advised the government in 1828 to oppose segregation of school children, and that view appears to have prevailed in official circles for the next decade.[90] At the tail end of the debate on the 1846 school bill, for example, government leader W.H. Draper explained to the House that he had been asked to provide for coloured children separately; he personally refused, but challenged any member who wished to introduce the measure to do so. No one did.[91] However the situation for blacks worsened as the new school legislation began to take effect, regulating the confusion of local common schooling and stabilizing its provisions by the introduction of property assessment. In many communities blacks were taxpayers and as their outrage at being deprived of what they were paying for increased, they appealed to the government for help.[92] The government, in turn, was forced to confront the deep prejudice against racial integration that existed in some quarters and that in some communities, was the majority voice. The white citizens of ss 3, Amherstburg, allegedly expressed their views with breathtaking frankness, avowing that 'sooner than they will send to School with niggers they will cut their children's heads off and throw them into the road side ditch.'[93] The fact that the school act did not permit the exclusion of black children from the common school on the grounds of race did not crimp the ingenuity of some white parents and school trustees. School boundaries were gerrymandered to produce racially segregated school districts; local common schools were declared to be private institutions; and, as a last resort, white parents simply withdrew their children from the common school, which invariably collapsed because of the drop in attendance. The official correspondence confirms that the education department supported black rights of access; however, as Ryerson reluctantly had to admit, 'prejudice, – especially, the prejudice of caste, – however unchristian and absurd, is stronger than law itself.'[94]

To counterbalance the injustice it could not stop, the government included in the 1850 school act provision for any group of five black families to request a separate 'coloured' school. The law thus provided national protection against prejudice, in that, since only blacks could apply for it, segregated schooling could not be imposed by the white community. Nothing much changed. Despite the torrent of new immigrants into the province, in communities such as West Flamborough where there were still too few black families to support a separate school, black children continued not going to school at all. Elsewhere whites became even more determined to harass their black neighbours into requesting a separate school. When such requests were made – albeit reluctantly – the result was sometimes a success, as in St Catharines, where the coloured school was purported to be the 'best furnished with maps and had the best Teacher in the Town.' But it would remain for court challenges in the 1850s and 1860s to clarify and confirm black access under the law. The legislation had helped to prevent the wholesale disruption of black schooling that seemed imminent in the circumstances of 1850; however it condemned many black children to attendance at poorer schools taught by the least-qualified teachers. Although a significant population from the black communities returned to the United States at the close of the Civil War, when the level of teacher qualifications was raised in the 1870s separate black schools were especially hard hit.[95]

The dominant black experience of separate schools in these decades was evidently one of intimidation and hardship, but that was not the sum of black schooling. Occasionally a black school was so successful that white parents enrolled their children in it. Brantford was just such a case in the late 1830s, and the superiority of the Buxton school in the 1850s (part of William King's Elgin settlement) drew students, white and black, from across the province and from the United States.[96] Elsewhere, school integration was never disturbed. As in the case of the Irish Catholics, the historian must acknowledge that myriad local particularities ultimately define the given instance; while the sources of social tension can be identified, the causes are never utterly predictable. Having said that, however, one recognizes that there were general conditions that apparently favoured racial integration in the common schools. Larger, socially heterogeneous communities with diversified economies, such as Hamilton or Toronto, were well placed to support integrated schools. But even there the weight of the moral conviction of individual school teachers and trustees proved critically important. The central administration of the common schools – which was feasible only in the larger towns and cities – was helpful. In Hamilton in the early 1840s local schools and local teachers had felt vulnerable when white working-class parents threatened to withdraw their children if blacks were admitted; under the central school system it was much harder for any group of parents to subvert a city-wide policy of integration.[97] Public gestures were important. The members of the Toronto Board of Common School Trustees and the city's politicians were committed to racial integration. At the annual public meeting each summer distinguished speakers invariably noted the successful performance of black children on the competitive examinations and generally applauded their colleagues and themselves for an enlightened policy.[98]

That is not to say, however, that black youngsters attended Toronto's schools without incident. The isolated glimpse we have suggests a larger question of some importance: from the school's point of view, could race ever be a simple or single problem? Lucy Greaves, 'a coloured girl,' attended various Toronto common schools during the spring and fall of 1859. Perhaps expelled from Louisa Street school, she certainly was expelled from Victoria Street in the late spring before she tried to get into Phoebe Street in the fall. Miss Round, the experienced teacher who expelled Lucy, considered her habits and language 'to be exceedingly bad.' While troubled by the fact that he had not been informed officially, the local superintendent saw a clear-cut case for the application of rule 13 (which provided for the expulsion of students prone to habitual disobedience and 'hopeless of reformation').[99] In effect her delinquent behaviour – not her racial origin – rendered Lucy unfit to attend the common schools. The controversial decision of the London school board in 1862 to segregate all its 'coloured' pupils (numbering somewhere between fifty and eighty) in separate classes further illuminates this point. London enjoyed something of a reputation as a centre of anti-slavery support in the 1850s, and this decision had obviously been made with difficulty. The minutes of the Board of Common School Trustees reveal just how divided the trustees were: the first motion was proposed in June 1861; discussion was suspended in December until after the trustees' election; a year later it had been accepted as a matter to be dealt with 'as soon as financially practicable,' and from there it dragged on.[100] In the meanwhile, however, it had become a *cause célèbre.* A respected conservative newspaper, the Toronto *Leader*, announced its unequivocal support for the school board's pro-segregation decision in a lengthy editorial on 12 December 1862. The argument reduces to one essential: 'there is no use in trying to turn a stream against its head.' Black children could only feel uncomfortable in their existing circumstances: the teachers lacked sympathy ('to use no

harsher term'), and their schoolmates called them names. Most importantly, the trustees reported that the trading of insults in the schoolyard
led to petty disputes in which 'parents frequently take part, complaints
are made, and will continue to be made by both parties, that their children
have been insulted; and, by the coloured parents, that theirs have been
harshly and perhaps unjustly treated.' One need not read between the
lines to see that the board had a management problem: rival parents
berating the administration, perhaps with justification, could not be tolerated.

Was parental meddling, then, the real problem? Had the racial issue
been something of a red herring for the board and / or for a certain
segment of London's white population? There is reason to think that that
might be so. In his judgment in the case of Dennis Hill *vs* the School
Trustees of Camden and Zone, one of the earliest of several school-
segregation cases launched in these years, Chief Justice John Beverley
Robinson noted how complex the reaction of white parents and teachers
might be to having black pupils in the same classroom. The prejudices
of the white population 'arise,' he observed, 'perhaps not so much from
the mere fact of difference of colour, as from an apprehension that the
children of the coloured people, many of whom have but lately escaped
from a state of slavery, may be, in respect to morals and habits, unfortunately worse trained than the white children are in general and that their
children might suffer from the effects of bad example.'[101] William King,
Henry Bibb, and other abolitionists who worked among and for fugitive
blacks would have recognized the problem to which Robinson alluded.
The challenge as they saw it was very much one of transforming ex-
slaves into disciplined, sober, and dependable workers. And with that as
the goal, there was a real problem. The values and habits appropriate to
black life in plantation society were not those increasingly being demanded of the urban working class in capitalist society. The gap between
these two worlds was enormous, but the need to learn new values and
work habits was not unique to ex-slaves or blacks: only the magnitude
of the task appeared daunting in their case.[102] Significantly, the compulsory taxation of real property in support of free common schools was
justified on the ground that the common school was the institution best
placed in a democratic society to effect this transition, to create a disciplined, civilized, and morally responsible populace. What was to be
done if the school could not cope with ragged clothes, unruly manners,
or belligerent parents? What if free schooling seemed to the very population for whose benefit the taxes were levied either uncomfortable or
irrelevant? Briefly, to Egerton Ryerson at least, these appeared to be
legitimate grounds for establishing yet another sort of separate school.

IV

Town and city boards of common school trustees were typically among the first to adopt the free school principle, for there the hackneyed image of the schoolmaster as policeman struck a chord for reasons yet only imagined in the rural townships. Pockets of utter destitution and chronic seasonal distress were not the monopoly of larger cities; but in the bigger centres these problems seemed more substantial and intractable, and the gradations in the material and moral circumstances of the working population more obvious. When the common schools became free, the issue of non-attendance gained prominence. Once the common school grant was apportioned on the basis of average attendance, there were financial consequences to the non-enrolment of a significant portion of the school-aged population and the sporadic attendance of those enrolled. By the mid-1850s non-attendance became an official issue through which rural teachers and local superintendents across the province shared in what was, in fact, largely an urban problem: the *apparent* failure of the free common school to reach the lower working class.[103]

The qualification *apparent* is necessary because it is impossible to know to what extent there was a 'fault' at all. Members of the black community wrote often and quite passionately to the education department about their desire for schooling; by contrast one hears very few voices of the most vulnerable of the white working class, and those there are come filtered through official channels. Much criticism of the school system assumed that children in the lower strata of the urban working class remained untaught and unschooled and that their parents were satisfied – indeed responsible, owing to their apathy or ignorance – for that state of affairs. It followed that the obvious, perhaps the only, institution capable of reaching those families was the common school, now free. These assumptions require close examination. The impression of failure on the part of the free school movement was created by statistics and nourished by social anxieties. A minor but curious feature of the mid-century quest for school improvement is that almost overnight none other than common schooling counted – literally. To the education department annually, and to their boards of school trustees periodically, urban school superintendents submitted collections of figures, comparing the estimated school-age population, the total common school enrolment, and the attendance averaged monthly. In time these were refined to distinguish Protestant from Roman Catholic, but always the dreaded or prized calculation was the percentage of the relevant school-age population on average attending the common schools. Rarely, after the early 1850s, did any one take serious note of the number of students who might be continuing what, after all, had been a tradition until the late 1840s: fee-paying private venture and parochial schooling of one sort or another.

In a long series of letters to the *Globe* in the winter of 1852, the Reverend John Roaf, a local Congregational minister, spoke eloquently of the close parental involvement in school management, discipline, and curriculum that was a feature of private venture schooling. 'The Free school system divests the Teacher of all proprietary and personal interests in his school,' he suspected, 'and will speedily render him sycophantic and servile to his trustees, but haughty and negligent towards his pupils' friends.'[104] Roaf spoke ostensibly for the mechanics of Yorkville, but his views had a wider currency. Four years later, the local superintendent in Toronto feared that these attitudes, prevalent among the city's working class, were damaging the schools' efforts. From a false sense of pride in not stooping to take charity, some parents avoided the schools; others, recent English immigrants, perhaps, confused publicly funded common schools with English board schools, which were notoriously rough and cheap. There were many, he reported, who 'insist that a teacher receiving a salary does not bring forward his pupils as well as one who is more dependent on public opinion (too often in school matters public caprice) for his daily bread.' These parents were a menace: they had notions about the relationship between the school, children, and parents that, in a large 'public school system,' were subversive. They interfered with the teacher and undermined the school's authority; they expected 'that a general system arranged for the good of all, ought to, and must, be set aside, to gratify individual whims, too often unreasonable demands.' Further, when they did not receive satisfaction, 'either the Teacher is vilified, or a grievance is nursed into active hostility, and then the School is complained against, and the child kept away.'[105]

There is no reason to suppose that only Toronto school officials felt a need to educate parents to the new school culture. Seen in this light the experience with racial tension of London's common school trustees in 1861 suggests that it was a commonplace problem at least for a while. Under considerable pressure to abandon the free school principle, in 1857 the Toronto board accepted the local superintendent's resignation instead and deliberately set out to solicit custom for the common schools. A widely circulated 'Address to Parents and Guardians' targeted among others parents who patronized Church of England parochial schools and the various private schools that competed for 'a class of persons in circumstances precisely like those who are attending our Schools.'[106] Church of England-sponsored day schools were not restricted to Toronto, but there Anglican parishioners contributed with exceptional generosity towards building parish schoolhouses. By the mid-1850s, upwards of three hundred children attended daily, and space for nearly one thousand was planned for the end of the decade. By all accounts these schools did indeed draw from the solid working class the common schools were determined to woo (and that by the mid-1860s, they would have captured).[107] Evidence of private schooling, especially as it shaded into the lower economic strata of the working class, is much more elusive. Some local superintendents and commentators continued to guess at what they termed 'private school' enrolment. In 1851, for example, the chairman of the Toronto Board of Common School Trustees added the number of 'public schools' to what he considered 'private schools' and reached a total of twenty-nine, but even together they apparently enrolled less than half the school-age population in the city. A decade later, however, despite a significantly greater measure of confidence in the common schools, there were seventy-one persons listed in the city directory under 'schools, school masters and teachers,' none of whom were employees of the common school board.[108] Something was going on that was not being counted. In Kingston in 1861, the local superintendent estimated that there were fourteen private schools with five hundred students in the city; two years later London's local superintendent took note in an off-hand manner of 'the few attending elementary private schools.'[109] Perhaps William Ormiston was being more honest than the others when he admitted in 1861 that he really did not know about the situation in Hamilton: there were 'a number of small private schools' in addition to a few ladies' schools and three classical schools.[110]

It does appear that after mid-century two processes were altering the educational landscape in the larger cities. The term 'private schooling' was swiftly losing its older meaning and now was used in a recognizably modern sense of schooling for the relatively prosperous and privileged minority; at the same time, private sector enrolments in this new sense of the term, as they became class specific, failed to keep pace with the expansion of public common schools.[111] Granted these general trends, however, sufficient fragmentary evidence exists to suggest a more substantial and longer-lived tradition of modest working-class private schooling in the major cities than historians have appreciated. Consider the census undertaken by the Toronto school board in 1863. Having tracked down the school habits of the population five to sixteen years of age, officials were quietly elated to find so few youngsters for whose absence from school no explanation could be given. Nevertheless, of the 7,058 Protestant school-age children in the city, 1,165 had not been enrolled in school in the past six months, and of the 5,077 who at some point were, only 3,000 – or 51 percent – were registered in the common schools.[112]

One can only suppose that Miss Cuyler knew her market when she resigned from the Toronto board's Park School in 1865 to open a private school in the neighbourhood.[113] And certainly some of the 'unlisted' private school ventures continued to be fairly humble. Alfred Sears, living in the lower end of Parliament Street at number 61, appeared fair game to Truant Officer Wilkinson on 14 May 1872, but Alfred had an excuse: his mother had withdrawn him from the common school and had sent the whole family 'to a private school.'[114]

However much the fleeting visibility of a sub-culture of working-class schooling may tease historians in the late twentieth century, it profoundly confused mid-nineteenth-century social critics. Quite simply, what was not counted was of little or no account. For some time into the 1860s the important role that the Sunday school movement could play in advancing basic literacy was acknowledged occasionally in the press. As late as 1867, the *Globe* believed that there were 'a surprising number in Toronto alone' who if not instructed in the Sabbath school *'will not be instructed at all.'* As a further supplement, evening schools became a more or less successful feature of town and even village life in the late 1850s and 1860s. But increasingly questions were raised about the other hours in the day and about the days of the week other than Sunday. The statistics of urban common school enrolment seemed incontrovertible: there must be a large population of youngsters in the major cities who were neither at school nor at work. Absence from school appeared to be a crime once the provision of free schools created a yardstick against which immorality and delinquency could be measured. Youngsters not attending school became known as 'street arabs': the racist overtones of the epithet conveyed the notion that the neglect and destitution of their lives signalled not merely an absence of stable family and school experience but an education in itself – in idleness and dissipation.

Juvenile crime and delinquency became a public issue in the cities in the late 1850s. Grand juries and justices of the high court publicized the number of boys arrested for petty crimes or for simply being neglected. It seemed that support for free schooling could be undermined by the controversy over whether common schools were responsible for salvaging and educating these street children. Three lines of argument emerged in the debate. Commentators, including many local school superintendents, who had the least firsthand experience of the problem favoured the position that the parents were to blame: they were apathetic, ignorant, even depraved, and should be compelled to send their children to school. The most astute observers recognized the extent to which street children were an integral part of the problem of entrenched urban poverty. Schools, as much as churches, were uncomfortable places when one was very poor.

Lastly, as they had in instances of proposed black integration, various Cassandras confidently predicted that, were the government to compel the neglectful parents of vagrant children to send their children to the common school, respectable working-class parents would withdraw their children.[115] The matter provoked a stormy but false crisis in 1862 when Ryerson, as chief superintendent, unexpectedly made public draft legislation to permit the various religious denominations to operate, with public financial support, separate 'ragged' schools for city urchins. The move was swiftly and roundly condemned in most quarters – the notable exception being Bishop Strachan's loyal associates in the Anglican Diocese of Toronto who thought they saw a long-sought-after legal basis for Church of England separate schools.[116]

The furore that predictably, by now, surrounded any mention of publicly funded denominational schools helped to discredit this new proposal for separate schools for neglected and vagrant children. However, a large measure of resistance also can be attributed to the public status the common school system now enjoyed. Significantly, the opposition of the newly formed provincial Teachers' Association was unanimous. Claiming a 'deep interest in the preservation and continued efficiency of the Common School system of Upper Canada,' the teachers concluded that 'the appropriation of the Common School funds to the support of schools connected with the various denominations, would be fraught with great danger to the educational interests of the Province.'[117] Neither the specific problem of attracting dishevelled street children into the common schools – or into any other institution catering to their needs – nor the more general one of persistent irregular attendance was much affected by this flurry of excitement in the summer of 1862. In the years that followed, local philanthropists launched new initiatives in the form of newsboys' homes, while public discussions leading to comprehensive school legislation by the end of the 1860s effectively translated the idea of compulsory education into a measure designed to enforce the regular attendance of ordinary pupils. For their part the teachers proposed that industrial schools be established to receive any vagrant, incorrigible, or refractory youngsters who might disrupt the common school classroom.[118] Charles R. Brooke, a Toronto common school trustee who courted publicity in the mid-1860s, outlined the essential issues of this controversy as it affected Toronto in a letter of 26 August 1865 to the editor of the *Globe*. 'The fact is,' he wrote, 'the city schools are not adapted to the wants of that [the vagrant] class; they are too respectable; these boys that roam about the wharfs and streets, ragged, shoeless and unemployed, ready to commit petty crimes, would be out of their element in our decent schools; it requires an entirely different organization to reach them.'

Through the late 1840s and early 1850s, editorial commentaries and public addresses favouring school reform often conveyed a note of urgency, a sense of crisis. The great enterprise of public instruction, publicists endlessly reminded their audiences, was directed to the future, which in a mere glance towards the United States one could discern. Touring the province in the fall of 1847 Egerton Ryerson had warned of a time of 'sharp and skillful competition and sleepless activity' and of the necessity for the 'rising generation' to be 'educated not for Canada as it has been, or even now is, but for Canada as it is likely to be half a generation hence.'[119] The image of life as a race that would be won or lost by individuals and communities galvanized more than one generation of Victorian Canadians to 'get on' and 'get ahead.' Increasingly, to do that demanded literacy, in the sense of the ability to read and write; but even more than that was required. Thus along with literacy the common schools assumed a critical role in disseminating to society's youth the values their governors perceived were appropriate to the future. In theory at least, through the discipline of attendance, the gradations of the curriculum (*Reader* after *Reader*), and endless recitations and class competition, pupils would learn the obedience, regularity, and precision valued in the public sphere. Muddled though the social, moral, and intellectual import of the curriculum might seem to a historian more than a century later, there was obviously very little confusion as to the prescribed tone of the school experience. *Respectability* was to be the key to the mid-Victorian schoolroom culture as it was to the new bourgeois social order. The passion aroused by demands for special consideration and by other circumstances that threatened to fragment the common school system was directly related to the urgency of the schools' agenda. However, as we have seen, whatever their particular constituencies, 'separate' schools typically allied themselves with the majority in the battle against idleness and immorality, for all that their existence refuted the common schools' fledgling claims to comprehensiveness. The entire provincial school system, while a key element, was nevertheless just part of a team of mid-nineteenth-century moral missionaries that included, among others, temperance crusaders, volunteer charity workers, and urban police officers, to name only the most obvious. Their shared objective, as the grounds defining social relationships in rural and urban communities shifted after mid-century, was to instil a work ethic and moral discipline appropriate to the new society. Many children and parents experienced this complex process of social redefinition most directly in and through the local school and there, often unwittingly, learned above all to accommodate to a different social reality than they had previously known. By 1870 *not being in school* mattered more, in the sense of being a greater social handicap, than whether the school one attended was a common or a separate one.

10 'I Wish I Were Not Here at the Present Juncture'

The changes transforming Ontario social life in the third quarter of the century were obscured in important ways from the vision of the education department. The remarkably long service of its key personnel and their responsible subordinates ensured continuity in the handling of day-to-day affairs, which in turn reinforced a deliberately conservative policy aimed at consolidating the school system.[1] Through the mid-century decades Egerton Ryerson continued to insist, as he had in the 1840s, that educational questions remain immune from the rival claims of theory or party (by the late 1860s he would prefer the word 'faction'); but that was not possible.[2] Rarely as we have seen, had there been more than an occasional moment in the colony's history when the school question was shielded successfully from partisan political scrutiny. For all its heat, however, the passionate debate about principles triggered by the legislation of the late 1840s and early 1850s did subside. By the middle of the 1850s government regulation and oversight of publicly funded common, separate, and grammar schools was a *fait accompli*. In succession local communities adopted and adapted to free schools. With success, however, public schooling became a bigger and more intrusive business, and much more about its regulation than such obviously political issues as denominational rights and racial segregation attracted public attention. In 1849 Ryerson had spoken confidently of the proper role of government and the law in the regulation of social affairs. 'It should be observed, that, according to the nature of things, government is merely the *instrument* to accomplish the *end* for which society exists; *Society* being the *principal*, *Government* the *agent*,' he assured the audience at a joint meeting of the mechanics' institutes of Niagara and Toronto in October 1849.[3] Experienced public administrator though he had become, by the 1860s Ryerson appears to have underestimated the complexity of the interests that increasingly would hold his educational policies and the education depart-

Egerton Ryerson, the elder statesman

ment to account. One says *his* policies advisedly: for more than a decade after the débâcle of the Cameron Act (with the notable exception of the separate school negotiations) educational policy and the regulations that gave it effect were largely the creation of the person. Changing circumstances eroded the influence of the Chief Superintendent, however, an experience that proved bewildering, humiliating, and finally, for the aging 'statesman in disguise,' politically fatal.

By the mid-1850s school improvement had grown into a substantial business enterprise whose repercussions were felt in local communities across the province. Government monies attracted more investment; better schoolhouses and qualified teachers cost more, but families and business investments were likely to be attracted to communities with superior educational facilities. When the log school was replaced, out went the crippling backless benches and the rough-hewn desks that had lined the walls, to be replaced by modern, manufactured two-seater desks and a specially designed teacher's table.[4] From there the list would grow to include major items, such as authentic blackboards (to replace the ones home-made by the teacher from a recipe supplied by the education department) and brass handbells, as well as minor necessities such as pens, nibs, and inkwells. The construction and outfitting of countless new schoolhouses annually generated employment and profit without, it seems, all that much controversy.[5] By comparison, the business of supplying common schools with the necessities for instruction – books and teaching apparatus of various sorts – proved considerably more contentious.

When the Educational Depository was established in 1850 to supply local schools with the newly authorized textbooks, the business interests most immediately affected, the province's booksellers, did not object. It was acknowledged to be too big a job for the private sector to handle.[6] A revolution of sorts had swept the book trade in England and the United States in the 1820s: cheap reading materials designed for the popular classes were now produced on a large scale. By the 1840s these developments were beginning to have an impact on the trade in Upper Canada but, outside the major cities and towns, recently published books and current periodicals remained in short supply. That situation changed dramatically in the 1850s as American book pedlars invaded the countryside. Prominent among the wares they hawked were dime novels and popular romantic fiction depicting the seamier side of life in New York City and adventures in the wild west or on pirate ships in the China seas. Some observers even feared that such 'vile trash' had begun to inundate the public schools before the depository got into full operation.[7] While the volume of book and periodical imports escalated – at the port of Toronto alone the value of these imports rose from £38,945.3.3. to £55,553.14.1 between 1854 and 1856 – confidence in the public's taste for reading materials and in the scruples of itinerant booksellers trying to make a sale did not increase. To those who worried about public morality, and they were numerous, the work of the Educational Depository became more, not less, essential.[8] What had begun almost as a stop-gap measure quickly became a fixture of the educational enterprise.

The depository operated as both wholesaler and retailer, purchasing on a large scale texts and other educational materials directly from British and American publishers and then selling them at prices well below what the commercial book trade in Upper Canada could sustain. While it seems not to have featured in his decision to establish the depository, Ryerson had had personal experience of starting just such a large-volume, cut-rate operation – in the form of the precursor of the Methodist book room

– when he was editor of the *Christian Guardian* in the early 1830s. Sermons, hymns, poetry, and various tracts were printed on the newspaper's press and, along with imported religious works, were sold through the book room 'at good discounts' to clergy, Sunday school teachers, and others.[9] The Educational Depository was a similar kind of operation on a larger scale. Authorized initially to supply the common schools, the depository quickly branched out, adding the Sunday schools and mechanics' institutes in 1851, the grammar schools in 1852, then the wider market of private schools and colleges and even the occasional direct sale to school children. Comparing the years 1855 and 1865, the number of volumes of textbooks and prize books distributed annually across the province increased from 27,320 to 48,483. Nevertheless the depository's remarkable success in supplying even the poorest and most remote school section with textbooks free of charge (delivered to the nearest railway station) was dwarfed by its business in supplying local public libraries.[10] The 1850 school act had provided for an annual grant in support of local public lending libraries and authorized the chief superintendent of education to dispense the monies upon request, provided the grant was at least matched by local sources.[11] Although the depository officials imposed a five-dollar minimum-order rule, once the public library operation got underway in 1853 the demand was brisk. In 1858 a new 231-page catalogue listed more than 3,000 titles in stock, each approved by the Council of Public Instruction. The purpose of the whole enterprise was explicitly didactic. From the outset the council avowed that 'no works of a licentious, vicious or immoral tendency, and no works hostile to the Christian religion should be admitted to the Libraries'; eventually, however, to woo the public from the 'deleterious trash which is brought to their doors by the Book Pedlars' the depository did resort to stocking novels and carefully vetted works of popular fiction. To critics Ryerson protested that the education department was only ensuring that the public's money was spent responsibly, by protecting local school managers against being imposed upon 'by itinerant or interested book dealers' and preventing any part of the library fund from being spent on the purchase or circulation of 'books having a tendency to subvert public morals or vitiate the public taste.'[12] In fact, if invited to do so, the depository's officials would select the books for their customers, having regard for 'the condition of the school, the number and age of the scholars, the character of the neighbourhood, whether old or new settlement, and the attainments of the pupils, the nature of the population, whether Protestant or Roman Catholic, or mixed nationality – whether Irish, Scotch or German etc., or any other peculiarity suggested by the parties sending the order or incident to the case.'[13] Such custom service was attractive; but private booksellers across the province were, understandably, increasingly incensed by the depository's practice.

The odd complaint had arisen, but it was the formal organization of the Booksellers' Association of Canada in the late fall of 1857 that gave weight to the objections. In a letter to Ryerson in early December, the Reverend John C. Geikie followed a year-long private correspondence with a public complaint in his new capacity as secretary-treasurer of the Booksellers' Association. He raised two points: the monopolistic practices of the depository amounted to unfair competition, in his view; and the employees of the education department seemed to benefit unduly from the patronage of the Council of Public Instruction in securing authorization for their own textbooks.[14] Ryerson deflected the criticism casually, but the matter did not end there. In fact an ideological gulf of some importance separated the Chief Superintendent from the members of the book trade. While the latter believed in the free market and in fair competition, Ryerson stoutly defended the education department's primary responsibility to promote the education of the people.[15] Innovative and aggressive marketing strategies on the part of the depository were to be applauded, for they served a purpose higher than mere commercial profit. In the spring of 1858 the booksellers went public, airing their grievances in a long letter to the editor of the *British Colonist* and in a petition to the legislature requesting the abolition of the depository. In reply, and on short notice, the department prepared statistics to show that the depository's impact on the book trade had been simultaneously over- and undervalued: in terms of the dollar value of imports it had been exaggerated; on the other hand the education department's policies had clearly stimulated an interest in books and reading and, by extension, had created a market for the private sector. There was a brief awkward moment when the matter was referred to a committee chaired by Ryerson's political adversary and the booksellers' advocate, George Brown, MPP, but for whatever reason his committee never reported. The commotion subsided and the depository officials appear to have made only one (slight) concession: henceforth they declined to fill orders from Japan and from local Sons of Temperance organizations.[16]

In 1866 the issue was revived, and this time the political consequences were damaging. While the argument was more elaborate, the substance was much the same. In the intervening years the provision of schoolbooks had become a highly lucrative business for booksellers throughout British North America. In Upper Canada, however, the market was severely restricted by the education department's policy of penalizing school trustees financially for using unauthorized textbooks. By the early 1860s the Irish national readers had more than shown their age, and efforts were launched to develop a substitute series of authorized texts for the common schools. Here was an opportunity not to be missed. New books – and, many argued, better books – were available, but the problem for the book trade was obtaining authorization from the Council of Public Instruction. The favouritism in that quarter seemed blatant. Three education department employees – John George Hodgins, J.H. Sangster, and T.J. Robertson – had together produced seven authorized texts since the late 1850s, and Ryerson's old publishing ally, John Lovell of Montreal, monopolized the new editions to the authorized list with his series of 'Lovell's texts.' By 1866 James Campbell, agent for the British publisher Thomas Nelson, a firm already heavily committed in the publishing and wholesale branches of the textbook trade, had become frustrated in his dealings with the education department. Determined to break into the Upper Canadian market, he launched a public attack on departmental favouritism by exposing the inferiority of recently authorized books. The fact that *Globe* publisher George Brown was the brother-in-law of Thomas Nelson, Jr, meant that political lines were drawn with razor sharpness. A deluge of charges and countercharges filled columns in the *Globe* throughout the spring. Campbell was not alone. In 1858, he had distanced himself from the majority of the Booksellers' Association, preferring at that time to support the depository, but now he had as allies the most successful and politically influential members of the trade. As their antipathy to Ryerson deepened so their critique of education department policy widened beyond matters relating to the depository to include proposed changes in the composition of the Council of Public Instruction and its functions.[17]

The education department rode out this storm as usual and perhaps for tidiness' sake, Ryerson arranged for a select committee of the new provincial legislature to examine the depository's operation in 1869. As expected it (and, by implication, he) was exonerated; but that was not really the issue any more. The political damage inflicted by the row with James Campbell and his friends was dangerous because it was insidious. The booksellers were not alone in becoming conscious of the fact that their interests conflicted with those of the education department, and defending the depository was only one of the many challenges Ryerson now faced. Fighting for increased salaries for departmental personnel was another; supporting Victoria College and other denominational colleges against the University of Toronto yet another; the list goes on, as does the list of antagonists with whom Ryerson battled in public, before legislative committees, and in the columns of the Toronto press. George Brown wielded obvious political power; as well, such prominent public figures as John Langton, Professor Daniel Wilson, and a future premier, Edward Blake, among others, begin to reappear through the 1860s as critics of one or another of Ryerson's policies. The effect on all the parties involved was inevitably cumulative.

Certainly, working behind the scenes in Quebec to help steer a grammar school bill through the Assembly in September 1865 convinced John George Hodgins that the booksellers' general unhappiness with Ryerson's policies and with the depository specifically was generating political opposition to this critically important piece of legislation. The puppet-master's hand belonged to George Brown, who had arranged for James Campbell and G. Mercer Adam to lobby the Hon. William McDougall (as provincial secretary responsible for education matters) with their grievances and suggestions for reform. In addition, various of Brown's allies in the House allegedly were primed to ask questions and prepare amendments to the grammar school bill.[18] The politicking, even if it produced no more than a momentary stall, was nevertheless disturbing, for Ryerson attached great importance to this bill. Nor did he want McDougall to be distracted. 'If Mr. McDougall gets the Bill through,' Ryerson wrote Hodgins on September 13, 'he will have done more for the school system in Upper Canada than we have got the Government and Legislature to do since Mr. Hincks left Canada.'[19]

The prospect of yet another delay rather than the intrinsic merit of this particular bill explains Ryerson's concern. Five years before, in March 1860, he had complained bitterly to his friend John A. Macdonald about the government's neglect of Upper Canadian school legislation. 'Three school Bills have been considered and passed in behalf of L.C. since any thing was done to aid the educational department of the public interests in U.C.,' he had calculated, 'though this is the fourth time and the fourth year I have solicited the attention of the Government to it.' Successive administrations were being cobbled together in these years as political deadlock deepened, none feeling strong enough to risk a major legislative initiative, all fearful of unwittingly stirring the embers of the separate school controversy.[20] Of all the loose ends in the Upper Canadian school system that deserved attention, the grammar schools were among the most needy.

Pressure to consider the role and administration of the grammar schools was coming from a number of directions. The education department's own officials, the grammar school inspectors, annually deplored the poor quality of the school accommodation and the insufficient resources generally that hampered the academic performance of the schools. Some county councils recklessly created new grammar schools, with the result that the government grant was fragmented to the point where it was woefully inadequate for the purpose. The 1853 grammar school act, which had brought the schools under a measure of central regulation and inspection, had restricted the power of the appointed boards of grammar school trustees to raise funds other than by pupil fees, while county, city, and town municipal councils were reluctant to raise the property assessment to support grammar schools. As late as 1864 only forty-nine of the ninety-five grammar schools in operation received any financial help from these quarters; and for those who did, the assistance was relatively modest. To overcome their financial difficulties, grammar school trustees increasingly united with the common school boards in their area to gain access to local tax revenue. It became a vicious circle, for in the rural counties such union schools invariably further depressed the quality of education. As early as 1856 it was evident that the grammar schools had to be placed on a more stable footing, in some manner comparable to that of the common schools.[21]

It had to be admitted at the same time that for all their limitations grammar schools were attracting students. While enrolments did not increase spectacularly, the pressure to found new schools testified to the willingness of parents to turn to the public school system for something more than (or instead of, in too many cases, Ryerson suspected) the common school. The overwhelming majority of grammar school pupils lived in the community where the school was located. By and large it seems that the ambitions of most of these youngsters (male and female) were modest. Only a small fraction pursued a grammar school education in order to matriculate at the university.[22] The others, disproportionately from families that considered themselves part of the middle class, went to school until the ages of fifteen or sixteen as much to grow up as to acquire specifically vocational skills.[23] Although grammar schools were permitted to offer commercial subjects such as bookkeeping, commercial arithmetic, and surveying, for some years to come most middle-class youths would acquire on-the-job informal training when they assumed full-time employment. In subtle ways, however, attendance at a grammar school did prepare youngsters for the adult worlds of work. Young women intending to teach until they married found a partial grammar school program to be an advantage when they came before the County Board of Examiners to obtain a teacher's certificate. And a liberal education was in a real sense 'vocational' for young men aspiring to a professional or business career and for the young women who in the future would manage – and grace – their homes. As in the common schools, of course, the grammar school routine tried to instil habits of punctuality, regularity, and industry and to foster ambition and competitiveness. General habits and values, then, rather than specific skills, linked the classroom to the world outside.[24]

There were, however, rumblings of discontent with the academic emphasis of the grammar school curriculum. John Langton raised the issue in 1860 with the select committee of the Legislative Assembly dealing with university affairs. 'There had been a growing conviction,' he reported, 'that from the narrow limits of the Studies of our Public Schools and Universities, they were not fitting men for the actual business of life.' The Board of Arts and Manufacture voiced similar concerns by the mid-1860s, deploring excessive 'brain work' and over-concentration on classics and the professions.[25] Preparation for the business world (if not 'for the actual business of life') was increasingly being offered in the private sector. The proprietors of the numerous private venture commercial colleges and academies that opened in the cities and towns after mid-century were confident that there was a market for courses in commercial law, business penmanship, and business correspondence, not to mention telegraphy and phonography (or 'short-hand writing'). Catering initially to men only, by the late 1860s some commercial schools directed their advertisements to both 'Young Men and Ladies' wishing to prepare as 'bookkeepers and for General Business.'[26]

The education department responded to another set of pressures, however. Ryerson had long maintained that it was the teaching of the classics, Latin and Greek, and other elements of the conventional classical curriculum that distinguished *grammar* schools from other schools. Grammar school studies were to be academically advanced (in the sense of 'harder'), to be sure, which was why there was an entrance requirement other than age, but ideally there should be an integrity to the program not duplicated by the advanced subjects that might be taught in a common school. Ideals were compromised somewhat by the 1855 regulations, which outlined a dual curriculum of classics *and* the advanced branches of an English education, designed to serve a minority of students as preparation for higher education of some sort and the majority as something akin to a 'finishing school.'[27] And ideals were undermined thoroughly by the real state of the schools in many communities. Even after a decade of improvement, not more than a handful, according to the inspectors, exceeded the minimal standard; a regular curriculum was rarely observed, and pupils or their parents chose the subjects they wanted. The quality of grammar schooling became a sensitive topic with Ryerson. John Langton, on assuming the vice-chancellorship of the University of Toronto in 1856, attempted to attract students by devising more realistic entrance requirements. Ryerson smarted visibly before the legislative select committee in 1860 at the suggestion that the university was responding to the failure of the grammar schools to prepare students adequately for matriculation.[28] He suspected, with considerable justification, that the ploy was designed to recruit students to University College at the expense of the denominational colleges. Nevertheless, the problem of the confusion of purpose with respect to the grammar schools remained.

In 1860 Ryerson proposed new school legislation with a view to tidying up some minor administrative details relating to common schools and increasing the efficiency of the grammar schools. The government, having survived a motion of want of confidence, unenthusiastically brought the school bill before the House, but Ryerson's bullying of John A. Macdonald did not make the government more committed to carrying through with Upper Canadian school legislation. Predictably, George Brown followed his own agenda; this time, Hodgins reported, rumour had it that 'Brown's policy would be to try and prevent the Government from passing the bill and then taunt them afterwards with not passing any good measures for U.C.'[29] The grammar school clauses not having survived second reading, Ryerson tried again in the spring of 1863. Now it seemed that all his irons were in the fire at once. In Quebec City himself for much of the time between February and May when the legislature was sitting, Ryerson became embroiled in promoting legislation relating to the university, separate schools, and grammar schools, as well as trying to improve his officials' salaries and defend them, the depository, and the department before a sub-committee of the Public Accounts Committee – chaired by George Brown – which was investigating the accounts of the education departments of Upper and Lower Canada. This time the grammar school bill survived long enough to be sent to a committee; however, the passing of R.W. Scott's Upper Canada separate school bill precipitated a political crisis for Premier John Sandfield Macdonald.[30] 'I wish I were not here at the present juncture,' Ryerson wrote Hodgins wearily in early May as he watched the government fall.[31]

Constitutional matters now dominated the political scene, diminishing the prospects for significant school legislation. The success of the Quebec Conference in the autumn of 1864 meant that much of the legislative session that began early in 1865 was taken up by the 'Confederation debate.' John A. Macdonald had warned in early January that no school measures could be attempted, and while William McDougall, the minister most closely involved, inclined to sympathize with Ryerson about the difficulties with the grammar schools, his best advice was to solve the problem by means of regulations from the Council of Public Instruction.[32] As the years dragged by and the grammar schools appeared to deteriorate, Ryerson was more determined than ever to proceed.

The problem in 1865, as it had been in 1860 when he first broached the question of new legislation in the public forum of his county convention tour, was at root financial. What was needed was a formula whereby the grammar schools could gain access to property-assessment revenue on terms comparable to that enjoyed by the common schools: once that was secured, a sequence of much-needed improvements inevitably would follow. Better teachers, better schoolhouses, higher standards, more legitimate grammar school work – the prospect was dazzling in its simplicity, but more difficult to engineer administratively. In 1860, in order to attract the broadest possible public support for further taxation for school purposes, Ryerson had proposed that the various grammar schools be *free* to all the youth in their respective counties.[33] To begin the process of improvement, however, all grammar schools had to be placed on an equal financial footing: the existing system of legislative grants perpetuated historical and often unjustifiable inequalities among schools. Here again, the experience of the common schools supplied the model for improved administration. Under the terms of the 1863 draft bill each grammar school was to receive a flat grant of $300 *plus* supplementary funds calculated on the *daily average attendance* of pupils 'studying the Latin, or Greek or French language, or such subjects of Agricultural Chemistry and Physical Science as may be prescribed according to law.'[34]

By the spring of 1865 halting the drift to union schools and a glorified elementary education had become the priority. New grammar school regulations, approved by the government, were issued by the Council of Public Instruction on 1 May, to be effective as of 1 January 1866. Ostensibly to 'protect' the common schools from unfair poaching of their students and program, the details and purpose of entrance requirements and the prescribed grammar school curriculum were clarified (and henceforth were to be monitored closely). As in the 1863 bill, the funding formula – the basis of apportioning the grammar school fund – provided the education department with the leverage to ensure compliance with the new regulations. However, since 1863 the range of studies that would count financially had shrunk; now the grant would be based on 'the average attendance at each Grammar School of pupils learning the Greek, or Latin language'; the specified minimum for the classics course was set at ten pupils. Moreover, there was to be no more 'padding' of the registers as now 'such attendance shall be certified by the Head Master and Trustees, and verified by the Inspector of Grammar Schools.'[35]

Registration in Latin or Greek technically had been the basis of counting pupils since 1855; the novelty was its proposed enforcement.[36] In this new legalistic context the 'classical requirement' appeared to be a conspicuously narrow and élitist basis on which to support what increasing numbers of parents were taking for granted as post-elementary schooling. Already by September, when Hodgins arrived in Quebec to oversee the passage of the long-sought-for revisions to the grammar school act, rumblings of opposition had been heard. The Teachers' Association, at its summer meeting, had debated and deplored the narrowness of the new curricular regulations,[37] and a majority of the legislators were at best sceptical. Hodgins anticipated momentarily the loss of 'Latin and Greek' as the basis for the grant, but in the event the bill passed.[38] Acknowledging some of the criticism of the prescribed curriculum, revised regulations issued 1 November 1865 (which superseded those of May) provided for a dual stream of studies; the classical course and a special course (with a stiffer entrance standard and no Latin) leading to surveying or civil engineering. In addition, girls were to be encouraged to learn French, but 'they were not to be returned, or recognized, as Pupils pursuing either of the prescribed Programmes of Studies for the Grammar schools.'[39]

It ought not to have come as a surprise to anyone who patronized most of the village and town grammar schools that the consequence of this attempted crackdown on 'standards' turned out to be a travesty of the intention. Enrolments in 'qualifying Latin' skyrocketed as of January 1866. Appalled, the grammar school inspector reported hordes of little boys and little girls dragooned into elementary Latin without the slightest ability or ambition to pursue a classical education. The presence of girls in the Latin class seemed especially outrageous; their mere existence in grammar schools had been acknowledged reluctantly, and then only to study English subjects and French. Now that girls taking Latin were 'worth something,' it seemed as though they were poised to overrun the schools. In 1865, 85 of the 102 grammar schools admitted girls; the remaining all-male hold-outs – typically the most serious classical schools – were being penalized inadvertently by the new funding formula. Nor had the special provisions for boys interested in mathematics proved particularly attractive: across the province by 1867 only seven boys had enrolled in the surveyor's option. Scrambling to control the situation, officials of the education department barely contained their fury at being taken advantage of by parents, headmasters, and trustees as they announced that a girl studying Latin would count only half as much as a boy, financially (a decision made, interestingly enough, while Ryerson was in Europe on his last grand tour). For 1868 it was proposed that girls be disqualified for grant purposes entirely.[40]

Of far greater significance than bureaucratic pique in the long run was the reaction of the Reverend George Paxton Young to the experience of inspecting the grammar schools in 1866. Young was exceptionally able and had a distinguished academic career; while inspector of grammar schools in the mid-1860s he provided much of the ammunition, as well as the design, for improving the schools. He had standards but was no snob. He appreciated that even the very best grammar schools in Upper Canada could not expect to be in the same league as the better mathematical and classical schools of Ireland and Great Britain: that would take time.[41] He did hope, however, to arrest the drift to downright *bad* schools and ill-prepared students. These concerns were clearly paramount and, on the basis of the perverse enrolment patterns in 1866, Young disavowed the scheme for a funding formula that he had had a large hand in creating. Standards would better be ensured by another strategy – 'payment by results' – which Hodgins had proposed while in Quebec in September 1865. As the name suggests, this complex grant formula included a performance component; it was in force in England (Hodgins had heard something of its workings from James Fraser) but in 1865 it had seemed to hinge on what appeared to be a too-costly inspectorate.[42] The issues of a proper classical curriculum and the presence of older girls in grammar schools were secondary but important concerns for Young. After November 1865, however, all the issues became muddled. The question of female education had become a topic of popular public discussion. And now there were countless parents who were not going to stop sending their daughters to the local grammar school, whatever the education department might decree.

Perhaps the most striking feature of girls' education in the mid-century decades was its variety. The prevailing notion of the 'separate spheres' appropriate for men and women ensured that Victorian Canadian parents characteristically shared quite different expectations of the futures for which their daughters and sons must be prepared. Nevertheless, the often harsh circumstances of colonial settlement made competence a prized quality in both sexes. 'Competence' could be defined in numerous ways, of course, and acquired under widely differing conditions. A considerable number of girls, from all social backgrounds, continued to receive most of, if not all, their education at home, having as their teacher a family member, a neighbour, or – if the family was especially privileged – a private tutor. By mid-century, as the quality of common schooling began to be more predictable, rural and village girls went to the local school, perhaps initially only in the 'off-season' when their brothers were working on the farm. In the towns and soon the major port cities, private venture schools of all sizes and expense continued to cater to a broad sector of the population, and families with serious aspirations to respectability patronized the numerous 'parlour schools,' run on a family basis, that offered a mixed curriculum of elementary literacy training, moral improvement, and social refinement.[43] A significant portion of this private market offered a superior or higher education for girls. Even the education department, in its most imperialistic mood, assumed that that market

Pinehurst Academy, Toronto, 1864

would hold for some time to come. While in absolute numbers private schools and their pupils were expected to decline as 'Public schools improve and increase,' the Chief Superintendent reported optimistically in 1852, 'superior Ladies' Seminaries' would be the exception.[44]

It was not unusual for a young girl to be taught at home and then, in her early teens, to be sent to school for as short a time as a term or for as long as a number of years. After that she might instruct her younger brothers and sisters if she did not actually teach in a school. Until recently historians have assumed that the education – and especially the home instruction – of Victorian middle-class girls was often frivolous and invariably inadequate. However, as we have seen, the range and level of instruction offered by one of the first experiments in institutional higher education for girls – the Methodist-sponsored co-educational Upper Canada Academy, which opened in Cobourg in 1836 – puts such a sweeping characterization in question. The 'Female Department' proved to be very popular. In 1840 there were 62 young ladies out of a total student body of 134. While entirely distinct from those in the 'Male Department,' the curricular offerings for girls from 1836 to 1841 (when the college incorporated as an all-male institution, Victoria College, with Egerton Ryerson as principal) included advanced languages and science as well as music and drawing.[45]

By mid-century this level of instruction was being matched in centres such as Toronto by relatively small household establishments that enjoyed a provincial reputation. Miss MacNally, 'a Dublin lady,' of considerable linguistic accomplishment ('speaking French, German and Spanish with equal facility' it was reported) assisted by her three sisters, ran a school for twelve years on the north side of Wellington Street in Toronto, until she married John Boyd, the principal of a local commercial academy in 1858. Her pupils came from some of Toronto's 'best families,' but also from as far away as Niagara. The renowned Mrs Forster, headmistress of 'Pinehurst' from 1853 to 1866, educated the daughters of numerous prominent Canadian families. One senses that here a pattern was being set: Pinehurst in the early 1860s was the apex of the world of girls' schools: the most privileged young ladies from larger centres such as Hamilton and London, where there were local 'ladies' schools,' nevertheless came all the way to Toronto to attend Mrs Forster's school. On a much-reduced scale, however, Miss Macartney's ladies' school, run out of a three-storey brick house at 325 King Street West, was patronized by families from Chippawa, Napanee, and Guelph as well as Toronto.[46] Miss Macartney also married and, as Mrs. Nixon, became principal of an Anglican-affiliated school. However neither her marriage nor her subsequent connection with a denominationally sponsored school for girls was exceptional by the 1860s. By then the number of more elaborate schools, in terms of curricula and physical amenities, had increased. Some still operated entirely as private venture establishments. Well known locally, Mrs Poetter, for example, held a concert and ball with her pupils at the St Lawrence Hall in Toronto on the evening of 27 April 1859; happily for such a pretentious occasion held in the depths of a financial depression, both 'passed off most successfully.'[47] Others developed unofficial links with a particular religious denomination, often through personal networks. More and more, however, various Protestant denominations founded or sponsored academically advanced schools for girls and, as the common schools improved and broadened their social appeal, it was the wealthier, more socially prominent families in the various local communities who patronized schooling in the private sector. Convent boarding schools had an established reputation among both Catholic and Protestant families as excellent finishing schools;[48] however growing sectarian animosity encouraged fears of possible religious conversion. Those 'wealthy, easy-going Protestants' who sent their daughters to such schools were

The Eclectic Female Institute, Brampton, 1863

'dangerously misguided,' one Methodist predicted gloomily; after all, 'the effect of education in convents was becoming apparent in the numerous perversions to Rome of Protestant girls.'[49] By the 1860s the Methodists and then the Anglicans – not to be outdone – had begun to compete in founding in various urban centres their own institutions for the superior education of young ladies.[50]

A number of factors came together in the 1860s to provoke serious interest in advanced schooling for young women. That the subject was 'in the air' proved enormously influential. A new generation of pioneering headmistresses was at work reforming the schooling of middle-class girls in England; in 1865 Cambridge University local examinations were opened to girls on the same terms as boys (although Cambridge did not admit women to formal membership in the university until 1947, some considerable time after Oxford in 1920). Closer to home, a clever accomplished daughter and / or wife was an obvious social asset – indeed increasingly a necessity – in the best circles of this maturing colonial society. An investment in a young girl's education was a form of dowry – at least so Egerton Ryerson wrote to his future son-in-law, Edward Harris, upon the latter's engagement to Sophie Ryerson in late 1859. He had spared no pains to make his daughter 'a well-educated, Christian and intelligent women, respectable in any circle, and worthy of the *respect* as well as affection of any man,' Ryerson assured Harris, for there was no fortune to leave her.[51] Most significantly, a positive view of the educated woman was shared by innumerable prosperous, respectable families in townships, villages, and towns across the province. For this audience reference to the influence of girls as future mothers could clinch an argument in favour of increased support for girls' schooling.[52]

Few any longer questioned (publicly at least) whether women had the brains to undertake serious study, although the wisdom of doing so would be debated for another two generations at least. In the mid-1860s public discussion focused on the issue of the perfect mix of useful, ornamental, and intellectual strands in the ideal female education.[53] In the ideal, of course, single-sex schools were simply assumed. On a practical level, however, the majority of even middle-class families could ill afford the increasingly hefty fees for the private girls' schools whose excellence gave rise to this particular academic debate. Indeed some parents would have scorned the implication of social climbing, while others undoubtedly were intimidated by these increasingly 'posh' establishments. Convinced of the utility of educating their adolescent daughters nonetheless, these parents turned to the education department and to the provincial school system for relief.[54]

To a limited extent in the few communities that had adopted the central-school model, their needs were met in the senior departments. Elsewhere – notably in Toronto, for example – efforts to establish a high school for girls floundered as common-school trustees were reluctant to absorb the additional expense.[55] Of course in Toronto, with the Girls' Model School and a large private sector, and to a lesser extent in Kingston and Bytown, with their traditional private school establishments, middle-class parents could find an affordable alternative to what they perceived as the socially dubious common school. In villages and small towns, however, few non-boarding options for girls existed. Granted, a 'ladies' private school or academy' with fees of twelve dollars per quarter opened late in 1860 with ten pupils in the still remote town of Owen Sound,[56] but most often the local grammar school provided the only recourse. The trustees of the Clinton Grammar School spoke for the ambitions of young women from middling social backgrounds across the province when they challenged the new regulations and funding provisions in 1867. Never had legislators specified that 'pupils' were only male, they argued. Some of the girls in the Clinton Grammar School were preparing to be teachers 'and others are influenced by the desire of their Parents that they should derive every possible advantage from the instruction given in the School.' Furthermore, as it had been alleged that females were a disruptive influence in grammar schools, why had no one objected to their presence in the senior classes of the common school? Not only had no one complained about that, but coeducation was favoured in the schools of the United States.[57]

They were quite right, of course. To debate the evils of coeducation when all but a handful of grammar schools took both boys and girls was to chase a red herring. And yet the issue – even today – finds champions for both sides. In all probability the vast majority of Victorian Canadian parents preferred single-sex schooling, at least for their older children. It accorded with widely shared attitudes about gender roles and common notions of propriety. Moreover the purported hazards of coeducation touched sexual anxieties that simmered very near the surface of bourgeois morality. Already the school system was frighteningly vulnerable, for the common schools were not without problems. The character of otherwise competent female teachers could seem subtly equivocal. Miss Armstrong, for example, 'appeared kind, orderly and diligent' in her management of the boys' gallery class at Park School in Toronto in 1859, but her limitations were noted: 'she is a young person of no great refinement, either mental or social,' James Porter observed, 'and is much better fitted to have the charge of little boys than of little girls.'[58] To become pregnant was quite unacceptable. The fact that the local teacher of ss 16, North Chatham disciplined the children by pounding them on the head was incidental: 'more than that,' the irate trustees informed the department in late May 1863, 'she is a Married Woman and is not in a proper state to appear with *decency* before a school as she expects to be confined in July.'[59] Trustees who hired male teachers ran other kinds of risks. Overtly sexual incidents were, if at all possible, covered up, but the allegations of at least questionable behaviour that surfaced in discipline cases, for example, suggest persistent parental anxiety about the relationship of pupils to teachers.[60] Occasionally that anxiety was warranted. One can feel some sympathy for the parents and trustees of ss 7, Sombra Village, Kent County, as the children returned home from school in 1868 with copies of a sixteen-page booklet entitled, *The Secret Friend or Warning to Young Men*, by Charles A. Stuart, MD. The long outline of the horrible consequences of masturbation might have spared some fathers an awkward fireside chat, but advertisements for 'Dr. Stuart's Rejuvenating Remedies' and details of the 'French Secret' for the prevention of conception and for guarding against disease were too much. That teacher was going to be fired.[61]

The isolated unfortunate incident was perhaps inevitable. But though instructing little boys and little girls together in the common schools was all very well in the view of the education department, teaching 'grown up' girls and 'grown up' boys together was another matter entirely. Even there, however, George Paxton Young argued, the matter was not clear cut. Should the teacher possess sufficient 'weight of character,' the experience could prove beneficial; the school would then resemble a family or an intimate social circle in which the mingling of young people of different sexes 'is universally admitted to be salutary.' Regrettably, with teachers of lesser character, girls from poorly disciplined homes were tempted to engage in rough play, to be insolent with the teacher, and generally to show off before the boys. Nothing less than a girl's moral character was at risk. 'It is not so much ... any gross and palpable departure from the ordinary moralities, that is to be feared in mixed schools,' Young (a perennial bachelor) primly assured his readers. 'I can hardly describe what I wish to indicate; but every one will understand it, who has been accustomed to associate with cultivated Women: – an ever present delicacy, married to an intelligence which at once strengthens it and liberates it from constraint.'[62] The Chief Superintendent understood it and agreed. Furthermore, he maintained, he had held these convictions since 1841 when, on assuming the principalship of Victoria College, he had disbanded the popular Female Department. But past history can be a fickle ally, as any good debater – which Ryerson was – knows all too well. His explanation for why coeducation prevailed in the common schools and – most tellingly – in the Normal School spoke eloquently to the present dilemma. If the requirement of separate-sex institutions proved impractical and unrealistic in those cases, it was equally so in the case of the grammar schools.[63]

By early 1868 it was clear that the issues of coeducation, a classical curriculum, and government funding formulas for post-elementary schooling would have to be tackled severally and face-on. The confusion had arisen because neither Ryerson nor Young had *seen* girls in the context of the grammar school. In 1860, Ryerson had repeated a speech as many as thirty-five times at county conventions around the province in which he proposed free grammar school tuition for farmers' *sons* and *young men* desiring a superior education.[64] Yet Ryerson was a man who prized the education of his daughters. The phenomenon of *not seeing* poses problems of interpretation for the historian. Teasingly it runs as a theme through Ryerson's career, suggesting an inability, or unwillingness, when it came to certain issues, to relate his private life to his public activity. In 1868, in a widely circulated letter to the press on the subject of the admission of girls to the grammar schools, he presented himself as a supporter of female education; but in doing so (unconsciously one assumes) he fibbed. Just as he relished telling the story of Lawrence Abbott's son and the Boston city hall door-keeper's son – all the while hoping to persuade son Charlie, at Upper Canada College, to aspire to go to a 'public school' in

England, just like Judge Hagarty's boy – so he wrote: 'For myself, I have never had a Daughter learn Latin but I am, of course, no rule for others.' The deception, if that is what it was, lay in the fact that in 1859 he had given Sophie instructions about learning Latin (she was to study with young Charlie).[65] George Paxton Young, whatever his initial idealism, *saw* quite quickly. The débâcle of the 1866 enrolments convinced him that, whatever his preference, girls would continue to attend the local grammar school, for there was no alternative.[66] Moreover it was only too obvious that studying Latin was as irrelevant to the vast majority of boys as it was to girls. What was needed – and in his post-retirement report for 1867 he sketched it – was a high school offering a solid English curriculum, more science, and the classics for the minority who might make some intellectual or professional use of them.[67] The age of the students would replace a distinctive curriculum as the defining feature of the proposed English high school: 'I consider it essential, that, in admission of Pupils to the high Schools, both age and attainments should be taken into account,' he wrote in July 1868, a telling prediction of the regimen of entrance examinations and prescribed courses of study that would accompany the translation of the grammar schools into high schools.

By December 1868 a new draft grammar school bill appeared, but the context now was a major legislative revision to create an articulated school system for the new province of Ontario. One needed a new vocabulary to describe it: public schools would replace 'common schools' at the elementary level; grammar schools would be eliminated; and high schools and collegiate institutes would be the secondary level. In itself, this development was unexceptional. In the various American states that traditionally influenced Canadian policy, coeducational high schools had long been an accepted feature of public school systems. One must ask, then: what point had there been to the fuss about Latin and girls, if in the end Ontario merely copied the Americans? A future for coeducation had been secured by all the fuss. With hindsight one can see that, for girls, that represented both a victory and a defeat. A victory, in that access to the 'superior' education that high schools provided allowed young women to aspire to quite different futures from those their mothers had known. Soon even the doors of the universities would be pried open by the adventurous few. The defeat, such as it was, lay in the relinquishing of the ideal of an education that could be not just separate but different and equal. For better or for worse, whether they attended public schools or private schools, girls increasingly would play the same game as the boys – but with boys' rules.

The mounting pressures in favour of acknowledging public responsibility for and public financial support of post-elementary schooling came from various directions. While in numerical terms a tiny minority in the province (and that would remain the case until at least the First World War), parents in a variety of circumstances sought access to high schools for their children: parents of boys as much as girls, and on the basis of a perception of social-class distinctions as much as academic ambition. Not a few old school promoters must have winced when they heard that the grammar school in Hamilton was no longer an integral part of the much-vaunted Central School, having been reconstituted on a separate basis in 1867 at the instigation of wealthy taxpayers who complained that they were forced to send their children 'abroad' for education or to private schools. 'Conceal it as we may, laud our own Central schools as we may,' the Hamilton *Spectator* intoned, 'the fact yet remains that we have not hitherto had such educational facilities as would induce persons of means and intelligence, and having a family of boys, to settle among us.'[68]

It is tempting to see the grammar school controversy of the mid-1860s as a 'comic interlude' provided by a bachelor intellectual unaccustomed to framing public policy and an aging, ailing, and frustrated administrator unwilling (more than unable) to abandon a pathetic colonial ambition. Such an interpretation would be not so much wrong as inadequate. Serious political myopia or miscalculation was at the centre of this issue. Expectations were rising; families well placed locally were making their voices heard; the education department failed to keep pace.[69] Ryerson was a commanding presence still, whose advanced age and increasing infirmity explain a portion of the problem. While he sensed that the political ground was shifting in the 1860s he seemed unable to do more than rail against a future of partisan politics and recall for his trusted lieutenant Hodgins how it once had been. Impatient with the government's inaction in 1860 Ryerson had recounted petulantly to John A. Macdonald the halcyon days of the early 1850s when Mr Baldwin and Mr Hincks seemed to have endless time and interest to spare for school legislation. In 1865 he remained sceptical of the importance of relying on the government's interest and influence, urging Hodgins to follow his tack of lobbying individual backbenchers.[70] Appealing to the people – tapping a grass-roots commitment to schooling – was a strategy Ryerson had pursued since the mid-1840s. For all that his critics considered his periodic convention tours to be 'mere bunkum' because 'all he seems to want is for the people to say, amen, and he is delighted,' Ryerson persisted.[71] At considerable cost to his own health he again stumped the province in the winter of 1869 and appeared, at least, still to believe in the power of the popular will, however carefully he orchestrated it. Either the old mechanisms no longer worked well, or he did not listen. He might better have heeded J.A. Macdonald's prediction that any last-minute school reforms 'might be all knocked on the head at the first session of the Upper Canadian Parliament.'[72]

Confederation created not only a new nation but a new Ontario legislature with responsibility for education. In the beginning, Premier John Sandfield Macdonald's government coalition of mismatched old reformers and erstwhile Tories partially masked the sharpening partisanship of the political process. But the factionalism Ryerson had always deplored was rife in the new legislature and no one played that game with greater relish or skill than Edward Blake, MPP for West Durham, and Sandfield Macdonald's successor as premier in 1871. The issue of new school legislation arose in time-honoured fashion, for the new government had no particular agenda and waited for Ryerson's suggestions. These came in a barrage, starting in the spring of 1868 with a special report 'on the Systems and State of Popular Education on the Continent of Europe, in the British Isles and the United States of America, with practical suggestions for the improvement of public instruction in the Province of Ontario,' a report on Institutions for the Education of the Deaf and Dumb and Blind, the Annual Report of the Normal Model, Grammar and Common Schools for 1867, and two draft bills respecting the common and grammar schools.[73] In November 1868, an unusually large select committee was established to examine the workings of the school system, and it was after this that the process started to go seriously awry. The select committee approved amendments to the draft bills, which were debated and further revised over the course of Ryerson's county tour, but when new draft legislation came before the legislature in November 1869 it was mutilated in what the *Globe* described as a free-for-all session.[74] On Ryerson's advice the government withdrew the legislation.

With still more time the process of policy making became more 'political' as well as more elaborate both within and outside the government. Members of the legislature, school trustees and officials, municipal politicians, newspaper editors, teachers (both pro and anti the education department) – even the chief justices – had their say. Writing in 1947, C.B. Sissons, Ryerson's modern biographer, saw in the whole exercise, from county conventions to legislative scrutiny, 'an admirable example of the making of law in a sober society.'[75] Quite so; but there are other elements in this extended débâcle that deserve to be highlighted, not least the estrangement of the Chief Superintendent from the government that accompanied, and outlived, this process. A fearful row in January 1869 between Ryerson and E.B. Wood, the provincial treasurer, over the financial arrangements of the education department, triggered the deterioration in working relations. Quickly other members of the department became embroiled. In April Hodgins felt forced to put his house up for rent and move to less expensive quarters, for example, because Blake had succeeded in having his salary cut by $500 annually.[76] More insidiously, department personnel would make new alignments independent of the Chief Superintendent. It is easy to plot the subsequent isolation of Ryerson, after 1871 particularly, in terms of personal animosity, Edward Blake being a prime culprit. But had that been the whole story, the influence of the Chief Superintendent would have been restored with the succession of Oliver Mowat to the premiership. Relations improved, but Ryerson did not regain his influence, largely because the issue had only partially ever been about him personally. It was primarily that he was of a generation of independent pioneer administrators who had to be tamed – indeed domesticated – to fit into the bureaucracy they themselves had created. A shift of critical importance occurred during the protracted process of framing the 1871 school bill; henceforth it would not be the department's policy but the government's policy, in ways that had never been true before.[77]

One ought not to be surprised that in the midst of the fray Ryerson, occasionally at least, realized not only what was at stake but what needed to be done. In what would prove to be the first of a series of letters of resignation, he wrote to the provincial secretary in December 1868 proposing that education be treated in a manner comparable to other government business by giving responsibility for it to a designated cabinet officer, a minister of public instruction. As had been so often the case in the past, he was ahead of his time: it would be more than seven years before the first 'Minister of Education,' Adam Crooks, was appointed.[78]

It has become something of a convention among historians to treat the 1871 school legislation as the 'coping stone' (to borrow C.B. Sissons's phrase) of Ryerson's career as a public administrator. In one sense – given its timing at the close of his career – this characterization is apt. However the connotation of 'crowning' conveyed by the word 'copestone' is inappropriate: the Common School Act of 1850 was a more significant benchmark in both Egerton Ryerson's public career and the development of the provincial school system. The school legislation of the early 1870s (the 1871 acts and the 1874 amending legislation) is best considered in conjunction with the regulations, some subsequently countermanded and revised, that streamed forth from the education department on the authority of the Council of Public Instruction. Certainly, as an administrative exercise, the drawing up of new regulations to cover, down to the minutest detail, the ways of 'doing business' for municipal councils, school trustees, teachers, ratepayers, etc., was a *tour de force*. As revision invariably entailed elaboration, one can almost see the tentacles of the education department inching forward with each successive circular. Substantively, however, this latest legislative and regulatory initiative was less conclusive. Over the next decade the government would retreat on some points – notably in the areas of curriculum and teacher certification, for example – which seemed significant in the early 1870s. Overall the new look given to the provincial school system after 1871 was *transitional*. Nevertheless, the confirmation of certain directions, previously only hinted at, in a few key areas proved to be extremely important.[79]

Undoubtedly the most obvious and memorable change was the vertical integration of an elementary and a secondary curriculum at the (renamed) public and high schools (and collegiate institutes). New subjects – mechanical arts, bookkeeping, and argicultural science – were added to the old common school curriculum. 'Limit tables,' applicable across the province, were issued detailing the various levels to be achieved for promotion, year by year, and the requisite hours each day to be allotted to each subject. Despite the department's assurance that 'it will be found that nothing has been introduced which is impracticable, or for mere show, but everything for practical use, and that which admits of easy accomplishment,' there was considerable confusion and dissatisfaction with the new order. Many parents, trustees, and ratepayers preferred the school to stick to the basics; teachers deplored excessive interference in when to teach what, particularly given the fact that much in the new curricular directives was irrelevant to one-room rural schools.[80] The new emphasis on science teaching appeared particularly problematic. Teachers felt threatened by a subject they did not know; they did not need George Paxton Young to tell them that 'many of the Public School Masters need to have their notions about Science entirely reconstructed.' In a real sense serious popular debate about the relevance of the school's curriculum dates from the early 1870s. Once started, discussion of what was best for farmers' sons or urban skilled workers proved to be almost endless.[81]

Difficulties inherent in revamping the course of study in the public schools were exacerbated by the introduction of a new hurdle: the transition to high school. Notions of how best to liberalize the old grammar school curriculum were readily at hand, the matter having been thoroughly aired by the grammar schoolmasters and the inspectors in the late 1860s. A modified classical option was now available in selected collegiate institutes, and an eclectic English and commercial program in the more numerous local high schools. When it came to translating the blueprint into practice, more hinged on the quality of the entering students than on the teachers' knowledge. The problem of defining and enforcing a province-wide *standard* had to be confronted. The education department developed a four-pronged strategy in the early 1870s, while relations with

The High School, Cayuga

the government were at best strained. The traditional oral inquisition required for grammar school entrance was replaced by *written answers*, the consequence of which was immediate: a preliminary introduction in 1871 of written answers to grammar questions *halved* the eligible intake.[82] Subsequently *uniform examinations* in all subjects were prepared and sent under seal to local authorities, who administered them according to strict guidelines. Uniform examinations without *centralized marking* made barely a dint in the problem, however. But on this issue the department and the government engaged in acrimonious negotiation after the regulations issued by the Council of Public Instruction were suspended by the government late in 1871 on the grounds that they misconstrued the respective powers of the inspectors and local examining boards. There would be further successful negotiation on that issue and on the matter of a passing minimum (50 per cent overall; 33 per cent minimum on each paper after 1873), but the problem remained that uniform examinations and centralized grading had to be based on some agreed-upon body of knowledge. What would that be? On this point the department appears to have suffered an enduring set-back. Pressure from parents and school trustees to lower the standard of the entrance examinations was intense; per-capita government funding of students in the high schools was approximately twenty-five to thirty times that of students in the public schools. By 1875 there was serious overlap in the academic work done in the two institutions. Students now could try the entrance exam after completing as little as half the course of study offered in the public school.[83] Having failed to staunch the flow of poorly qualified students into the local high schools, the education department simply threw up a new hurdle: the Intermediate Examination. While, as a consequence, the high school curriculum shed a year-by-year strait-jacket of prescribed study and re-formed with a horizontal division between lower and upper school, the results of the Intermediate Examination, which bridged that divide, formed the basis of the calculation of the 'payment by results' component of high school funding after 1876. Written examinations were firmly entrenched. Despite the potential hazards of cramming, which they acknowledged, the high school inspectors in 1875 marvelled at what had been achieved. 'It is difficult to overestimate the value of this [written testing of work] in giving accuracy and precision to thought and expression,' they boasted. Moreover the public schools were rising to the challenge and 'a stream of newly oxygenated blood has begun to flow through the arteries of the body scholastic, which must, ere long,' they predicted, 'impart a measure of life to the remotest extremity.'[84]

The teachers had a good deal to contend with in keeping up with parental expectations and new departmental requirements; in addition the 1871 legislation notionally streamlined and raised teachers' qualifications. Following consultation with the Teachers' Association the department redefined the various categories of certification: now first- and second-class provincial certificates conveyed what was tantamount to a life-time licence to teach anywhere in the province. All certificates, provincial and county, were to be based on written examinations. Predictably, the results of the first round revealed a depressingly high failure rate, and a clamour against 'too high standards' ensued. The department both gave and held the line. The third-class county certificate valid locally for one year, which it hoped to abolish, in fact flourished: there was simply too great a demand for teachers. The notion of a hierarchy of certification was maintained, however. The value of the provincial certificates was protected by a centrally administered examination process so effective that it provoked various charges of examination fraud.[85]

The education department's interest in improving teacher qualifications, while genuine, was undoubtedly paced by the increasingly self-conscious Ontario Teachers' Association whose voice was listened to seriously in government circles in the 1870s. The forces promoting professionalism made their most significant gain with the changing status of the inspectorate. In the mid-1860s the Reverend James Fraser had identified the system of local county superintendents as 'one of the weak points of the Canadian system,' not least because the inspectors had dubious qualifications for the job and existed in a limbo somewhere between the municipal authorities who employed them and the education department whose policies they were to promote and superintend. Not all the contradictions in the position were resolved in 1871. Incumbents in office for more than three years were to be carried forward and exempted from the new qualifications and examinations. Moreover all inspectors remained employees of local municipal authorities (county or city), but were henceforth protected from dismissal except 'for misconduct or inefficiency.' The main point – the professionalization of the inspectorate – was secured, however. For men embarking on a career in teaching there was now another rung on the hierarchical ladder to which to aspire. And there is no doubt that the new inspector, armed with sheafs of new regulations issued by the Council of Public Instruction, made a formidable impression on many local school trustees in the 1870s.[86]

The Council of Public Instruction itself was soon to be a major casualty of the post-1871 arrangements, although it must be admitted that beyond a tight circle very few people would have noticed. Long a bone of contention among the critics of various departmental policies, this appointed advisory body of unrepresentative citizens had been living on borrowed time. The *raison d'être* of the council dated from the 1840s, and its careful balancing of religious and political interests reflected the schisms of that era. One has the impression that Ryerson in his heyday in the 1850s used the council less as a sounding board than as a rubber stamp. By the 1870s the 'politics' of education had become muddied by competing professional interests as much as by a more sophisticated political style. To humble the education department, Edward Blake subjected the council's operations to a humiliating scrutiny in 1872, demanding justification for virtually every pronouncement. Oliver Mowat, on succeeding Blake as premier, opened the council's membership to three elected representatives of the high school, public and separate school teachers, and public school inspectors, respectively. Despite the growing sense of professionalism in the ranks, however, each constituency chose a distinguished outsider – Professor Daniel Wilson, Sam Wood, MPP, and Goldwin Smith – which probably complicated the matter. Certainly the tactic of pouring 'new wine into old bottles' did not work. The last meeting of the council on 13 November 1875 was attended by only three members.[87]

Egerton Ryerson's retirement as chief superintendent and the appointment of Adam Crooks as minister of education in February 1876, came hard on the heels of the demise of the Council of Public Instruction.

Egerton Ryerson is so closely identified with the development of public schooling that it is all too easy to characterize these events as marking the end of an era for both the individual and the school system. Retirement did close a controversial chapter in the life of a truly remarkable Upper Canadian. However, issues of public policy are ongoing and less amenable than individual careers to being categorized in eras. The best evidence of this is, perhaps, another often-noted feature of the 1870s legislation: compulsory education. The relevant clauses of the 1871 act, requiring the education of children seven to twelve years of age for a minimum of four months a year, were utterly ineffectual and remained so for decades, despite further legislative provisions for establishing industrial schools. By the turn of the century, it would be the shrinking of alternatives, more than compulsion or even the attractions of going to school, that would secure virtual universal enrolment, if not regular attendance.[88]

What is significant, however, about the 1870s is that there was no John Roaf (as there had been in 1850) to question the very premise of a provincial, publicly supported, centrally administered school system. Edward Blake and others argued, justifiably, that compulsory measures were unworkable. But such criticism merely highlights the distance that had been travelled since mid-century. There would continue to be debate and negotiation over detail; but by the early 1870s the basic structure of the school system was taken for granted by all parties: ratepayers, teachers, parents, children, and government.

conclusion

The educational landscape at the close of Egerton Ryerson's career was markedly different from what it had been at the beginning. Not only was there more of everything – pupils, teachers, schoolhouses, textbooks, blackboards – but, overall, there was greater uniformity and more formality in the regular organization of learning. The experience of growing up had become more predictable also. By the mid-1870s more and more children at much the same ages attended school for at least part of the year; a smaller but growing number attended a good deal of the time; and by and large their experiences of school became increasingly similar. Invariably, of course, general trends can be misleading, for often the exceptions are at least as interesting as the rule. It is equally clear, for example, that despite the blandishments of the education department elements of the older, more flexible, more familial style of schooling and learning persisted after mid-century in many communities through the 1860s; and well after that they reappeared on the new frontiers of Muskoka, Haliburton, and Algoma, as the pioneer experience of a previous half-century repeated itself.[89] On certain measures of material improvement, differences in schooling between rural and urban communities were accentuated, in time. However, to state it so baldly is to imply that only time and some quantifiable measure of social development (ideally expressed in terms of rateable property values, perhaps) stood in the way of perfect provincial uniformity. Such is the substance of a bureaucrat's fantasy: it is not history. On the one hand, the cultural diversity entrenched with settlement and the varied local economies upon which town and country dwellers depended discouraged uniformity. On the other hand, pressures of agrarian capitalism modified rural family forms in many of the same ways as a maturing commercial and early industrial capitalism affected urban family life. In both rural and urban worlds what had only recently been an informal transition from school to work had become more regulated and formalized.

Contrary to the impression created by Victorian school advocates, neither legislation nor the rules, regulations, and exhortations of an education bureaucracy ushered in the era of popular education in Upper Canada. As we have seen, schooling of some sort and for some portion of time had long been a common feature of most children's lives. The novelty, by the 1870s, lay in the virtual monopoly of schooling enjoyed by the provincial school system in which ordinary taxpayers had now invested heavily with both their money and their faith. The process of school 'improvement,' unpredictable and irregular though it had been, and dependent as it was upon the attitudes as much as upon the material prosperity of the population, had clearly made an impact. The Ontario public school system was firmly in place.

Looking back over the decades since Upper Canada's beginnings, one is astonished by the staggering variety of ideas and forms that the public school system had replaced. There was no lack of theories about education in Upper Canada's early and mid-century years; models for schooling the young were almost as numerous as the children themselves. Yet in the end, one constellation of ideas predominated. How had this come about?

The reasons, at one level, are fairly obvious. After mid-century, the carrot was the government school fund. Any community that wanted government money to help pay the teacher had learned that it had to follow provincial education department rules. Any school board that wanted cheap textbooks subsidized by the department now knew that these had to be bought from the approved list. But this was not all. The education department of Upper Canada had also done a gigantic job of salesmanship. Government schooling, it could be said, was the original state consumer product. Who could resist the propaganda that the education department churned out by the ton and the textbooks, maps and globes, and blackboards that educational authorities said were so essential? These things, if you had them and others did not, made it plain that you had a better school in Section 1 than your neighbours had in Section 2. If it was not plain, the education department helped to make it so, by publishing the facts at least once a year: which townships had few or no blackboards in their schools; which school had no globe; who paid the lowest average salaries to their male or female school teachers; and who spent the least, in any given year, on their schools. As Egerton Ryerson had once pointed out, good education created new wants; and one of those wants was more and better education.

Assiduously, the education department promoted competition among the localities, as school sections, townships, villages, and towns were urged to compete for better schools than the schools of their neighbours. The message of competition was directed not only to the province as a whole and to local school communities, but to individuals and occupational groups. What was to become of the sons and daughters of Upper Canada if they failed to acquire a proper education, in an age when apprenticing children to oneself or to neighbours or friends was clearly no longer an adequate preparation for their future? To succeed in the new era of commercial capitalism, it seemed necessary to acquire what only improved schools could provide. Schools were seen to inculcate in children not only the deference to authority and love of punctuality and order they needed if they were to become efficient workers in the new industrial era, but also the energy and skills they needed to compete, to get on in the world.

If Upper Canadians bought the message, it was partly because it was sold so well; and partly because they felt too poor to pay for the schooling they wanted for their children themselves. By 1850, the law had already provided for the common school fund to be distributed on the basis of average attendance. Local communities could also tax themselves to make the school free. A sparsely settled rural community with no free school could hardly compete with the local town where in all probability the school was free and children were able to attend more regularly. The incentive to fall into line must have been very great indeed.

This said, there was a dramatic disjuncture between what government school promoters said was happening and what was really happening. The continuities are striking. To illustrate this point, it is useful to look at the school and teaching experiences of a child of Ontario in the 1860s and 1870s. Elizabeth Smith, of Winona, kept a diary, beginning in 1872 when she was thirteen.[90] In it she tells us a little about her life as a pupil in an Ontario common school and much more about her life and feelings as a teacher in two different Ontario rural schools, when she was eighteen and twenty years old. What was remarkable about both her schooling and her teaching was their sporadic nature. Elizabeth did not attend school regularly. She had to stay home to mind her new baby sister when she was thirteen; the weather and the condition of the roads also played a role in keeping her at home. Her sisters and brothers too were irregular in their attendance. A brother stayed at home for long periods when his eyes were giving him trouble; a sister, who attended a 'ladies' college' for a while, did so only between the months of October and February. Elizabeth's teaching was perhaps more regular on a daily or weekly basis. But she taught for only a year at a time, and her 'career' in teaching lasted for little more than two years.

Despite its brevity, Elizabeth's experience of teaching has a great deal to say about the old and the new world of Ontario schooling in the 1870s. There was, first of all, her intense involvement with the communities of which her schools were a part. In one of them, this meant enduring a 'scandal' perpetrated and spread by the first family she boarded with, when they were angered by her decision to move to cheaper accommodation that was also a shorter distance from the schoolhouse. It meant the sometimes amusing, sometimes irritating attentions of local swains, one of whom became a serious suitor, although, in the end, Elizabeth discouraged him because she was reluctant to become seriously involved with a Roman Catholic. It meant mixed feelings not only about suitors but about obligatory visits to the homes of her pupils, about playing the organ for a nearby Catholic church, and about a decision to found a Methodist Sunday school. In the latter case, her ambivalence stemmed from a sense of having undertaken too many duties on Sunday, coupled with a gnawing suspicion that she would have been made superintendent of the Sunday school had she been a young man.

The teaching itself she found monotonous, on the whole, and the children she taught hard to bring forward. In her second school she wondered what would happen should she have to 'rule by fear' as she did 'over *some at least* by love.' It did seem ridiculous to have to look up to one of her scholars, a 'great brawny man of a fellow' who was only a year younger than herself. Outside supervision was noted in the visit of the inspector, an experience that if not traumatic was certainly stressful. The 'little knowledge' of the children, whom Elizabeth regarded as 'deplorably ignorant' to begin with, 'flew out the window' when the inspector 'came in at the door.' The diarist confessed to an urge to beat some of the children, on this occasion, and lamented their inability to retain what she had taught them. 'If they would only remember what they learn,' was the substance of her complaint. But, in the end, she admitted that the whole process of teaching defeated her. She guessed that the scholars had little interest in retaining the old lessons once she gave them a new one, but could not imagine why.

An early school photo: ss 7, Scarborough, some time before the schoolhouse was destroyed by fire in 1870

Yet Elizabeth Smith became fond of her pupils, and both she and the girls in one of her schools cried when the schoolmistress left to attend Hamilton Collegiate Institute. The two public rituals of the school year, the 'Christmas Tree' and the spring examination, the diarist believed had been gloriously successful, and, in the latter case, she had been placed 'on a pedestal of fame' and 'become a shining light.' When she had a daguerrotype made of her 'school and flock,' we see that a new era had begun: the era of the class photo. Perhaps even more interesting is Elizabeth's distinction between her school, now obviously the house in which she offered her lessons, and her 'flock' or the pupils who came to the school to be taught. The scholars and their teacher were no longer the school. The latter had become an entity, a building, an institution.

Although much in Elizabeth Smith's life is suggestive of the old world of schooling – her own and her brothers' and sisters' irregular attendance at school, for example, or the obviously small scale and sociable nature of her teaching experience and its rootedness in what seemed, on the surface at least, stable agricultural communities – there was also much that was new. From Elizabeth Smith's diary, we can extrapolate something of the legacy of the nineteenth-century school revolution to our own time.

A school photo from the early 1870s

Two themes emerge as particularly deserving of attention. First of all, Elizabeth Smith taught not just in schools, but in a system of schools. By the 1870s a majority of her fellow teachers in Upper Canada were, like herself, young women, many of whom saw their work as temporary. Her work was supervised by a hierarchy of male officials, of which the inspector was only perhaps the most awe-inspiring. The school, which in Mary O'Brien's or Thomas Appleton's day had been a teacher and his or her scholars, was now a building, property owned by the school corporation and controlled by its elected trustees. The female teacher was not only at the bottom of a growing hierarchy of male officialdom, she was also an employee of the state that this hierarchy represented. Parents came to the school only on set days to see what the teacher displayed, at Christmas or in the spring examination. Finally, the teacher was often not a member of the community. Motivated by her own inner need to compete and succeed, she tried to do well by her pupils, but she sometimes regarded them as alien and ignorant and incapable of learning.

At the same time, teaching – indeed the whole classroom enterprise –

was changing. Elizabeth Smith, unlike Mary O'Brien or Anne Langton, was not in complete control of her school; nor, however, were the parents of her pupils, who were beginning to get the message that their children were not welcome in school if they came late. Unlike the old teacher from the Gore District so deplored by District Superintendent Patrick Thornton in the late 1840s, Elizabeth Smith certainly did not lie down on a bench to teach. She probably stood at the front of the room and employed the new educational technology of the day – a blackboard, provincial readers, and perhaps even maps and a globe. She was aware of and tried to employ the energizing pedagogy of love. She referred to her pupils as 'little shrimps' and clearly cared for them. Indeed her boredom and loneliness in teaching only produced a sense of guilt. Why could she not perform her duties more cheerfully, she seemed to be asking herself? Ah well, carrying on was at least just what she needed: a discipline that would do her good. Yet, teaching was not just a discipline for Elizabeth Smith. She hoped through teaching to make her way in the world, and to fulfill an ambition to go to university and study medicine.

The creation of Ontario's school system was a complicated (if always flawed) process in which all sorts of people, some of whom were eager, others somewhat afraid to face the future, attempted to deal with the education of their own and other people's children. To regard either Elizabeth Smith, nineteenth-century schoolmistress, or her pupils, some of whom (especially the girls) evidently came to her school with eagerness, as targets of concerted efforts to control and / or marginalize either the working classes or the young women who taught them, is obviously to simplify. Images of 'class conspiracy' and central administrative 'dictatorship' are frankly implausible and must be discarded. Yet one cannot underestimate the power of the institution that had been created in the provincial school system. Inevitably the values it represented and promoted were rooted in the social structures of the liberal capitalist society that was Ontario. Current social, racial, and gender stereotypes were reinforced, in some cases with devastating effects. The school system would prove to be no more tolerant than society at large of ambitions or behaviour that deviated too far from the norm.

It is hard to imagine a society without schools. Our own take up more and more days of the year and years of our lives. Yet it is important to remember that 150 years ago few people sent their children to school for more than a few years, and then not consistently throughout the school year. It took a long time for the competitive quest for educational improvement to permeate society. It is also critically important to recognize that the ever-increasing march of school attendance, school building, and educational system development that ensnared the Elizabeth Smiths of nineteenth-century Ontario reflected and responded to shifting rhythms in the lives of young people. Quite simply, in their world, there were fewer and fewer alternatives to going to school. The myriad family responsibilities that had absorbed so much of the waking hours of children and young people in earlier times had diminished. When once the time spent at school was fitted around the demands of family time, now the situation was reversed. Increasingly, the regulated hours of the school day, week, and year would dictate the routines of family life.

Notes

Abbreviations Used in the Notes

AO	Archives of Ontario
ARUC	*Annual Report of the Normal, Model, Grammar and Common Schools in Upper Canada* (titles vary); also known as the *Annual Report of the Chief Superintendent of Schools for Upper Canada*
CHR	*Canadian Historical Review*
DCB	*Dictionary of Canadian Biography*
DHE	John George Hodgins, comp., *Documentary History of Education in Upper Canada, from the Passing of the Constitutional Act of 1791 to the Close of Dr. Ryerson's Administration of the Education Department in 1876* 28 vols (Toronto: Warwick Bros and Rutter 1894–1910)
Fraser Report	Great Britain, Schools Inquiry Commission, *Report to the Commissioners Appointed by Her Majesty to Inquire into the Education Given in Schools in England Not Comprised within Her Majesty's Two Recent Commissions, and to the Commissioners Appointed by Her Majesty to Inquire into the Schools in Scotland on the Common School System of the United States and of the Provinces of Upper and Lower Canada*, by the Rev. James Fraser, *British Parliamentary Papers* 1867
HS/SH	*Histoire sociale / Social History*
JEUC	*Journal of Education of Upper Canada*
MTCL	Metropolitan Toronto Reference Library
OH	*Ontario History*
OISE	Ontario Institute for Studies in Education
PAC	Public Archives of Canada
PAC RG5	Records of the Provincial and Civil Secretaries' Offices, Upper Canada and Canada West, Public Archives of Canada
RG2	Education Records of the Archives of Ontario
TBEHC	Toronto Board of Education Historical Collection

Preface

1 Egerton Ryerson, *First Lessons in Christian Morals for Canadian Families and Schools* (Toronto 1871) Lesson V, 30–2n
2 See especially Samuel Bowles and H. Gintis, *Schooling in Capitalist America: Education and the Contradictions of Economic Life* (New York: Basic Books 1976); and Michael B. Katz, 'The Origins of Public Education: A Reassessment,' *History of Education Quarterly* (Winter 1976) 381–408.

PART ONE *Interpreting Pioneer Schooling*

1 Upper Canada Central School, *First Annual Report* (York 1822)
2 James J. Talman, ed., *Loyalist Narratives from Upper Canada* (Toronto: Champlain Society 1946) ix, xxv; *A Letter from a Gentleman to His Friend in England, Descriptive of the Different Settlements in the Province of Upper Canada* (Philadelphia 1795) 14; Edward Allen Talbot, *Five Years' Residence in the Canadas*, vol. 2 (London 1824) 18; Adam Fergusson, *Practical Notes Made during a Tour in Canada and a Portion of the United States in 1831, with Added Notes Made during a Second Visit to Canada in 1833* (Edinburgh 1834) 118; 'Memoirs of Colonel John Clarke, of Port Dalhousie, C.W.,' *OH* 7 (1906) 175. On the uses of travel literature as a source for early Upper Canada (and some of the problems associated with it) see James J. Talman, 'Travel Literature as Source Material for the History of Upper Canada,' Canadian Historical Association *Report and Papers* (1929–30) 111–20; also Gerald M. Craig, *Early Travellers in the Canadas 1791–1867* (Toronto: Macmillan 1955).
3 Charles E. Phillips, *The Development of Education in Canada* (Toronto: Gage 1957) 100
4 R.D. Gidney, 'Elementary Education in Upper Canada: A Reassessment,' *OH* 65 (Sept. 1973) 170, reprinted in Michael B. Katz and Paul H. Mattingly, eds, *Education and Social Change: Themes from Ontario's Past* (New York: New York University Press 1975)
5 Alison Prentice, *The School Promoters: Education and Social Class in Mid-Nineteenth Century Upper Canada* (Toronto: McClelland and Stewart 1977) 49
6 *Claims of the Churchmen and Dissenters of Upper Canada Brought to the Test: In a Controversy between Several Members of the Church of England and a Methodist Preacher* (Kingston 1828) 17, 74
7 Upper Canada Central School, *First Annual Report*. Students of the manuscript census returns have documented extraordinary mobility. See Michael B. Katz, *The People of Hamilton, Canada West: Family and Class in a Mid-Nineteenth Century City* (Cambridge, Mass.: Harvard University Press 1975) ch. 3; and David Gagan, *Hopeful Travellers: Families, Land, and Social Change in Mid-*

Victorian Peel County, Canada West (Toronto: University of Toronto Press 1981) 114–25.

8 V.C. Fowke, 'The Myth of the Self-Sufficient Canadian Pioneer,' *Transactions of the Royal Society of Canada* 56, series 3, section 2 (June 1962) 32, 33; Anna Jameson, *Sketches in Canada and Rambles among the Red Men* (London 1852) 91–5, reprinted in Beth Light and Alison Prentice, eds, *Pioneer and Gentlewomen of British North America, 1713–1867* (Toronto: New Hogtown Press 1980) 19–22; 'The Bell and Laing School Papers,' *Lennox and Addington Historical Society Papers* vol. 5 (1914) 24n; Fred Landon, ed., 'Selections from the Papers of James Evans, Missionary of the Indians,' *OH* 26 (1930) 479. For discussion of Upper Canadian native peoples' reactions to the early-nineteenth-century schools provided for them by missionaries or government-appointed teachers, see J. Donald Wilson, ' "No Blanket to Be Worn in School": The Education of Indians in Early Nineteenth-Century Ontario,' *HS/SH* 14 (Nov. 1974) 293–305, reprinted in Jean Barman et al., eds, *Indian Education in Canada, I: The Legacy* (Vancouver: University of British Columbia Press 1986) ch. 4.

9 *Kingston Gazette* 12 Feb. 1811

10 John Strachan, *A Letter to the Rev. A.N. Bethune, Rector of Cobourg, on the Management of Grammar Schools* (York 1829)

CHAPTER I *Family and State in Upper Canadian Education*

1 For a discussion of literary sources and the insight they give into the history of Upper Canadian family life and child rearing, see David Gagan, ' "The Prose of Life": Literary Reflections of the Family, Individual Experience and Social Structure in Nineteenth-Century Canada,' *Journal of Social History* 9 (Spring 1976) 367–81.

2 Charles R. Sanderson, ed., *The Arthur Papers, Being the Canadian Papers Mainly Confidential, Private and Demi-official of Sir George Arthur, KCH, Last Lieutenant-Governor of Upper Canada in the Manuscript Collection of the Toronto Public Libraries* 3 vols (Toronto: University of Toronto Press 1957) *passim*

3 PAC, Sir Allan Napier MacNab Papers, Public Archives of Canada. The diary has been published in Charles Ambrose Carter and Thomas Malville Bailey, eds, *The Diary of Sophia MacNab* (Hamilton, Ont. 1974), and 'Rules for Sophie and Minnie,' in Beth Light and Alison Prentice, eds, *Pioneer and Gentlewomen of British North America 1713–1867* (Toronto: New Hogtown Press 1980) 30–2.

4 Letitia Youmans, *Campaign Echoes* (Toronto, 3rd ed. 1893) 28

5 Letitia Youmans does not mention this employment in her autobiography. But her name appears in the 1861 manuscript census as the assistant in the grammar school in Colborne. A search for the Youmans household in the same census return turned up a husband with the correct name and occupation. It is very

unlikely that there could have been two highly educated Letitia Youmanses in Upper Canada during the 1860s, each married to an identical spouse. It seems safe to conclude therefore that the Youmanses made Colborne their home for a period in the 1860s and that Letitia did in fact return briefly to school teaching.

6 AO, Diaries Collection, MU840, Thomas Dick Diary 1867–94

7 This was the case in Hamilton at least. See Michael B. Katz, *The People of Hamilton, Canada West: Family and Class in a Mid-Nineteenth Century City* (Cambridge, Mass.: Harvard University Press 1975).

8 Joseph F. Kett, *Rites of Passage: Adolescence in America, 1790 to the Present* (New York: Basic Books 1977). Kett stresses the tendency of rural youths in the early nineteenth century to use schools seasonally or periodically over even longer time spans than a year. Periods of school for most young men, then, were interspersed with periods of employment. If 'employment' is taken to mean productive occupation (with or without pay), then the same was clearly true for rural girls as well.

9 AO, Strachan Papers, John Strachan to Dr Brown, 13 July 1806; Richard Cartwright, *Life and Letters of the Late Honourable Richard Cartwright* (Toronto 1876) 98; Edward Allen Talbot, *Five Years' Residence in the Canadas* (London 1824) vol. 2, 119

10 Frances Stewart, *Our Forest Home*, completed and edited by her daughter, E.S. Dunlop (Toronto 1889)

11 Frederick F. Thompson, 'Reflections upon Education in the Midland District, 1810–1816,' *Historic Kingston* 11 (Mar. 1963) 10, 12

12 Philippe Ariès, *Centuries of Childhood: A Social History of Family Life* (New York: Random House 1962)

13 Ross W. Beales, 'Anne Bradstreet and Her Children,' in Barbara Finklestein, ed., *Regulated Children, Liberated Children: Education in Psychohistorical Perspective* (New York: Psychohistory Press 1979). See also N. Ray Hiner's contribution to the same volume; J.H. Plumb, 'The New World of Children in Eighteenth-Century England,' *Past and Present* 67 (May 1975) 64–93; and Linda A. Pollack, *Forgotten Children: Parent-Child Relations from 1500–1900* (Cambridge: Cambridge University Press 1983).

14 Expressions of grief about the death of children are to be found in the verse of a Cobourg Loyalist, dating from 1797, cited in Clara C. Field, 'Literary Landmarks of Several Counties,' *OH* 25 (1929) 220, and in a letter by John Strachan concerning the loss of a young daughter. Strachan to Brown, Dec. 1818, in George W. Spragge, ed., *The John Strachan Letterbook, 1812–1834* (Toronto: University of Toronto Press 1946) 184. On Strachan's delight in his children, see J.L.H. Henderson, *John Strachan, 1778–1867* (Toronto: University of Toronto Press 1960) 52. MTCL, Boulton Papers, Letters of William Boulton, 21 Feb. 1834, 45

15 University of King's College, Toronto, Upper Canada, *Proceedings at the Ceremony of Laying the Foundation Stone April 23, 1842 and at the Opening of*

the University, June 8, 1843 (Toronto 1843) 55–6 and 61, 62; Richard Cockrell, *Thoughts on the Education of Youth* (Newark, Upper Canada 1795; Toronto: Bibliographical Society of Canada 1949) 7, 8. See also *DHE* vol. 1, 34–5, for a comment on the tenderness of the infant mind, dating from 1799; Alison Prentice, *The School Promoters: Education and Social Class in Mid-Nineteenth Century Upper Canada* (Toronto: McClelland and Stewart, 1977) ch. 2; and J. Donald Wilson 'Richard Cockrell,' *DCB* vol. 6, 158–60.

16 Cockrell, *On the Education of Youth* 8; Israel Lewis, *A Class Book, for the Use of Common Schools and Families, in the United Canadas, Entitled the Youth's Guard against Crime* (Kingston 1844) vii; C.B. Sissons, *Egerton Ryerson: His Life and Letters* (Toronto: Clarke, Irwin and Oxford University Press 1937) vol. 1, 126; Gerald E. Boyce, ed., *Hutton of Hastings* (Belleville: Mika Publishing 1972) 38, 79, 83–4, 126, 131. On the responsibilities of fathers for the education of their children see also Alison L. Prentice and Susan E. Houston, eds, *Family, School and Society in Nineteenth Century Canada* (Toronto: Oxford University Press 1975) 10–11.

17 Rev. G.J. Mountain, *A Sermon on the Education of the Poor, the Duty of Diffusing the Gospel, and, More Particularly, on the Importance of Family Religion* (Quebec 1822) 19; Rev. J.H. Harris, *A Sermon Preached at St. James' Church, York, on Sunday, March 17th, 1833, in Aid of the Sunday School Society for the Diocese of Quebec* (York nd) 8; Rev. John S.C. Abbott, 'The Management of Boys by Mothers,' *Canada Temperance Advocate* 15 (16 July 1849) 220. A growing American literature on the idealization of and growing emphasis on the mother's role in child-rearing includes Barbara Welter, 'The Cult of True Womanhood 1820–1860,' *American Quarterly* 18 (1966) 151–74; Nancy Cott, *The Bonds of Womanhood: 'Woman's Sphere' in New England, 1780–1835* (New Haven: Yale University Press 1977); and Mary P. Ryan *The Cradle of the Middle Class: The Family in Oneida County, New York, 1790–1865* (Cambridge: Cambridge University Press 1981) especially 157–63 and the lists of evangelical and reform periodicals on 196–7.

18 Boyce, ed., *Hutton of Hastings* 103–4; Sanderson, ed., *The Arthur Papers* vol. 1, 482

19 *British Colonist* 19 Jan. 1847; Peter N. Moogk, 'Apprenticeship of Edward Davis, an Abandoned Child, by the Town Wardens of Waterloo to Christian Schwartzentruber, A Farmer of Wilmot Township, 1 June 1839,' *Waterloo Historical Society Annual* 57 (1969) 80–1. It is interesting that Robert Gourlay, in his *Statistical Account of Upper Canada* (London 1822), found the law permitting wardens to apprentice abandoned youngsters unfortunate: 'This act seems humane; but it is just one of those meddling laws which have done so much mischief in England and would be better expunged' (vol. 2, 372–3). Gourlay did not explain the mischief but argued that, although in Scotland such 'legal interferences' were non-existent, no orphans were utterly abandoned. On the other hand, another

Scottish visitor to Upper Canada in the early 1820s, the Reverend William Bell, noted that orphans were never left destitute in the colony since farmers 'readily' took them and brought them up for the 'benefit they receive[d] for their labour,' implying that elsewhere this may *not* have been the case. See Rev. William Bell, *Hints to Emigrants in a Series of Letters from Upper Canada* (Edinburgh 1824).

20 The indenture for Mary Ann Thompson, AO, Nelles Family Papers, is reproduced in Light and Prentice, eds, *Pioneer and Gentlewomen* 318–19; Moogk, 'Apprenticeship of Edward Davis,' 80–1. For advertisements for apprentices, see the *Gore Gazette* 17 Mar. 1827, and the *Belleville Antidote* 13 Aug. 1833. In the *Cobourg Star* of 18 July 1832, the Emigrant Society advertised its willingness to place emigrants' children in apprenticeships. An indenture of a shoemaker's apprentice, dating from 1824, may be found in *OH* 41 (1949) 217–18.

21 R.D. Gidney, 'Elementary Education in Upper Canada: A Reassessment,' *OH* 65 (Sept. 1973) 175; *Gore Gazette* 17 Mar. 1827, 4; *Bytown Gazette* 16 Aug. 1837, 3; Sanderson, ed., *The Arthur Papers* vol. 1, 482; A.S. Miller, ed., *The Journals of Mary O'Brien 1828–1838* (Toronto: Macmillan 1968). The Mary O'Brien manuscript, 'Mary Sophia O'Brien Journal,' is in AO, and sections of the journal are reproduced in Light and Prentice, eds, *Pioneer and Gentlewomen* 71–2.

22 *Cobourg Star* 24 Apr. 1839, 3. Earlier that year, in the *Cobourg Star* for 18 Jan. 1839, 'A LADY, of the highest respectability' advertised for two or three children to board and be educated 'with her own family,' suggesting again that the practice was not uncommon.

23 Alison Smith, 'John Strachan and Early Upper Canada, 1799–1814,' *OH* 52 (Sept. 1960) 159–75; H. Clarke, *Friendly Advice to Emigrants, by an Old Countryman* (Montreal 1834) 10, 21

24 François, Duc de La Rochefoucault-Liancourt, *Tour through Upper Canada, in 1795* (Toronto nd) 121; Janet Carnochan, 'Niagara Library, 1800–1820,' Niagara Historical Society, *Report and Papers* 6 (1900); Adam Fergusson, *Practical Notes Made during a Tour in Canada and a Portion of the United States in 1831, with Added Notes Made during a Second Visit to Canada in 1833* (Edinburgh 1834) 118. For libraries, book societies, and newsrooms in the 1830s, see *Cobourg Star* 26 Sept. 1832, 293, and 10 Dec. 1833, 4; *Picton Traveller* 20 Jan. 1837, 3; and *Bytown Gazette* 24 Jan. 1838, 3.

25 David V.J. Bell, 'The Loyalist Tradition in Canada,' *Journal of Canadian Studies* 5 (May 1971) 22–33; Lawrence A. Cremin, *American Education: The Colonial Experience, 1607–1783* (New York: Harper Torchbooks 1970) ch. 6, and R.D. Gidney, 'Making Nineteenth-Century School Systems: The Upper Canadian Experience and Its Relevance to English Historiography,' *History of Education* 9: 2 (1980) 111–12

26 In 'Legal Education in Upper Canada 1785–1889: The Law Society as Educator,' David H. Flaherty, ed., *Essays in the History of Canadian Law* (Toronto: Os-

goode Society 1983) 49–142, G. Blaine Baker argues that in Upper Canada apprenticeship quickly became a formality to aspiring lawyers, as Law Society lectures, term-keeping at court, and residence in Osgoode Hall assumed critical importance in the law student's training. Apprenticeship appeared to be important until at least the 1830s, however. See also Baker's 'The Juvenile Advocate Society, 1821–1826: Self-Proclaimed Schoolroom for Upper Canada's Governing Class,' *Historical Papers* (1985) 74–101. On the training of American lawyers and doctors in the early nineteenth century, see William R. Johnson, 'Education and Professional Life Styles: Law and Medicine in the Nineteenth Century,' *History of Education Quarterly* 14 (Summer 1974). The training of doctors in Lower Canada during the same period is analysed in Barbara Tunis, 'Medical Education and Medical Licencing in Lower Canada: Demographic Factors, Conflict and Social Change,' *HS/SH* 27 (May 1981) 67–91. Both articles emphasize the importance of apprenticeship in professional training during the periods examined.

27 A.E. Cruikshank, ed., *Simcoe Papers* vol. 1, 143–4, 179; Gerald Craig, *Upper Canada: The Formative Years* (Toronto: McClelland and Stewart 1963) 25

28 J. Donald Wilson, 'Richard Cockrell,' *DCB* vol. 6, 159. Spragge, ed., *John Strachan Letterbook* 29; Smith, 'John Strachan and Early Upper Canada'; George W. Spragge, 'The Cornwall Grammar School under John Strachan,' *OH* 34 (1942)

29 AO, John Strachan Papers, John Strachan to Dr Brown, 9 Oct. 1808; Smith, 'John Strachan and Early Upper Canada,' 170; Gerald Craig, 'John Strachan,' *DCB* vol. 9, 753

30 MTCL, S 61, Daniel Wilkie Papers, John Whitelaw to Daniel Wilkie, 31 July 1810

31 An Act to Establish Public Schools in Each and Every District of this Province, 47 George III (1807) cap. 6, in *DHE* vol. 1, 60–1

32 *DHE* vol. 1, 68, 72, 122

33 Cartwright, *Life and Letters* 34; John Mills Jackson, *A View of the Political Situation of the Province of Upper Canada in North America* (London 1809) 8–9; Gourlay, *Statistical Account of Upper Canada* vol. 2, 374. See also *DHE* vol. 3, 142.

34 *DHE* vol. 1, 76–7; Thompson, 'Reflections upon Education,' 12

35 PAC RG5, District Trustees to the Office of the Lieutenant-Governor, 21 Nov., 19 Sept., 30 Aug., and 1 Sept. 1816, in reply to circular dated 19 Aug.

36 *Letters from an American Loyalist* (Halifax 1810) 38; *DHE* vol. 1, 76–7

37 Strachan to Marquis of Wellesley, 1 Nov. 1812, in Spragge, ed., *John Strachan Letterbook* 29; J.D. Purdy, 'John Strachan's Educational Policies, 1815–1841,' *OH* 64 (Mar. 1972) 46–7

38 Strachan, 'Report on Education, February 26th, 1815,' in Spragge, ed., *John Strachan Letterbook*

39 An Act Granting to His Majesty a Sum of Money, to be Applied to the Use of

Common Schools throughout this Province, and to Provide for the Regulation of Said Common Schools, 56 George III (1816) cap. 36, in *DHE* vol. I, 102–4

40 Charles E. Phillips, *The Development of Education in Canada* (Toronto: Gage 1957) 112

41 *DHE* vol. I, 94, 104; James Strachan, *A Visit to the Province of Upper Canada in 1819* (Aberdeen 1820) 129

42 Purdy, 'John Strachan's Educational Policies,' 50–3; Phillips, *Education in Canada* 112, 114, 129; *DHE* vol. I, 197–8; Allan Greer, 'The Sunday Schools of Upper Canada,' *OH* 67 (Sept. 1975) 175

43 R.D. Gidney has pointed out the continuity of this tradition. 'It was exercised anywhere in the empire that *raisons d'état* demanded it, and it was transferred to British North America as part of the Governors' royal instructions from the 1760s onwards ... The licensing powers ... continued in force into the nineteenth century except where superseded by a provincial statute.' See his 'Making Nineteenth-Century School Systems,' 111–12.

44 Purdy, 'John Strachan's Educational Policies,' 53–4; RG2 A, *Minutes of the General Board of Education* 1823–1833

45 Sir Peregrine Maitland to Lord Bathurst, *DHE* vol. I, 178–9; RG2 A, *Minutes of the General Board of Education* 1823

46 Ibid., *Minutes of the General Board of Education* Jan. 1829, 57–66. See also *DHE* vol. I, 268 ff.

47 Upper Canada Central School, *First Annual Report* (York 1822)

CHAPTER 2 *Creating Schools and Scholars*

1 E.J. Lajeunesse, ed., *The Windsor Border Region* (Toronto: University of Toronto Press 1960) 136–47, reproduces letters from Dufaux to his superiors describing his efforts in connection with the school. See also R. Godbout, 'Les Franco-Ontariens et leurs écoles de 1791 à 1844,' *Revue de l'Université d'Ottawa* 33 (Sept. 1963) 477. Godbout argues that the school at Assumption was the first school in what was to become Upper Canada, but at least four others have been cited for 1786: two in Kingston founded by the Rev. John Stuart and the Rev. M. Donovan and two more in the Bay of Quinte, at Fredericksburgh and Ernesttown. See Frank Eames, 'Pioneer Schools of Upper Canada,' *OH* 18 (1920) 92–6; and F.P. Smith, 'Early Schools in Kingston,' *Historic Kingston* 5 (Oct. 1956) 25. Godbout identifies as '*l'école mère de l'Ontario*' the school for girls and boys founded by La Salle at Fort Frontenac in the third quarter of the seventeenth century.

2 Eames, 'Pioneer Schools,' 92–6

3 John Ross Robertson, *Landmarks of Toronto* (Toronto: *Evening Telegram* 1894) vol. I, 295; Beth Light and Alison Prentice, eds, *Pioneer and Gentlewomen*

of British North America, 1713–1867 (Toronto: New Hogtown Press 1980) 71–2; Letitia Youmans, *Campaign Echoes* (Toronto 1893); AO, Personal Diaries Collection, Ms 475, vol. 3, John Tidey Diary, 1838–45; 'Lydia Case Ranney, 1800–1901,' from *Outstanding Women of Oxford County*, by Brenda Dyer et al. (Oxford County Board of Education 1979), reprinted in *Canadian Women's Studies* 3:1 (1979) 51; *Cornwall Constitutional* 31 Oct. 1850, 3

4 John Strachan, *A Letter to the Rev. A.N. Bethune, Rector of Cobourg, on the Management of Grammar Schools* (York 1829)

5 On definitions of private and public in early-nineteenth-century schooling, see R.D. Gidney, 'Elementary Education in Upper Canada: A Reassessment,' *OH* 65 (Sept. 1973), reprinted in Michael B. Katz and Paul H. Mattingly, eds, *Education and Social Change: Themes from Ontario's Past* (New York: New York University Press 1975) 21; Carl F. Kaestle, *Evolution of an Urban School System: New York, 1750–1850* (Cambridge, Mass.: Harvard University Press 1973) 16–18.

6 Eames, 'Pioneer Schools,' 92–6

7 Ibid.; Edith G. Firth, ed., *The Town of York, 1793–1815: A Collection of Documents of Early Toronto* Champlain Society (Toronto: University of Toronto Press 1962) 192. Edward Allen Talbot argued in 1824 that Cockrell's school remained for many years one of the province's two schools 'of any note.' The other would have been John Strachan's. *Five Years' Residence in the Canadas* (London 1824) vol. 2, 120

8 Smith, 'Early Schools in Kingston,' 27–8

9 *Niagara Gleaner* 15 Sept. 1823; *Cobourg Star* 7 June 1843, 3

10 *Cornwall Observer* 12 Aug. 1847, 1, and 26 Oct. 1835, 3; *Niagara Reporter* 30 Apr. 1841, 3; *Cobourg Star* 15 Feb. 1832, 37

11 *DHE* vol. 2, 127; Edith G. Firth, ed., *The Town of York, 1815–1834: A Further Collection of Documents of Early Toronto* Champlain Society (Toronto: University of Toronto Press 1966) 171–3; *Cobourg Star* 9 July 1834

12 *Cornwall Observer* 6 May 1836, 3; *Niagara Gleaner* 1 Jan. 1831, 3, and 6 Oct. 1823, 3; *Bytown Gazette* 27 Oct. 1836, 3

13 Lajeunesse, *Windsor Border Region* 137; Robertson, *Landmarks* vol. 1, 124–5; David Newlands, 'The Yonge Street Quaker School, 1806–1826,' *York Pioneer* (Fall 1976) 12–16

14 Janet Carnochan, 'The Early Schools of Niagara,' Niagara Historical Society *Reports and Papers* 6 (1900) 37–8, 43–4; 'The Indian Village,' *Cobourg Star* 31 Jan. 1849, 2. See also the discussion of an Indian school in the *Cobourg Star* 22 Feb. 1831.

15 Patrick Campbell, *Travels in the Inhabited Parts of North America in the Years 1791 and 1792*, H.H. Langton, ed. (Toronto 1937) 166; Adam Fergusson, *Practical Notes Made During a Tour in Canada and a Portion of the United States in 1831, with Added Notes Made during a Second Visit to Canada in 1833* (Edinburgh 1834) 135; William Case to James Evans, 22 Nov. 1829, in 'Selections

from the Papers of James Evans, Missionary to the Indians,' Fred Landon, ed.,
OH 26 (1930) 476–9; 'The Indian Village,' *Cobourg Star* 31 Jan. 1849, 2. On
industrial schooling for native children, see J. Donald Wilson, ' "No Blanket to
Be Worn at School": The Education of Indians in Early Nineteenth-Century
Ontario,' *HS/SH* 14 (Nov. 1974) 293–305, reprinted in Jean Barman et al, eds,
Indian Education in Canada, I: The Legacy (Vancouver: University of British
Columbia Press 1986) ch. 4.

16 *DHE* vol. 2, 127

17 *Niagara Gleaner* 28 Oct. 1819

18 Robert Gourlay, *Statistical Account of Upper Canada* (London 1822) vol. 1, 471;
F.F. Thompson, 'Reflections upon Education in the Midland District, 1810–
1816,' *Historic Kingston* 11 (Mar. 1963) 18; Charles E. Phillips, *The Development
of Education in Canada* (Toronto: Gage 1957) 122; *DHE* vol. 1, 90–3; PAC RG5
B11, George Okill Stuart, President of the Midland District School Society, to
His Excellency Sir Peregrine Maitland, nd; W.P.J. Millar, 'The Remarkable Rev.
Thaddeus Osgood: A Study in the Evangelical Spirit in the Canadas,' *HS/SH* 19
(May 1977) 64–6; also her biography of Osgood, *DCB* 8 (1985), 665–7; Queen's
University Archives, Midland District School Society, Board of Trustees, minutes
1818 ff

19 Ibid.; *DHE* vol. 1, 90; J.D. Purdy, 'John Strachan's Educational Policies, 1815–
1841,' *OH* 64 (Mar. 1972) 52

20 Upper Canada Central School, *First Annual Report*; George W. Spragge, 'The
Upper Canada Central School,' *OH* 32 (1937) 179–80; biography of Thomas Appleton, *DCB* 6 (1987), 11–12

21 Smith, 'Early Schools in Kingston,' 28–9

22 Allan Greer, 'The Sunday Schools of Upper Canada,' *OH* 67 (Sept. 1975) 170–3

23 Ibid.; Phillips, *Education in Canada* 111, 181; 'Sunday Schools,' *Cobourg Star*
25 Jan. 1832, 13

24 For recent studies, see J.D. Purdy, 'The English Public School System in Nine-
teenth-Century Ontario,' in F.A. Armstrong et al., eds, *Aspects of Nineteenth-
Century Ontario* (Toronto: University of Toronto Press 1974) 237–52; Marion
Royce, 'Methodism and the Education of Women in Nineteenth Century Ontario,'
Atlantis 3: 2, Pt 1 (Spring 1978) 131–43, and 'Education for Girls in Quaker
Schools in Ontario,' *Atlantis* 3: 1 (Fall 1977) 181–92; Richard P. Howard, *Upper
Canada College, 1829–1979: Colborne's Legacy* (Toronto: Macmillan 1979);
D.C. Masters, *Protestant Church Colleges* (Toronto: University of Toronto Press
1966). The portrait of the voluntary school movement sketched by R.D. Gidney
and W.P.J. Millar in 'From Voluntarism to State Schooling: The Creation of
the Public School System in Ontario,' *CHR* 66 (Dec. 1985) 442–73, begins the
process of analysing the collective impact of these schools.

25 *DHE* vol. 1, 42, and vol. 2, 262. In her discussion of the origins of American
women's colleges, Helen Lefkowitz Horowitz distinguishes between the 'academy'

and the 'seminary,' arguing that in the early-nineteenth-century United States the latter was the newer usage and connoted both a greater 'seriousness' and the goal of professional preparation. *Alma Mater: Design and Experience in the Women's Colleges from Their Nineteenth-Century Beginnings to the 1930s* (Boston: Beacon Press 1984) 11. This distinction does not appear to hold for Upper Canada, however.

26 Robert S. Sullivan to Egerton Ryerson, 20 July 1843, Ryerson Correspondence, United Church Archives; Anson Aylesworth, 'Newburgh,' *Lennox and Addington Historical Society Papers and Records* (reprinted Belleville: Mika Publishing 1974) vol. 2, 35–6

27 *Annual Circular of the Cobourg Ladies' Seminary* (Cobourg 1845); *Catalogue of the Officers and Students of the Burlington Ladies' Academy of Hamilton, Canada West* (Hamilton 1847). Hodgins listed the academies taught by the following women: Mrs Hurlburt, Mrs Vannorman (Van Norman), and Mrs Crombie in Cobourg; Mrs G. Ryerson, Mrs Cockburn, Misses Skirving, and Misses Winn in Toronto; Mrs Hermann Poetter in Kingston; Miss Coates in Niagara; Miss Felton in Hamilton; Mrs King in Cornwall. *DHE* vol. 5, 101

28 The headmasters, certainly, were always men, and only two grammar schools that hired women have so far been discovered: Dundas Grammar School in 1846, and Colborne in 1861. See 'Dundas District School,' *Cornwall Observer* 18 June 1846, 3, and 1861 Manuscript Census for Northumberland County. On Letitia Youmans's employment as an assistant in the Colborne Grammar School, see ch. 1, n5.

29 Strachan, *On the Management of Grammar Schools* 3

30 MTCL, S 61, Daniel Wilkie Papers, John Whitelaw to Daniel Wilkie, various letters. Whitelaw seems to have turned his school over to the monitors entirely when he was sick and, in a letter to the trustees of the Midland District School, dated 29 Oct. 1816, indicated his belief that the six monitors employed in the school were capable of running it should he be permitted to take leave in order to attend university for a period of time. Strachan also mentions the use of monitors in his pamphlet on the management of grammar schools.

31 Phillips, *Education in Canada* 111; J.A. Bannister, *Early Educational History of Norfolk County* (Toronto: University of Toronto Press 1926) 52–3, 131; Eames, 'Pioneer Schools,' 99

32 Michael Smith, *A Geographical View of the Province of Upper Canada* (Philadelphia 1813) 10–19; J.D. Wilson, R.M. Stamp, and L-P. Audet, eds, *Canadian Education: A History* (Scarborough: Prentice-Hall 1970) 207; Greer, 'Sunday Schools of Upper Canada,' 173

33 Douglas McCalla and Peter George, 'Measurement, Myth and Reality: Reflections on the Economic History of Nineteenth Century Ontario,' *Journal of Canadian Studies* 21 (Autumn 1986) 76; Mary Larratt Smith, *Young Mr Smith in Upper Canada* (Toronto: University of Toronto Press 1980) 10, 33

34 Royce, 'Education for Girls in Quaker Schools,' 183; *Upper Canada Academy, Circular* (1841); Ryerson to Lord Glenelg, 18 Apr. 1837, *DHE* vol. 3, 105; T.R. Preston, *Three Years' Residence in Canada from 1837 to 1839* (London 1840) vol. 2, 104; *Cobourg Star* 17 Sept. 1845, 3. Gidney and Millar report a cost of £55.0.0 to an Upper Canadian parent who sent his son to Upper Canada College for three quarters in 1833, however ('From Voluntarism to State Schooling,' 449).

35 *Catalogue ... Burlington Ladies' Academy*; *Cornwall Observer* 2 June 1842, 3, and 9 Jan. 1845, 3; *Cobourg Star* 11 Jan. 1831; *Niagara Chronicle* 24 Dec. 1846, 3

36 *Brockville Recorder* 26 July 1833; *Cornwall Observer* 2 June 1842 and 18 June 1846, 3

37 Charles R.N. Rubridge, *A Plain Statement of the Advantages Attending Emigration to Upper Canada* (London 1838) 37

38 Ernesttown Common School Register, reproduced in 'The Bell and Laing School Papers,' *Lennox and Addington Historical Society Papers* vol. 5 (1914) 29–37

39 A typical boarding school of this type was Mr and Mrs Twigg's. The Twiggs received boarders and day pupils 'at their house' in Kingston in 1826. *Niagara Gleaner* 19 Aug. 1826, 3

40 *Farmers' Journal* 9 July 1828, 3; *DHE* vol. 2, 126; Robertson, *Landmarks* vol. 1, 124; *Gore Gazette* 12 July 1828. See also Eames, 'Pioneer Schools,' 98.

41 Ernest J. Hathaway, 'Early Schools of Toronto,' *OH* 23 (1926) 314; *Niagara Gleaner* 5 Jan. 1833, 3

42 MTCL, Boulton Papers, Letters of William Boulton, 25 Dec. 1833 and 21 Feb. 1834. The Streets evidently landed on their feet. In 6 August 1834, an ad in the *Cobourg Star* (p. 3) announced that Mrs and the Misses Street were ready to receive pupils in their school in Ancaster, which was now 'under the patronage of Lady Colborne and the Bishop of Quebec.'

43 *Cobourg Star* 12 Sept. 1838

44 *Picton Traveller* 12 Aug. 1836, 3, and 26 Feb. 1836, 2

45 *Niagara Gleaner* 15 June 1833, 2; *Cobourg Star* 11 Mar. 1840, 3

46 Robertson, *Landmarks* vol 1, 295; *Niagara Gleaner* 6 Apr. 1829, 3; RG2 A, *Minutes of the General Board of Education* 30 Apr. 1829, 78–9. The difficulty of survival once a large investment had been made in buildings and grounds is graphically illustrated in the case of Grantham Academy. For a brief account of the struggles to maintain this school, see Gidney and Millar, 'From Voluntarism to State Schooling,' 457. On the 'monumental' in Upper Canadian academy and college architecture, see Dana Johnson, 'For the Privileged Few: The Private and Specialist Schools of Ontario, 1800–1930,' Parks Canada *Research Bulletin* 215 (Feb. 1984) 2–6.

47 Firth, ed., *The Town of York, 1793–1815* lxxiv; Hathaway, 'Early Schools of Toronto,' 321; Robertson, *Landmarks* vol. 1, 464; W.H. Cole, 'The Local History

of Brockville,' *OH* 12 (1914) 39; Frank Eames, 'Gananoque's First Public School, 1816,' *OH* 17 (1919) 102; R. Louis Gentilcore and C. Grant Head, *Ontario's History in Maps*, Ontario Historical Studies Series (Toronto: University of Toronto Press 1984) Pt vi

48 Eames, 'Gananoque's First Public School,' 97–8; Mr Howard Campbell, Mrs Victor Ross, and Mrs Albert Pearsall, comps, *A History of Oro Schools* (np, nd) 4; John Barnett, 'An Early Red School House and Its Record Book,' *OH* 48 (Winter 1956) 8

49 Frederic Burrows, 'Early Education,' *Lennox and Addington Historical Society Papers and Records* vol. 2, 10; MTCL, Alice Maud Mills Papers, Letters of Hon. David Mills to his Youngest Daughter, Alice Maud Lovett Mills; Campbell et al., *Oro Schools* 4

50 Ibid.; Gerald E. Boyce, ed., *Hutton of Hastings* (Belleville: Mika Publishing 1972) 181–90

51 'Ladies' Seminary,' *Cobourg Star* 3 May 1843, 3

52 F.H. Armstrong, 'John Strachan, Schoolmaster, and the Evolution of the Elite in Upper Canada / Ontario,' in J. Donald Wilson, ed., *An Imperfect Past: Education and Society in Canadian History* (Vancouver: Centre for the Study of Curriculum and Instruction, University of British Columbia 1984) 154–69

53 Patrick Shirreff, *A Tour through North America, Canada and the United States* (Edinburgh 1835) 190; Ian E. Davey, 'Trends in Female School Attendance in Mid-Nineteenth Century Ontario,' *HS/SH* 16 (Nov. 1975) 250

54 R.D. Gidney, 'Making Nineteenth-Century School Systems: The Upper Canadian Experience and Its Relevance to English Historiography,' *History of Education* 9: 2 (1980), especially 108–11

55 *Cobourg Star* 31 May 1831, 166; *Bytown Gazette* 23 Aug. 1837; *Cobourg Star* 21 July 1841, 4

56 *Niagara Gleaner* 2 Jan 1830; *Globe* 27 Sept. 1849; MTCL, Boulton Papers, Letter of William Boulton, 8 July 1833

57 Alison Smith, 'John Strachan and Early Upper Canada, 1799–1814,' *OH* 52 (Sept. 1960); Youmans, *Campaign Echoes* 45–9; Boyce, ed., *Hutton of Hastings* 124, 158

58 RG2 A, *Minutes of the General Board of Education* 23 Feb. 1831, 17 Nov. 1830, and 26 Nov. 1830, 131–2, 136–7, 147; *DHE* vol. 2, 346

59 Hazel C. Mathews, *Oakville and the Sixteen* (Toronto: University of Toronto Press 1953) 108

60 RG2 C-6-C, Fredericksburgh, 11 Apr. 1842

CHAPTER 3 *Schoolmistresses and Schoolmasters*

1 Hugh Douglass, 'The Story of Rockwood Academy,' *Wentworth Bygones* 8 (1969) 48; J.D. Wilson, 'The Teacher in Early Ontario,' in F.A. Armstrong et al., eds, *Aspects of Nineteenth-Century Ontario* (Toronto: University of Toronto Press 1974) 219–21

2 *Bytown Gazette* 21 Feb. 1838, 3

3 *Cobourg Star* 24 May 1831. This 'Cobourg Ladies' Academy' evidently bore no relation to either the academy or the seminary founded in Cobourg, in the early 1840s, by Mrs Hurlburt and Mrs Van Norman respectively (see ch. 2, n27 and ch. 3, pp. 67–8). It may well have been the same Miss Radcliffe of the Niagara school for young ladies whose 1818 fee schedule has come down to us (see p. 48).

4 *Niagara Gleaner* 14 Aug. 1830, 3, and 28 Jan. 1832, 3; *Cobourg Star*, 18 Mar. 1846, 3

5 *Bytown Gazette* 19 Dec. 1838, 2

6 *Niagara Spectator* 16 Oct. 1817, 1; *Cobourg Star* 16 Dec. 1835, 2; *Cornwall Observer* 5 Sept. 1839, 3

7 *Cobourg Star* 28 Mar. 1832, 35, 29 May 1833, 132, 13 Mar. 1833, 65, and 6 Nov. 1833, 3; *Niagara Gleaner* 26 June 1830, 3, 17 Sept. 1831, 4, and 13 Apr. 1833, 2; *Niagara Spectator* 21 Mar. 1817, 3

8 Discussion of Barnabas Bidwell's character appears in the *Kingston Gazette* 16, 23, and 30 Apr. 1811. See also J.E. Rea, 'Barnabas Bidwell: A Note on the American Years,' *OH* 60 (1968) 31–7. On the Reverend Moses Marcus, see the *Picton Traveller* 21 Oct. 1836, 3.

9 Ads specifically requesting 'a man' are to be found in the *Niagara Spectator* 20 Jan. 1819 ('the St. Catharines School'); *Niagara Gleaner* 28 Mar. 1826, 4 ('the common school at Stanford'); *Cobourg Star* 13 Nov. 1833, 3 ('Village of Grafton'), and *Bytown Gazette* 12 Dec. 1839, 2 ('Township of Fitzroy').

10 *DHE* vol. 2, 125; H.H. Langton, ed., *A Gentlewoman in Upper Canada: The Journals of Anne Langton* (Toronto: Clarke, Irwin 1950); A.S. Miller, ed., *The Journals of Mary O'Brien, 1828–1838* (Toronto: Macmillan 1968); *Canadian Argus and Niagara Spectator* 2 Mar. 1820, 1

11 George W. Spragge, ed., *The John Strachan Letterbook, 1812–1834* (Toronto: University of Toronto Press 1946) 70; RG2 A, *Minutes of the General Board of Education* 31 Mar. 1829, 69

12 Spragge, ed., *John Strachan Letterbook* 203

13 Charles Fothergill, *A Sketch of the Present State of Canada* (York: Upper Canada 1822) 94

14 Bishop Mountain to the Society for the Propagation of the Gospel, 16 Oct. 1801, in Edith Firth, ed., *The Town of York, 1793–1815: A Collection of Documents of Early Toronto* Champlain Society (Toronto: University of Toronto Press 1962) 193–4

15 Rev. William Bell, *Hints to Emigrants in a Series of Letters from Upper Canada* (Edinburgh 1824). For ads by clergymen anxious to take in scholars, see *Gore Gazette* 14 June 1828 and *Niagara Gleaner* 12 May 1827, 3.

16 *Cornwall Observer* 24 June 1841, 2; Frank Eames, 'Pioneer Schools of Upper

Canada,' *OH* 18 (1920) 95; Isabel Skelton, *A Man Austere: William Bell, Parson and Pioneer* (Toronto: Ryerson Press 1947) 182; AO, Diaries Collection, Ms 275, John Tidey Diary, 1838–45

17 John Ross Robertson, *Landmarks of Toronto* (Toronto: *Evening Telegram* 1894) vol. 1, 294–5. On the subject of young teachers and competition for wages, see ch. 6.

18 Marjorie Theobald, ' "Mere Accomplishments"'? Melbourne's Early Ladies' Schools Reconsidered,' *History of Education Review* 13: 2 (1984) 15–28, and 'Women and Schools in Colonial Victoria, 1840–1910' (PH D diss., Monash University 1985)

19 R.D. Gidney and W.P.J. Millar, 'From Voluntarism to State Schooling: The Creation of the Public School System in Ontario,' *CHR* 66 (Dec. 1985) 472

20 Robertson, *Landmarks* vol. 1, 295; *Cornwall Constitution* 31 Oct. 1850

21 Letitia Youmans, *Campaign Echoes* (Toronto 1893) 73–4; Margaret W. Bayne, *Centenary of First Woman Teacher in Zorra: Lillias Macpherson Rose, 1835–1843* (Woodstock North: Braemar and Embro Women's Institutes 1935)

22 Andrew F. Hunter, *A History of Simcoe County* (Barrie, Ont. 1909) 14

23 Report of the Committee on Education: Appendix B to the Fifth Report of the General Board, 3 Vict. (1840) *DHE* vol. 3, 243–83

24 *Niagara Chronicle* 21 Aug. 1851, 1; *Cobourg Star* 26 July 1848, 3. For other family schools, see *Cobourg Star* 1 Dec. 1832, 339, and 2 July 1848, 3; *Cornwall Observer* 5 Dec. 1836, 3; *Niagara Chronicle* 25 Oct. 1849, 3.

25 *Niagara Herald* 11 Sept. 1828, 3; *Cobourg Star* 9 Mar. 1836, 2

26 Henry Scadding, *Toronto of Old: Collections and Recollections* (Toronto 1983) 104. John Beverley Robinson was one of the key pupils Strachan was anxious to see go forward in the community. See the discussion of Strachan and his pupils in F.H. Armstrong, 'John Strachan, Schoolmaster, and the Evolution of the Elite in Upper Canada / Ontario,' in J. Donald Wilson, ed., *An Imperfect Past: Education and Society in Canadian History* (Vancouver: Centre for the Study of Curriculum and Instruction, University of British Columbia 1984) 154–69. Whitelaw's correspondence with his former pupil Daniel Wilkie lasted for at least a decade. MTCL, S 61, Daniel Wilkie Papers

27 Janet Carnochan, 'The Early Schools of Niagara,' Niagara Historical Society *Reports and Papers* 6 (1900) 39; Firth, ed., *The Town of York, 1793–1815* 198–200

28 F.F. Thompson, 'Reflections upon Education in the Midland Districts, 1810–1816,' *Historic Kingston* 11 (Mar. 1963) 13; *Niagara Gleaner* 1 Sept. 1832; Hunter, *History of Simcoe County* 289

29 William Case to Evans, Dec. 1830, cited in Fred Landon, 'Selections from the Papers of James Evans, Missionary to the Indians,' *OH* 26 (1930) 476; Petition of Henry Goff, Schoolmaster, 20 Feb. 1835, Goff to Colborne, 24 July 1835, and

Taylor to Colborne, 22 May 1835, cited in James H. Love 'Social Stress and Education Reform in Mid-Nineteenth Century Upper Canada' (PH D diss., University of Toronto 1978) 56–7

30 F.F. Thompson, 'Reflections upon Education,' 9; *Niagara Gleaner* 7 Jan. 1825, 4; Richard Cockrell, *Thoughts on the Education of Youth* (Newark, Upper Canada 1795; Toronto: Bibliographical Society of Canada 1949); *British Colonist* 18 Sept. 1839, 1

31 *Picton Traveller* 8 Apr. 1836, 3; *Cornwall Observer* 5 Oct. 1837, 3; *Bytown Gazette* 9 Sept. 1837, 3

32 On the practical focus of early arithmetic education, see Donald Vander Klok, 'From Practical Application to Mental Discipline: Mathematics Education in the United States from 1620 to 1890' (MA diss., University of Toronto 1982).

33 Alison Smith, 'John Strachan and Early Upper Canada, 1799–1814,' *OH* 52 (Sept. 1960) 162–4; John Strachan, *A Letter to the Rev. A.N. Bethune, Rector of Cobourg, on the Management of Grammar Schools* (York 1829), especially 5, 10–13, 21–3, 41–2, and 45

34 J.D. Purdy, 'John Strachan's Educational Policies, 1815–1841,' *OH* 64 (Mar. 1972) 54; *DHE* vol. 3, 213

35 Upper Canada Central School, *First Annual Report* (York 1822). See also *DHE* vol. 1, 178.

36 See Alison Prentice, 'From Household to School House: The Emergence of the Teacher as Servant of the State,' *Material History Bulletin* 20 (Fall 1984).

37 Douglass, 'Rockwood Academy,' 47; Allan Greer, 'The Sunday Schools of Upper Canada,' *OH* 67 (Sept. 1975) 171–2, 183–4; William Case to James Evans, 9 Jan. 1830, in Landon, 'Selections from the Papers of James Evans' 477

38 Bruce Curtis, 'The Speller Expelled: Disciplining the Common Reader in Canada West, 1846–50,' *Canadian Review of Sociology and Anthropology* 22 (Aug. 1985) 346–68

39 *Cobourg Star* 8 Jan. 1840, 3, 13 June 1832, 178, and 19 Aug. 1835, 3

40 *British Colonist* 17 Jan 1839, 4; Charles E. Phillips, *The Development of Education in Canada* (Toronto: Gage 1957) 203

41 *Kingston Gazette* 26 Mar. 1811; *Farmers' Journal* 5 Aug. 1829, 3, and 28 Oct. 1829, 3

42 *Cobourg Star* 24 Apr. 1839, 3; *Circular of the Upper Canada Academy* (1841)

43 *Niagara Gleaner* 29 July 1826, 3; Gerald E. Boyce, ed., *Hutton of Hastings* (Belleville: Mika Publishing 1972) 45–7, 56

44 *Canadian* (Niagara) 17 Aug. 1825, 1; *Cornwall Observer* 20 Nov. 1835, 3; *Niagara Chronicle* 23 Aug. 1843, 1; *Bytown Gazette* 28 or 20 Aug. 1839, 3

45 Marion Royce, 'Methodism and the Education of Women in Nineteenth Century Ontario,' *Atlantis* 3:2 Pt 1 (Spring 1978) 137 and 141; Theobald, ' "Mere Accomplishments"?' especially 17

46 Robertson, *Landmarks* vol. 1, 378 ff; Phillips, *Education in Canada* 141; *Cobourg Star* 31 Jan. 1849

47 AO, Strachan Papers, John Strachan to Dr Brown, 20 Oct. 1807; *DHE* vol. 1, 34; *Cobourg Star* 16 Dec. 1835, 2; *Cornwall Observer* 11 July 1833; *Cobourg Star* 15 Mar. and 11 Apr. 1838; *Christian Guardian* 2 May and 9 May 1838

48 *Bytown Gazette* 19 June 1839, 3. On a teacher's reputation and parents' interest, see *Niagara Gleaner* 2 June 1827, 3. On the York infant school examination, see Edith G. Firth, ed., *The Town of York, 1815–1834: A Further Collection of Documents of Early Toronto* (Toronto: University of Toronto Press 1966) 171–3; *Cobourg Star* 13 Feb. 1839 and 23 Dec. 1835

49 MTCL, S 61, Daniel Wilkie Papers, John Whitelaw to Daniel Wilkie, 8 Dec. 1810 and 30 Jan. 1811

50 Hazel C. Mathews, *Oakville and the Sixteen* (Toronto: University of Toronto Press 1953) 109, 233; Robertson, *Landmarks* vol. 1, 379–80

51 Edward Allen Talbot, *Five Years' Residence in the Canadas* (London 1824) vol. 2, 119. On the removal to new locations of schools, see *Cobourg Star* 14 May 1834, 2. A teacher's irregular attendance is recorded in PAC RG5 B11, the Reply from Trustees, Eastern District School, to Lt Governor's Circular, 19 Sept. 1816. Pupil registers indicate a constant coming and going of children. See, for example, AO, George Okill Stuart Papers, the 'Account Book of the Home District Grammar School, 1806–1811'

52 Early comments by parents are hard to find, as diaries and letters (for the period before 1830 especially) are rare. For concerned parents of the 1830s and 1840s, see Charles R. Sanderson, ed., *The Arthur Papers* 3 vols (Toronto: University of Toronto Press 1957); Boyce, ed., *Hutton of Hastings*; and RG2 C-6-C, 'Incoming Correspondence' file of the education department, in which letters from parents to the central authorities occasionally surface.

53 Concern about school children's health was a mid-nineteenth-century constant and would continue to be characteristic of the century. Maria Baldwin wrote to her father from a convent school in Lower Canada that he need not worry about her health, suggesting that in fact he *was* likely to worry. Robert Sullivan expressed concern about the health of pupils at the Upper Canada Academy, and one of Egerton Ryerson's daughters died of tuberculosis, evidently contracted when she was boarding at a convent school. MTCL, Baldwin Papers, Maria Baldwin to Robert Baldwin, Quebec, 24 Jan. 1843; Robert B. Sullivan to Egerton Ryerson, 20 July 1843, Ryerson Correspondence, United Church Archives; C.B. Sissons, *Egerton Ryerson: His Life and Letters* 2 vols (Toronto: Clarke, Irwin 1937, 1947) vol. 2, 165–8 and 183–5; Clara Thomas, *Ryerson of Upper Canada* (Toronto, Ryerson Press 1969) 111

54 MTCL, S 61, Daniel Wilkie Papers, Whitelaw to Wilkie, 18 Feb. 1811 and 30 Jan. 1810; *DHE* vol. 1, 76–7

55 Ernest J. Hathaway, 'Early Schools of Toronto,' *OH* 23 (1926) 323–4, 326; *DHE*

vol. 2, 29, 82, 121, 178, 249; *DHE* vol. 3, 175, 314; Margaret H. Zieman, 'Private Schools in Upper Canada, between 1786 and 1860' (Unpublished paper, OISE nd)

56 *DHE* vol. 5, 138; Robertson, *Landmarks* vol. 1, 379–80

57 MTCL, S 61, Daniel Wilkie Papers, Whitelaw to Wilkie, 2 Mar. 1814 and 4 Apr. 1814; PAC RG5 B11, London District, Mr Hutchison, to Lt Governor reply, 20 Nov. 1816

58 John Strachan was among those who disapproved of girls' attending grammar schools and argued that their presence in these schools was only a temporary 'inconvenience.' RG2 A, *Minutes of the General Board of Education* Jan. 1829, 59. The attendance of girls at York's grammar school was said to have eventually 'dropped off,' *DHE* vol. 3, 211. See also Scadding, *Toronto of Old* 185; *Cornwall Observer* 4 Feb. 1841, 2.

59 Youmans, *Campaign Echoes* 72–3; Robertson, *Landmarks* vol. 1, 296

60 Leo A. Johnson, *The History of the County of Ontario* (Whitby, Ont.: Corporation of the County of Ontario 1973) 63; Harvey J. Graff, *The Literacy Myth: Literacy and Social Structure in the Nineteenth Century City* (New York: Academic Press 1979) 61, 64

61 See Harvey J. Graff, *The Legacies of Literacy: Continuities and Contradictions in Western Culture and Society* (Bloomington: Indiana University Press 1987).

62 Mary O'Brien Diary, 13 May 1829, in Marion Royce, 'Notes on Schooling for Girls in Upper Canada from the Pre-Conquest Period until the Mid-Nineteenth Century,' Canadian Women's History Series, 10 (Toronto: OISE Press, Women in Canadian History Project 1978) 8

63 F.P. Smith, 'Early Schools in Kingston,' *Historic Kingston* 5 (Oct. 1956) 27; RG2 A, *Minutes of the General Board of Education* Jan. 1829, 59

64 Strachan, *On the Management of Grammar Schools* 23; *Circular of the Upper Canada Academy* (1841) 12–13

65 *Cobourg Star* 8 Sept. 1841, 1. The headmistresses of the Cobourg Ladies' Seminary and the Cobourg Ladies' Academy eventually moved on to found schools in other places, however. Mrs D.C. Van Norman, of the seminary, founded Burlington Ladies' Academy with her husband in 1845. In 1847, the Cobourg Ladies' Academy's Mrs Hurlburt moved with her husband to Toronto, where they opened the Adelaide Academy. See Royce, 'Methodism and the Education of Women,' 142.

PART TWO *Mid-Nineteenth-Century School Reform*

1 Charles R.N. Rubridge, *A Plain Statement of the Advantages Attending Emigration to Upper Canada* (London 1838) 26

2 *Cobourg Star* 19 Jan. 1842

3 AO, Diaries Collection, Ms 275, John Tidey Diary, 1838–45

4 Tidey appears to have been superintendent for the township of Norwich North. For two of his reports see *ARUC* 1858 and 1861. Further information on Tidey and his family may be found in the Amelia Poldin Collection of Oxford County material, in AO.

5 Gerald E. Boyce, ed., *Hutton of Hastings* (Belleville: Mika Publishing 1972) 83–4, 120

6 Ibid. 122, 203–5

7 RG2 C-6-C, James Ryan and John Murphy to Egerton Ryerson, 22 Nov. 1853

8 RG2 C-6-C, James Ryan and John Stewart to Ryerson, 5 June 1855

9 RG2 C-6-C, John Murphy to Ryerson, 14 June 1855, 18 July 1856, and 10 Mar. 1859; Architects of the Normal School to John George Hodgins, 19 Oct. 1855

10 Letter to the Editor, *Globe* 2 July 1855; RG2 C-6-C, John Murphy to Hodgins, 19 July 1855; Patrick Freeland to Ryerson, 7 June 1859; James Moore to Ryerson, 11 July 1859; Alfred Otter to Hodgins, 12 July 1859, and to Ryerson, 25 July 1859

11 J. Harold Putman, *Egerton Ryerson and Education in Upper Canada* (Toronto: William Briggs 1912); C.B. Sissons, *Egerton Ryerson: His Life and Letters* 2 vols (Toronto: Clarke, Irwin 1937, 1947); Charles E. Phillips, *The Development of Education in Canada* (Toronto: Gage 1957). For a discussion of this early work see Alison Prentice, *The School Promoters: Education and Social Class in Mid-Nineteenth Century Upper Canada* (Toronto: McClelland and Stewart 1977) 9–15.

12 The reinterpretation of mid-nineteenth-century school reform began in the 1960s. The first fruits appeared in two collections, J.D. Wilson, R.M. Stamp, and L-P. Audet, eds, *Canadian Education: A History* (Scarborough: Prentice-Hall 1970) and Michael B. Katz and Paul H. Mattingly, *Education and Social Change: Themes from Ontario's Past* (New York: New York University Press 1975), among other shorter studies. Revisionist approaches to the topic and to the history of Canadian education generally have been analysed in a number of interpretive and historiographical articles. See Bruce Curtis, 'Preconditions of the Canadian State: Educational Reform and the Construction of a Public in Upper Canada, 1837–1846,' *Studies in Political Economy* 10 (Winter 1983) 99–121; Chad Gaffield, 'Going Back to School: Towards a Fresh Agenda for the History of Education,' *Acadiensis* (Spring 1986); R.D. Gidney, 'Making Nineteenth-Century School Systems: The Upper Canadian Experience and Its Relevance to English Historiography,' *History of Education* 9: 2 (1980) 101–16; Patrick J. Harrigan, 'A Comparative Perspective on Recent Trends in the History of Education in Canada,' *History of Education Quarterly* 26 (Spring 1986); J. Donald Wilson, 'Some Observations on Recent Trends in Canadian Educational History,' in J. Donald Wilson, ed., *An Imperfect Past: Education and Society in Canadian History* (Vancouver: Centre for the Study of Curriculum and Instruction, University of British Columbia, 1986).

CHAPTER 4 *Towards a Government School System*

1 For a mid-nineteenth-century Upper Canadian commenting on the absence of fathers whose work took them out of the home on weekdays and the consequent elevation of mothers to a position of sole guardianship in the home, see Walter Eales, *Lectures on the Benefits to Be Derived from Mechanics Institutes* (Toronto 1851) 11; Susan E. Houston, 'Victorian Origins of Juvenile Delinquency,' in Michael B. Katz and Paul H. Mattingly, eds, *Education and Social Change: Themes from Ontario's Past* (New York: New York University Press 1975); Joseph F. Kett, *Rites of Passage: Adolescence in America, 1790 to the Present* (New York: Basic Books 1977); and Mary P. Ryan, *The Cradle of the Middle Class: The Family in Oneida County, New York, 1790–1865* (Cambridge: Cambridge University Press 1981).

2 Susan E. Houston, 'Politics, Schools, and Social Change in Upper Canada,' *CHR* 53 (Sept. 1972) 251–2, 255

3 *Journals of the House of Assembly of Upper Canada* 1836, App. 35, 57–60

4 On the environmental origins of social problems as perceived by early and mid-nineteenth-century reformers, see David J. Rothman, *The Discovery of the Asylum: Social Order and Disorder in the New Republic* (Boston: Little, Brown 1971).

5 *ARUC* (1847) App. A, 84; *ARUC* (1848) Pt 1, 38; 'Educational Intelligence: Canada,' *JEUC* 16:3 (Mar. 1861) 47; *DHE* vol. 12, 90–1; *ARUC* (1857) Pt 1, 47

6 Certainly school superintendents from rural Upper Canada provided evidence that it was not just urban children that were poor. See the appendices of *ARUC*, containing local superintendents' reports.

7 Alison Prentice, *The School Promoters: Education and Social Class in Mid-Nineteenth Century Upper Canada* (Toronto: McClelland and Stewart 1977) 49, 120

8 Bruce Curtis, 'Preconditions of the Canadian State: Educational Reform and the Construction of a Public in Upper Canada, 1837–1846,' *Studies in Political Economy* 10 (Winter 1983) 99–121. Curtis has elaborated on the theme in *Building the Educational State: Canada West, 1836–1871* (London, Ont.: Falmer Press / Althouse Press 1988). This comprehensive exploration of the way in which state-subject relations were constructed through the building of the school system appeared after our own manuscript was completed, but adds intriguing detail and a somewhat different perspective to the picture of legal and administrative change summarized here. See also John Brewer and John Styles, eds, *An Ungovernable People: The English and Their Law in the Seventeenth and Eighteenth Centuries* (London: Hutchinson 1980); and Philip Corrigan and Derek Sayer, *The Great Arch: English State Formation as Cultural Revolution* (Oxford: Basil Blackwell 1984).

9 Prentice, *The School Promoters* 50, 122

10 On the power of teachers over children, see RG2 C-6-C, Memorial of the District

Council of Colborne, 1848; *DHE* vol. 1, 126–7; *DHE* vol. 2, 87; Egerton Ryerson, *Report on a System of Public Elementary Instruction for Upper Canada* (Montreal 1847) 160; 'Circular to Each Teacher,' 14 Aug. 1850, *The Common School Acts of Upper Canada; and the Forms, Instructions, and Regulations for Executing Their Provisions; together with the Circulars Addressed to the Various Officers Concerned with the Administration of the School Law, by the Chief Superintendent of Schools* (Quebec 1853) 95

11 On American teachers, see J. Donald Wilson, 'The Pre-Ryerson Years,' and James Love, 'The Professionalization of Teachers in Mid-Nineteenth-Century Upper Canada,' in Neil McDonald and Alf Chaiton, eds, *Egerton Ryerson and His Times* (Toronto: Macmillan 1978) 13, 110.

12 'Memorial to the Legislature of the Gore District Council against the Common School Act of 1846,' *DHE* vol. 7, 115; RG2 C-6-C, Memorial of the District Council of Colborne, 1848

13 *Forms, Regulations, and Instructions for Making Reports, and Conducting All the Necessary Proceedings under the Act 7th Victoria, Cap. XXIX and for the Better Organization and Government of Common Schools in Upper Canada* (Cobourg 1845) 30; 'Rules for Teachers,' *JEUC* 2 (Apr. 1849) 50; 'Deportment in the Teacher,' *JEUC* 2 (July 1849) 98

14 *Doctor Charles Duncombe's Report upon the Subject of Education* (New York: R. Publishers, Johnson Reprint Corp. 1966) 40–1

15 RG2 C-6-C, Henry Lively to Egerton Ryerson, 27 Oct. 1846, and Alexander Allen et al., to Ryerson, nd, answered 29 Sept. 1846

16 John Lalor, Esq., 'Respect for School Teachers the Interest of Society,' *JEUC* 1 (Mar. 1848) 79; RG2 C-6-C, William Frazer to Egerton Ryerson, 29 May 1849. See also 'The Dignity of the Teacher's Work ,' *JEUC* 7 (June 1854) 80.

17 'The Importance of Education to a Manufacturing, and a Free People,' *JEUC* 1 (Oct. 1848) 297; 'Address on Agricultural Education,' *DHE* vol. 13, 38

18 Prentice, *The School Promoters*, especially chs 3 and 4

19 See Edith G. Firth, ed., *The Town of York, 1815–1834: A Further Collection of Documents of Early Toronto* Champlain Society (Toronto: University of Toronto Press 1966) 224–5; Susanna Moodie, *Roughing It in the Bush* (Toronto: McClelland and Stewart 1923) 458–73. Recent research into the early and mid-nineteenth-century Ontario economy has challenged the view that Upper Canadian agricultural communities were self-sufficient or that the economy was driven by the staple sector alone. See especially Douglas McCalla, 'The "Loyalist" Economy of Upper Canada, 1784–1806,' *HS/SH* 32 (Nov. 1983) 279–304; 'Forest Products and Upper Canadian Development, 1815–1846,' *CHR* 68 (June 1987) 159–98; and Douglas McCalla and Peter George, 'Measurement, Myth and Reality: Reflections on the Economic History of Nineteenth Century Ontario,' *Journal of Canadian Studies* 21 (Autumn 1986) 71–86.

20 Bruce Curtis, 'Schoolbooks and the Myth of Curricular Republicanism: The State of the Curriculum in Canada West, 1820–1850,' *HS/SH* 32 (Nov. 1983) 305–30

21 'Duty of Public Men of All Classes in Reference to Common Schools,' *JEUC* 2 (May 1849) 72; *DHE* vol. 8, 286

22 'Dr. Ryerson's Address on the Advantages of Free Schools, 1850,' *DHE* vol. 9, 81.

23 For a more detailed account of the discussions, legislative efforts, and reports of the 1830s, see Houston, 'Politics, Schools, and Social Change.'

24 An Act to Repeal Certain Acts therein Mentioned, and to Make Further Provision for the Establishment and Maintenance of Common Schools throughout the Province, 4 and 5 Vict. (1841) cap. 18, *DHE* vol. 4, 48–55. Much of the discussion that follows draws on R.D. Gidney and D.A. Lawr, 'The Development of an Administrative System for the Public Schools: The First Stage, 1841–50,' in McDonald and Chaiton, eds, *Egerton Ryerson and His Times* 160–83.

25 *Cobourg Star* 19 Jan. 1842, 2

26 RG2 F2, Superintendent of Emily Township, report for period 30 July 1842; RG2 C-6-C, F. McAnnarry to Robert Murray, 2 Dec. 1842, David McLaren et al., to Murray, 2 Dec. 1842, copy of letter from James Cunningham to W.M. Shaw (sent to Murray, 19 Nov. 1842), copy of letter from chairman of school commissioners, Waterloo, 25 Oct. 1842, and Richard Fowler Budd to Murray, 8 Nov. 1942

27 An Act for the Establishment and Maintenance of Common Schools in Upper Canada, 7 Vict. (1843) cap. 21, in *DHE* vol. 4, 251–62

28 Gidney and Lawr, 'Development of an Administrative System,' 172

29 C.B. Sissons, *Egerton Ryerson: His Life and Letters* (Toronto: Clarke, Irwin 1947) vol. 2, ch. 2

30 (Montreal 1847) *DHE* vol. 6, 140–211

31 See especially the essays by Goldwin S. French, Albert S. Fiorino, Neil McDonald, and Alison Prentice in McDonald and Chaiton, eds, *Egerton Ryerson and His Times*; Prentice, *The School Promoters*; and David Onn, 'Egerton Ryerson's Philosophy of Educator,' *OH* 61 (June 1969).

32 An excellent brief study of Ryerson the man and the career educator is R.D. Gidney's essay on Ryerson in *DCB* vol. 11 (1881–90) 783–95. See also Clara Thomas, *Ryerson of Upper Canada* (Toronto: Ryerson Press 1969), and Sissons, *Egerton Ryerson*. The latter remains valuable for the wealth of original material quoted in its pages, as well as for Sissons's reconstruction of the events of Ryerson's life.

33 *DHE* vol. 6, 205, 213. For further discussion of Ryerson's views on administration, see Alison Prentice, 'The Public Instructor: Ryerson and the Role of the Public School Administrator,' in Chaiton and McDonald, eds, *Egerton Ryerson and His Times* 129–57.

34 'Introductory Sketch of the System of Public Elementary Instruction in Upper Canada,' *DHE* vol. 10, 2

35 An Act for the Better Establishment and Maintenance of Common Schools in Upper Canada, 9 Vict. (1846) cap. 20, *DHE* vol. 6, 59–69

36 RG2 CI, Letterbook C, Egerton Ryerson to George Henry, Superintendent of the Brock District, 12 Mar. 1847, 274

37 RG2 CI, Letterbook C, Egerton Ryerson to William Millar, Superintendent of the Eastern District, 18 Mar. 1847, 263

38 R.D. Gidney and D.A. Lawr have commented on how effective some of the early district superintendents were, calling attention particularly to William Hutton, Jacob Keefer, Dexter D'Everardo, John Steele, Elias Burnham, and Hamnet Pinhey. Certainly most of these men kept up a significant correspondence with the education department, and several had strong views on the school system that they passed on to the provincial superintendent. Further analysis of the superintendents' role may be found in Philip Corrigan and Bruce Curtis, 'Education, Inspection and State Formation: A Preliminary Statement,' Canadian Historical Association *Historical Papers* (Montreal 1985).

39 *DHE* vol. 6, 299–304

40 An Act for Amending the Upper Canada School Act of 1846, 10 and 11 Vict. (1847) cap. 29 in *DHE* vol. 7, 26–8

41 See ch. 6 below, and Alison Prentice, ' "Friendly Atoms in Chemistry": Women and Men at Normal School in Mid-Nineteenth-Century Toronto,' in David Keane and Colin Read, eds, *Metropolis and Hinterland: Essays on Nineteenth-Century Ontario Presented to J.M.S. Careless* (Toronto: Dundurn Press forthcoming).

42 Prentice, 'The Public Instructor,' 136–7

43 RG2 CI, Letterbook D, 131–2

44 'Memorial of the Gore District Council,' *DHE* vol. 7, 113–16, 119, 197–8, 201–2; Egerton Ryerson to William Draper, 12 Apr. 1847, *DHE* vol. 8, 61–2; RG2 CI, Ryerson to Draper, 10 Nov. 1847

45 *DHE* vol. 7, 114–15, 196; *DHE* vol. 8, 63; *Globe* 19 July 1849

46 Details of Toronto's reaction to the 1847 act are to be found in AO, Toronto City Council Papers, 'Second Report of the Standing Committee on Education, City of Toronto, May 1, 1848.' See also Peter Ross, 'The Free School Controversy in Toronto, 1848–1852,' in Katz and Mattingly, eds, *Education and Social Change* 57–80.

47 AO, Toronto City Council Papers, 'Report of the Standing Committee on Education,' 14 and 26 June 1848; see also Ross, 'The Free School Controversy,' 59–61

48 'Free Schools in the City of Toronto,' *JEUC* 2:6 (June 1849) 96; Michael B. Katz, *The People of Hamilton, Canada West: Family and Class in a Mid-Nineteenth Century City* (Cambridge, Mass.: Harvard University Press 1975) ch. 5

CHAPTER 5 *The Battle for Control over Public Schools*

1 The term 'incipient bureaucracy' was coined by Michael Katz to describe the early stages of bureaucratic development in the Boston school system. See 'The

Emergence of Bureaucracy in Urban Education: The Boston Case,' *History of Education Quarterly* (Summer and Fall 1968) 155–88, 319–57.

2 RG2 CI, Letterbook E, Egerton Ryerson to the *Examiner* 31 Dec. 1849, 93–7. See also *DHE* vol. 8, 226, 238.

3 An Act for the Better Establishment and Maintenance of Public Schools in Upper Canada, and for Repealing the Present School Act, 12 Vict. (1849) cap. 83, *DHE* vol. 8, 167–85. Hodgins's commentary is on pages 167 and 233.

4 Minutes of the board reveal no action taken without Ryerson's direction, and it was generally believed that appointments to the board were made on Ryerson's advice.

5 *DHE* vol. 8, 226

6 *Copies of Correspondence between Members of the Government and the Chief Superintendent of Schools on the Subject of the School Law for Upper Canada and Education Generally* (Toronto 1850) 36–44

7 Egerton Ryerson to Robert Baldwin, 14 July 1849, *DHE* vol. 8, 233–8

8 RG2 CI, Letterbook E, Egerton Ryerson to William Frazer, 23 Oct. 1849, and to Provincial Secretary, 7 Dec. 1849, 58, 74–7; RG2 C-6-C, Provincial Secretary to Ryerson, 15 Dec. 1849

9 *Globe* 20 Dec. 1849; *Ottawa Citizen* 12 Jan. 1850, 2; RG2 T, *Examiner* 20 Dec. 1849; *Bathurst Courier* 4 Jan. 1850; and other unidentified newspaper clippings

10 RG2 CI, Letterbook E, Egerton Ryerson to Peter Grant, 2 Feb. 1850, and to James Coyne, 21 Feb. 1850, 121, 132. See RG2 C-6-C, Trustees, SS 5, Guelph, to Ryerson, Mar. 1850, for an example of local school officers pressured by taxpayers in the community.

11 RG2 C-6-C, Trustees, Johnston District to Egerton Ryerson, 28 Jan. 1850; Rev. Johnston Nielson to John George Hodgins, 17 Feb. 1850; Robert Douglas to Ryerson, 4 Mar. 1850; Benjamin Hayter to Hodgins, 3 Feb. 1850; Trustees, SS 5, Guelph, to Ryerson, Mar. 1850; Dexter D'Everardo to Ryerson, Apr. 1850

12 RG2 C-6-C, M. McDonnell to Hincks, 30 May 1850; *DHE* vol. 9, 54–71; *DHE* vol. 10, 282

13 Act for the Better Establishment and Maintenance of Common Schools in Upper Canada, 13 and 14 Vict. (1850) cap. 48, *DHE* vol. 9, 31–49

14 At least to readers with no specific training in legal history. This is, perhaps, the place to raise the need for investigation into the history of nineteenth-century school reform from the point of view of the law. David Tyack has estimated a total of some 3,000 lawsuits involving schools during the nineteenth century for the whole United States, a number that he considers indicates a low level of court activity. (Letter to Alison Prentice, 1982.) In contrast, Upper Canada seems to have produced an enormous number of suits, particularly in the two decades following the school act of 1850. Ryerson's comment that his law was simpler than the Cameron Act is to be found in RG2 CI, Letterbook E, Egerton Ryerson to Angus Stewart, Mar. 1850, 139.

15 'Explanatory Circulars in Regard to the Local Administration of the School Law, 1852,' *DHE* vol. 10, 251

16 RG2 C-6-C, William Hutton to Egerton Ryerson, 3 June 1850

17 See *DHE* vol. 10, 102, 107.

18 Angus Dallas, *Statistics of the Common Schools: Being a Digest of the Evidence Furnished by the Local Superintendents and the Chief Superintendent of Schools in Their Reports for 1855, by a Protestant* (Toronto 1857); Adam Townley, *Seven Letters on the Non-Religious Common School System of Canada and the United States* (Toronto 1853)

19 Most of the circulars are reproduced in *ARUC*.

20 On the *JEUC*, see Alison Prentice, 'The Public Instructor: Egerton Ryerson and Public School Administration,' 149–68, and R.D. Gidney and D.A. Lawr, 'The Development of an Administrative System for the Public Schools: The First Stage, 1841–50,' in Neil McDonald and Alf Chaiton, eds, *Egerton Ryerson and His Times* (Toronto: Macmillan 1978) 129–83.

21 Dallas, *Statistics of the Common Schools* iii

22 *Niagara Chronicle* 17 July 1851, 3; *Niagara Mail* 23 July 1851

23 An Act Supplementary to the Common School Law of 1850, 16 and 17 Vict. (1853) cap. 185, *DHE* vol. 10, 133–40; also An Act to Amend the Laws Relating to Separate Schools in Upper Canada, 18 Vict. (1855) cap. 131, *DHE* vol. 11, 129–31

24 An Act to Amend the Law Relating to Grammar Schools in Upper Canada, 16 and 17 Vict. (1853) cap. 86, *DHE* vol. 10, 140–45; and An Act to Make Further Provision for the Grammar and Common Schools of Upper Canada, 18 Vict. (1855) cap. 132, *DHE* vol. 11, 128–9. For Ryerson's comments, see *DHE* vol. 8, 291.

25 Charles E. Phillips, *The Development of Education in Canada* (Toronto: Gage 1957) 197–9; *ARUC* (1854) App. E, 152–8; RG2 B, *Minutes of the Council of Public Instruction* 26 Dec. 1854 and 22 June 1855, 311–21, 368–9

26 *ARUC* (1855) Pt 1, 23

27 *Niagara Chronicle* 27 Nov. 1844, 2; *Cobourg Star* 24 June 1846, 2

28 'Permanency and Prospects of the System of Common Schools in Upper Canada,' *DHE* vol. 10, 38–41

29 *Census of Canada, 1851–52*. Personal Census. vol. 1 (Quebec: John Lovell 1853) 310–11

30 This topic is explored in Prentice, 'The Public Instructor.'

31 See discussions of American state departments of education in Carl F. Kaestle, *Pillars of the Republic: Common Schools and American Society, 1780–1860* (New York: Hill and Wang 1983), and Wayne E. Fuller, *Old Country School: The Story of Rural Education in the Middle West* (Chicago: University of Chicago Press 1982) ch. 8.

32 Gidney and Lawr, 'Development of an Administrative System,' 161. Ryerson

was aware that there was also a huge increase in the number of local authorities that his office dealt with. By 1861 these amounted to 'about 420 municipal councils and treasurers and local school superintendents – 30 County Boards of Public Instruction and 3,500 school corporations in all 4,200.' *DHE* vol. 16, 312

33 *JEUC* I (Feb. 1848) 44

34 RG2 CI, Letterbook D, Ryerson to D. Brodie, Esq., 24 Jan. 1848

35 'Duties of Local Superintendents,' *JEUC* (Jan. 1856) 11

36 Gerald E. Boyce, ed., *Hutton of Hastings* (Belleville: Mika Publishing 1972) 165; J. Harold Putman, *Egerton Ryerson and Education in Upper Canada* (Toronto: William Briggs 1912) 152

37 'Local Superintendent's Visitation of Schools,' *JEUC* 14 (Apr. 1861) 56

38 RG2 CI, Letterbook C, Ryerson to Provincial Secretary, 27 Mar. 1847, 305, and RG2 CI, Letterbook D, 14 Oct. 1848, 310–11. See also *DHE* vol. 7, 194.

39 RG2 CI, Letterbook C, Ryerson to Provincial Secretary, 27 Mar. 1847, 302–3

40 RG2 CI, Letterbook E, Circular to County Wardens, 31 July 1850, 237–40

41 'Difficulties and Salaries of District Superintendents,' *JEUC* I (May 1848) 154

42 RG2 C-6-C, Charles Fletcher to Ryerson, 1 Apr. 1850

43 RG2 C-6-C, A. Vervais to Ryerson, 1 Oct. 1850

44 RG2 C-6-C, Aaron Gelner and Abraham O. Clemens to Ryerson, 20 July 1859

45 Tht Kirwan, Rural Dean, R.C. Pastor of London and Williamstown, to Egerton Ryerson, 26 Oct. 1852, *Copies of Correspondence between the Chief Superintendent of Schools for Upper Canada and Other Persons, on the Subject of Separate Schools* (Toronto 1855). This letter and the remainder of the lengthy correspondence between Kirwan and Ryerson over this situation may be found in Alison L. Prentice and Susan E. Houston, eds, *Family, School and Society in Nineteenth Century Canada* (Toronto: Oxford University Press 1975) 144–58.

46 RG2 C-6-C, Hamnet Pinhey to Ryerson, 12 Feb. 1850

47 *ARUC* (1864) App. A, 8

48 RG2 C-6-C, Superintendent of Common Schools, Dalhousie, to Ryerson, 7 Feb. 1847

49 RG2 C-6-C, Superintendent of Common Schools, West Oxford, to Ryerson, 20 Sept. 1850; Cecil Mortimer to Ryerson, 6 Mar. 1850

50 RG2 F-3-B, Alexander Dick to Ryerson, 1850; Matilda Superintendent to Ryerson, 1852; RG2 C-6-C, Charles Manson to Ryerson, 10 June 1852; James Stevenson to Ryerson, 28 Feb. 1859; John Radcliff to Ryerson, 11 Apr. 1852

51 RG2 C-6-C, James Stevenson to Ryerson, 28 Feb. 1859

52 RG2 C-6-C, Robert Galbraith to Ryerson, 17 Jan. 1859, and Superintendent, Caledon, to Ryerson, 22 Jan. 1859

53 RG2 C-6-C, A.S. Holmes to Ryerson, 24–9 Dec. 1846, and Joseph Wheeler to Ryerson, 22 Apr. 1850. For an expression of another local superintendent's sense that he was responsible to Ryerson and to no one else, see Township Superintendent, Charlottenburgh, Glengarry, to Ryerson, 23 Apr. 1850.

54 RG2 C-6-C, Superintendent, Charlottenburgh, to Ryerson, 3 July 1850; *ARUC* (1857) App. A, 179–80

55 *ARUC* (1863) App. A, 100; *ARUC* (1868) App. A, 31

56 *ARUC* (1858) App. A, 42; *ARUC* (1861) App. A, 161; RG2 C-6-C, C. J. Henderson to Ryerson, 18 May 1850

57 *ARUC* (1866) App. A, 61; *ARUC* (1865) App. A, 3

58 RG2 C-6-C, Superintendent, Ottawa, to Ryerson, 8 Feb. 1862; *ARUC* (1863) App. A, 147

59 *ARUC* (1861) App. A, 106

60 *ARUC* (1869) App. D, 71

61 For further discussion of this point and elaboration on the remarks of Hutton and the other superintendents, see Alison Prentice, *The School Promoters: Education and Social Class in Mid-Nineteenth Century Upper Canada* (Toronto: McClelland and Stewart 1977) 157–61.

62 RG2 C-6-C, J.G. House to Hodgins, 5 Dec. 1859

63 *ARUC* (1861) App. G, 238

64 *ARUC* (1869) App. D, 52, 63

65 *ARUC* (1860) App. A, 186; *ARUC* (1866) App. A, 6

66 *ARUC* (1866) App. A, 25–6

67 RG2 C-6-C, Robert Hodger to Ryerson, 17 Jan. 1859, William Inglis to Ryerson, 7 Jan. 1860, and Thos Chambers to Ryerson, 1 Jan. 1862

68 *ARUC* (1861) App. A, 156; *JEUC* 8 (Dec. 1855) 183–4

69 RG2 CI, Letterbook C, Ryerson to Stephen Young, 8 May 1847, 362

70 RG2 T, *North American* 18 Feb. 1853

71 RG2 T, Hamilton Hunter to the Editor, *Examiner*, 10 Mar. 1847

72 RG2 C-6-C, Trustees of SS 7, Haldimand, to Ryerson, 11 Jan. 1849

73 RG2 C-6-C, William Pennington to Ryerson, 18 Jan. 1869

74 RG2 C-6-C, Benj. Hammond to Ryerson, 15 Nov. 1859, London trustees to Ryerson, 2 Jan. 1852, Windham trustees to Ryerson, 21 Mar. 1860

75 RG2 CI, Letterbook C, Ryerson to Archibald Fletcher, 15 Jan. 1846, 17

76 RG2 CI, Letterbook D, Ryerson to W.C. Boyd, 26 Feb. 1849, 403

77 *ARUC* (1851) App. C, no. 8, 177–8

78 RG2 C-6-C, Robert Hodger to Ryerson, 17 Jan. 1859

79 *DHE* vol. 12, 11

80 *ARUC* (1852) App. G, 272–4; *JEUC* 8 (Mar. 1855) 42

81 *Hamilton Gazette* 21 June 1852

82 *JEUC* 14 (Jan. 1861) 8–9

83 RG2 CI, Letterbook C, Ryerson to Hamilton Hunter, 7 Feb. 1847, 10 Feb. 1847, 263, 238–9

84 RG2 CI, Letterbook E, Ryerson to Ch. Fletcher, 6 Aug. 1849, 25

85 RG2 CI, Letterbook D, Ryerson to E. Burnham, 4 Apr. 1849, 424–5

86 RG2 C-6-C, John Flood to Ryerson, 18 Oct., 24 Dec. 1849; RG2 CI, Letterbook E, Ryerson to Flood, 7 Feb. 1850, 122

87 RG2 CI, Letterbook C, Ryerson to Mr Waldon et al., 14 Apr. 1847, 329, and Letterbook E, Ryerson to Morgan Jellett, 14 Aug. 1849, 33

88 RG2 CI, Letterbook C, Ryerson to Patrick Thornton, 15 July 1846, 108

89 RG2 CI, Letterbook D, Ryerson to Thornton, 19 May 1848, 241; Letterbook C, 6 Aug. 1846, 124; and Letterbook D, 19 Aug. 1848, 271–2

90 RG2 CI, Letterbook D, Ryerson to Thornton, 23 Nov. 1848, 13 Jan. 1849, 27 Mar. 1849, 340, 369, 420–1; RG2 CI, Letterbook D, Ryerson to Leslie (Provincial Secretary) 9 July 1849, 495–6; RG2 C-6-C, Leslie to Ryerson, 5 July 1849

91 RG2 C-6-C, Thornton to Ryerson, 2 July 1848 and 22 Feb. 1849

92 RG2 C-6-C, Thornton to Ryerson, 5 Nov. 1846; RG2 CI, Letterbook C, Ryerson to Thornton, 10 Nov. 1846, 165–6

93 *Cornwall Constitutional* 29 May 1851, 3, and 16 July 1851, 5; *Aylmer Times* 29 Aug. 1856, 3

94 Ryerson to Geo. Gurnett, 18 Apr. 1849; *Niagara Mail* 23 July 1856, 3

95 R.D. Gidney and D.A. Lawr, 'Bureaucracy *vs.* Community?: The Origins of Bureaucratic Procedures in the Upper Canadian School System,' *Journal of Social History* 13 (Spring 1980) 438–57

96 Donald H. Akenson, *Being Had: Historians, Evidence and the Irish in North America* (Toronto: P.D. Meany Publishers 1985) 149–52

CHAPTER 6 *Forging a Public School Teaching Force*

1 *The Normal School for Ontario: Its Design and Functions* (Toronto 1871) 71, 74

2 Ibid. 68, 70

3 Ibid. 73

4 *The Normal School for Ontario*, for example, was printed in its entirety in *ARUC* (1869) and then reissued in pamphlet form in 1871. See also *Toronto Normal School, Jubilee Celebration* (Toronto 1898) 23 for a description of the opening ceremonies and early days at the school.

5 *Proceedings at the Ceremony of Laying the Chief Cornerstone of the Normal and Model School and Education Offices for Upper Canada* (Toronto 1851)

6 *Normal School for Ontario* 70–4

7 *DHE* vol. 15, 293

8 *Globe* 28 Sept. 1850; *DHE* vol. 10, 7; *Normal School for Ontario* 73, 79

9 RG2 B, *Minutes of the Second General Board of Education / Council of Public Instruction* vol. 2, 23 Jan. 1851 and 12 Oct. 1852, 157–60, 237–9

10 *DHE* vol. 10, 6

11 Angus Dallas, *The Common School System: Its Principle, Operation and Results* (Toronto 1855) vi

12 *Normal School for Ontario* 59, 63, 73; *DHE* vol. 10, 169

13 *Toronto Normal School Jubilee* 28; RG2 B, Letterbook A, *Board of Education Minutes* vol. 2, 25–8. RG2 C-6-C, T.C. Young to J. George Hodgins, 3 June 1847

14 Boarding with families was the system followed in 'Holland, Scotland and the neighbouring States,' according to Ryerson (*DHE* vol. 7, 99). For further discussions of boarding arrangements and the presence of women, see Alison Prentice, 'Education and the Metaphor of the Family: The Upper Canadian Example,' in Michael B. Katz and Paul H. Mattingly, eds, *Education and Social Change: Themes from Ontario's Past* (New York: New York University Press 1975) 120–8, and ' "Friendly Atoms in Chemistry": Women and Men at Normal School in Mid-Nineteenth Century Toronto,' in David Keane and Colin Read, eds, *Metropolis and Hinterland: Essays on Nineteenth Century Ontario Presented to J.M.S. Careless* (Toronto: Dundurn Press forthcoming).

15 Although the claim at first was that Toronto would follow 'the Dublin system of Normal School instruction,' by 1859 Toronto's headmaster was arguing, at least according to one education department correspondent, that the Canadian normal school's system and Ireland's differed 'materially.' RG2 B, Letterbook A, 2, and RG2 C-6-C, Jeremiah Gallivan to Egerton Ryerson, rec'd 31 Oct. 1859

16 *Toronto Normal School Jubilee* 24; *DHE* vol. 7, 101; 'Return to an Address of the Legislative Assembly,' 8 Nov. 1869, no. 176, *ARUC* (1869) 151; *Globe* 9 Mar. 1850

17 RG2 C-6-C, Peter Nicol to Egerton Ryerson, 14 Feb. 1859

18 Thomas Robertson, 'Inspection and Supervision of Schools,' *JEUC* 3:2 (Feb. 1850) 17; RG2 C-6-C, Robertson to the Council of Public Instruction, 14 Jan. 1851

19 RG2 B, vol. 2, *Board of Education Minutes* 31 Oct. 1848, 69; RG2 B, *Council of Public Instruction Minutes* vol. 2, 5 July 1853, 30 June and 4 Aug. 1854, 265–6, 287–8, 295

20 *DHE* vol. 10, 21, citing the *Council of Public Instruction Minutes* for 12 Aug. 1851

21 Ryerson to Lord Metcalfe, 9 May 1846, Ryerson Correspondence, United Church Archives

22 RG2 C-6-C, Joseph Bell to Ryerson, 10 Nov. 1849, and W.H. Poole to Hodgins, 9 Nov. 1849. (See also George Snider to Ryerson, 29 Oct. 1849; Rev. Thos. Williams to Ryerson, 10 Nov. 1849, and Jane McLennan to Ryerson, 12 Nov. 1849.)

23 RG2 B, *Council of Public Instruction Minutes*, 28 Feb. and 26 Oct. 1852, 219, 241–2

24 RG2 C-6-C, Archibald Macallam to Ryerson, 11 July 1855

25 RG2 B, vol. 2, *Board of Education Minutes* 4 Jan. 1848 and 30 Mar. 1849, 40, 88; RG2 C-6-C, Robertson to Ryerson, 29 June 1859, and Geo. McVittie to Ryerson, 30 Apr. 1850

26 RG2 CI, Letterbook D, 80, 83

27 RG2 B, Letterbook A, vol. 2, Ryerson to Joshua Webster, Esq., 26 Aug. 1851, and Ryerson to Mr John Borden, 21 Nov. 1851, 124, 132

28 RG2 B, *Board of Education Minutes* vol. 2, 21 Oct. 1848, 12 Apr. 1850, and 21 May 1852, 66, 113, 230–1. See also the circular dated 17 June 1847, ibid. 24–5. In January 1849, a Mr Joseph Hugill 'retired' from the school. Ryerson had refused to pay him the usual student housing subsidy because no certificate of moral character had been forthcoming. RG2 C-6-C, Hugill to Robertson, 3 Jan. 1849, and RG2 B, vol. 2, *Board of Education Minutes* 9 Jan 1849, 250

29 RG2 B, *Board of Education Minutes* vol. 2, 19 May, 30 June, and 4 July 1848, and 17 Nov. 1852, 49, 54, 55, 248; 10 July 1860, vol. 3, 37–8. See also *ARUC* (1847) 98 and *ARUC* (1854) 112; *DHE* vol. 16, 76.

30 E.C. Guillet, *In the Cause of Education: A Centennial History of the Ontario Education Association, 1861–1960* (Toronto: University of Toronto Press 1960) 61–2

31 *DHE* vol. 10, 14, 24; *DHE* vol. 11, 23–4; *ARUC* (1858) 128–9; RG2 B, *Council of Public Instruction Minutes* vol. 2, 5 July 1853 and 12 Apr. 1855, 266–7. For further discussion, see Prentice ' "Friendly Atoms in Chemistry." '

32 RG2 B, Letterbook A, Ryerson to Robertson, 4 July 1848; RG2 B, Letterbook A, *Council of Public Instruction Minutes* vol. 2, 29 Apr. 1851 and 13 Apr. 1852, 175, 226

33 RG2 B, *Board of Education Minutes* vol. 2, 4 July 1848 and 28 July 1848, 56–7, and 60; RG2 C-6-C, Robertson to Ryerson, 13 Dec. 1848; RG2 B, Letterbook A, Ryerson to innkeepers and to Rev. Waddell, 4 Dec. 1848 and 5 Jan. 1849

34 RG2 C-6-C, Robertson to Ryerson, 12 Mar. 1849; Robertson and Hind to Ryerson, 12 Mar. 1849, and Robertson to Ryerson, 15 Dec. 1849; RG2 B, *Board of Education Minutes* vol. 2, 18 Dec. 1849, *Council of Public Instruction Minutes* 7 May 1851 and 18 June 1851, 105–6, 118–19, 184; RG2 B, *Council of Public Instruction Minutes* vol. 2, 16 July 1852 and 18 Jan. 1853, 235, 252; RG2 B, Robert Yathy to Ryerson, 26 Mar. 1849; loose paper in RG2 B, Letterbook A, vol. 1, Ryerson to Robertson, 24 Aug. 1852. See also Prentice, ' "Friendly Atoms in Chemistry." '

35 Anxious inquiries were received about admission dates and requirements and very soon aspiring students whose credentials were deemed inadequate were being turned away. For the summer session beginning in June 1849, for example, only 106 of the 123 applicants (83 males and 23 females) were accepted, the remainder having been rejected for 'want of literary qualifications.' A decade later the school rejected 49 or 21 per cent of the 232 who applied for entry in the winter term. See *JEUC* 2:6 (June 1849) 87; RG2 C-6-C, Robertson to Ryerson, 18 Feb. 1859. Detailed discussion of the students admitted to the school, their social backgrounds and subsequent histories, may be found in Prentice, ' "Friendly Atoms in Chemistry." ' For a discussion of the school's approach to pedagogy, see ch. 9 of this volume.

36 See for example, RG2 C1, Letterbook E, Ryerson to the *Examiner*, 2 Dec. 1850, 97–9.
37 'Normal School Examinations,' the *Globe*, reprinted in *JEUC* 1:10 (Oct. 1848) 318
38 Dallas, *The Common School System* 27
39 *ARUC* (1857) 11; *DHE* vol. 13, 303, and *DHE* vol. 15, 125
40 *DHE* vol. 8, 265–6; Dallas, *The Common School System* 26; RG2 C-6-C, Pennock to Ryerson, 5 Nov. 1849, and D.Y. Hoit to Hodgins, 15 Dec. 1849. See also *DHE* vol. 16, 9.
41 RG2 T, *Huron Signal* 17 Jan. 1850
42 RG2 C-6-C, John Ransom to Sir Francis Hincks, 13 Apr. 1850
43 See the Report of the Grammar School Inspector, *ARUC* (1867) 65.
44 RG2 C1, Letterbook D, Ryerson to James D. Cathy, 2 Mar. 1849, 407–8
45 On the Toronto Board's antipathy to the school, see RG2 C-6-C, Fred Cumberland to Ryerson, 5 Jan. 1859, and Dallas, *The Common School System* 25.
46 *ARUC* (1863) App. A, 141; *DHE* vol. 9, 147; *ARUC* (1860) App. A, 181
47 *ARUC* (1864) App. A, 40; *ARUC* (1861) App. A, 160; *ARUC* (1867) Pt 1, 5
48 Undated clipping entitled 'My Dear David' and signed 'Peter Pan,' glued to back cover of *Proceedings at the Ceremony of Laying the Chief Cornerstone* (1851), Thomas Fisher Rare Book Library, University of Toronto; 'Reminiscences of Superannuated Common School Teachers, 1843–45,' *DHE* vol. 5, 297; RG2 C-6-C, Robert Elliott to Ryerson, 17 Nov. 1849; Joseph King to Ryerson, 12 July 1850; Thomas Gayton to Ryerson, 3 Aug. 1850; John H. Leonard to Ryerson, 10 July 1850
49 W.H. Landon, *Report of the Superintendent of Schools for the Brock District* (Woodstock 1848) 3–4; RG2 C-6-C, Otto Klotz to Ryerson, 25 Feb. 1851; *ARUC* (1865) App. A, 46
50 *DHE* vol. 4, 264; *ARUC* (1863) App. A, 106; *ARUC* (1864) App. A, 34
51 RG2 C1, Letterbook D, Egerton Ryerson to John Monger, 26 Dec. 1848, 360; RG2 C-6-C, C.W.D. De L'Armitage to Ryerson, 27 June 1849, Meade N. Wright to Ryerson, 29 June 1859, and Teacher to Ryerson, 1 Apr. 1859
52 *JEUC* 14:3 (Mar. 1861) 40; AO, Local Education Records, RG51, 108–16, Trustee Minute Book, SS 1, North-west Oxford, 1845–59 and 1867–79; *ARUC* (1865) App. A, 53. But see RG2 C-6-C, for the complaint of a trustee who could get no one to agree on who should clean the school: William Thompson to Ryerson, 16 Dec. 1865.
53 'Resolutions of the School Association of the Eastern District,' in RG2 C-6-C, D.P. McDonald to Ryerson, 9 July 1850; *DHE* vol. 7, 130; RG2 C-6-C, Superintendent, Scott Township, to Ryerson, 22 Feb. 1851; RG2 C1, Letterbook C, Ryerson to John Hendry, 7 Nov. 1846, 160
54 *Remarks on the State of Education in the Province of Canada by 'L'* (Montreal 1849) 24–5. For an interesting discussion of the blurred distinctions between the social position of nineteenth-century women teachers and servants, see Jeanne

Peterson, 'The Victorian Governess: Status Incongruence in Family and Society,' in Martha Vicinus, ed., *Suffer and Be Still: Women in the Victorian Age* (Bloomington and London: Indiana University Press 1973) 3–20.

55 'Address to the Trustees of Common Schools,' Feb. 1848, *DHE* vol. 7, 225; 'General Regulations and Instructions,' *JEUC* 1:11 (Nov. 1848) 349; 'Address to the Trustees of Common Schools,' *JEUC* 1:3 (Mar. 1848) 74; 'County School Corrections in Upper Canada, 1860,' *DHE* vol. 16, 182

56 *DHE* vol. 3, 274; RG2 C-6-C, James Mavis to Ryerson, 30 June 1846; Henry Lively to Ryerson, 27 Oct. 1846 and 17 Mar. 1850

57 RG2 C-6-C, John Ransome to the Hon. Francis Hincks, 13 Apr. 1850 and George Graftey to Ryerson, 24 Jan. 1859

58 RG2 CI, Letterbook C, Ryerson to J. Neilson, 4 Mar. 1847, 260

59 *The School Book Question: Letters in Reply to the Brown-Campbell Crusade against the Education Department* (Montreal 1866) 10

60 A history of teacher certification, giving the details of shifting categories and classes of certificates over the years, may be found in J.G. Althouse, *The Ontario Teacher: A Historical Account of Progress 1800–1910* (D PAED diss., University of Toronto 1929; Ontario Teachers' Federation 1967).

61 *Proceedings at the Ceremony of Laying the Chief Cornerstone* 9; *DHE* vol. 9, 219; *ARUC* (1864) App. A, 55; RG2 C-6-C, James Carswill to Ryerson, 25 Jan. 1859 and 'Philomath' to Ryerson, no. 4199, 1865; *ARUC* (1869) App. D, 67; 'Central Board of Examiners: Upper Canada Teachers' Association,' *JEUC*, 18:10 (Oct. 1865) 151

62 *ARUC* (1863) App. A, 129, 143; *ARUC* (1864) App. A, 18; Althouse, *The Ontario Teacher* 86

63 *Report on a System of Public Elementary Instruction for Upper Canada* (Montreal 1847) 188; 'Circular to Each Teacher,' 14 Aug. 1850, *The Common School Acts of Upper Canada* (Toronto 1853) 93, 95

64 'Circular to Each Teacher'; RG2 C-6-C, R.I. Henderson to Ryerson, 6 Aug. 1850, and T.J. Robertson to Ryerson, 10 June 1850; Althouse, *The Ontario Teacher* 32–3

65 Guillet, *In the Cause of Education*

66 'Dr. Wilson's Address,' *JEUC* 18:10 (Oct. 1865) 146. For a more detailed discussion of the interests and activities of teacher associations in nineteenth-century Upper Canada and Ontario, see Harry John Smaller, 'Teachers' Protective Associations, Professionalism and the "State" in Nineteenth Century Ontario' (PH D diss., University of Toronto 1988).

67 'Circular to Each Teacher,' 93; *Forms, Regulations and Instructions for Making Reports and Conducting All the Necessary Proceedings under the Act 7th Victoria cap. 29 and for the Better Organization and Government of Common Schools in Upper Canada* (Cobourg 1845) 55–6; *ARUC* (1845–6) 1; *ARUC* (1863) Pt 1, 17

68 Landon, *Report of the Superintendent ... Brock District* 3–4; 'Report of the

Standing Committee on Education of the Home District,' *DHE* vol. 5, 265. For later complaints about continuing low wages, see *ARUC* (1858) App. A, 71, *ARUC* (1861) App. B, 212, and *ARUC* (1864) App. A, 20.

69 *ARUC* (1852), App. A, 90–1; RG2 C-6-C, Henry Livesly to Ryerson, 27 Oct. 1846

70 *DHE* vol. 8, 266–7; *ARUC* (1863) App. A, 131; *ARUC* (1862) App. A, 107; *ARUC* (1869) App. D, 69; RG2 C-6-C, Henry Livesly to Ryerson, 27 Oct. 1846

71 *Report on a System of Public Elementary Instruction* 56; RG2 C-6-C, Rev. R.N. Taylor to Ryerson, 29 Sept. 1849; *ARUC* (1858) App. A, 33; *ARUC* (1864) App. A, 26–8

72 RG2 C-6-C, Trustee, Bathurst District, to Ryerson, Nov. 1849

73 See 'Legislative Provision in Aid of Worn-Out Common School Teachers,' *JEUC* 6:5 (May 1854) 86, for a discussion of whether or not the fund degraded its recipients and made old teachers into paupers. Evidence that it was not popular among teachers may be found in *JEUC* 18:10 (Oct. 1865) 144.

74 RG2 C-6-C, Henry Livesly to Ryerson, 27 Oct. 1846

75 *ARUC* (1858) App. A, 5, and RG2 C-6-C, M. Gallagher to Ryerson, 9 June 1860

76 See *ARUC* (1866) App. A, 231; RG2 C-6-C, James Marrs to Ryerson, 20 June 1846, and Thomas Scott and Charles Westley to Ryerson, 5 Feb. 1850

77 For a more detailed discussion of these factors, see Marta Danylewycz, Beth Light, and Alison Prentice, 'The Evolution of the Sexual Division of Labour in Teaching: A Nineteenth-Century Ontario and Quebec Case Study,' *HS/SH* 31 (May 1983), especially 93–8.

78 Marta Danylewycz and Alison Prentice, 'Teachers, Gender and Bureaucratizing School Systems in Nineteenth Century Montreal and Toronto,' *History of Education Quarterly* 24 (Spring 1984) 75–100

79 *ARUC* (1847) 6; *ARUC* (1866) Pt 1, 5; *JEUC* 20 (Mar. 1867) 55; *Remarks on the State of Education in the Province of Canada by 'L'* 129–30. Inquiries came to the education department from couples planning to teach school together; wives and also daughters and sons sometimes assisted in their husbands' or fathers' schools. See RG2 C-6-C, Hannah Scarlett to Ryerson, 12 May 1849, and Samuel Wilson to Ryerson, 7 May 1849.

80 An Act for the Best Establishment and Maintenance of Common Schools in Upper Canada, 1850, cl. 48, *DHE* vol. 9, 49; RG2 CI, Letterbook C, Ryerson to H.A. Clifford, 10 Mar. 1847, 267; 'Revised Terms of Admission into the Normal School, 1851,' *DHE* vol. 10, 20, adopted 31 July 1851; 'Programme of the Examination and Classification of Teachers of Common Schools,' 3 Oct. 1850, *The Common School Acts of Upper Canada* (Toronto 1853) 102

81 *ARUC* (1868) App. A, 44; RG2 C-6-C, Blair to Ryerson, 27 Mar. 1867, and Dick Gater to Ryerson, 21 Nov. 1868; *ARUC* (1860) App. A, 190; *ARUC* (1869) App. D, 86

82 RG2 CI, Letterbook D, Ryerson to Mr Benjamin Jacobs, 1 Feb. 1848, 151; *DHE* vol. 7, 276; *ARUC* (1865) Pt 1, 7; *ARUC* (1866) Pt 1, 4–5

83 Danylewycz, Light, and Prentice, 'Evolution of the Sexual Division of Labour in Teaching,' 96–101

84 Ibid. and Danylewycz and Prentice, 'Teachers, Gender and Bureaucratizing School Systems,' 82–8

85 Danylewycz and Prentice, 'Teachers, Gender and Bureaucratizing School Systems,' 91–2

86 AO, Local Education Records, RG51, 108–16, Trustee Minute Books, SS 1, Northwest Oxford, 1845–59 and 1867–79 and SS 11, Norwich North, 1863–79

87 Susan Laskin, Beth Light, and Alison Prentice, 'Studying the History of an Occupation: Quantitative Sources on Canadian Teachers in the Nineteenth Century,' *Archivaria* 14 (Summer 1982) 81–2

88 Smyth Carter, *The Story of Dundas* (Iroquois, Ont.: St Lawrence News Publishing House 1905) 128; RG2 C-6-C, Elizabeth Ann Inglis to Egerton Ryerson, 29 Dec. 1849

89 The proportions of teachers with Normal School certificates, decade by decade, were 7.1 per cent of all teachers in 1851, 10 per cent in 1861, 12.5 per cent in 1871, and 24.2 per cent in 1881. *ARUC* (1851, 1861, 1871, and 1881)

90 For evidence and discussion, see Prentice, ' "Friendly Atoms in Chemistry." ' The research by Susan Laskin on the origins of Normal School students and the distribution of teachers with Normal School certificates also illustrates these points. 'The Training and Certification of Elementary School Teachers in Ontario, 1847–1875,' *Historical Atlas of Canada*, vol. 2 (forthcoming)

91 For a history of the model schools, see John Stewart Hardy, 'Training Third Class Teachers: A Study of the Ontario Model School System, 1877–1907' (PH D diss., University of Toronto 1981) ch. 1.

92 Richard M. Bernard and Maris A. Vinovskis, 'The Female School Teacher in Ante-Bellum Massachusetts,' *Journal of Social History* 10 (Spring 1977) 332–45

PART THREE *Behind the Schoolroom Door*

1 Richard Johnson, 'Elementary Education: The Education of the Poorer Classes,' in Celina Fox et al., eds, *Education, Government and Society in Nineteenth Century Britain: Commentaries on British Parliamentary Papers* (Dublin: Irish University Press 1977) 8

2 J. George Hodgins, ed., *'The Story of My Life' by the late Rev. Egerton Ryerson* (Toronto 1883) xiv–xv; Rev. Dr Dewart, *Christian Guardian* 22 Feb. 1882, 604. See also Daniel Calhoun, *The Intelligence of a People* (Princeton, NJ: Princeton University Press 1973) 68–70; Lee Soltow and Edward Stevens, *The Rise of Literacy and the Common School in the United States: A Socio-economic Analysis to 1870* (Chicago: Chicago University Press 1981) chs 4, 5; Harvey J. Graff, *The Literacy Myth: Literacy and Social Structure in the Nineteenth Century City* (New York: Academic Press 1979). For a more recent (1984) reflection by Graff

on the state of historical research into literacy, see 'The History of Literacy: Toward the Third Generation,' *Interchange* 17 (Summer 1986) 122–34.

3 Teachers' Convention, 1863, *JEUC* 16 (Aug. 1863) 125; also, E.C. Guillet, *In the Cause of Education: A Centennial History of the Ontario Education Association, 1861–1960* (Toronto: University of Toronto Press 1960) 29

4 *Fraser Report* 275, 277. Fraser's assessment is given a twist by Bruce Curtis in ' "'Littery Merrit,' Useful Knowledge," and the Organization of Township Libraries in Canada West, 1840–1860,' *OH* 78 (Dec. 1986) 285–312.

5 *ARUC* (1861) Pt 2, table O, 101n; see also Allan Smith, 'The Imported Image: American Publications and American Ideas in the Evolution of the English-Canadian Mind, 1820–1900' (PH D diss., University of Toronto 1971) 71–4; Paul Rutherford, *A Victorian Authority: The Daily Press in Late-Nineteenth-Century Canada* (Toronto: University of Toronto Press 1982) 24–35

6 Paul Craven, 'Law and Ideology: The Toronto Police Court, 1850–1880,' in David H. Flaherty, ed., *Essays in the History of Canadian Law* vol. 2 (Toronto: The Osgoode Society 1983) especially 286–99; John Choules, 'The Periodic Necessity of Example: Deterrence and the Dramaturgy of Public Executions in Ontario 1792–1869' (Major research paper, York University Graduate Program in History 1986)

7 See especially Myra C. Glenn, *Campaigns against Corporal Punishment: Prisoners, Sailors, Women and Children in Antebellum America* (Albany: State University of New York Press 1984); Bruce Curtis, *Building the Educational State: Canada West, 1836–1871* (London, Ont.: Falmer Press / Althouse Press 1988) 58–60.

8 *ARUC* (1856) 283

9 AO, Education Papers Collection, MU 975, 1860–9, Box 6, no. 6, Maria Payne Notebooks

10 RG2 C-6-C – the education department incoming correspondence – contains details of numerous discipline cases. For examples see Samuel Nash to Egerton Ryerson (hereafter E.R.), Kingston, 13 Nov. 1855; John Hudson to E.R., William Begg to E.R., SS 3, Township of London, 5 May 1860; A.J. Campbell to E.R. Carlisle, 25 May 1860; Wm Thomson to E.R., Caledonia, 19 June 1862.

11 Ibid. J.H. Johnson to E.R., 10 Apr. 1860; also *Brockville Recorder* 12 Apr. 1860, and editorial, *Globe* 13 Apr. 1860

12 TBEHC, James Porter Diary, vol. 1, 10 May 1859; vol. 2, 14–15 Jan. 1861. Local Superintendent Porter's diaries indicate that in Toronto suspension was used so frequently that after 1859 Porter restricted authority to send pupils home to the head teacher of each school. Parents often objected strenuously to the suspension (Mrs Pullen, the wife of the city bell-ringer, was outraged when Angelina was sent home for having lice in her hair on 1 July 1864, for example), but if that did not accomplish its purpose they frequently pleaded to have the child reinstated. In the Pullen case, Angelina was taken back but proved to be a hazard of

another sort. On 30 May 1865 she fell asleep and could not be roused by her teacher. The *Globe* ran the story, reporting Angelina as having 'dropped dead' (30 May 1865).

13 Alison L. Prentice and Susan E. Houston, eds, *Family, School and Society in Nineteenth Century Canada* (Toronto: Oxford University Press 1975) 107–15

14 *DHE* vol. 28, 247–8

15 Simcoe County Archives, Neil J. Campbell Ms, 60

16 Dunnville *Independent* 1 Jan. 1857

17 In addition to the references cited above, see *ARUC* (1858) App. A., Goderich, 80; James Porter Diary, vol. 3, 8 Sept. 1865, 9 Feb. 1866.

18 James Porter Diary, vol. 1, 18 May, 7 Sept. 1859; vol. 3, 6, 16 Feb. 1866; vol. 4, 11 Sept. 1871. See also Porter entry, *DCB* vol. 10, 599.

19 *Report of the Past History and Present Condition of the Common or Public Schools of Toronto* (Toronto 1859) 115; James Porter Diary, vol. 1, 12 Apr. 1859; vol. 2, 9, 13 Mar. 1863; vol. 3, 6, 13 June 1864; 11, 13, 17 Feb. 1865; *Leader* 13 June 1864

CHAPTER 7 *Going to School*

1 Egerton Ryerson to W.H. Draper, 20 Apr. 1846, in C.B. Sissons, *Egerton Ryerson: His Life and Letters* vol. 2 (Toronto: Clarke, Irwin 1947) 101

2 *ARUC* (1875) table Q, *DHE* vol. 27, 213–15; 'Special Educational Statistics,' Ontario, *Sessional Papers* 13 (1873); Ian E. Davey, 'Educational Reform and the Working Class: School Attendance in Hamilton, Ontario, 1851–1891' (PH D diss., University of Toronto 1975) table 5.5; also 'The Rhythm of Work and the Rhythm of School,' in Neil McDonald and Alf Chaiton, eds, *Egerton Ryerson and His Times* (Toronto: Macmillan 1975) 221–53

3 Carl F. Kaestle and Maris A. Vinovskis, *Education and Social Change in Nineteenth-Century Massachusetts* (New York: Cambridge University Press 1980) chs 1, 2

4 R.D. Gidney and W.P.J. Millar, 'From Voluntarism to State Schooling: The Creation of the Public School System in Ontario,' *CHR* 66 (Dec. 1985) 442–73

5 Ian E. Davey, 'On School Attendance,' *ANZHES Journal* 6 (Autumn 1977) 1–12; Michael B. Katz, 'Who Went to School?' in Michael B. Katz and Paul H. Mattingly, eds, *Education and Social Change: Themes from Ontario's Past* (New York: New York University Press 1975) ch. 11

6 Ian E. Davey, 'Trends in Female School Attendance in Mid-Nineteenth Century Ontario,' *HS/SH* 16 (Nov. 1975) 243

7 David Gagan, *Hopeful Travellers: Families, Land, and Social Change in Mid-Victorian Peel County, Canada West*, Ontario Historical Studies Series (Toronto: University of Toronto Press 1981); Michael B. Katz, *The People of Hamilton, Canada West: Family and Class in a Mid-Nineteenth Century City* (Cambridge, Mass.: Harvard University Press 1975); Michael B. Katz, Michael T. Doucet,

and Mark J. Stern, *The Social Organization of Early Industrial Capitalism* (Cambridge, Mass.: Harvard University Press 1982)

8 Gagan, *Hopeful Travellers* 83, 134

9 AO Mss Misc. Coll., Eliza Blain Keyes memoirs, 1844; R.D. Gidney and D.A. Lawr, 'Bureaucracy *vs.* Community?: The Origins of Bureaucratic Procedures in the Upper Canadian School System,' *Journal of Social History* 13 (Spring 1980) 443; Wayne E. Fuller, *The Old Country School: The Story of Rural Education in the Middle West* (Chicago: University of Chicago Press 1982) ch. 4

10 Gerald E. Boyce, 'The Bayside Property and the School, 1784–1874,' *OH* 64 (1972) 181–200

11 Chad Gaffield, *Language, Schooling, and Cultural Conflict: The Origins of the French-Language Controversy in Ontario* (Kingston and Montreal: McGill-Queen's University Press 1987) 101–7; and 'Demography, Social Structure and the History of Schooling,' in David C. Jones et al., eds, *Approaches to Educational History* (Winnipeg: University of Manitoba 1981) 85–112

12 *ARUC* (1856) App. A, 151

13 RG2 C-6-C, George Murray to E.R., 9 June 1857. See also the case of West Tilbury, 3 Mar. 1864 *vs* 19 Aug. 1853.

14 *ARUC* (1863) App. A, 98

15 RG2 C-6-C, O.K. Weese, Geo. Orr, and J. Graham to E.R., 22 June 1858

16 *ARUC* (1866) Pt I, 25

17 E.R. to Provincial Secretary, 2 Apr. 1872, *DHE* vol. 24, 192

18 RG2 C-6-C, Frederick Burrowes to J.G. Hodgins, 31 Aug. 1872, cited by Dana Johnson, 'Going to School in Rural Ontario,' Parks Canada *Research Bulletin 212* (Dec. 1983)

19 *ARUC* (1850) App. A, 196–7

20 Ibid. 188; University of Western Ontario Regional Collection M315, London School Board Minutes vol. 2, 8 July 1858

21 TBEHC, James Porter Diary, vol. 3, 1 May 1866. Average attendance at Centre Street School dropped from 174 in 1865 to 126 in 1866. See also Honora M. Cochrane, ed., *Centennial Story: The Board of Education for the City of Toronto, 1850–1950* (Toronto: Thomas Nelson 1950) 55

22 TBEHC, Toronto Board of School Trustees, Sites and Building Committee Minutes 1864; W.C. Wilkinson Diary, vol. 3. Bureau of Municipal Research, Biographies of Individual Schools under the Toronto Board of Education, vol. 2: *Park School* (Toronto 1921) 49; TBEHC, James Porter Diary, vol. 4, 5 Apr. 1869

23 *ARUC* (1863) App. A, 150

24 Minor epidemics were commonplace occurrences reported by local superintendents: L.T. Spalding, comp., *The History and Romance of Education* (Hamilton 1972) 16, cited in Davey, 'The Rhythm of Work,' n69; TBEHC, Toronto Board of School Trustees, Minutes, vol. 2, 4 May, 20 June 1960; *Annual Report of the Local Superintendent ... Toronto* (1860) 28. The smallpox epidemic of 1860 activated perennial divisions among Toronto school trustees. A motion to require

a medical certificate of vaccination for all pupils returning after the summer holidays was adopted by the board in May; however in June the question was reopened and a parent's certificate was deemed sufficient. See also Barbara L. Craig, 'State Medicine in Transition: Battling Smallpox in Ontario, 1882–1885,' *OH* 75 (Dec. 1983) 319–47, and Paul Bator, 'The Health Reformers *vs.* the Common Canadian: The Controversy over Compulsory Vaccination against Smallpox in Toronto and Ontario, 1900–1920,' *OH* 75 (Dec. 1983) 348–73

25 Gidney and Lawr, 'Bureaucracy *vs.* Community?' 450–1; Alison Prentice, *The School Promoters: Education and Social Class in Mid-Nineteenth Century Upper Canada* (Toronto: McClelland and Stewart 1977) 161; RG2 C-6-C, Superintendent, Usborne, to E.R., 15 June 1861

26 *DHE* vol. 24, 293; see also, for example, the previously cited report of Local Superintendent Edward Scarlett of Northumberland County. In his view, seats and desks were 'as if purposely got up to inflict punishment on youthful delinquents' *ARUC* (1856) App. A, 151.

27 Prentice, *The School Promoters* 159

28 Gerald Killan, *David Boyle: From Artisan to Archaeologist* (Toronto: University of Toronto Press 1983) 28, 36; RG2 C-6-C, 27 July 1861, Bagot SS 1, Renfrew County, also 7 Mar. 1862, SS 5, Rear Leeds and Lansdowne County. Arson was suggested sometimes in correspondence with the education department: cf RG C-6-C, 17 Feb. 1868, 20 Jan. 1858; also Bruce Curtis, 'Patterns of Resistance to Public Education: England, Ireland and Canada West 1830–1890,' paper given at Comparative and International Education Society, Mar. 1986.

29 J.G. Hodgins, *The School House: Its Architecture, External and Internal Arrangements* (Toronto: Lovell and Gibson 1857); *ARUC* (1869) in *DHE* vol. 22, 77

30 'Ontario Teachers' Association Meeting, 1869,' *DHE* vol. 21, 295 ff

31 *DHE* vol. 28, 281

32 Letter to the editor and editorial, *Globe* 22 Oct. 1858

33 Katz, Doucet, and Stern, *Social Organization of Early Industrial Capitalism* table 7–2, 253

34 *ARUC* (1865) App. A, 63; *ARUC* (1868) App. A, 42. See also *ARUC* (1871) App. A, Whitby, 116, and Prentice, *The School Promoters* 150–1

35 *Annual Report of the Local Superintendent ... Toronto* (1865) 86; ibid. (1869) 6–9. See also Cochrane, ed., *Centennial Story* 56–7; TBEHC, James Porter Diary, vol. 4, 5 Apr., 21 May, 3, 4 Sept. 1869.

36 *DHE* vol. 21, 296

37 Ibid. 297. See also 'Abbreviated Report, for 1872, of the Truant Officer,' *Annual Report of the Local Superintendent ... Toronto* (1872) 15–16, 63–5.

38 'Report to the Government on the School Law of 1846 and 1847, Accompanied by a Draft of Bill for Their Improvement, October, 1848,' *DHE* vol. 8, 83–93

39 Davey, 'On School Attendance,' 6, 9; Gagan, *Hopeful Travellers* 83, and table 30, 84

40 For example, see RG2 C-6-C, John J. Tilley, 17 Mar. 1873 (Box 218, no. 3998); *ARUC* (1874) App. B, 80. For general Ontario patterns, see Davey, 'The Rhythm of Work'; for New England, Joseph F. Kett, *Rites of Passage: Adolescence in America, 1790 to the Present* (New York: Basic Books 1977).

41 Marvin McGinnis and Heather Tremble, 'School Attendance of Farm Children in 1861 Ontario: A Preliminary Work' (Ms, 25 Nov. 1982)

42 RG2 C-6-C, Charlotteville, 21 Mar. 1860; *ARUC* (1868) 26

43 RG2 C-6-C, Westmeath, 25 Feb. 1863 (no. 1876); also Chad Gaffield, 'Schooling, the Economy and Rural Society in Nineteenth-Century Ontario,' in Joy Parr, ed., *Childhood and Family in Canadian History* (Toronto: McClelland and Stewart 1982) 69–92

44 *ARUC* (1874) App. B, 101; George Peters, *DHE* vol. 28, 275; RG2 C-6-C, J.A. Murdoch, 8 Feb. 1861

45 *ARUC* (1861) App. A, 176, cited by Davey, 'The Rhythm of Work,' n63

46 RG2 C-6-C, J. Holmes, 9 Mar. 1857; also Ottawa, 25 Jan. 1866

47 TBEHC, Wilkinson Diary, vol. 2, 20 Feb. 1873; vol. 3, 26 Feb. 1873. There is now an extensive literature on geographical mobility in nineteenth-century North American society; see especially Katz, *People of Hamilton* ch. 3, and Gagan, *Hopeful Travellers*.

48 On the importance of the issue of student transfers from one school to another, see H.P. Bamman, 'Patterns of School Attendance,' in Katz and Mattingly, eds, *Education and Social Change* 217–45; and H.P. Bamman and Ian E. Davey, 'Ideology and Space in the Toronto Public School System' (Paper presented to the Conference on Historical Urbanization in North America, York University 1973). Also 'Local Superintendents' Speech,' *Globe* 8 Nov. 1854; editorial, *Globe* 8 Dec. 1854; TBEHC, James Porter Diary, vol. 1, 11 Oct. 1859, Park School Male Department; 16 May 1860, Phoebe Street Male Department

49 *Annual Report of the Local Superintendent ... Toronto* (1866) 45–55; see also RG2 C-6-C, Ottawa, 25 Jan. 1866

50 For a discussion of nineteenth-century attitudes towards 'job-hopping' on the part of young men, see Joseph F. Kett, 'The Adolescence of Vocational Education,' in Harvey Kantor and David B. Tyack, *Work, Youth and Schooling: Historical Perspectives on Vocationalism in American Education* (Palo Alto, Ca.: Stanford University Press 1982) 100.

51 *Globe* 23 Sept. 1871; Katz, *People of Hamilton* 289; M.B. Katz and Ian E. Davey, 'Youth and Early Industrialization in a Canadian City,' in John Demos and S.S. Boocock, eds, *Turning Points: Historical and Sociological Essays on the Family* (Chicago: University of Chicago Press 1978) s81–119

52 Erastus Wiman, *Annual Report of the Board of Trade, with a Review of the*

Commerce of Toronto for 1862 (Toronto 1863); TBEHC, James Porter Diary, vol. 3, 2 June 1864

53 Gagan, *Hopeful Travellers*; Chad Gaffield and David Levine, 'Dependency and Adolescence on the Canadian Frontier: Orillia,' *History of Education Quarterly* (Spring 1978) 35–47; Gaffield, 'Schooling, the Economy and Rural Society'; D.H. Akenson, *The Irish in Ontario: A Study in Rural History* (Montreal: McGill-Queen's University Press 1984)

54 *ARUC* (1874) App. B, 71, cited in Davey, 'The Rhythm of Work,' n57

55 'Ninth Annual Report of the Board of Arts and Manufactures,' *Journal of the Board of Arts and Manufactures* vol. 6 (1866) 33–4; *Annual Report of the Canadian Labour Union* (Toronto 1876)

56 Katz, Doucet, and Stern, *Social Organization of Early Industrial Capitalism* 35, 97–101, 254–7

57 *Globe* 11 July 1871; *Census of Canada 1870–71* vol. 3, table 28

58 Katz, Doucet, and Stern, *Social Organization of Early Industrial Capitalism* 281

59 'Report of the Grammar School Inspectors for 1860,' *DHE* vol. 16, 143–6; Gidney and Millar, 'From Voluntarism to State Schooling,' 457. On grammar school development generally, see Walter N. Bell, *The Development of the Ontario High School* (Toronto: University of Toronto Press 1918) chs 7, 8.

60 'Grammar School Inspectors' Report,' *DHE* vol. 12, 83, 328–33; vol. 16, 144

61 RG2 C-6-C, W.F. Checkley, 12 Jan. 1857; 'Provincial Teachers' Association Meeting, 1862,' *DHE* vol. 18, 88

62 *DHE* vol. 17, 6 ff; Mary Larratt Smith, *Young Mr Smith in Upper Canada* (Toronto: University of Toronto Press 1980) 177; RG2 C-6-C, Harron to J.G.H., 9 Mar. 1859

63 First letter from the Chairman of the Toronto Grammar School Board to the Provincial Secretary, 6 May 1853, *DHE* vol. 11, 205–11; TBEHC, Toronto Grammar School Board Minutes, 4 Jan. 1854; Grassett to Charles Daly, *c.* 1860; Joseph Sheard to the board, 8 Oct. 1860

64 W.S. Wallace, introd., 'A Tassie Boy: Fragment of an Autobiographical Sketch by the Rev. W.G. Wallace,' *OH* 46 (1954) 169–78; 'Grammar School Regulations,' *DHE* vol. 13, 202

65 Provincial Teachers' Association Annual Meeting, *DHE* vol. 19, 60

66 'Grammar School Inspectors' Report, 1860,' *DHE* vol. 16, 145; Prentice, *The School Promoters* 143–4

67 Egerton Ryerson to the Provincial Secretary, 27 Mar. 1847, *DHE* vol. 7, 189; An Act for Amending the Upper Canada Common School Act of 1846, 10 and 11 Vict. (1847) cap. 19, *DHE* vol. 7, 26–8

68 Egerton Ryerson, 'Special Report on the Supply to the Schools of Maps, Apparatus and Library Books,' *DHE* vol. 13, 299–300

69 The most authoritative studies of Hamilton's schools in the nineteenth century are by Ian E. Davey: 'School Reform and School Attendance: The Hamilton Central

School, 1853–61' (MA diss., University of Toronto 1972); 'Educational Reform and the Working Class'; and in collaboration with Michael B. Katz. For documentation on the early years of the Central School, see J.H. Smith, *The Central School Jubilee Reunion: Aug., 1903, and Historical Sketch* (Hamilton 1905); 'Board of Common School Trustees, Hamilton, to Egerton Ryerson, 29 March, 1856,' *DHE* vol. 13, 74–5; *ARUC* (1855) App. A, 278–85. For a complementary analysis of the London Central School, see Michael Murphy, 'The Union Central School and London Education: A Socio-economic Profile, 1870' (Unpublished paper, University of Western Ontario).

70 Ian E. Davey, 'School Reform and School Attendance: The Hamilton Central School, 1853–1861,' in Katz and Mattingly, eds, *Education and Social Change* 294–314

71 For analysis of Toronto schools from the mid-nineteenth century, see Peter N. Ross, 'The Free School Controversy in Toronto, 1848–52,' in Katz and Mattingly, eds, *Education and Social Change* 57–80; Bamman, 'Patterns of School Attendance'; Susan E. Houston, 'Social Reform and Education: The Issue of Compulsory Schooling, Toronto, 1851–71,' in McDonald and Chaiton, eds, *Egerton Ryerson and His Times* 254–76

72 AO, Charles Clarke Papers, Riddell to Clarke, 15 Mar. 1868; *JEUC* 21:6 (June 1868) 92; *Globe* 6 July 1867

73 *ARUC* (1869) App. D, London, 109–10; *JEUC* 21 (Sept. 1868) Belleville, Kingston; Brooke to the editor, *Globe* 31 July; 3, 8, 12, 16, 26 Aug.; 11, 19, 30 Sept.; 6, 14 Oct. 1865; *Annual Report of the Local Superintendent ... Toronto* (1865) 8–10, 52–8

74 *Globe* 7 Dec. 1865 carried a detailed report of both the Reverend Mr Porter's remarks and the trustees' decision; see also *Annual Report of the Local Superintendent ... Toronto* (1865) 58–79, especially 65, 72.

75 A similar quest by American and British historians has proved equally fruitless. See Carl F. Kaestle, *Pillars of the Republic: Common Schools and American Society, 1780–1860* (New York: Hill and Wang 1983), and J.S. Hurt, *Elementary Schooling and the Working Classes, 1860–1918* (London: Routledge and Kegan Paul 1979) Pt 3. Bruce Curtis made the case for resistance in his paper 'Patterns of Resistance to Public Education.'

76 Chad Gaffield speculates on the attractions of schooling for young people in eastern Ontario in 'Schooling, the Economy and Rural Society,' 91–2.

CHAPTER 8 *What One Might Teach and Another Learn*

1 *ARUC* (1864) App. A, 63. Robert Stamp, *The Schools of Ontario 1876–1976*, Ontario Historical Studies Series (Toronto: University of Toronto Press 1982)

2 *ARUC* (1868) App. A, 45; TBEHC, James Porter Diary, vol. 3, 24 Sept. 1868

3 'E.R. to Higginson, 30 Apr. 1845,' *DHE* vol. 5, 240; E. Ryerson, *Special Report*

on the Means which Have Been Adopted for the Establishment of a Normal School and for Carrying into Effect Generally the Common School Act (Montreal 1847) 14–15; J. Donald Wilson, 'Common School Texts in Use in Upper Canada prior to 1845,' Bibliographical Society of Canada *Papers* 9 (1970) 36–53; Viola E. Parvin, *The Authorization of Textbooks for the Schools of Ontario, 1846–1950* (Toronto: University of Toronto Press 1965) 29; Bruce Curtis, 'Schoolbooks and the Myth of Curricular Republicanism: The State of the Curriculum in Canada West, 1820–1850,' *HS/SH* 32 (Nov 1983) 305–30; James H. Love, 'Anti-Americanism and Common School Education Reform in Mid-Nineteenth Century Upper Canada: The Niagara District as a Case Study' (PH D diss., University of Toronto 1978) and 'Cultural Survival and Social Control: The Development of a Curriculum for Upper Canada's Common Schools in 1846,' *HS/SH* 30 (Nov. 1982) 357–82

4 E. Ryerson, 'Circular Addressed to District Superintendents ... December 1846,' *DHE* vol. 6, 267; *A Brief History of Public and High School Text-books Authorized for the Province of Ontario 1846–1889*, Prepared by the Education Department (Toronto: Warwick and Sons 1890); 'Proceedings of the Board of Education, Oct. 30, 1846,' *DHE* vol. 6, 245; *ARUC* (1847) *DHE* vol. 7, 162; George L. Parker, *The Beginnings of the Book Trade in Canada* (Toronto: University of Toronto Press 1985) 112 ff. An inventory of the books actually used in the common schools across the province could be compiled on the basis of information surviving in manuscript form for the period 1855–70 in the local superintendents' annual reports, RG2 F-3-B.

5 Donald H. Akenson, *The Irish Education Experiment: The National System of Education in the Nineteenth Century* (London: Routledge and Kegan Paul 1970) 227–30; Dianna S. Cameron, 'John George Hodgins and Ontario Education, 1844–1912' (MA diss., University of Guelph 1976) 113–15; J.M. Goldstrom, *The Social Content of Education, 1808–1870: A Study of the Working Class School Reader in England and Ireland* (Shannon: Irish University Press 1972); also 'The Content of Education and the Socialization of the Working Class Child, 1830–1860,' in Phillip McCann, ed., *Popular Education and Socialization in the Nineteenth Century* (London: Methuen 1977) 93–109; 'Proceedings of the Board of Education Oct. 9, 1846,' *DHE* vol. 6, 242–5

6 *JEUC* 1 (Nov. 1848) 337; Curtis, 'Schoolbooks and the Myth of Curricular Republicanism,' 328; William Sherwood Fox, 'School Readers as an Educational Force: A Study of a Century of Upper Canada,' *Queen's Quarterly* 39 (1932) 688–703

7 Goldstrom, *The Social Content of Education*; Ruth Miller Elson, *Guardians of Tradition: American Schoolbooks of the Nineteenth Century* (Lincoln: University of Nebraska Press 1964)

8 *The First Book of Lessons for the Use of Schools* (Montreal and Toronto: James Campbell 1867) sect. 2, lessons 6, 7, 10

9 *The Second Book of Lessons for the Use of Schools* (London 1858) sect. 4, lesson 11

10 Fox, 'School Readers'; *A Sequel to the Second Book of Lessons for the Use of Schools* (1864) 13; reprinted in Parvin, *Authorization of Textbooks* 27; TBEHC, James Porter Diary, vol. 4, 10 May 1872

11 In Hamilton in 1868, 3.7 per cent of students in the common school system were in Book 5; in Toronto in 1875 the figure was 5 per cent; cf 'E. Ryerson to the Provincial Secretary 18 Mar. 1872,' *DHE* vol. 24, 210–11. See also R.D. Gidney and W.P.J. Millar, 'From Voluntarism to State Schooling: The Creation of the Public School System in Ontario,' *CHR* 66 (Dec. 1985) table 3, 473.

12 J.M. Goldstrom, 'Richard Whately and Political Economy in School Books, 1833–1880,' *Irish Historical Studies* 15 (1966) 133–46; also *The Social Content of Education* 83–5; and 'The Content of Education and the Socialization of the Working Class Child,' 102–3

13 *The Third Book of Lessons for the Use of Schools* (Toronto 1851) sect. 3, lesson 10

14 *The Fourth Book of Lessons for the Use of Schools* (Montreal: R. and A. Hiller 1853) 229

15 Compare *First Book* sect. 3, lesson 22; *Second Book* sect. 2, lessons 8, 11; sect. 3, lessons 5, 7; sect. 4, lessons 1, 6.

16 Sharon Dyas, 'The World View Presented to Children of Toronto Schools, 1862–67' (Ms, Department of History, York University 1978), an analysis of vols 2 and 3 of James Porter's diary

17 Cf Elson, *Guardians of Tradition*, and Goldstrom, 'The Content of Education and the Socialization of the Working Class Child.'

18 Parvin, *Authorization of Textbooks* 39–40; *A Brief History* 7

19 *ARUC* (1847) *DHE* vol. 7, 162–3; Curtis, 'Schoolbooks and the Myth of Curricular Republicanism'

20 Wilson, 'Common School Texts,' 41, 46–7; 1,162 of the 2,727 common schools reported using Walkingame's arithmetic, *ARUC* (1847) *DHE* vol. 7, 163. See also W.B. Gray, 'The Teaching of Mathematics in Ontario, 1800–1941' (D PAED diss., University of Toronto 1948) chs 2, 3

21 J.H. Sangster, *National Arithmetic in Theory and Practice: Designed for the Use of Canadian Schools* (Montreal: Lovell 1859); *Series of National Schoolbooks. First Book of Arithmetic: For the Use of Schools*, rev. ed., Adapted to the New Decimal Currency (Toronto: Robert McPhail 1860); Parvin, *Authorization of Textbooks* 38–9; *Annual Report of the Local Superintendent … Toronto* (1865) 50; TBEHC, James Porter Diary, vol. 3, Mar. 1866

22 Cf Elson, *Guardians of Tradition* 2, and Bruce Curtis, 'The Speller Expelled: Disciplining the Common Reader in Canada West, 1846–50,' *Canadian Review of Sociology and Anthropology* 22 (Aug. 1985) 346–68

23 E. Ryerson 'Report on a System of Public Elementary Instruction for Upper

Canada,' *DHE* vol. 6, 170–1; Robert Sullivan, *The Spelling-Book Superseded; Or, a New and Easy Method of Teaching the Spelling, Meaning, Pronunciation and Etymology of All the Difficult Words in the English Language with Exercises on Verbal Distinctions* 18th ed. (Dublin 1850)

24 Alison Prentice, *The School Promoters: Education and Social Class in Mid-Nineteenth Century Upper Canada* (Toronto: McClelland and Stewart 1977) 76–9; C.E. Phillips, 'The Teaching of English in Ontario, 1800–1900' (D PAED diss., University of Toronto 1935); Margaret Hoddinott, 'On the Teaching of Writing in Upper Canada in the First Half of the Nineteenth Century' (Ms, Department of History, York University 1985). There were no desks for *Second Book* pupils in Toronto until 1874 (*ARUC* [1874] App. B, 84).

25 E. Ryerson, 'Public Elementary Instruction,' *DHE* vol. 6, 182–5; *JEUC* 18 (June 1865) 96; 'E.R. to Chas. Coburn, Pennsylvania,' *DHE* vol. 19, 67–9; Parvin, *Authorization of Textbooks* 33–4, 38–9; *A Brief History* 8; A.G. Croal, 'The History of the Teaching of Science in Ontario, 1800–1900' (D PAED diss., University of Toronto 1940) chs 2, 3; E.J. Quick, 'The Development of Geography and History Curricula in the Elementary Schools of Ontario, 1846–1966' (D ED diss., University of Toronto 1967) chs 2, 3

26 *DHE* vol. 6, 193, 299–300

27 *ARUC* (1847) *DHE* vol. 7, 165; *ARUC* (1857) 18–21; R.D. Gidney and D.A. Lawr, 'Bureaucracy *vs.* Community?: The Origins of Bureaucratic Procedures in the Upper Canadian School System,' *Journal of Social History* 13 (Spring 1980) 445, 449–50; W.D. Edison Matthews, 'The History of the Religious Factor in Ontario Elementary Education' (D PAED diss., University of Toronto 1950) 103–5

28 Simcoe County Archives, Neil J. Campbell Ms (Diary and school census SS 7, Oro Township) 82; *Fraser Report* 293 ff, and see especially 248–51, in which Fraser reproduces all mention of religious instruction in 152 local superintendents' reports for 1863.

29 E. Ryerson, 'Public Elementary Instruction,' *DHE* vol. 6, 193

30 *ARUC* (1850) App. A, 156

31 'Minimum Qualifications for Second Class Teachers, 1850,' *DHE* vol. 9, 220. On 31 Dec. 1858 the Council of Public Instruction officially prescribed a course of study for each of the three divisions in the common school, *DHE* vol. 14, 63–4.

32 *Fraser Report* 206, 241, 242

33 Toronto Board of School Trustees, *Report of the Past History and Present Condition of the Common or Public Schools of the City of Toronto* (Toronto 1859) 58–63, 108–25; *Annual Report of the Local Superintendent ... Toronto* (1875) table H; 'Nineteen Years' Progress of the Hamilton City Schools, 1850–1869,' in J. George Hodgins, ed., *Schools and Colleges of Ontario, 1792–1910* (Toronto 1911) vol. 1, 75–6; *ARUC* (1868) London, App. A, 108–11; Rev. George Blair,

Address to the School Trustees, Parents and Common School Teachers of the County of Durham C.W. (Bowmanville 1866); Honora M. Cochrane, ed., *Centennial Story: The Board of Education for the City of Toronto 1850–1950* (Toronto 1950)

34 Prentice, *The School Promoters* 152–3; Dyas, 'The World View Presented to Children'; Toronto Board, *Report of the Past History and Present Condition* 61; Cochrane, *Centennial Story* 43, 45

35 *DHE* vol. 17, 236; *ARUC* (1863) 18–19; ibid. App. A, 151; *DHE* vol. 18, 93

36 *Globe* 14 Nov. 1853; *ARUC* (1866) App. A, 46; also Pt 1, 26

37 'Report and Suggestions with Respect to the County Grammar (now High) Schools of Ontario for the Year 1870,' *DHE* vol. 22, 246

38 Reminiscences, *DHE* vol. 28: George Peters 275; Hugh Lucas 277; Ellen Bowes 261

39 Bruce Curtis, 'Curricular Change and the Red Readers: History and Theory' (Paper presented at the Goodson Seminar, University of Western Ontario, 2–3 Oct. 1986). Cf David Vincent, *Bread, Knowledge and Freedom: A Study of Nineteenth Century Working Class Autobiography* (London: Methuen 1982) ch. 7.

40 Bowes, *DHE* vol. 28, 260; TBEHC, James Porter Diary, vol. 1, 11 Apr. 1859; *Annual Report of the Local Superintendent ... Toronto* (1874) 20

41 Cf Stamp, *Schools of Ontario* 9 ff; Bruce Curtis, 'Preconditions of the Canadian State: Educational Reform and the Construction of a Public in Upper Canada, 1837–1846,' *Studies in Political Economy* 10 (Winter 1983) 108–10; Prentice, *The School Promoters* ch. 1; *DHE* vol. 6, 160, 159

42 *Toronto Normal School, Jubilee Celebration* (Toronto 1898) 24; TBEHC, James Porter Diary, vol. 1, 11 Apr. 1859. See also, W.P. McCann and Francis Young, *Samuel Wilderspin and the Infant School Movement* (London: Croom Helm 1982).

43 Daniel Calhoun, *The Intelligence of a People* (Princeton, NJ: Princeton University Press 1973) 108–11

44 E. Ryerson, 'Circular to Local Superintendents of Schools on the Sub-apportionment of the Legislative School Grant, 1855,' *DHE* vol. 11, 213; J. George Hodgins, *The School House: Its Architecture, External and Internal Arrangements* (Toronto: Lovell and Gibson 1857), 84

45 TBEHC, James Porter Diary, vol. 3, 26 May 1864, 8 May, 20 June 1866

46 *ARUC* (1861) App. to ch. 7, *DHE* vol. 17, 42

47 '7th Annual Convention of the Teachers' Association of the Province of Ontario,' *JEUC* 20 (Oct. 1867) 163

48 AO, Education Papers Collection, MU975 1860–9, Box 6, no. 6, Maria Payne Notebooks

49 TBEHC, James Porter Diary, vol. 3, 6 Mar. 1865

50 RG2 F-3-B, James Fotheringham to E.R., 27 Mar. 1871

51 'Report of Local Superintendent to County Council, United Counties of Northumberland and Durham, Jan. 1856,' *DHE* vol. 13, 21; RG2 C-6-C, J.H. Knight to editor of *JEUC* 17 Sept. 1861

52 George Paxton Young, 'Report with Regard to County Grammar Schools for 1867,' *DHE* vol. 20, 127; *The Normal School for Ontario: Its Design and Functions* (Toronto 1871) 75

53 'Report of the Committee on School Management,' *Annual Report of the Local Superintendent ... Toronto* (1865) 45–6

54 'Teachers' Association Annual Meetings,' *JEUC* 20 (Oct. 1867) 163

55 Blair, *Address* 7; C.B. Sissons, *Egerton Ryerson, His Life and Letters* vol. 2 (Toronto: Clarke, Irwin 1947) 630n1

56 Reminiscences, *DHE* vol. 6, 285–6, 306; Canniff Haight, *Country Life in Canada Fifty Years Ago: Personal Recollections and Reminiscences of a Sexagenarian* (Toronto: Hunter, Rose 1885) 159; University of Toronto, Thomas Fisher Rare Book Library, John George Hodgins, 'School Children's Manners: Official Regulations,' Ms nd

57 RG2 F-2, ser. 1, 1842–8: envelope 1, Sept. 1842; envelope 3

58 See especially Hodgins, 'School Children's Manners'; RG2 B, *Council of Public Instruction Minutes* vol. 2, 123, 327; *The Common School Acts of Upper Canada; and the Forms, Instructions and Regulations for Executing Their Provisions; together with the Circulars Addressed to the Various Officers Concerned in the Administration of the Law, by the Chief Superintendent of Schools* (Toronto 1853); J. George Hodgins, ed., *The Laws Relating to Common Schools in the Rural Sections of Upper Canada, together with the Forms, General Regulations and Instructions for Executing Their Provisions* (Toronto 1859); 'General Regulations for the Organization, Government and Discipline of Common Schools in Upper Canada,' *ARUC* (1858) App. E; Toronto Board, *Report of the Past History and Present Condition* 66–8; 'Address to Parents and Guardians,' *Annual Report of the Local Superintendent ... Toronto* (1869) 86–91; ibid. (1875) 51–6

59 For example, Reminiscences, *DHE* vol. 28, 255–60, 265; RG2 C-6-C, Otto Plotz to E.R., 27 June 1861; John Fletcher to E.R., 5 Apr. 1861; Binbrook and Saltfleet, 29 Jan. 1868 (no. 1151); *Fraser Report* 208; 'Visit of the Prince of Wales, 1860,' *DHE* vol. 16, 118–35; *JEUC* 20 (Jan. 1867) 1

60 *ARUC* (1874) App. B, 84; TBEHC, James Porter Diary, vol. 3, 23 Feb., 22 Mar. 1865; Prentice, *The School Promoters* 149 ff

61 *ARUC* (1869) *DHE* vol. 22, 79–80

62 For reaction see: RG2 C-6-C, Wm Ormiston, Hamilton, to E.R., 1 Mar. 1861; *ARUC* (1860) App. A, especially 170, 190; *ARUC* (1861) App. A, 168; *ARUC* (1863) App. A, 144; *ARUC* (1864) App. A, 64

63 'Waterloo, 1854,' *DHE* vol. 13, 72–3; 'Prize Books Given, 1857–61,' *ARUC* (1861) Pt 2, 123

64 *ARUC* (1865) Pt 1, 9; *JEUC* 18 (May 1865) 65–9

65 Bowes, *DHE* vol. 28, 261

66 Carl F. Kaestle, *Pillars of the Republic: Common Schools and American Society, 1780–1860* (New York: Hill and Wang 1983) 67–9

67 *ARUC* (1869) *DHE* vol. 22, 78–9

68 The evidence on this point is scattered and impressionistic. For a sampling, cf RG2 C-6-C, Hawkesville, 4 Mar. 1861; TBEHC, James Porter Diary, vol. 3, 13 July 1864; *Niagara Observer* 1 July 1867; 'Toronto City Common Schools,' *JEUC* 16 (Aug. 1863) 126–7.

69 RG2 C-6-C, Markham, 11 Apr. 1856. The heavy use of occasional teachers in Toronto certainly undercut the notional advantage a large city school system might enjoy in terms of permanency of appointments.

70 *Shorter Oxford English Dictionary* vol. 2, 2000 (1711 usage)

71 'Inspectors' General Report on the State of the Grammar Schools in 1856,' *DHE* vol. 12, 329

72 'Report and Suggestions with Respect to the County Grammar Schools,' *ARUC* (1866) Pt 1, 28–9; see also 'Inspectors' Report and Suggestions,' *ARUC* (1865) App. B, 75–6; *ARUC* (1867) Pt 1, 53–5, 62–3

73 TBEHC, James Porter Diary, vol. 1, 26 May 1859; 'Report and Suggestions,' *DHE* vol. 23, 163; Prentice, *The School Promoters* 76–8

74 'Ontario Teachers' Association Meetings, 1869,' *DHE* vol. 21, 292; Ontario Grammar School Masters' Association, *DHE* vol. 21, 306; Calhoun, *Intelligence of a People* 79–81, 130; 'Report and Suggestions,' *ARUC* (1868) Pt 1, 30

75 TBEHC, James Porter Diary, vol. 1, 2, 3 Sept. 1859; *Annual Report of the Local Superintendent ... Toronto* (1864); ibid. (1868) 11; 'The Public Schools of Ontario,' *Canadian Monthly and National Review* 1 (June 1872) 487

76 'Ontario Teachers' Association Meetings,' *DHE* vol. 25, 222

77 'Programme of Course of Study for Public Schools, 1871,' *DHE* vol. 23, 83

78 'Communications from Edwin Chadwick, Esq., C.B., Respecting Half-time and Military and Naval Drill, and on the Time and Cost of Popular Education on a Large and a Small Scale,' and 'Letter to N.W. Senior, Esq., One of Her Majesty's Commissioners for Inquiring into the State of Popular Education,' *Parliamentary Papers* 43 (1862) Pt 1, 1–159; E.A. Meredith, *Short School Time, with Military or Naval Drill, in Connection Especially with the Subject of an Efficient Militia System* (Quebec 1865); also *DHE* vol. 19, 145–8. Meredith's private life is portrayed in Sandra Gwyn's *The Private Capital: Ambition and Love in the Age of Macdonald and Laurier* (Toronto: McClelland and Stewart 1984); see also Harold Silver, 'Ideology and the Factory Child: Attitudes to Half-time Education,' in McCann, *Popular Education* 141–66, especially 154.

79 'Ontario Teachers' Association Meetings, 1869,' *DHE* vol. 21, 291, 292

80 Gillian Sutherland, *Policy Making in Elementary Education, 1870–95* (Oxford: Oxford University Press 1973) 7–8

81 *Fraser Report* 238–40

82 Ibid. 242; also *DHE* vol. 18, 98–9

83 'Inspector's Report upon the State of the County Grammar Schools of the Eastern Half of the Eastern Section of Upper Canada for the Year 1860,' *DHE* vol. 16, 148–9

CHAPTER 9 *Exceptions to the Rule*

1 *Globe* 13 Jan. 1852, also *DHE* vol. 10, 274–7. It is intriguing to compare the version of this story that Professor Goldwin Smith, ever sceptical of Ryerson's educational policies, included in his presidential address to the Ontario Teachers' Association in 1873: 'No sight gave him greater pleasure than to see in the Chicago schools the children of wealthy Parents sitting side by side with the shoeless children of Emigrants. If they could introduce a feeling of brotherhood into society he would hail the day joyfully,' he told his audience, 'but they must not attempt to do it by force.' *DHE* vol. 26, 64

2 Susan E. Houston, 'Politics, Schools, and Social Change in Upper Canada,' *CHR* 53 (Sept. 1972) 264–5

3 *ARUC* (1852) 130

4 An Act to Make further Provision for the Establishment of Common Schools throughout the Province, 4 and 5 Vict. (1841) cap. 18. esp. sect. 11; see also Supreme Court of Ontario Court of Appeal, 'Respecting Bill 30: Howland C.J.O. and Robins J.A. (dissenting),' 10–11; Robert M. Stamp, 'The Historical Background to Separate Schools in Ontario: Final Report' (Toronto: Ministry of Education, Ontario, June 1985) 2.

5 *DHE* vol. 10, 176

6 John S. Moir, *Church and State in Canada West: Three Studies in the Relation of Denominationalism and Nationalism 1841–1867* (Toronto: University of Toronto Press 1959) 132

7 Ibid. ch. 6; Franklin A. Walker, *Catholic Education and Politics in Upper Canada: A Study of the Documentation Relative to the Origin of Catholic Elementary Schools in the Ontario School System* (Toronto: Federation of Catholic Education Associations of Ontario 1955)

8 Moir, *Church and State* 132

9 An Act for the Establishment and Maintenance of Common Schools in Upper Canada, 7 Vict. (1843) cap. 29, sect. 55, 56

10 An Act for the Better Establishment and Maintenance of Common Schools in Upper Canada, 13 and 14 Vict. (1850) cap. 48, sect. 24; also E.R. to Stephen Lett, 27 Apr. 1858, *DHE* vol. 13, 227

11 Estimates vary. Cf E.R., 'Circular to the Town Reeves, 1850,' *DHE* vol. 9, 208: *ARUC* (1850) 14–15; *ARUC* (1852) 20; *Mirror* 15 Aug. 1851, 22 Apr. 1853; Moir, *Church and State* 144

12 Angus Dallas, *The Common School System: Its Principle, Operation and Results*

(Toronto 1855); *Appeal on the Common School Law: Its Incongruety and Malad-
ministration, Setting forth the Necessity for a Minister of Public Instruction
Responsible to Parliament* (Toronto: Office of the Catholic *Citizen* 1858). A Protestant (pseud.), *Statistics of the Common Schools: Being a Digest and Comparison of the Evidence Furnished by the Local Superintendents and the Chief
Superintendent ... in a Series of Seven Letters to the Hon. J.A. Macdonald*
(Toronto: Office of the Catholic *Citizen* 1857); *Suggestions on the Organization
of a System of Common Schools ... in a Series of Three Letters to Hon. J.A.
Macdonald* (Toronto: Office of the Catholic *Citizen*); Adam Townley, *Seven Letters on the Non-Religious Common School System of Canada and the United
States* (Toronto: Henry Russell 1853)

13 An excellent recent study of American education is Carl Kaestle, *Pillars of the
Republic: Common Schools and American Society, 1780–1860* (New York: Hill
and Wang 1983).

14 Loyal Orange Association of British North America, *Grand Lodge Annual Report,
1849* (Toronto 1849) 13–14

15 *Echo and Protestant Episcopal Recorder* 7 Mar., 28 May, 6 June 1856; Proceedings of the Synod of the Diocese of Toronto, June 1858, *DHE* vol. 13, 273–6.
Moir, *Church and State* 161–2. It is impossible to gauge the extent to which local
school trustees might have bent the regulations to accommodate their Catholic
neighbours. In Collingwood in the mid-1860s, apparently in order to avoid a sectarian split, the regulations were compromised to the extent that the Bible was
used as the reading book one day a week. *ARUC* (1866) App. A, 60. The Rev.
James Fraser, visiting British schools commissioner, analysed all the material
in the local superintendents' reports for 1863 pertaining to religious instruction;
Fraser Report 250–1

16 *Copies of Correspondence between the Roman Catholic Bishop of Toronto and
the Chief Superintendent of Schools on the Subject of Separate Schools in Upper
Canada: With an Appendix* (Quebec 1852); *Copies of Correspondence between
the Chief Superintendent of Schools for Upper Canada and Other Persons on the
Subject of Separate Schools* (Toronto 1855); *Controversy between Dr. Ryerson,
Chief Superintendent of Education in Upper Canada and Rev. J.M. Bruyère,
Rector of St. Michael's Cathedral, Toronto, on the Appropriation of the Clergy
Reserves Fund, Free schools vs. State Schools, Public Libraries and Common
Schools, Attacked and Defended* (Toronto: Leader in Patriot Steam Press 1857);
*Dr. Ryerson's Letter in Reply to the Attacks of Foreign Ecclesiastics against
the Schools and Municipalities of Upper Canada* (Toronto 1857); *Dr. Ryerson's
Letters in Reply to the Attacks of the Hon. George Brown M.P.P.* (Toronto 1859)

17 Egerton Ryerson, *Special Report on the Separate Schools Provision of the School
Law of Upper Canada* (Quebec 1858) 18; Stamp, 'Historical Background to
Separate Schools'; Alison Prentice and Susan Laskin, 'Ontario Separate Schools,
1856–1891,' *Historical Atlas of Canada*, vol. 2, forthcoming

18 The literature is too extensive to survey here. In addition to the works previously cited, see Franklin A. Walker, *Catholic Education and Politics in Ontario: A Documentary Study* (Toronto: Thomas Nelson 1964); *Report of the Royal Commission on Education in Ontario, 1950*, J.A. Hope, chairman (Toronto: King's Printer 1950); E.F. Henderson et al., *Historical Sketch of the Separate Schools of Ontario and the Catholic Separate School Minority Report* (Toronto: English Catholic Education Association of Ontario 1950); C.B. Sissons, *Egerton Ryerson, His Life and Letters* (Toronto: Clarke, Irwin 1947) vol. 2, 254–60, 327–31.

19 Walker, *Catholic Education ... in Upper Canada* 79–83

20 The discussion of Irish migration that follows is indebted to the work of Donald Harmon Akenson, *The Irish in Ontario: A Study in Rural History* (Kingston and Montreal: McGill-Queen's University Press 1984) ch. 1.

21 *Mirror* 12 Dec. 1856

22 The phrase is borrowed from Charlotte J. Erickson, *Invisible Immigrants: The Adaptation of English and Scottish Immigrants in Nineteenth Century America* (Coral Gables, Fla.: University of Miami Press 1972). See also Gordon A. Darroch and Michael Ornstein, 'Ethnicity and Occupational Structure in Canada in 1871: The Vertical Mosaic in Historical Perspective,' *CHR* 61 (Sept. 1980) 305–30; and 'Ethnicity and Class: Transitions over a Decade: Ontario 1861–71,' Canadian Historical Association *Annual Report* (1984) 111–37.

23 The local press is the best source for details on the impact of the Famine migration; see especially Toronto *Mirror* 18 Feb. 1848, 5 Oct. 1849; *Globe* 21 June, 1, 22 July 1848; G.J. Parr, 'The Welcome and the Wake: Attitudes in Canada West toward the Irish Famine Migration,' *OH* 64 (1974) 101–13.

24 Akenson, *Irish in Ontario* 34; also *Being Had: Historians, Evidence and the Irish in North America* (Toronto: P.D. Meany Publishers 1985)

25 Moir, *Church and State* 144–5

26 J.S. Moir concluded that Bishop Power shared Egerton Ryerson's view that separate Catholic schools were 'an unfortunate necessity' (ibid. 138); Franklin Walker disagreed, dating Catholic commitment to the principle of Catholic education from the early 1840s (*Catholic Education ... in Upper Canada* 54–5, 313); J. Donald Wilson concluded that 'the attitude remained unchanged but pressure mounted' with the arrival of Bishop de Charbonnel (J.D. Wilson, R.M. Stamp, and L-P. Audet, *Canadian Education: A History* [Toronto: Prentice-Hall 1970] 235). D.H. Akenson has sketched a parallel between the positions adopted by influential Irish prelates in the 1840s and 1850s and the Canadian case, in *Being Had* 174–80.

27 *DHE* vol. 10, 90–1, 266–70; vol. 11, 80–9; *Copies of Correspondence between the Bishop and the Chief Superintendent* (1852) App. 28, 55–6; *Copies of Correspondence between the Chief Superintendent and Other Persons* (1855), 168–77, 209–26; Walker, *Catholic Education ... in Upper Canada*, 95–108

28 E.R. to Hon. Francis Hincks and Dr John Rolph, 1 Aug. 1851, *DHE* vol. 10, 90–1

29 De Charbonnel to E.R., 1 May 1852, *Copies of Correspondence between the Bishop and the Chief Superintendent* (1852)

30 E.R. to J.G. Hodgins, 13 Mar. 1851, Sissons, *Egerton Ryerson* vol. 2, 220

31 Akenson, *Being Had* ch. 6; also *A Protestant in Purgatory: Richard Whately, Archbishop of Dublin* (Hamden, Conn.: Archon Books for Conference on British Studies and Indiana University 1981) 166–7; and *The Irish Education Experiment: The National System of Education in the Nineteenth Century* (London: Routledge and Kegan Paul 1970)

32 Carl Kaestle, *Evolution of an Urban School System: New York City, 1750–1850* (Cambridge, Mass.: Harvard University Press 1973) 151–8; Selwyn K. Troen, *The Public and the Schools: Shaping the St. Louis System, 1838–1920* (Columbia: University of Missouri Press 1975) ch. 2. The Toronto *Mirror* noted Bishop (soon Archbishop) Hughes's statements on Catholic schooling; see especially 17 Nov. 1854.

33 *Copies of Correspondence between the Bishop and the Chief Superintendent* (1852) 245; Walker, *Catholic Education ... in Upper Canada* 117–20; for reminiscences of its use in the 1850s and 1860s, see *DHE* vol. 28, 243, 245, 278, 280.

34 Lingard's *History of England* was allegedly censored by Protestant school trustees, *Mirror* 8, 15 Feb. 1856.

35 Walker, *Catholic Education ... in Upper Canada* 182; also Township of Williams case, *Copies of Correspondence between the Chief Superintendent and Other Persons* (1855) 209–26

36 Ibid.

37 RG2 C-6-C, Adam Ullman to E.R., 6 Dec. 1869

38 Walker, *Catholic Education ... in Upper Canada* 106–7

39 See, for example, the many letters from local Catholic trustees complaining of the 1853 act, and Ryerson's replies: *Copies of Correspondence between the Chief Superintendent and Other Persons* (1855) 55–232; Hon. J. Elmsley to E.R., 4 Mar. 1857, *DHE* vol. 13, 164–8; Alison Prentice, *The School Promoters: Education and Social Class in Mid-Nineteenth Century Upper Canada* (Toronto: McClelland and Stewart 1977) 73–7; *Canadian Freeman* 1 Mar. 1865.

40 J. George Hodgins, ed., *'The Story of My Life' by the late Rev. Egerton Ryerson* (Toronto 1883) ch. 45; Sissons, *Egerton Ryerson* vol. 2, 342–3; C.B. Sissons, ed., *My Dearest Sophie: Letters from Egerton Ryerson to His Daughter* (Toronto: Ryerson Press 1955) xxix, xxxi–xxxii

41 In 1955 Franklin Walker offered a significantly different assessment of Ryerson's handling of the separate school issue: 'Much bitterness would have been prevented if Ryerson had shown more readiness to compromise, and to understand

the Catholic position. But the basic difference could not be met: Ryerson so disliked the very notion of separate schools that he thought they necessarily must be in an inferior position.' *Catholic Education ... in Upper Canada*, 314

42 RG2 C-6-C, James Feagan to E.R., 5 Mar. 1859; reprinted in Alison L. Prentice and Susan E. Houston, eds, *Family, School and Society in Nineteenth Century Canada* (Toronto: Oxford University Press 1975) 158–9

43 Akenson, *Irish in Ontario* 276; Walker *Catholic Education ... in Ontario*, 15n32

44 E.R. to Pierre Chauvreau, 3 May 1864, *DHE* vol. 18, 197–8; *ARUC* (1870) *DHE* vol. 22, 81–2

45 RG2 C-6-C, F. Rynn to J.G.H., 19 Jan. 1861. The issues of common school teachers who were allegedly only nominal Catholics but whose presence precluded the founding of a separate school arose sporadically; cf *Mirror* 22 Apr. 1853, 27 May, 25 Aug. 1854.

46 *ARUC* (1865) 24; Walker, *Catholic Education ... in Upper Canada*, 295n13

47 RG2 C-6-C, J.A. Murdock, Bathurst, to E.R., 7 Mar. 1857; also Akenson, *Irish in Ontario* 276–7

48 'Reminiscences of Superannuated School Teachers, 1850–51,' *DHE* vol. 9, 300

49 Marvin McInnis and Heather Tremble, 'School Attendance of Farm Children in 1861: A Preliminary Work' (Ms 1983) 17

50 David Gagan, *Hopeful Travellers: Families, Land and Social Change in Mid-Victorian Peel County, Canada West*, Ontario Historical Studies Series (Toronto: University of Toronto Press 1981) 82–3

51 Rev. M.M. O'Shea to Bishop John Farrell, 18 July 1864, cited in Walker, *Catholic Education ... in Ontario* 23n51; see also 24–9

52 For a general discussion of the 'inferiority' of separate schools, see Walker, *Catholic Education ... in Ontario*, 13–21.

53 'Reminiscences of superannuated teachers,' *DHE* vol. 28, 276–7. For a general characterization of Catholic elementary textbooks of the period, see J.M. Goldstrom, *The Social Content of Education, 1808–1870: A Study of the Working Class School Reader in England and Ireland* (Shannon: Irish University Press 1972) 118–19, 130.

54 Bruce W. Hodgins, 'John Sandfield Macdonald,' in J.M.S. Careless, ed., *The Pre-Confederation Premiers: Ontario Government Leaders, 1841–1867*, Ontario Historical Studies Series (Toronto: University of Toronto Press 1980) 258–9; see also *Mirror* 4 Apr. 1856

55 *Mirror* 11 June 1847; also 5, 12 Feb., 11 Oct. 1847. The issue of the relative extent of the economic and social marginality of Irish Catholics in Upper Canadian towns and cities in the decade of the 1850s has not been resolved by historians. In addition to the works by Akenson and Darroch and Ornstein previously cited, see especially Michael B. Katz's two volumes on the social structure of Hamilton in this period: *The People of Hamilton, Canada West: Family and Class in a*

Mid-Nineteenth Century City (Cambridge, Mass.: Harvard University Press 1975) and M.B. Katz, M.T. Doucet, and M.J. Stern, *The Social Organization of Early Industrial Capitalism* (Cambridge, Mass.: Harvard University Press 1982).

56 Letter to the editor from Guelph, *Mirror* 11 Apr. 1856

57 Letter to the editor, *Mirror* 28 Mar. 1856

58 *Mirror* 20 Mar., 3 Apr. 1857

59 Walker, *Catholic Education ... in Ontario* 19; Murray W. Nicolson, 'Irish Catholic Education in Victorian Toronto: An Ethnic Response to Urban Conformity,' *HS/SH* 34 (Nov. 1984) 287–306

60 *Toronto in Camera: A Series of Photographic Views of the Principal Buildings in the City of Toronto* (Toronto 1868) no. 46

61 Jessie Middleton, *The Municipality of Toronto* (Toronto: Dominion Publishing 1923) vol. 2, 592–3; J.R. Teefy, *Jubilee Volume, 1842–92: The Archdiocese of Toronto and Archbishop Walsh* (Toronto: Geo. T. Dixon 1892) 268–72

62 RG2 F-3-F, Box 1, Roman Catholic Separate School Annual Reports 1852–71, Kingston; L.J. Flynn, *At School in Kingston 1850–1873* (1973) ch. 3; John K.A. Farrell, 'The History of the Roman Catholic Church in London, Ontario, 1826–1931' (MA diss., University of Western Ontario 1949) App. H: First Annual Report of the Roman Catholic Separate School Board, Dec. 31 1858; T.J. O'Neil to Board of School Trustees, Toronto, 20 Apr. 1852, *Copies of Correspondence between the Bishop and the Chief Superintendent* (1852) App. 29; Nicolson, 'Irish Catholic Education,' 295; Walker, *Catholic Education ... in Upper Canada* 152–3

63 Ian E. Davey, 'School Reform and School Attendance: The Hamilton Central School, 1853–61' (MA diss., University of Toronto 1972) 64; 'Apportionment of the Legislative School Grant for Common Schools, 1868,' *JEUC* (June 1868) 83; TBEHC, James Porter Diary, vol. 1, 15 Apr. 1859; *Mirror* 4 Apr. 1856; Nicolson, 'Irish Catholic Education,' 296n37. It was estimated that the opening of separate schools in Hamilton drew 1,000 students or potential students (roughly 20 per cent) from the central system, J.G. Hodgins, ed., *Schools and Colleges of Ontario, 1792–1910* (Toronto: King's Printer 1910) vol. 2, 149.

64 Walker, *Catholic Education ... in Upper Canada* 181

65 William R. Bigg, Esq., Brockville, to E.R., *ARUC* (1873) Ontario, *Sessional Papers* 3 (1874) 75; RG2 C-6-C, H.H. Oliver, Paris, to E.R., 1 Mar. 1857; 'Report of the Grammar School Inspector,' *ARUC* (1865) 78–9; 'Report of the Select Committee on School Attendance, Toronto Board of School Trustees,' *Globe* 16 Nov. 1865; J.G. Hodgins to Remigius Elmsley, 31 Jan. 1876, summarized in Walker, *Catholic Education ... in Ontario,* 18, 33

66 A Citizen to the *Mirror: Letter* IV, *The Question of Separate Schools, Discussed in a Series of Letters and Other Articles that Appeared in the Toronto* Mirror *and Montreal* True Witness *in Consequence of the Publication of the Correspondence*

between His Lordship the Rt. Rev. Dr. De Charbonnel, Bishop of Toronto, and the Rev. Dr. Ryerson (Toronto 1853) 11; Walker, *Catholic Education ... in Ontario* 20; Katz, *People of Hamilton* 286–7, 289–90

67 Franklin Walker concluded that there was 'little foundation' to allegations of coercion; in the 1870s there may well have been restless 'murmurings,' however, as the *Canadian Freeman* alleged (31 Aug. 1871) *Catholic Education ... in Ontario* 20–2.

68 Nicolson, 'Irish Catholic Education,' 291

69 TBEHC, W.C. Wilkinson Diary, vol. 2, 21 Feb. 1873; also vol. 1, 14, 17, 29, 30 May, 4, 6, 12, 25 June, 6 Sept. 1872. For recent analyses of the antipathy between Orange and Green, see Gregory S. Kealey, 'Orangemen and the Corporation,' in Victor L. Russell, ed., *Forging a Consensus: Historical Essays on Toronto* (Toronto: University of Toronto Press for the Toronto Sesquicentennial Board 1984) 41–86; 'The Orange Order in Toronto: Religious Riot and the Working Class,' in G.S. Kealey and Peter Warrian, eds, *Essays in Canadian Working Class History* (Toronto: McClelland and Stewart 1976) vol. 1, 13–54; J.R. Miller, 'Anti-Catholic Thought in Victorian Canada,' *CHR* 66 (Dec. 1985) 474–94. The most exhaustive work to date on the Orange Order is Cecil Houston and William J. Smyth, *The Sash Canada Wore: A Historical Geography of the Orange Order in Canada* (Toronto: University of Toronto Press 1980).

70 Nicolson, 'Irish Catholic Education,' 296–302

71 *Mirror* 19 Dec. 1856; 7 Dec. 1855. By the late 1850s the *Mirror* kept a watchful eye on the performance of separate school youngsters. The paper's correspondent flinched at the brogue used in a play performed by the pupils of the Sisters of St Joseph (25 July 1856) considering that at least part of the school's function was to eradicate its use among the Irish in Canada; deplored a certain hastiness in the replies of the boys at a Christian Brothers school (19 Mar. 1858); and applauded the Brothers' determination to enforce discipline by demanding notes from home when students had been absent (25 May 1855).

72 Toronto Board of School Trustees, *Report of the Past History and Present Condition of the Common or Public Schools of the City of Toronto* (Toronto 1859) 43; *Copies of Correspondence between the Bishop and the Chief Superintendent* (1852) 25; *Copies of Correspondence between the Chief Superintendent and Other Persons* (1855) 50; *Dr. Ryerson's Letters ... to Foreign Ecclesiastics* 47

73 *ARUC* (1857) 24

74 *Mirror* 22 Aug. 1851, 23 Apr. 1858

75 For background see Robin W. Winks, *The Blacks in Canada* (New Haven, Conn.: Yale University Press 1971). Indispensable are two well-known contemporary sources: Benjamin Drew, *North-side View of Slavery: The Refugee, or the Narratives of Fugitive Slaves Related by Themselves, with an Account of the History and Condition of the Coloured Population of Upper Canada* (Cleveland: John P.

Jewett and Co. 1856); and Samuel Gridley Howe, *The Refugees from Slavery in Canada West: Report to the Freedmen's Inquiry Commission* (Boston 1864).

76 William H. Pease and Jane H. Pease, *Black Utopia: Negro Communal Experiments in America* (Madison: State Historical Society of Wisconsin 1963) 49

77 Daniel G. Hill, 'Negroes in Toronto, 1793–1865,' *OH* 55 (1963) 76–8; see also F.H. Armstrong, 'The Toronto Directories and the Negro Community in the late 1840s,' *OH* 61 (June 1969) 111–19.

78 Howard Law, ' "Self-reliance Is the True Road to Independence": Ideology and the Ex-Slaves in Buxton and Chatham,' *OH* 77 (June 1985) 107–21; Fred Landon, 'The Work of the American Missionary Association among the Negro Refugees in Canada West, 1848–1864,' *OH* 21 (1924) 198–205

79 Pease and Pease, *Black Utopia* esp. 66–7

80 Ibid. ch. 5; Victor Ullman, *Look to the North Star: A Life of William King* (Boston and Toronto: Beacon Press / Saunders 1969) 103–230

81 Pease and Pease, *Black Utopia* 98

82 For a discussion of the extradition proceedings under the terms of the Webster-Ashburton Treaty of 1842 in the case of John Anderson, see Patrick Brode, *Sir John Beverley Robinson: Bone and Sinew of the Compact* (Toronto: The Osgoode Society 1984) 264–7; Fred Landon, 'Social Conditions among the Negroes in Upper Canada before 1865,' *OH* 22 (1925) 144–6; Pease and Pease, *Black Utopia* 8.

83 Law, ' "Self-Reliance," ' 108; *Liberator* 10 Oct. 1851. Apparently the black residents of St Catharines were forcibly relocated from Queenston Street to North Street in the 1850s; eventually many ended up on Welland Street. *St. Catharines Standard* 22 Nov. 1960

84 Ibid.; Landon, 'Social Conditions,' 157–8

85 Law, ' "Self-Reliance," ' 117

86 *Provincial Freeman* 26 Feb. 1852, cited in Hill, 'Negroes in Toronto,' 31–2

87 Pease and Pease, *Black Utopia* ch. 4; letter to the editor from 'Diogenes,' *Globe* 3 Jan. 1863, reprinted in Prentice and Houston, *Family, School and Society* 236–40; Landon, 'Social Conditions,' 156–7; Robin W. Winks, 'Negro School Segregation in Ontario and Nova Scotia,' *CHR* 50 (June 1969) 171

88 Quoted in Hill, 'Negroes in Toronto,' 88

89 *Voice of the Fugitive* 1 Jan. 1852, quoted in Landon, 'Social Conditions,' 151

90 John Strachan to John Macaulay, 9 Aug. 1838, cited in Wilson, Stamp, and Audet, *Canadian Education* 232n49

91 *Mirror of Parliament of the Province of Canada March 20–June 9, 1846* (Montreal 1846) 21 Apr. 1846, 87

92 See especially the correspondence respecting the petition from Hamilton, 1843, *DHE* vol. 4, 312–13.

93 Isaac J. Rice to E.R., Amherstburg, 23 Jan. 1846, *DHE* vol. 6, 294

94 Winks, 'Negro School Segregation,' 176–80; *DHE* vol. 7, 211

95 E.R. to J.G.H., Kingston, 27 Feb. 1860, *DHE* vol. 16, 94–5; RG2 C-6-C, Box 174, 209–10, 212

96 Winks, 'Negro School Segregation,' 171; Ullman, *Look to the North Star* 146–56; Law, ' "Self-Reliance," ' 113

97 Hamilton petition, *DHE* vol. 4, 313; Teachers' Association annual meeting, 1864, 1865, E.C. Guillet, *In the Cause of Education: A Centennial History of the Ontario Education Association, 1861–1960* (Toronto: University of Toronto Press 1960) 31, 35

98 *Annual Report of the Local Superintendent ... Toronto* (1864) 35; ibid. (1869) 40

99 TBEHC, James Porter Diary, vol. 1, 3 Oct. 1859; Toronto Board, 'School Discipline as to Teachers,' *Past History and Present Condition* 65–6

100 University of Western Ontario Regional Collection M315, London School Board, Minutes 1861–3

101 Francis G. Carter, *Judicial Decisions on Denominational Schools* (Toronto: Ontario Separate School Trustees Association 1962) 132–5; 'Dennis Hill *vs.* Camden and Zone,' reprinted in Prentice and Houston, *Family, School and Society* 240–4; see also editorial and letter to the editor from 'Diogenes,' *Globe* 3 Jan. 1863; H.W. Arthurs, 'Civil Liberties, Public Schools, Segregation of Negro Students,' *Canadian Bar Review* 41 (Sept. 1963).

102 Law, ' "Self-Reliance" ' 110, 116–17

103 The consequences of the funding formula appeared straightforward: 'any irregularity of attendance on the part of pupils of our Schools, not merely affects their progress in useful Knowledge, but by diminishing our averages, decreases our share of the Grant, and, by consequence, adds to the amount required to be raised by taxation for School purposes.' Report of Finance Committee for 1855, *Copies of Documents Relating to the Common Schools of the City, Forwarded by the Board of School Trustees to the City Council* (Toronto 1858) 21

104 John Roaf to the editor, *Globe* 31 Jan., 3, 5, 7, 17, 28 Feb. 1852

105 'Report #10, 6 May, 1856,' *Copies of Documents* 14–15, reprinted in Prentice and Houston, *Family, School and Society* 99–101

106 Toronto Board, *Past History and Present Condition* 71–2; 'Report #25, 1 Dec. 1857,' reprinted in Prentice and Houston, *Family, School and Society* 102

107 Susan E. Houston, 'School Reform and Education: The Issue of Compulsory Schooling, Toronto 1851–71,' in Neil McDonald and Alf Chaiton, eds, *Egerton Ryerson and His Times* (Toronto: Macmillan 1978) 264; *Globe* 19 June 1862

108 *Brown's Toronto General Directory, 1861* (Toronto W.C. Chewett and Co. 1861)

109 *ARUC* (1863) 156

110 RG2 C-6-C, Wm Ormiston to E.R., 1 Mar. 1861

111 R.D. Gidney and W.P.J. Millar, 'From Voluntarism to State Schooling: The Creation of the Public School System in Ontario,' *CHR* 66 (Dec. 1985) 442–73

112 *ARUC* (1863) 150–5

113 TBEHC, James Porter Diary, vol. 2, 24 Apr. 1865
114 TBEHC, W.C. Wilkinson Diary, vol. 1, 14 May 1872, reprinted in Prentice and Houston, *Family, School and Society* 167
115 Houston, 'School Reform and Education,' 254–76. See especially the annual reports of Samuel Woods, local superintendent in Kingston 1867–70, *ARUC* (1867) App. A, 45; *ARUC* (1869) App. D, 107; 'Report of an Annual Lecture by Mr. Samuel Woods,' *JEUC* 20 (June 1867) 110–11.
116 *DHE* vol. 17, 175–91
117 Report of the Teachers' Association, Hamilton, 6 Aug. 1862, *Globe* 7 Aug. 1862
118 Houston, 'School Reform and Education,' 267–70
119 Egerton Ryerson, 'The Importance of Education to a Manufacturing and a Free People,' *JEUC* (Oct. 1847) 300

CHAPTER 10 *'I Wish I Were Not Here at the Present Juncture'*

1 Egerton Ryerson, despite threatening to do so since 1869, did not retire until January 1876; John George Hodgins served as deputy minister until 1890; E.R. to J.G.H., 5 Mar. 1866, *DHE* vol. 19, 164: 'the efficiency and interests of the school system now requires that our policy should be consolidating and conservative.'
2 'Lecture on the Social Advancement of Canada,' Oct. 1849, *JEUC* 2 (Dec. 1849) 150; United Church Archives, Ryerson Papers, E.R. to Sophie, 31 July 1868
3 *JEUC* 2 (Dec. 1849) 147
4 Manufacturing school furniture had become 'a new branch of trade,' according to Ryerson in 1865, *DHE* vol. 19, 157.
5 R.D. Gidney and D.A. Lawr, 'Bureaucracy *vs.* Community?: The Origins of Bureaucratic Procedures in the Upper Canadian School System,' *Journal of Social History* 13 (Spring 1980) 438–57
6 George L. Parker, *The Beginnings of the Book Trade in Canada* (Toronto: University of Toronto Press 1985). The discussion that follows relies heavily on pages 97, 130, 137.
7 Hon. Peter De Blaquière to J.G.H., *JEUC* 13 (Nov. 1860) 167; Parker, *Beginnings of the Book Trade* 130. See also, Michael Denning, *Mechanic Accents: Dime Novels and Working Class Culture in America* (London: Verso 1987).
8 *Christian Guardian* editorial reprinted in *JEUC* 18 (Nov. 1865) 163–4; cf *JEUC* 14 (Apr. 1861) 49–51; (Toronto) *Ecclesiastical and Missionary Record* (1850) 171; London School Board Minutes, 6 Dec. 1864
9 Parker, *Beginnings of the Book Trade* 123
10 'Special Report on the Separate School Provision of the School Law of Upper Canada and the Measures which Have Been Adopted to Supply the Municipalities with School Textbooks, Apparatus and Libraries,' *Journal of the Legislative Assembly* (1858) App. 43; also *DHE* vol. 13, 280–306; Dianne Cameron,

'J. George Hodgins and Ontario Education, 1844–1912' (MA diss. University of Guelph 1976) ch. 3, especially 116

11 13 and 14 Vict. cap. 48, sect. 8, 9, 10. Under 18 Vict. (1855) cap. 132 the value of the annual legislative library grant was raised to £3,500.

12 *A General Catalogue of Books in Every Department of Literature for Public School Libraries in Upper Canada* ... (Toronto 1857) 236; *DHE* vol. 20, 94–5; 'Special Report ... Textbooks, Apparatus and Libraries,' 28

13 *ARUC* (1869) App. G, 130

14 RG2 C-6-C, John C. Geikie to E.R., 1 Dec. 1857; see also, C.B. Sissons, *Egerton Ryerson: His Life and Letters* (Toronto: Clarke, Irwin 1947) vol. 2, 524–7; Cameron, 'J. George Hodgins,' 125–7.

15 *British Colonist* 19 Mar. 1858; *DHE* vol. 13, 315

16 Cameron, 'J. George Hodgins,' 127

17 Cf Sissons, *Egerton Ryerson* vol. 2, 524–7; Linda Wilson Corman, 'James Campbell and the Ontario Education Department, 1858–1884,' *Papers of the Bibliographical Society of Canada / Cahiers de la société bibliographique du Canada XIV, 1975* (Toronto: Bibliographical Society 1976) 17–52, especially 46 ff; Cameron, 'J. George Hodgins,' 130–5

18 J.G.H. to E.R., 4, 13 Sept. 1865, Sissons, *Egerton Ryerson* vol. 2, 510–12. George Brown subsequently disclaimed any involvement in Ryerson's controversy with James Campbell and the booksellers; George Brown to E.R., 24 Mar. 1868, Sissons, *Egerton Ryerson* vol. 2, 556

19 Sissons, ibid. 512n1

20 E.R. to J.A. Macdonald, 21 Mar. 1860, Sissons, *Egerton Ryerson* vol. 2, 450

21 *ARUC* (1856); Walter N. Bell, *The Development of the Ontario High School* (Toronto: University of Toronto Press 1918) 62–4

22 *Fraser Report* 269. Of a total of 5,332 pupils enrolled, 4,013 (75 per cent) lived locally; 70 matriculated at university, one-half of those at University of Toronto. See also W.E. Macpherson, *The Ontario Grammar Schools*, Bulletin of the Department of History and Political and Economic Science, Queen's University, no. 21 (Kingston 1916) 17–18.

23 For a provocative study of middle-class family strategies in relation to schooling, see Mary P. Ryan, *The Cradle of the Middle Class: The Family in Oneida County, New York 1790–1865* (New York: Cambridge University Press 1981) 164–5, 170–1. For a different interpretation, see R.D. Gidney and D.A. Lawr, 'Egerton Ryerson and the Origins of the Ontario Secondary School,' *CHR* 60 (1979) 442–65, especially 454.

24 Cf Daniel T. Rodgers and David B. Tyack, 'Work, Youth and Schooling: Mapping Critical Research Areas,' in Harvey Kantor and David B. Tyack, eds, *Work, Youth and Schooling: Historical Perspectives on Vocationalism in American Education* (Palo Alto, Ca.: Stanford University Press 1982) 269–96.

25 *DHE* vol. 15, 183. Langton pursued the topic in a lengthy address to the Literary

and Historical Society of Quebec: 'Some General Remarks on Education,' *Transactions of the Literary and Historical Society of Quebec for 1864–65* (Quebec 1866) 1–36; *Journal of the Board of Arts and Manufactures* 5 (1865) 1–2; 7 (1867) 169–71.

26 Advertisements are too numerous to cite. See, for example, J.G. Hodgins, ed., *The Establishment of Schools and Colleges in Ontario 1792–1910* (Toronto: King's Printer 1910) vol. 3, 362–3; MTCL, Baldwin Room, *The Toronto Academy* (nd); James Papers, s53, Box 2: Canadian Collegiate Institute (prospectus), Georgetown, Ontario; 'Day's Commercial College and High School Toronto,' *Canadian Almanac for 1868* 108; 'Benedict's Commercial School,' *Cobourg Star*, 29 Jan. 1868.

27 Egerton Ryerson, 'Second Circular to Boards of Grammar School Trustees,' 17 Feb. 1855, *DHE* vol. 15, 200; Gidney and Lawr, 'Origins,' 445–6

28 Sissons, *Egerton Ryerson* vol. 2, 400–19; *DHE* vol. 15, 121; *DHE* vol. 18, 203

29 J.G.H. to E.R., 30 Apr. 1860, Sissons, *Egerton Ryerson* vol. 2, 452

30 Sissons, ibid. 476–87; Bruce W. Hodgins, 'John Sandfield Macdonald,' in J.M.S. Careless, ed., *The Pre-Confederation Premiers: Ontario Government Leaders 1841–1867*, Ontario Historical Studies Series (Toronto: University of Toronto Press 1980) 274–80

31 E.R. to J.G.H., 20 May 1863, Sissons, *Egerton Ryerson* vol. 2, 486

32 Sissons, ibid. 497, 503

33 *DHE* vol. 16, 81

34 A Bill for the Further Improvement of Grammar Schools in Upper Canada, sect. 11, *DHE* vol. 17, 300; see also, Circular to Members of Both Houses of the Legislature, 27 March 1863, *DHE* vol. 17, 294–8

35 Ibid. vol. 18, 253

36 E.R. to Teachers' Educational Association meeting, 1865, ibid. vol. 19, 60; Sissons, *Egerton Ryerson* vol. 2, 513

37 *DHE* vol. 19, 60–2

38 J.G.H. to E.R., 5, 13 Sept. 1865, *DHE* vol. 19, 33, 35; Sissons, *Egerton Ryerson* vol. 2, 504; An Act for the Further Improvement of Grammar Schools in Upper Canada, 29 Vict. (1865) cap. 23, *DHE* vol. 19, 25–7

39 Revised Programme of Studies and General Rules and Regulations for the Government of Grammar Schools in Upper Canada, Nov. 1865, *DHE* vol. 19, 46–9

40 *ARUC* (1867) *DHE* vol. 20, 148–50

41 *Annual Report of the Grammar School Inspector* (1864), *DHE* vol. 18, 203; see also Young biography, *DCB* vol. 11, 942–3

42 See especially *Annual Report of the Grammar School Inspector* (1866), *DHE* vol. 20, 104–7; also J.G.H. to E.R., 5 Sept. 1865, *DHE* vol. 19, 33–4, vol. 23, 144–6, vol. 24, 90–100. By the mid-1870s, however, 'payment by results' was introduced in Ontario high schools.

43 Kate Rousmaniere, 'To Prepare the Ideal Woman: Private Denominational Girls'

Schooling in Late Nineteenth-Century Ontario' (MA diss., University of Toronto 1984) 37–40. See also Deborah Gorham, *The Victorian Girl and the Feminine Ideal* (Bloomington, Ind.: Indiana University Press 1982) Pt 1; Carol Dyhouse, *Girls Growing Up in Late Victorian and Edwardian England* (London: Routledge and Kegan Paul).

44 *ARUC* (1851) *DHE* vol. 10, 29

45 *Christian Guardian* 27 Dec. 1837, quoted in Marion Royce, 'Methodism and the Education of Women in Nineteenth Century Ontario,' *Atlantis* 3:2, Pt 1 (Spring 1978) 137.

46 John Ross Robertson, *Landmarks of Toronto* vol. 3, 33–4

47 Ibid. 336–7. See also 'A Protestant,' *Globe* 18 Sept. 1863. The fact that Egerton Ryerson's daughter Lucille and two female cousins attended a convent in Montreal in order to improve their French suggests something of the measure of the problem posed by the lack of comparable Protestant institutions. C.B. Sissons, ed., *My Dearest Sophie: Letters from Egerton Ryerson to His Daughter* (Toronto: Ryerson Press 1955) xxix

48 'A Watchman,' *Leader* 19 Sept. 1863

49 T. Webster, *History of the Methodist Episcopal Church in Canada* (Hamilton 1870) 407, cited by J.R. Miller, 'Anti-Catholic Thought in Victorian Canada,' *CHR* 66 (Dec. 1985) 490n84; 'Meeting of the Church of England Synod, Toronto,' *Globe* 17 June 1865

50 Rousmaniere, 'To Prepare the Ideal Woman,' 41–52; Ian E. Davey, 'Trends in Female School Attendance in Mid-Nineteenth Century Ontario,' *HS/SH* 16 (Nov. 1975) 238–54; Carolyn Gossage, *A Question of Privilege: Canada's Independent Schools* (Toronto: Peter Martin 1977). For a discussion of an earlier commitment to coeducational denominational sponsorship of schools, see Marion Royce, 'Education for Girls in Quaker Schools in Ontario,' *Atlantis* 3:1 (Fall 1977).

51 Sissons, ed., *My Dearest Sophie* 4 (editorial note). See also Felicity Hunt, ed., *Lessons for Life: The Schooling of Girls and Women, 1850–1950* (Oxford: Basil Blackwell 1987).

52 Egerton Ryerson, *A Special Report on the Systems and State of Popular Education on the Continent of Europe, in the British Isles, and the United States of America, with Practical Suggestions for the Improvement of Public Instruction in the Province of Ontario* (Toronto 1868) 192

53 'Address to Parents on the Education of Girls: By Mrs. Holiwell, of "Elm House" School for the Education of Young Ladies' (Toronto 1865), reprinted in Alison L. Prentice and Susan E. Houston, eds, *Family, School and Society in Nineteenth Century Canada* (Toronto: Oxford University Press 1975) 244–52. While music and drawing 'extras' were among the mainstays of the girls' private school curriculum, French was virtually mandatory; see Alexander Marling, ed., *The Canada Educational Directory and Yearbook for 1876 …* (Toronto 1876) 73–87.

54 Editorial, *Christian Guardian* 22 June 1864; editorial, *Globe* 28 May 1864, 6
   July 1867
55 An all-girls' school was first proposed for Toronto in 1843; see J.E. Middleton,
   Municipality of Toronto (Toronto 1922) vol. 1, 227. A serious proposal for a high
   school for girls, in 1864, apparently involved a self-consciously 'ornamental'
   curriculum with an emphasis on 'drawing, music & c.' The Hon. John McMurrich
   in 1870 deplored that aspect of the proposal; by then he and others preferred a
   version of higher education for girls 'who had shown equal capacity to the boys'
   that was comparable if not identical. See *Annual Report of the Local Superintendent ... Toronto* (1864) 42; ibid. (1870) 37–8; also 'Address of the Rev. E.H.
   Dewart, Ontario Teachers' Federation, 1870,' *DHE* vol. 22, 145–6.
56 RG2 F-3-B, Annual Reports of Local Superintendents, Owen Sound, 1861
57 H. Hale, Chairman, Clinton Board of Grammar School Trustees to E.R., 23 Dec.
   1867, *DHE* vol. 20, 238–40. Petitions were also received from Colborne, Iroquois, and Lindsay: see Ann Margaret Gray, 'Continuity in Change: The Effects
   on Girls of Co-educational Secondary Schooling in Ontario, 1860–1910' (MA
   diss., University of Toronto 1979) 30.
58 TBEHC, James Porter Diary, vol. 1, 5 Apr. 1859
59 RG2 C-6-C, Box 49, item 3618
60 Ibid., case of SS 11, Aldborough Township, 23 Mar.–1 June 1863, Box 47–49
61 Ibid. 14 July 1868, Box 134, item 5690
62 *Annual Report of the Inspector of Grammar Schools* (1865) *DHE* vol. 19, 97–8;
   ibid. (1866) *DHE* vol. 20, 108; Marion Royce, 'Arguments over the Education of
   Girls – Their Admission to Grammar Schools in This Province,' *OH* 67 (Mar.
   1975) 1–13, especially 5
63 *ARUC* (1867) *DHE* vol. 20, 150; Gray, 'Continuity in Change,' 31–4
64 'Proceedings of the County School Conventions, 1860,' *DHE* vol. 16, 81
65 'Circulars to the Newspaper,' *DHE* vol. 20, 246; also report on the local county
   convention, *St. Thomas Weekly Dispatch* 25 Feb. 1869; Sissons, ed., *My Dearest
   Sophie* 24 Sept. 1859, 3–4; 2 Jan. 1862, 38
66 The members of the Legislative Assembly came to much the same conclusion,
   DHE vol. 20, 237–8.
67 *Annual Report of the Late Inspector of Grammar Schools* (1867) *DHE* vol. 20,
   109–28, especially 116
68 *JEUC* 20 (Mar. 1867) 56, and *DHE* vol. 22, 50–3. See also J. Anthony C.
   Ketchum, ' "The Most Perfect System": Official Policy in the First Century of
   Ontario's Government Secondary Schools and Its Impact on Students between
   1871 and 1910' (ED D diss., University of Toronto 1979).
69 Gidney and Lawr, 'Origins,' 459–65
70 E.R. to J.A.M., 21 Mar. 1860, Sissons, *Egerton Ryerson* vol. 2, 449–50; E.R.
   to J.G.H., 8 Sept. 1865, *DHE* vol. 19, 35
71 Letter to editor, *Peterborough Examiner* 11 Mar. 1869

72 Sissons, *Egerton Ryerson* vol. 2, 447–8, 515–24, 564–73; Egerton Ryerson to the editors of the Toronto daily newspapers, 16 Jan. 1868, *DHE* vol. 20, 247–8; J.A.M. to E.R., 30 Jan. 1865, Sissons, *Egerton Ryerson* vol. 2, 497

73 See especially *DHE* vol. 20, 293–7, 303 ff, vol. 21, 1–33, vol. 22, 17–31.

74 *Globe* 15 Dec. 1869

75 Bruce W. Hodgins, 'John Sandfield Macdonald,' 297–8; Sissons, *Egerton Ryerson* vol. 2, 585

76 Sissons, ibid. 565; *DHE* vol. 21, 144, 168; Cameron, 'J. George Hodgins,' 91–4

77 Joseph Schull, *Edward Blake: The Man of the Other Way* (Toronto: Macmillan 1975) 58–9, 72–3, 83–4; Sissons, *Egerton Ryerson* vol. 2, 594–7, 603. In an editorial note, *DHE* vol. 24, 149, J. George Hodgins commented bitterly 'that practically the Government of the day allowed neither the Chief Superintendent nor the Council of Public Instruction any freedom or discretion, in framing Regulations and Instructions for carrying out the provisions of the Comprehensive School Law of 1871.' Egerton Ryerson was among a distinguished company of mid-Victorian civil servants who were brought to heel, cf George Kitson Clark, 'Statesmen in Disguise: Reflections on the History of the Neutrality of the Civil Service,' *Historical Journal* 2 (1959) 19–39.

78 Sissons, *Egerton Ryerson* vol. 2, 563, 578. A second letter of intention was dated 10 Feb. 1872, the third, and final, 12 June 1875; in between there were various conversations 'around' the subject. Adam Crooks's role as minister is addressed by Robert M. Stamp in *The Schools of Ontario, 1876–1976*, Ontario Historical Studies Series (Toronto: University of Toronto Press 1982) ch. 1.

79 The 1874 amending legislation, 37 Vict. (1873) cap. 27 and 28, is reprinted in *DHE* vol. 26, 1–29, 30–98. See also Sissons, *Egerton Ryerson* vol. 2, 582–9; Stamp, *Schools of Ontario* 22–3, 32–45.

80 'Circular of the Chief Superintendent to the Inspectors of Public Schools in Ontario, 1871,' *DHE* vol. 23, 136; cf 'Programme of Course of Study for Public School, 1871,' ibid. 83–4. The education department's incoming correspondence files document widespread critical reaction, which ranged from mild scepticism to downright refusal to follow the new regulations; see, for example, RG2 C-6-C, Box 209, items 49, 51, 284, 285; also 'Ontario Teachers' Association Annual Meeting, 1875,' *DHE* vol. 27, 63.

81 'Proceedings of the Ontario Teachers' Association, 1871,' *DHE* vol. 23, 147. For a sampling of well-placed reservations about the appropriateness of the schools' curriculum, cf remarks of President Samuel Nelles to the Ontario Teachers' Association, 1870, to the effect that schooling was 'too bookish, too abstract and too remote from living realities' *DHE* vol. 22, 163; *The Weekly Leader* 23 Dec. 1870; *Ontario Teacher* 1 (Sept. 1873) 270; Archbishop Lynch's remarks on the disturbing effect of high schools on farmers' sons, quoted by Franklin Walker in *Catholic Education and Politics in Ontario: A Documentary Study* (Toronto: Thomas Nelson 1964) 9.

82 'Report and Suggestions with Respect to the High Schools and Collegiate Institutes of Ontario for 1871,' *DHE* vol. 23, 170

83 Ibid. vol. 25, 144–75, vol. 26, 198–202

84 Ibid., vol. 26, 249, 251, vol. 27, 262–4, vol. 28, 102–5

85 Ibid. vol. 23, 74–9, 129–30, 153. On third-class certificates, see 'Orders in Council, 6 Sept. 1876,' *DHE* vol. 18, 78. The commission of inquiry into the conduct of the Rev. H.J. Borthwick, Inspector of Public Schools and Chairman of the Board of Examiners, Ottawa, in 1875 proved to be particularly revealing, *DHE* vol. 27, 266–7.

86 *Fraser Report* 214; *DHE* vol. 22, 122, vol. 23, 120. New regulations in respect of 'adequate' school accommodation were especially intimidating, although they stimulated a significant increase in expenditure on school repairs, furnishing, and replacements. In 1870 almost half a million dollars was spent on these items across the province; in 1875 the total figure was $1,234,980, see *DHE* vol. 27, 211.

87 *DHE* vol. 24, 1–13, 127–33, 149–55, 159–74, vol. 25, Introduction, 107–18; Sissons, *Egerton Ryerson* vol. 2, 603; Sissons, ed., *My Dearest Sophie* 264n

88 Susan E. Houston, 'School Reform and Education: The Issue of Compulsory Schooling,' in Neil McDonald and Alf Chaiton, eds, *Egerton Ryerson and His Times* (Toronto: Macmillan 1978) 271–3; Sissons, *Egerton Ryerson* vol. 2, 585. See also W.M. Landes and L.C. Salomon, 'Compulsory Schooling Legislation: An Economic Analysis of the Law and Societal Change in the Nineteenth Century,' *Journal of Economic History* 32 (1972) 54–91.

89 John R. Abbott, 'Educational Policy Formation and Implementation on the Ontario Resource Frontier: The Case of the District of Algoma, 1903–1922' (PH D diss., University of Toronto 1983); 'Hostile Landscapes and the Spectre of Illiteracy: Devising Retrieval Systems for "Sequestered" Children in Northern Ontario, 1875–1930,' in J. Donald Wilson, ed., *An Imperfect Past: Education and Society in Canadian History* (Vancouver: Centre for the Study of Curriculum and Instruction, University of British Columbia 1984)

90 Veronica Strong-Boag, ed., *'A Woman with a Purpose': The Diaries of Elizabeth Smith, 1872–1884* (Toronto: University of Toronto Press 1980). Elizabeth Smith Shortt (1859–1949) was a member of the first class of women graduates in medicine at Queen's University, Kingston, in 1884.

Index

Numbers in bold type refer to pages on which illustrations appear.